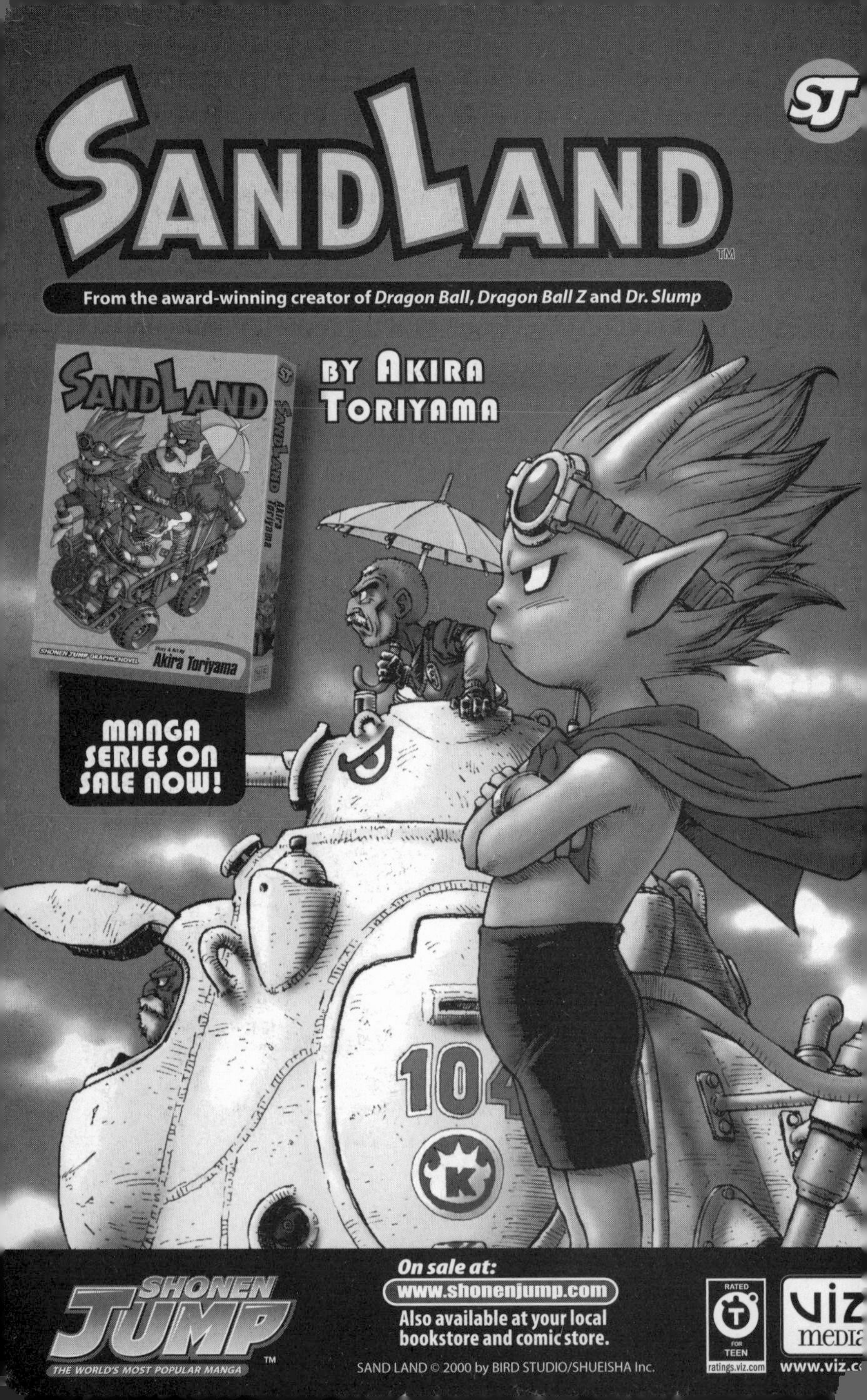
SJ
SAND LAND™
From the award-winning creator of Dragon Ball, Dragon Ball Z and Dr. Slump
SAND LAND
SAND LAND Akira Toriyama
SHONEN JUMP GRAPHIC NOVEL
Story & Art by Akira Toriyama
BY AKIRA TORIYAMA
MANGA SERIES ON SALE NOW!
104
K
SHONEN JUMP™
THE WORLD'S MOST POPULAR MANGA
On sale at:
www.shonenjump.com
Also available at your local bookstore and comic store.
SAND LAND © 2000 by BIRD STUDIO/SHUEISHA Inc.
RATED T FOR TEEN
ratings.viz.com
VIZ media
www.viz.c

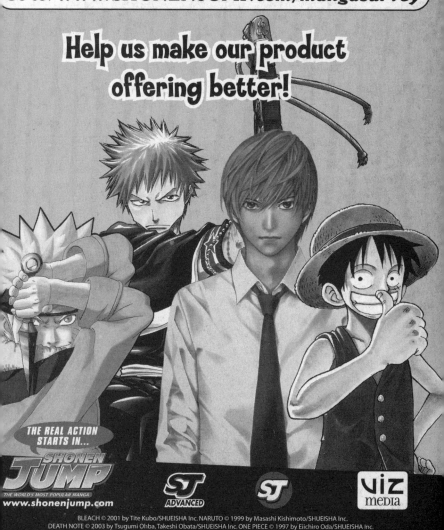

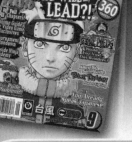
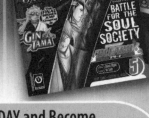

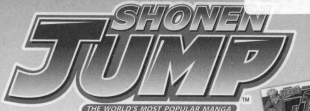

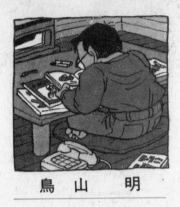

鳥 山 明

I can't sit around doing nothing. I don't feel relaxed unless I'm totally involved in something. Kinda like how sharks have to keep swimming or they die. I need to be immtersed in something no matter how pointless it may be. But because of this, when I don't have anything to do, I get really restless and pace around in my room. It would really be nice if "work" was one of those things I could really get involved in…

—*Akira Toriyama, 1991*

Widely known all over the world for his playful, innovative storytelling and humorous, distinctive art style, **Dragon Ball** creator Akira Toriyama is also known in his native Japan for the wildly popular **Dr. Slump**, his previous manga series about the adventures of a mad scientist and his android "daughter." His hit series **Dragon Ball** ran from 1984 to 1995 in Shueisha's **Weekly Shonen Jump** magazine. He is also known for his design work on video games such as **Dragon Warrior**, **Chrono Trigger** and **Tobal No. 1**. His recent manga works include **Cowa!**, **Kajika**, **Sand Land**, **Neko Majin**, and a cildren's book, **Toccio the Angel**. He lives with his family in Japan.

DRAGON BALL Z VOL. 12
The SHONEN JUMP Manga Edition

This graphic novel is number 28 in a series of 42.

STORY AND ART BY
AKIRA TORIYAMA

ENGLISH ADAPTATION BY
GERARD JONES

Translation/Lillian Olsen
Touch-Up Art & Lettering/Wayne Truman
Cover Design/Sean Lee
Graphics & Design/Sean Lee
Senior Editor/Jason Thompson
Managing Editor/Elizabeth Kawasaki

Editor in Chief, Books/Alvin Lu
Editor in Chief, Magazines/Marc Weidenbaum
VP of Publishing Licensing/Rika Inouye
VP of Sales/Gonzalo Ferreyra
Sr. VP of Marketing/Liza Coppola
Publisher/Hyoe Narita

Printed in Canada

In the original Japanese edition, DRAGON BALL and DRAGON BALL Z
are known collectively as the 42-volume series DRAGON BALL. The
English DRAGON BALL Z was originally volumes 17-42 of the Japanese
DRAGON BALL.

Published by VIZ Media, LLC
P.O. Box 77010 • San Francisco, CA 94107

The SHONEN JUMP Manga Edition
10 9 8 7 6 5 4 3
First printing, July 2003
Third printing, February 2008

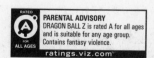

PARENTAL ADVISORY
DRAGON BALL Z is rated A for all ages
and is suitable for any age group.
Contains fantasy violence.
ratings.viz.com

THE WORLD'S
MOST POPULAR MANGA

www.viz.com

www.shonenjump.com

SHONEN JUMP MANGA

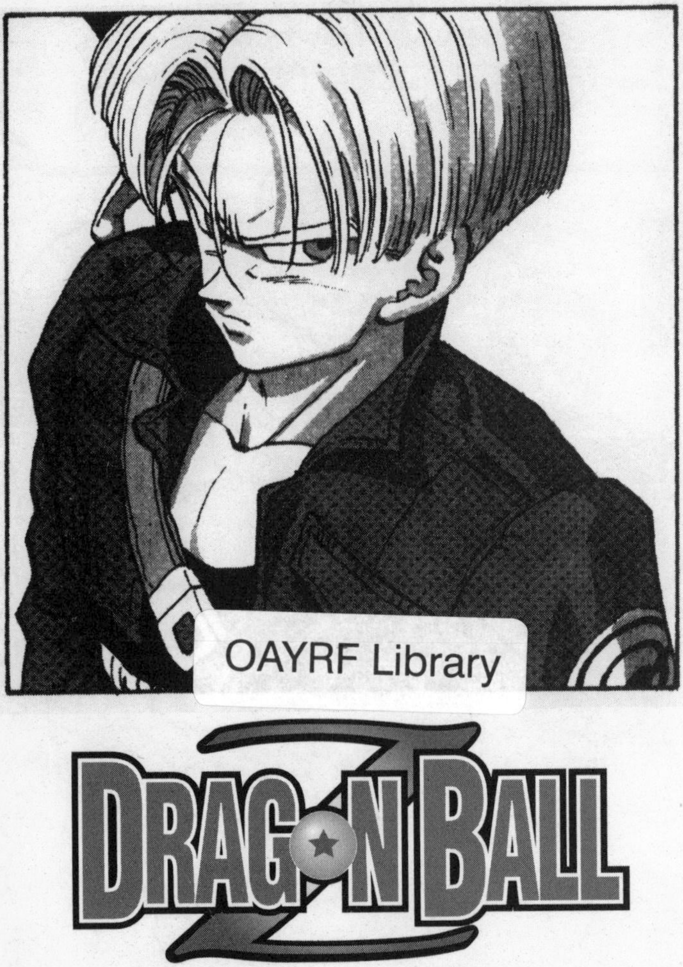

DRAGON BALL Z

Vol. 12

DB: 28 of 42

STORY AND ART BY
AKIRA TORIYAMA

THE MAIN CHARACTERS

Bulma

Goku's oldest friend, Bulma is a scientific genius. She met Goku while on a quest for the seven magical Dragon Balls which, when gathered together, can grant any wish.

Son Goku

The greatest martial artist on Earth, he owes his strength to the training of Kame-Sen'nin and Kaiô-sama, and the fact that he's an alien Saiyan. To get even stronger, he has trained under 100 times Earth's gravity.

Kaiô-sama

The "Lord of Worlds," he is Kami-sama's superior in the heavenly bureaucracy. He taught Goku the *kaiô-ken* and other amazing martial arts techniques.

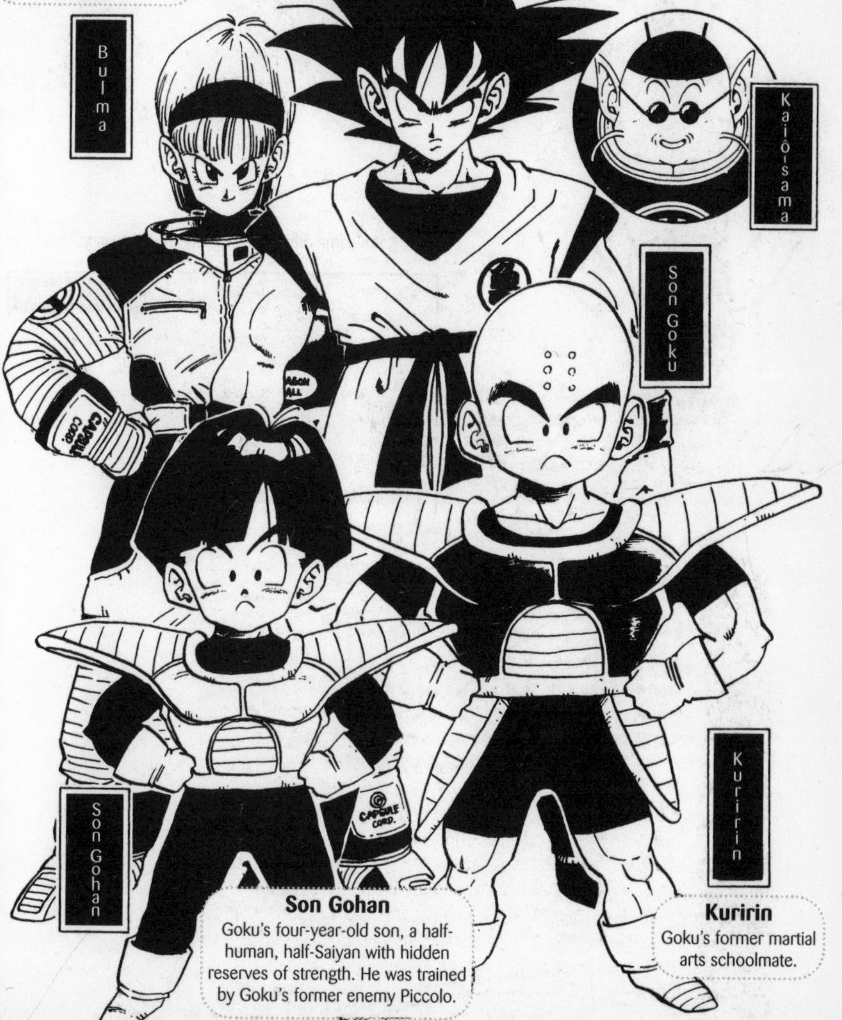
Bulma
Kaiô-sama
Son Goku
CAPSULE CORP.
Kuririn
Son Gohan
CAPSULE CORP.

Son Gohan

Goku's four-year-old son, a half-human, half-Saiyan with hidden reserves of strength. He was trained by Goku's former enemy Piccolo.

Kuririn

Goku's former martial arts schoolmate.

Freeza

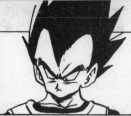

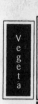

Vegeta

The evil Prince of the Saiyans. He teamed up with our heroes hoping to use them to become a "Super Saiyan" and defeat Freeza, so he could rule the universe himself. Freeza killed him in the battle on Namek, but the Dragon Balls brought him back to life.

Vegeta

Piccolo

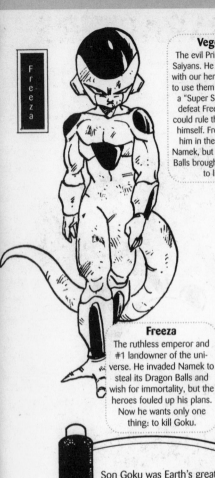

Piccolo

Goku's former arch-enemy, the Namekian Piccolo is the darker half of Kami-sama, the deity who created Earth's Dragon Balls. If Piccolo dies, Kami-sama dies too, and if Kami-sama dies, Earth's Dragon Balls will vanish.

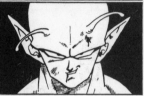

The Great Elder

The Great Elder

The oldest living Namekian. It created Namek's Dragon Balls in the same way that Kami-sama created Earth's Dragon Balls. The Great Elder's guardian, Nail, merged with Piccolo to make him strong enough to fight Freeza.

Freeza

The ruthless emperor and #1 landowner of the universe. He invaded Namek to steal its Dragon Balls and wish for immortality, but the heroes fouled up his plans. Now he wants only one thing: to kill Goku.

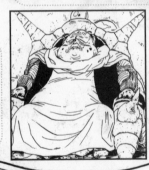

Son Goku was Earth's greatest hero, and the Dragon Balls—which can grant any wish—were Earth's greatest treasure. But when the Dragon Balls were destroyed, Goku and his friends had to travel to Planet Namek, where the Dragon Balls were originally made. There they met the monstrous Freeza, who had invaded the planet to steal Namek's Dragon Balls and wish for immortality. Freeza seemed unbeatable, but just when all hope seemed lost, Goku transformed into the Super Saiyan, the legendary strongest warrior in existence. While his friends fled Namek with the Dragon Balls, Goku chose to stay behind to defeat Freeza fair and square. Now only Goku and Freeza remain on the dying planet, fighting in the scarce minutes before war-torn Namek explodes...

DRAGON BALL Z 12

THE CONTENTS, IF YOU PLEASE ...
OHO HOH HOH HOH HOH ...!

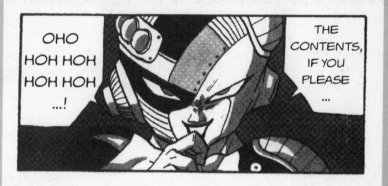

DRAGON BALL

DBZ:132 • Son Goku's Choice

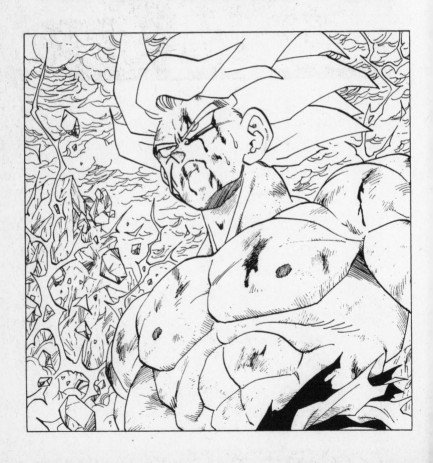

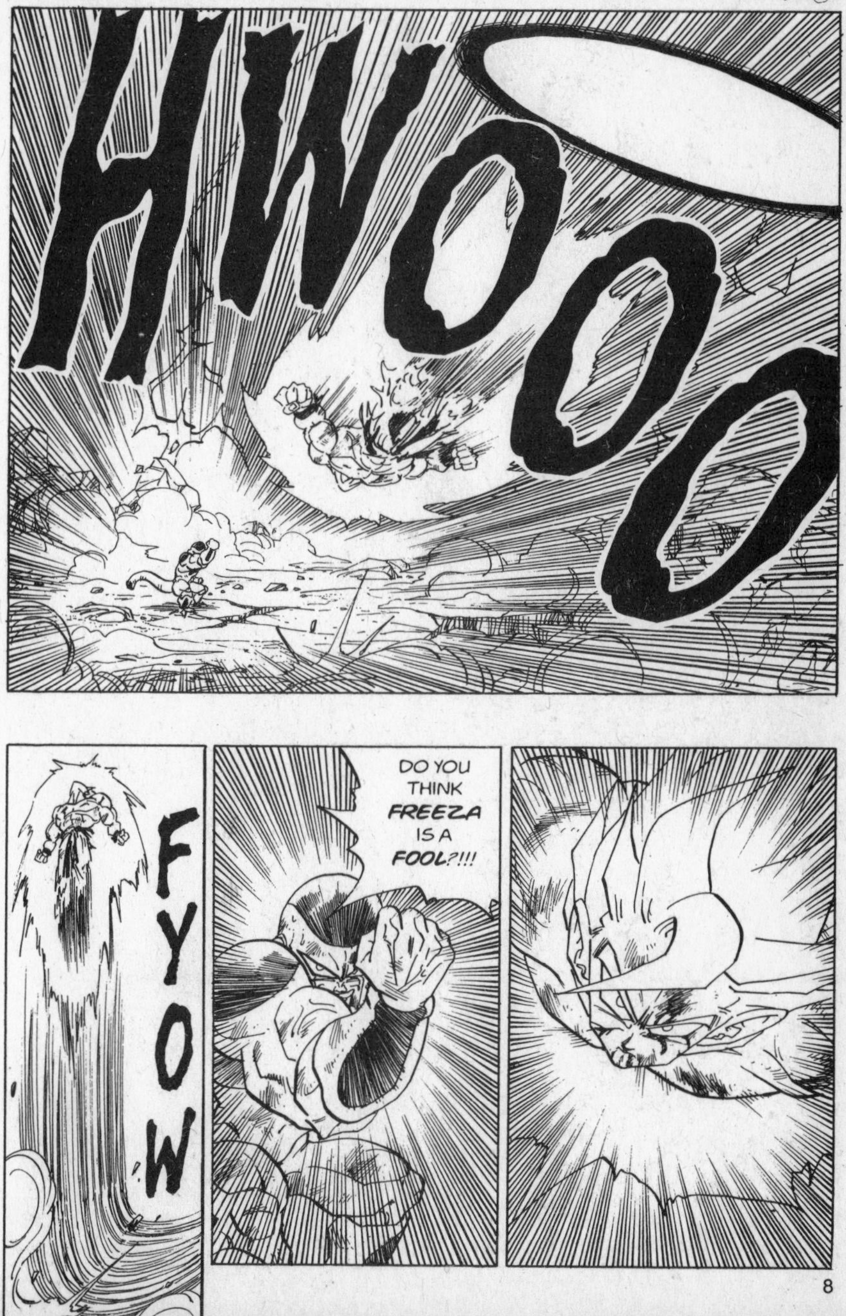
HWOOOO
DO YOU THINK FREEZA IS A FOOL?!!!
FYOW

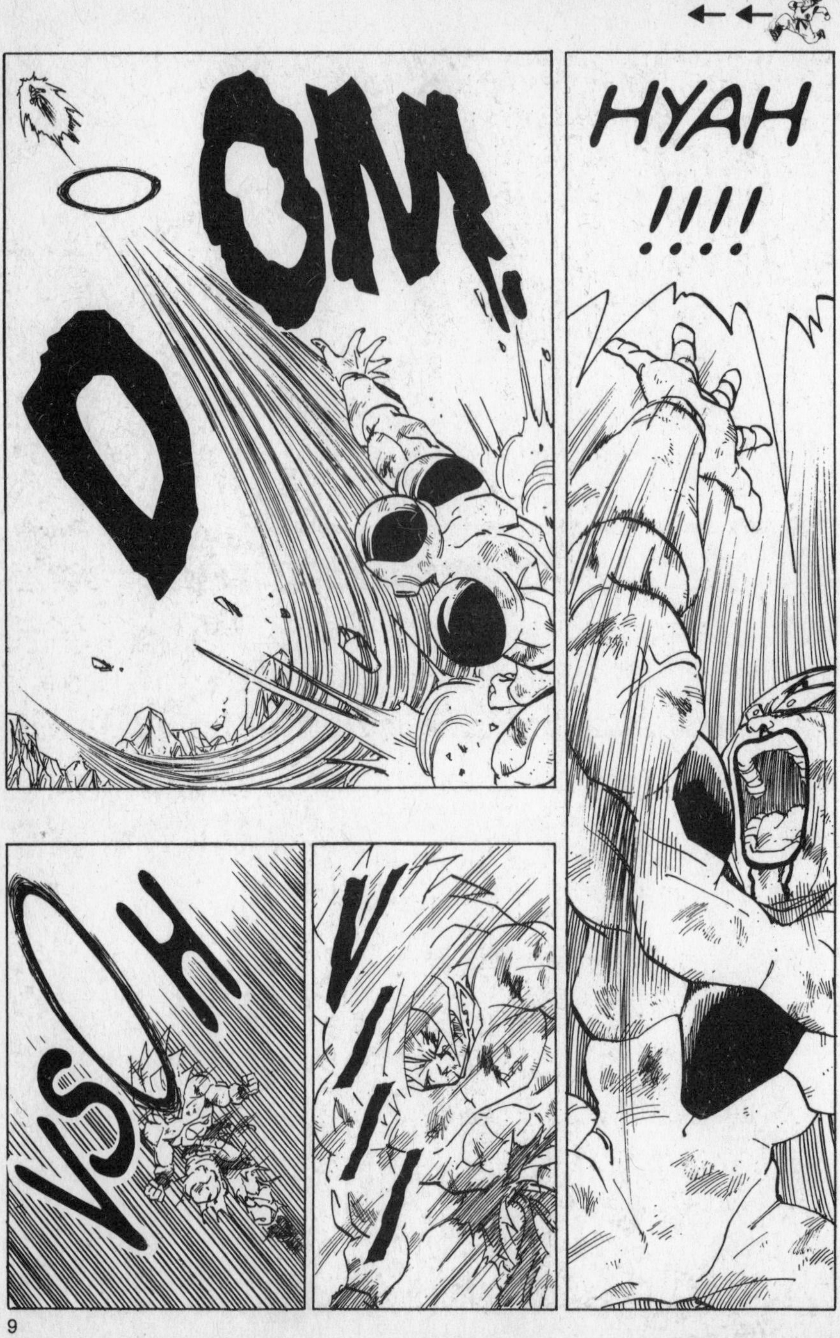
HYAH
!!!!
DOOM!
VSH

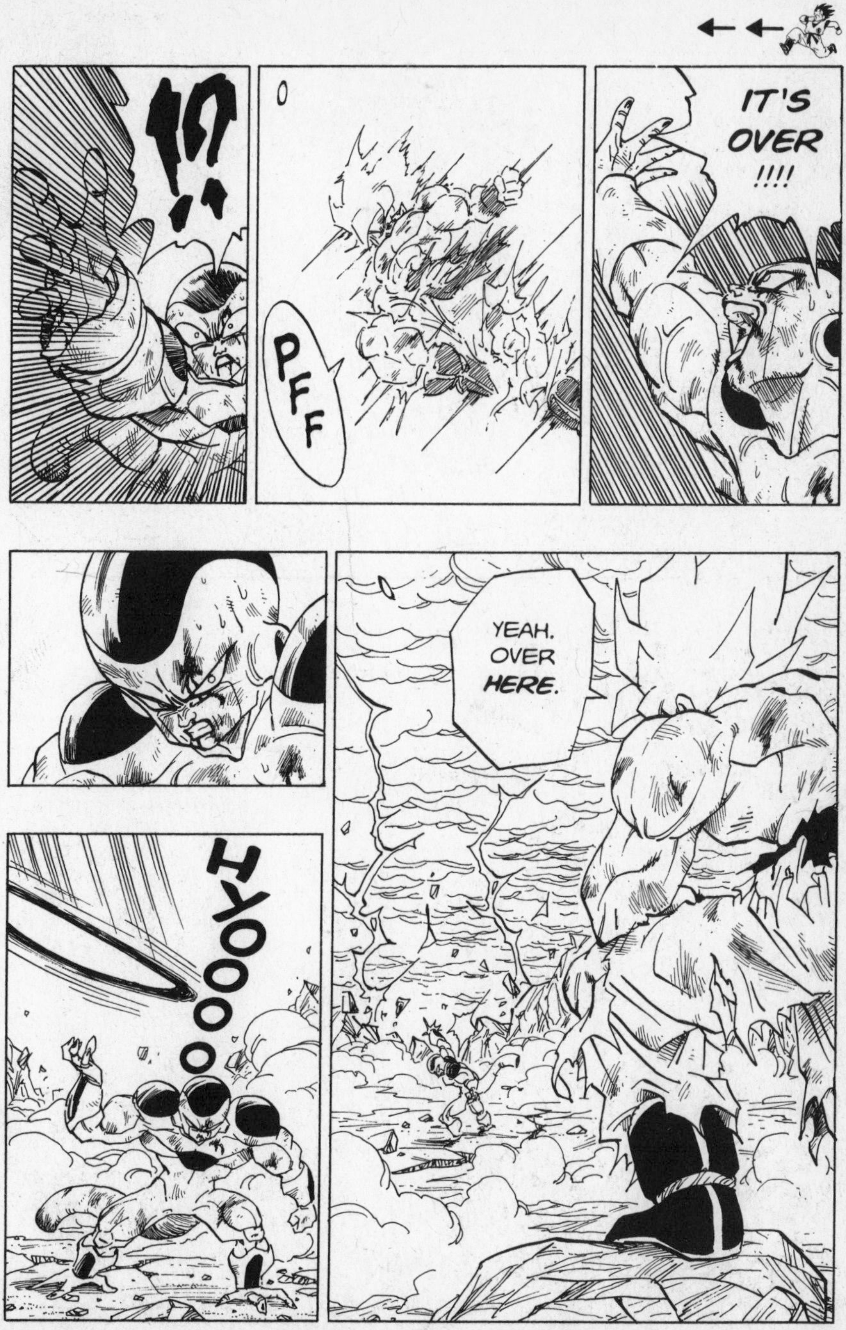
IT'S OVER !!!!
PFF
!?
YEAH. OVER HERE.
HYOOOOO

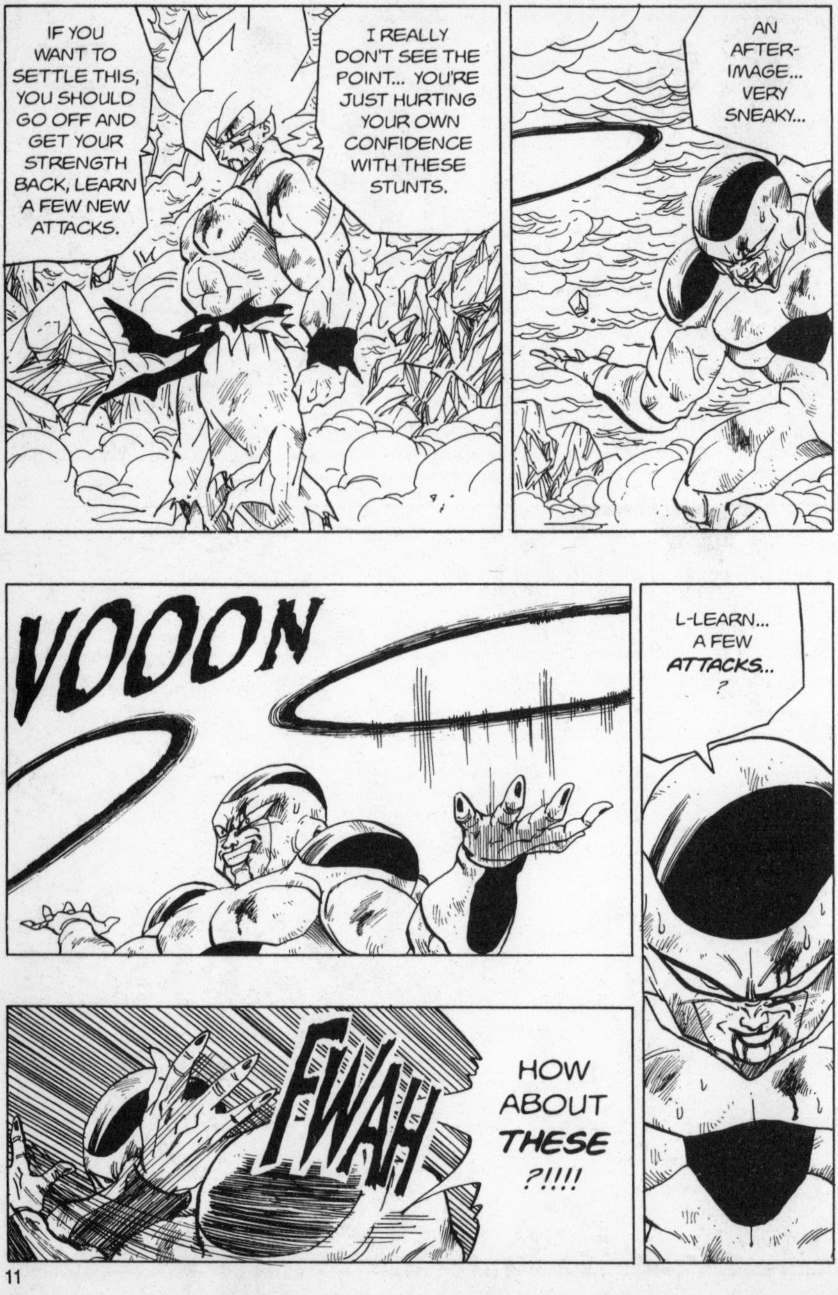
AN AFTER-IMAGE... VERY SNEAKY...
I REALLY DON'T SEE THE POINT... YOU'RE JUST HURTING YOUR OWN CONFIDENCE WITH THESE STUNTS.
IF YOU WANT TO SETTLE THIS, YOU SHOULD GO OFF AND GET YOUR STRENGTH BACK, LEARN A FEW NEW ATTACKS.
L-LEARN... A FEW ATTACKS...?
VOOON
HOW ABOUT THESE?!!!!
FWAH

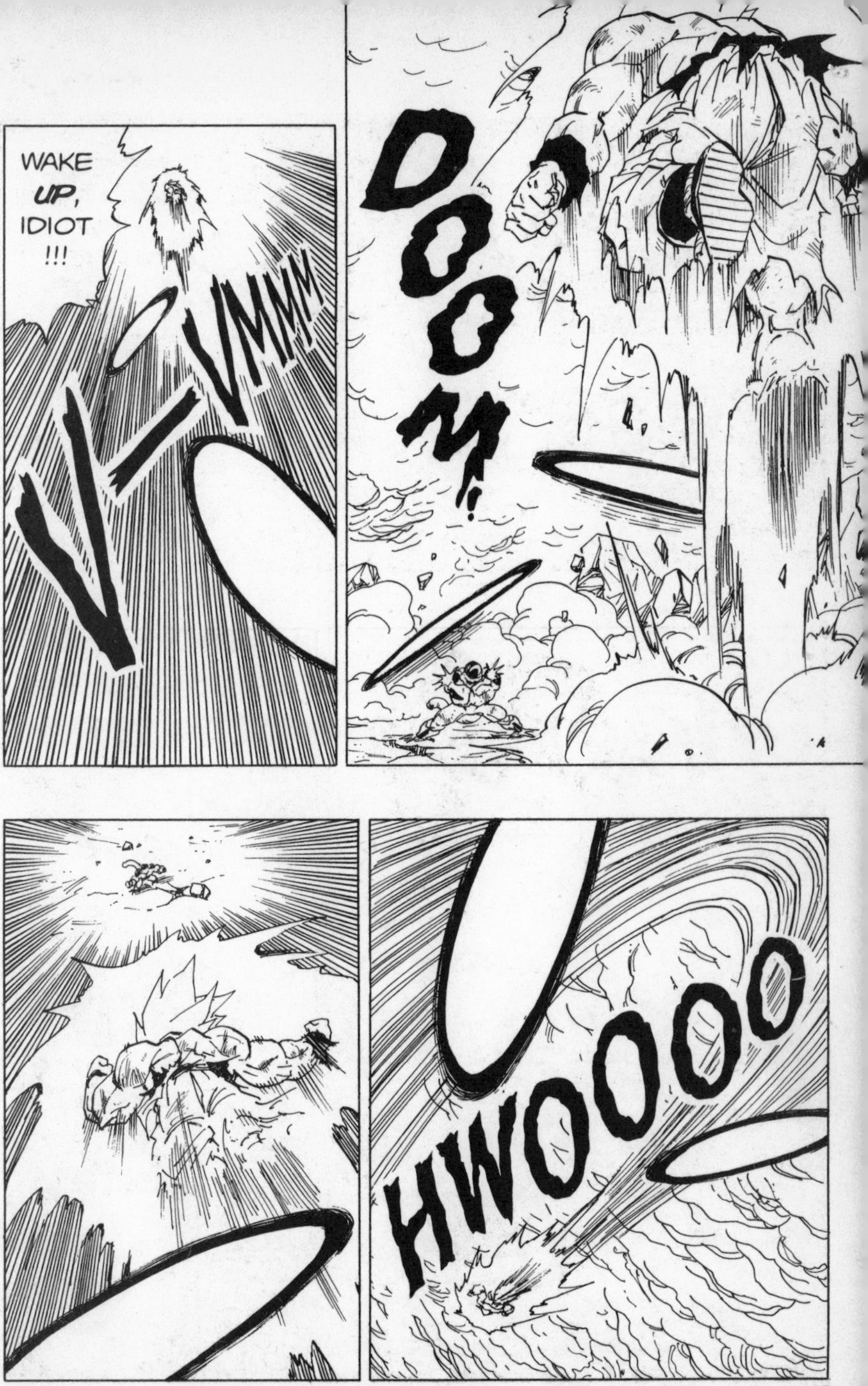
DOOOM!!
WAKE UP, IDIOT!!!
VOVMMM
HWOOOOOO

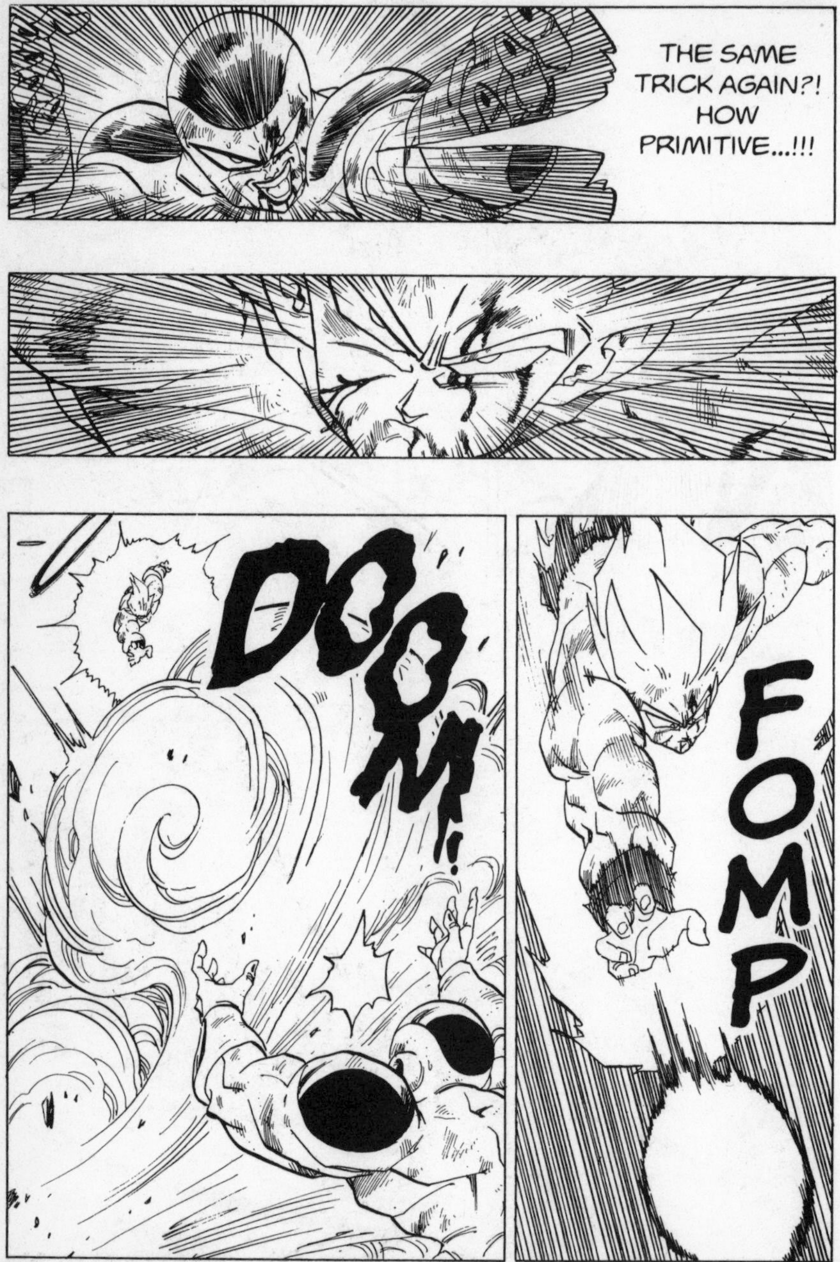
THE SAME TRICK AGAIN?! HOW PRIMITIVE...!!!
FOMP
DOOM!!

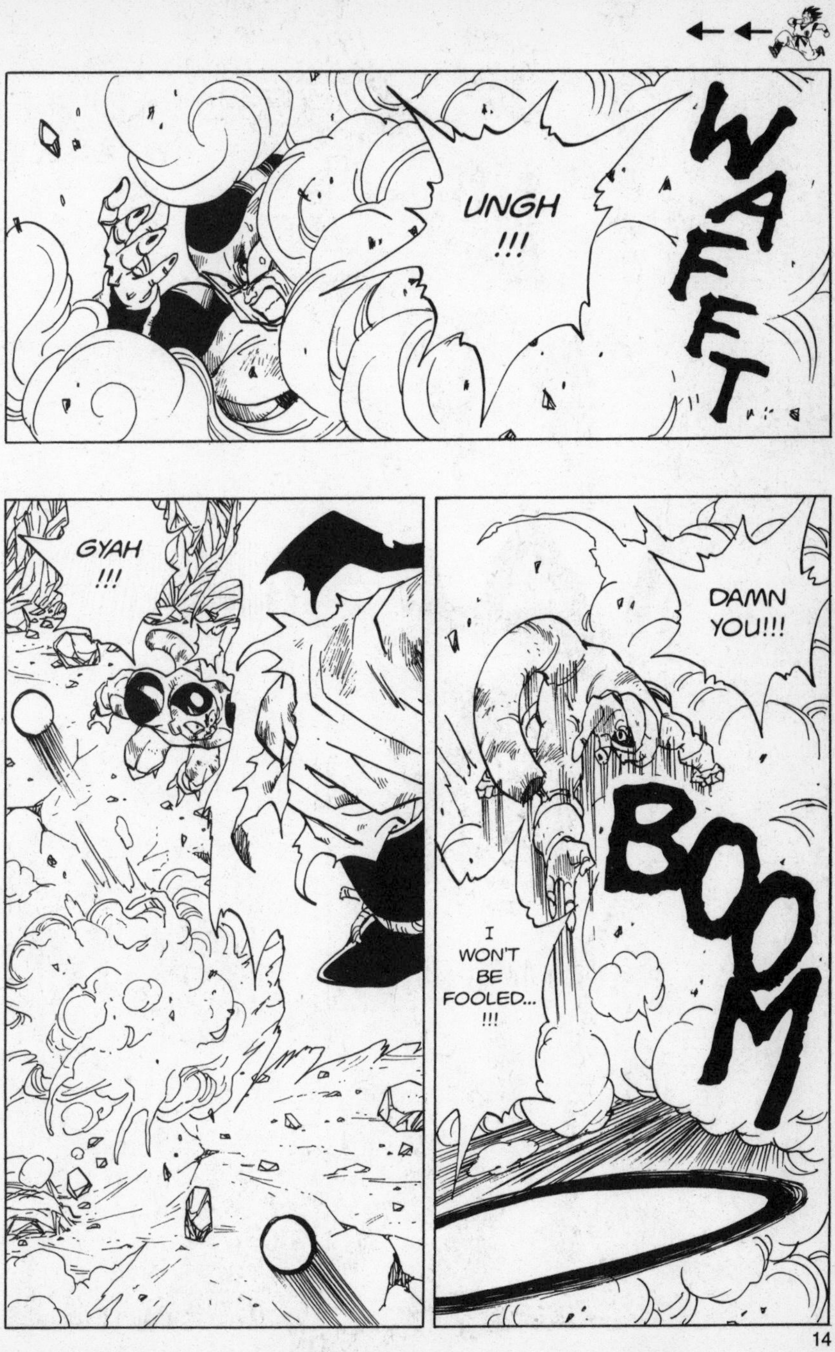
WAFFT
UNGH!!!
DAMN YOU!!!
BOOM
I WON'T BE FOOLED...!!!
GYAH!!!

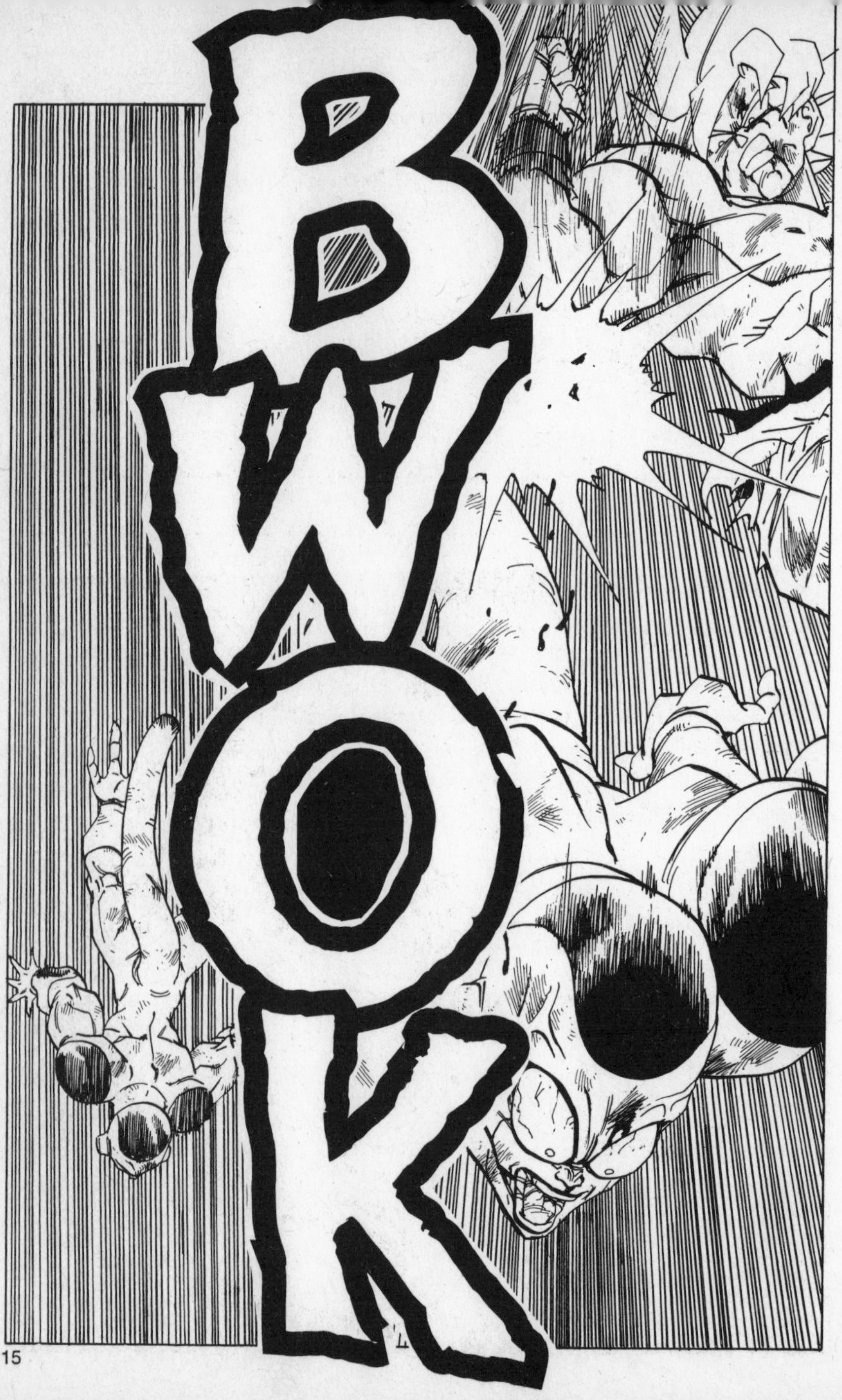
BWOK

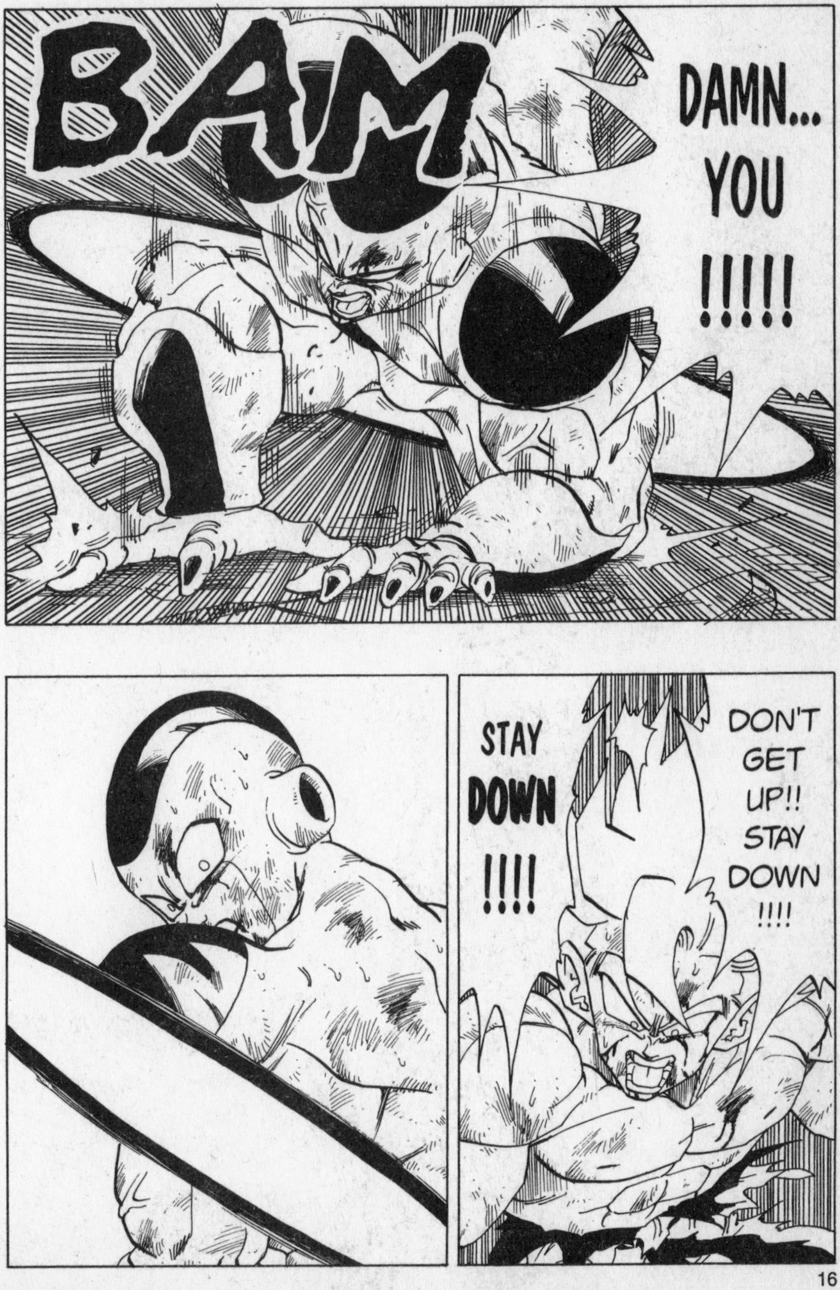
BAM
DAMN... YOU !!!!!
DON'T GET UP!! STAY DOWN !!!!
STAY DOWN !!!!

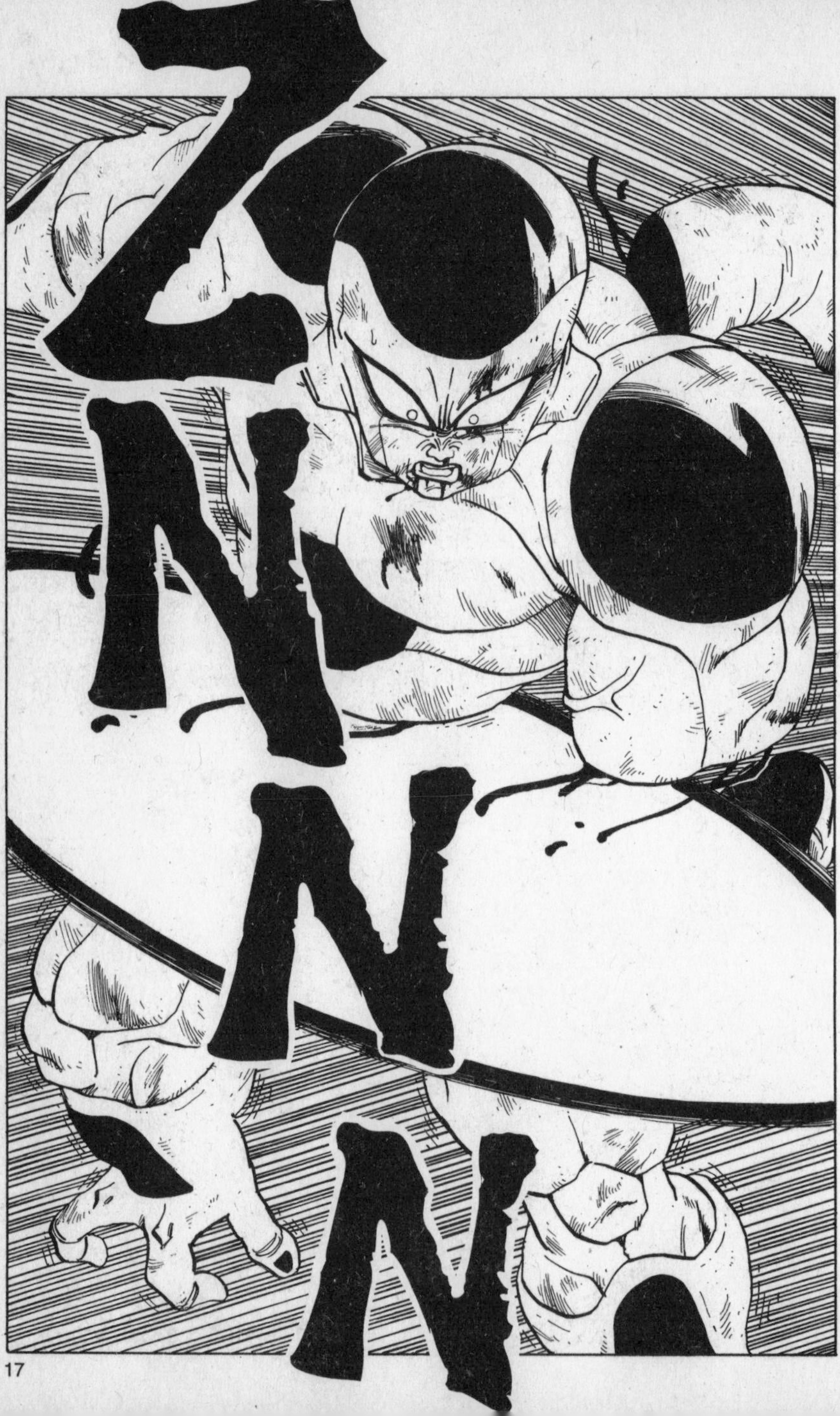
ZNNN

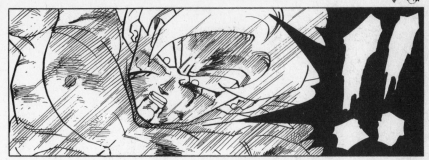

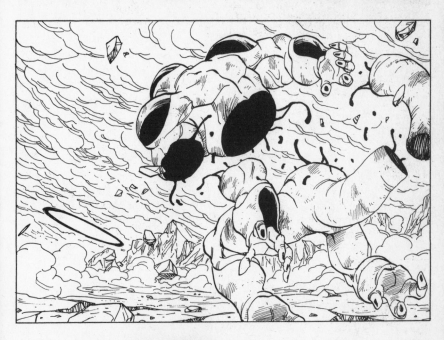

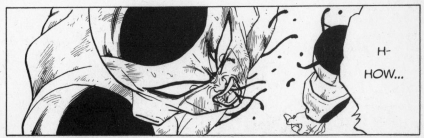

H- HOW...

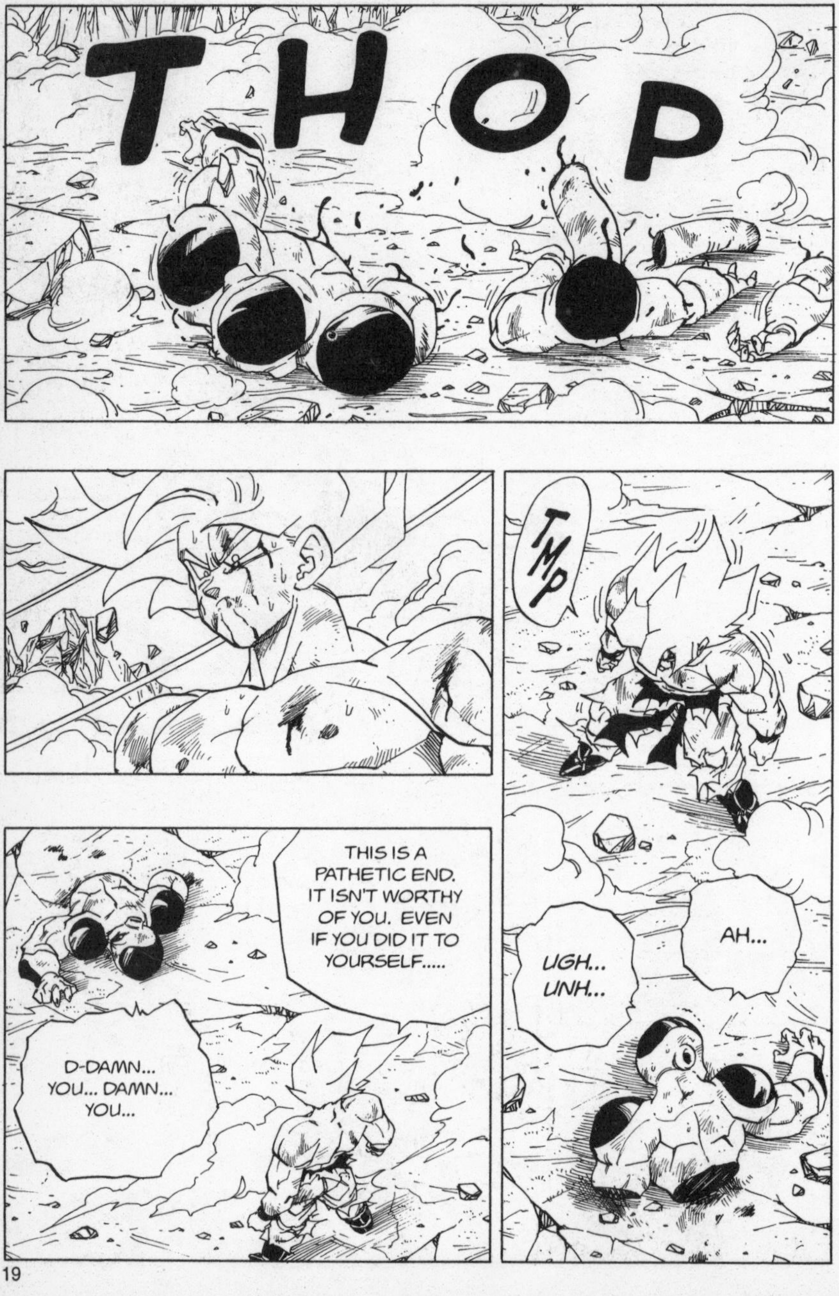
THOP
TMP
AH...
UGH... UNH...
THIS IS A PATHETIC END. IT ISN'T WORTHY OF YOU. EVEN IF YOU DID IT TO YOURSELF.....
D-DAMN... YOU... DAMN... YOU...

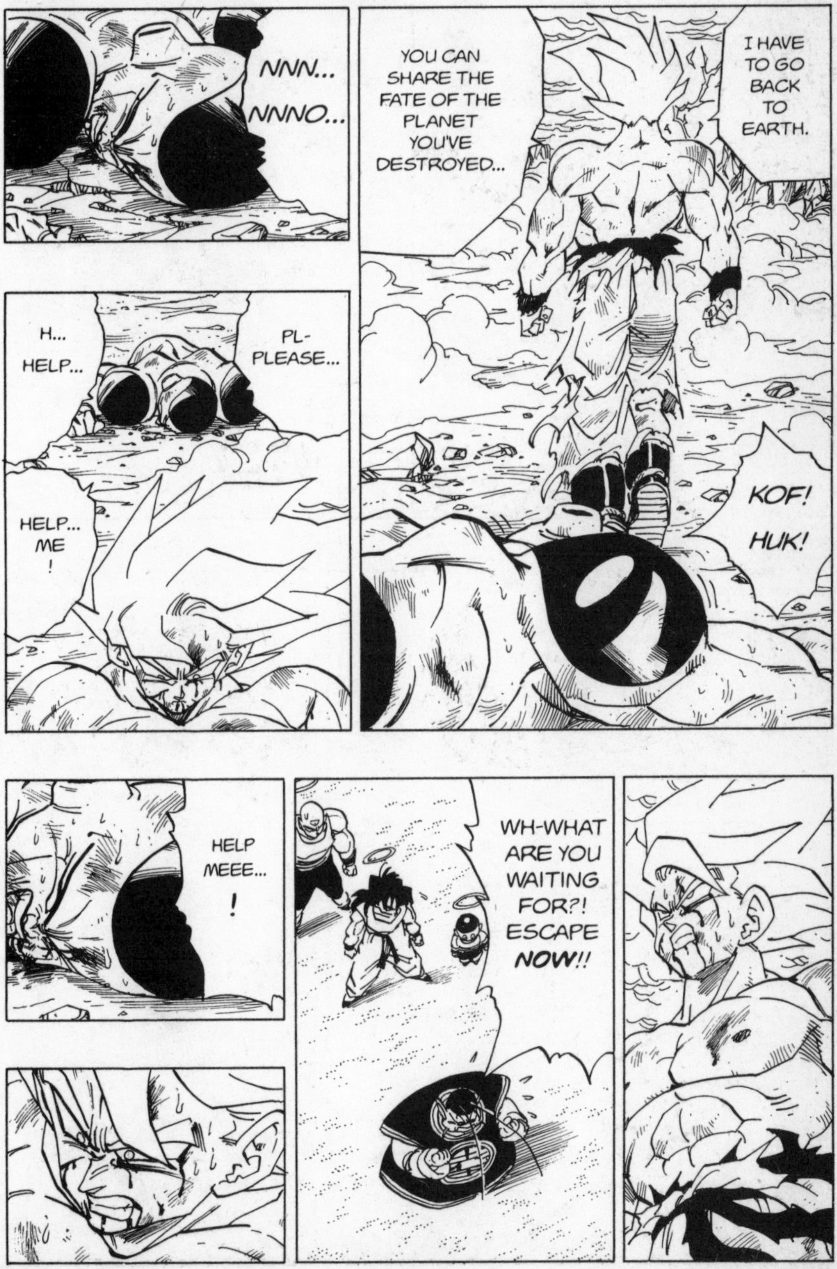
I HAVE TO GO BACK TO EARTH.
YOU CAN SHARE THE FATE OF THE PLANET YOU'VE DESTROYED...
KOF!
HUK!
NNN...
NNNO...
PL- PLEASE...
H... HELP...
HELP... ME !
WH-WHAT ARE YOU WAITING FOR?! ESCAPE *NOW!!*
HELP MEEE...
!

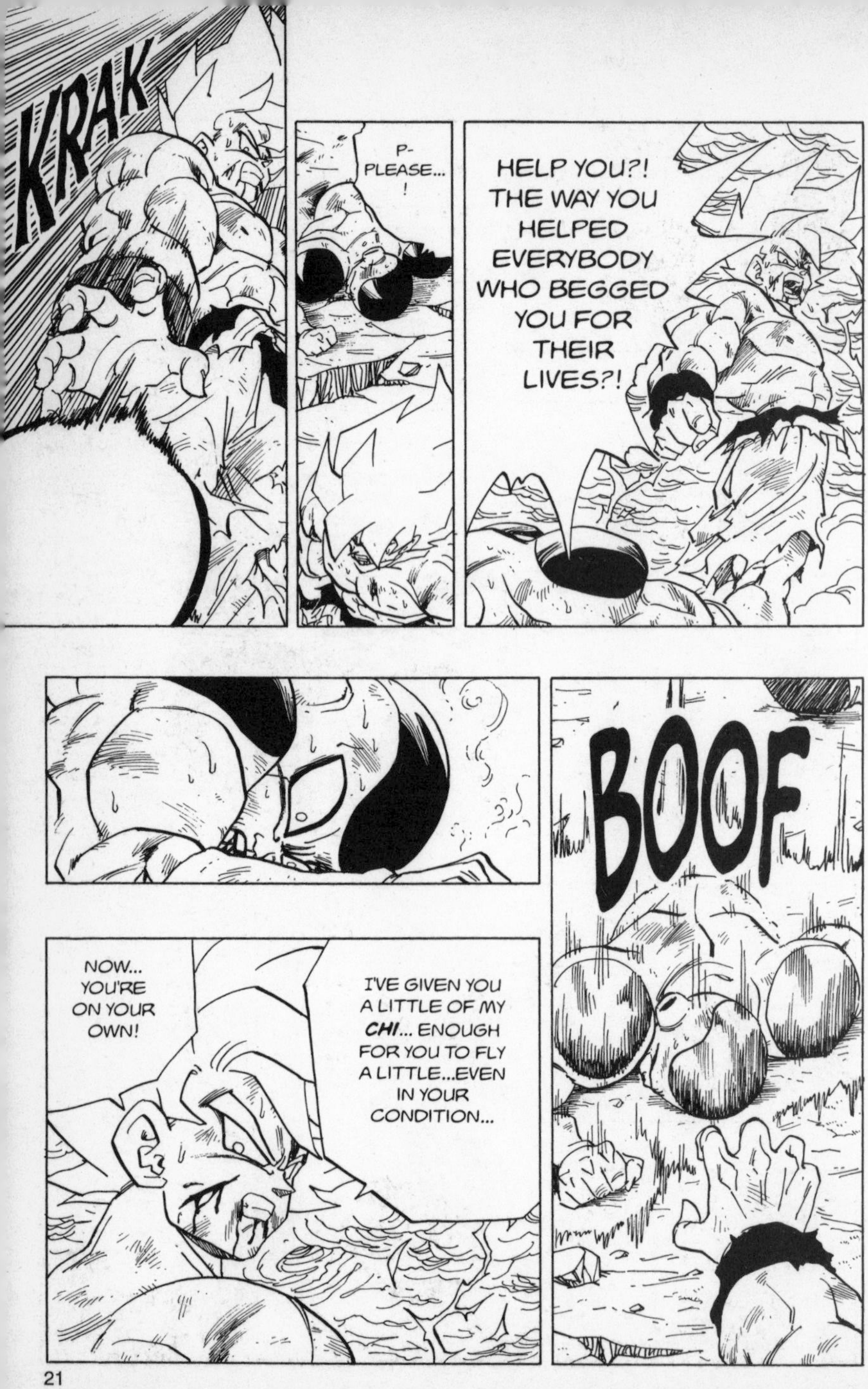
HELP YOU?! THE WAY YOU HELPED EVERYBODY WHO BEGGED YOU FOR THEIR LIVES?!
P-PLEASE...!
KRAK
BOOF
I'VE GIVEN YOU A LITTLE OF MY *CHI*... ENOUGH FOR YOU TO FLY A LITTLE...EVEN IN YOUR CONDITION...
NOW... YOU'RE ON YOUR OWN!

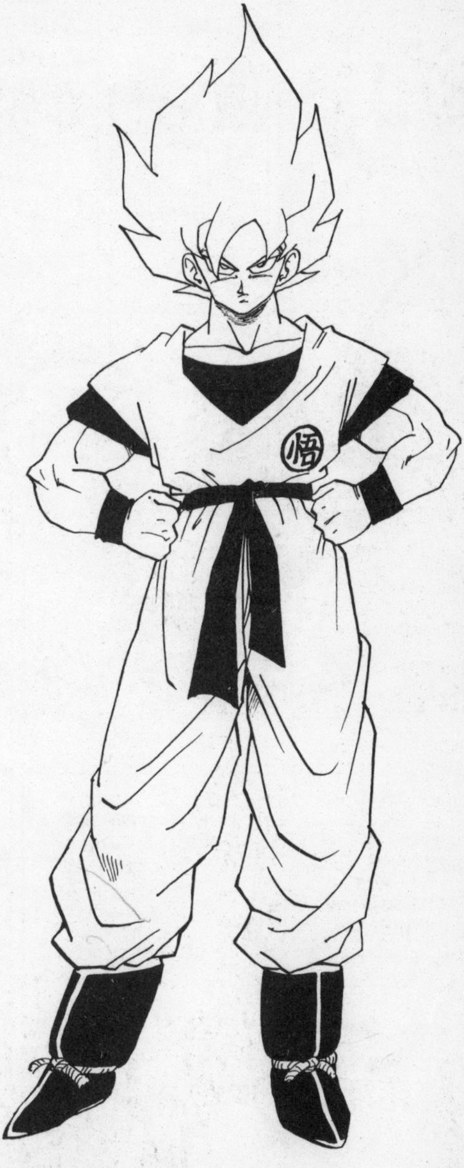
悟

DBZ:133 • The End of Everything

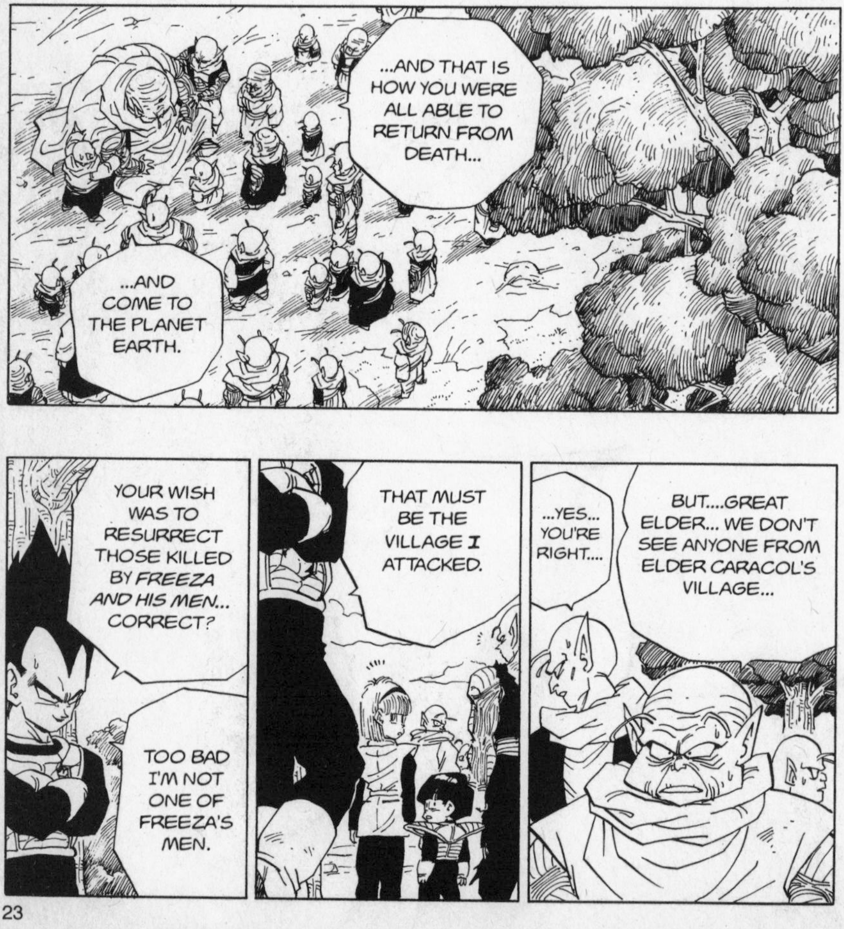
...AND THAT IS HOW YOU WERE ALL ABLE TO RETURN FROM DEATH...
...AND COME TO THE PLANET EARTH.
BUT....GREAT ELDER... WE DON'T SEE ANYONE FROM ELDER CARACOL'S VILLAGE...
...YES... YOU'RE RIGHT....
THAT MUST BE THE VILLAGE I ATTACKED.
YOUR WISH WAS TO RESURRECT THOSE KILLED BY *FREEZA AND HIS MEN...* CORRECT?
TOO BAD I'M NOT ONE OF FREEZA'S MEN.

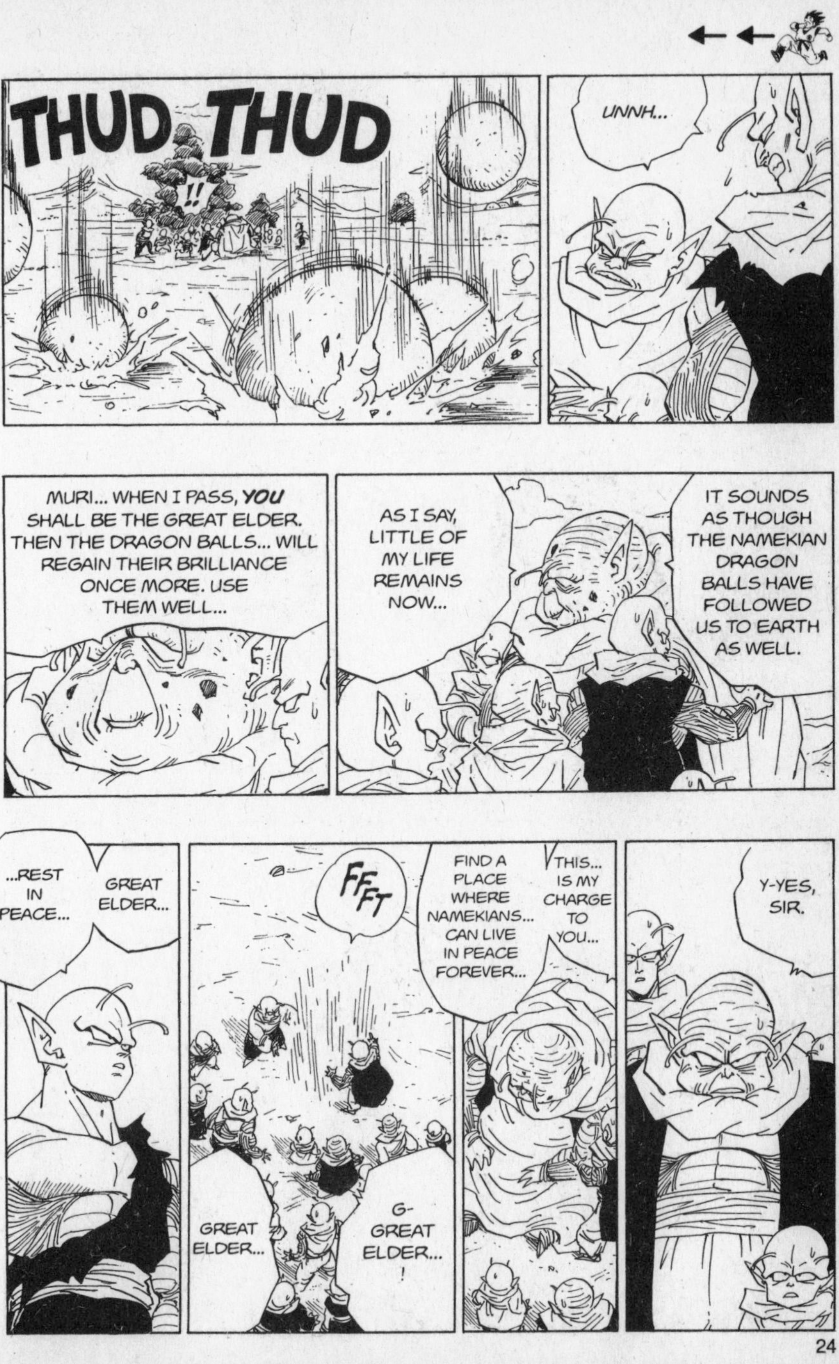
UNNH...
THUD THUD
!!
IT SOUNDS AS THOUGH THE NAMEKIAN DRAGON BALLS HAVE FOLLOWED US TO EARTH AS WELL.
AS I SAY, LITTLE OF MY LIFE REMAINS NOW...
MURI... WHEN I PASS, ***YOU*** SHALL BE THE GREAT ELDER. THEN THE DRAGON BALLS... WILL REGAIN THEIR BRILLIANCE ONCE MORE. USE THEM WELL...
Y-YES, SIR.
THIS... IS MY CHARGE TO YOU...
FIND A PLACE WHERE NAMEKIANS... CAN LIVE IN PEACE FOREVER...
FFFT
G-GREAT ELDER...!
GREAT ELDER...
GREAT ELDER...
...REST IN PEACE...

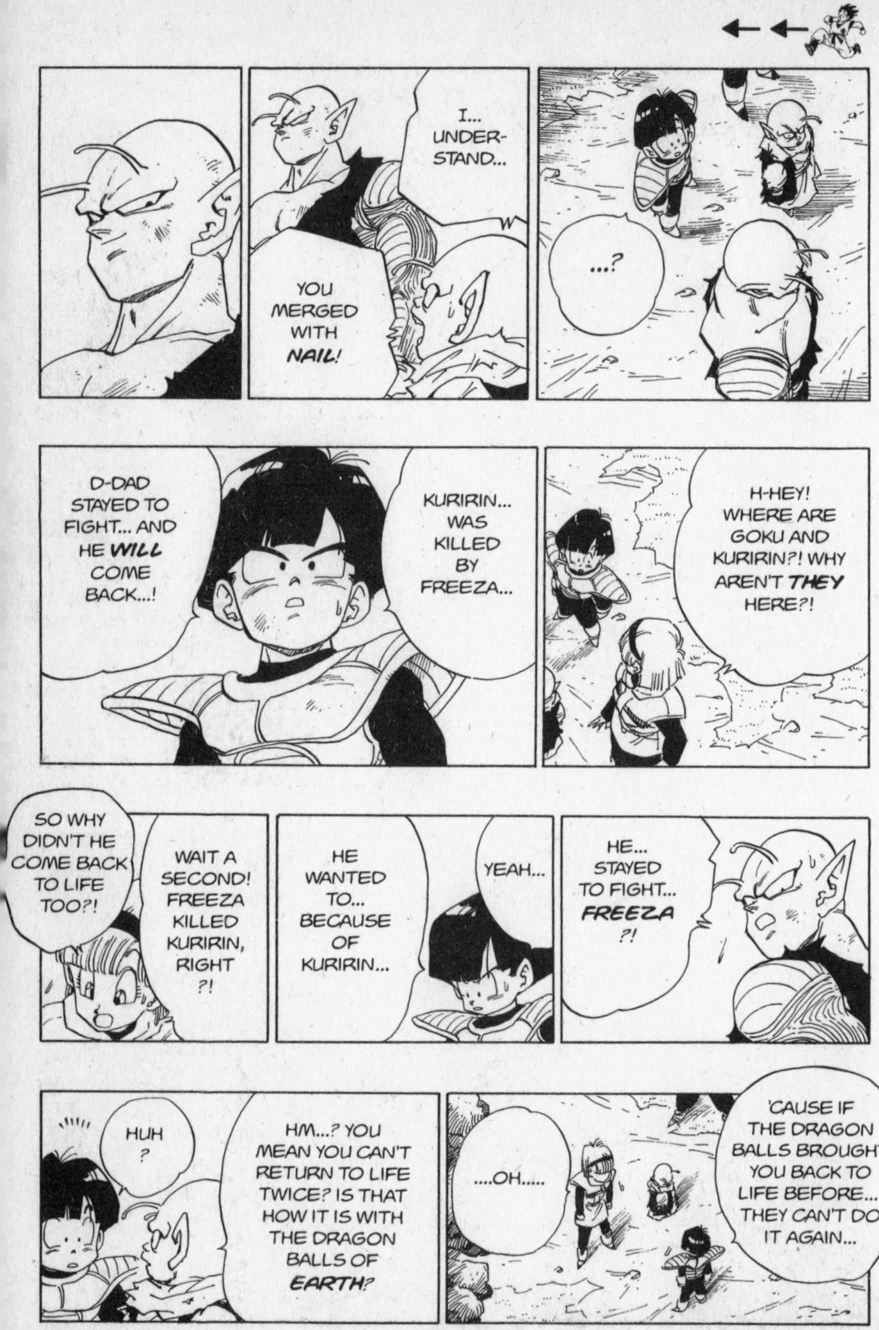
...?
I... UNDERSTAND...
YOU MERGED WITH NAIL!
H-HEY! WHERE ARE GOKU AND KURIRIN?! WHY AREN'T THEY HERE?!
KURIRIN... WAS KILLED BY FREEZA...
D-DAD STAYED TO FIGHT... AND HE WILL COME BACK...!
HE... STAYED TO FIGHT... FREEZA?!
YEAH...
HE WANTED TO... BECAUSE OF KURIRIN...
WAIT A SECOND! FREEZA KILLED KURIRIN, RIGHT?!
SO WHY DIDN'T HE COME BACK TO LIFE TOO?!
'CAUSE IF THE DRAGON BALLS BROUGHT YOU BACK TO LIFE BEFORE.... THEY CAN'T DO IT AGAIN...
....OH.....
HM...? YOU MEAN YOU CAN'T RETURN TO LIFE TWICE? IS THAT HOW IT IS WITH THE DRAGON BALLS OF EARTH?
HUH?

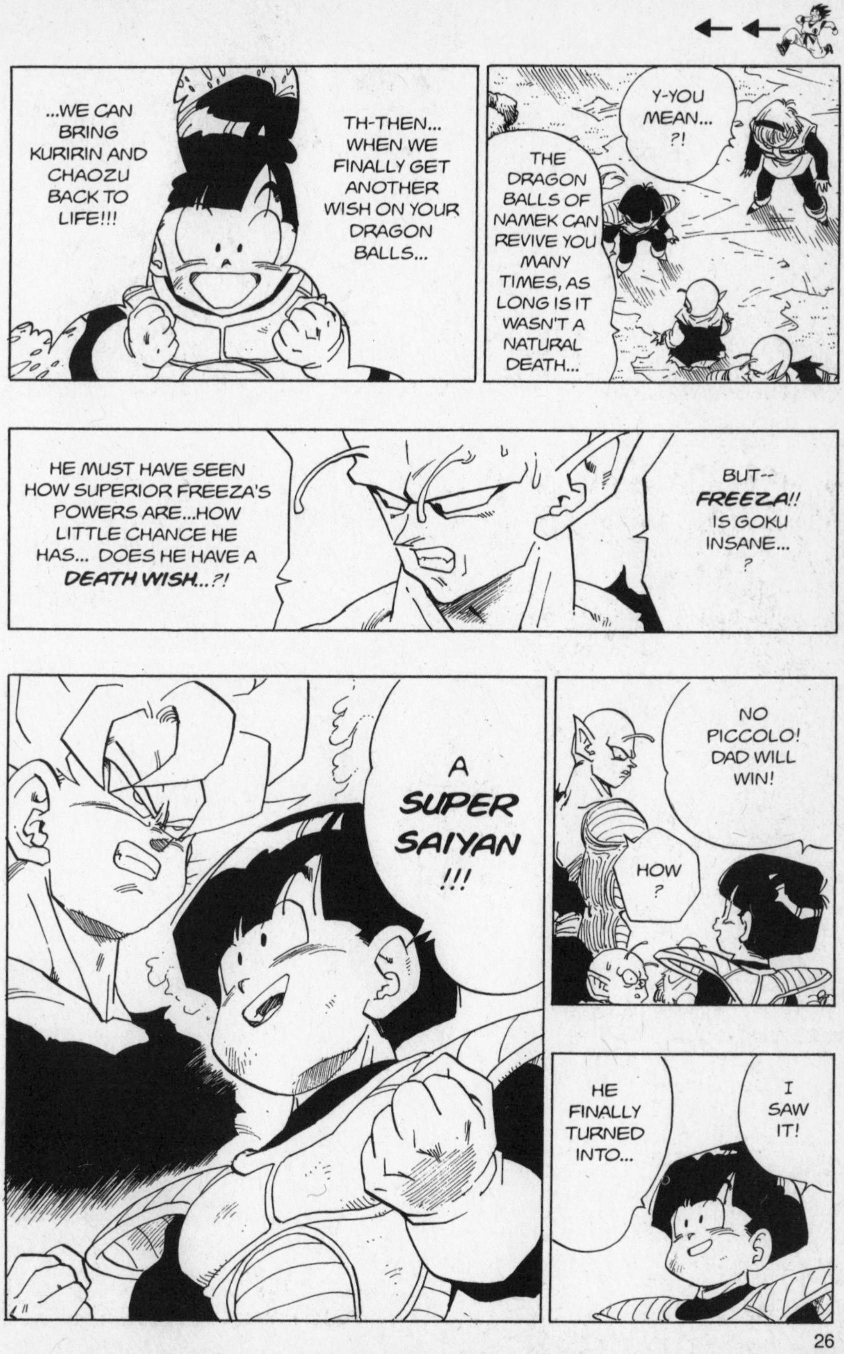
Y-YOU MEAN...?!
THE DRAGON BALLS OF NAMEK CAN REVIVE YOU MANY TIMES, AS LONG IS IT WASN'T A NATURAL DEATH...
TH-THEN... WHEN WE FINALLY GET ANOTHER WISH ON YOUR DRAGON BALLS...
...WE CAN BRING KURIRIN AND CHAOZU BACK TO LIFE!!!
BUT-- FREEZA!! IS GOKU INSANE...?
HE MUST HAVE SEEN HOW SUPERIOR FREEZA'S POWERS ARE...HOW LITTLE CHANCE HE HAS... DOES HE HAVE A DEATH WISH...?!
NO PICCOLO! DAD WILL WIN!
HOW?
I SAW IT!
HE FINALLY TURNED INTO...
A SUPER SAIYAN!!!

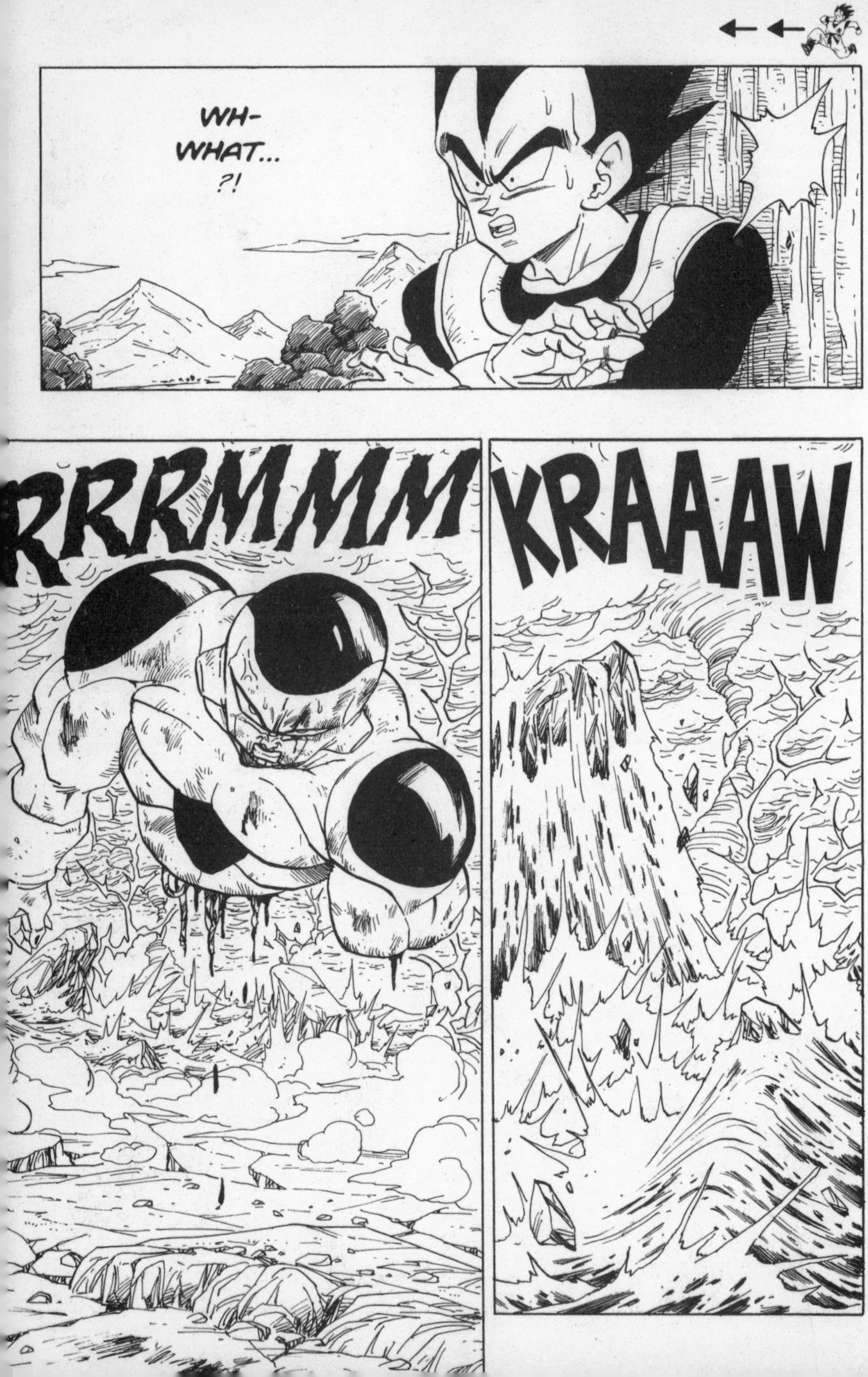
WH- WHAT... ?!
KRAAAW
RRRMMM

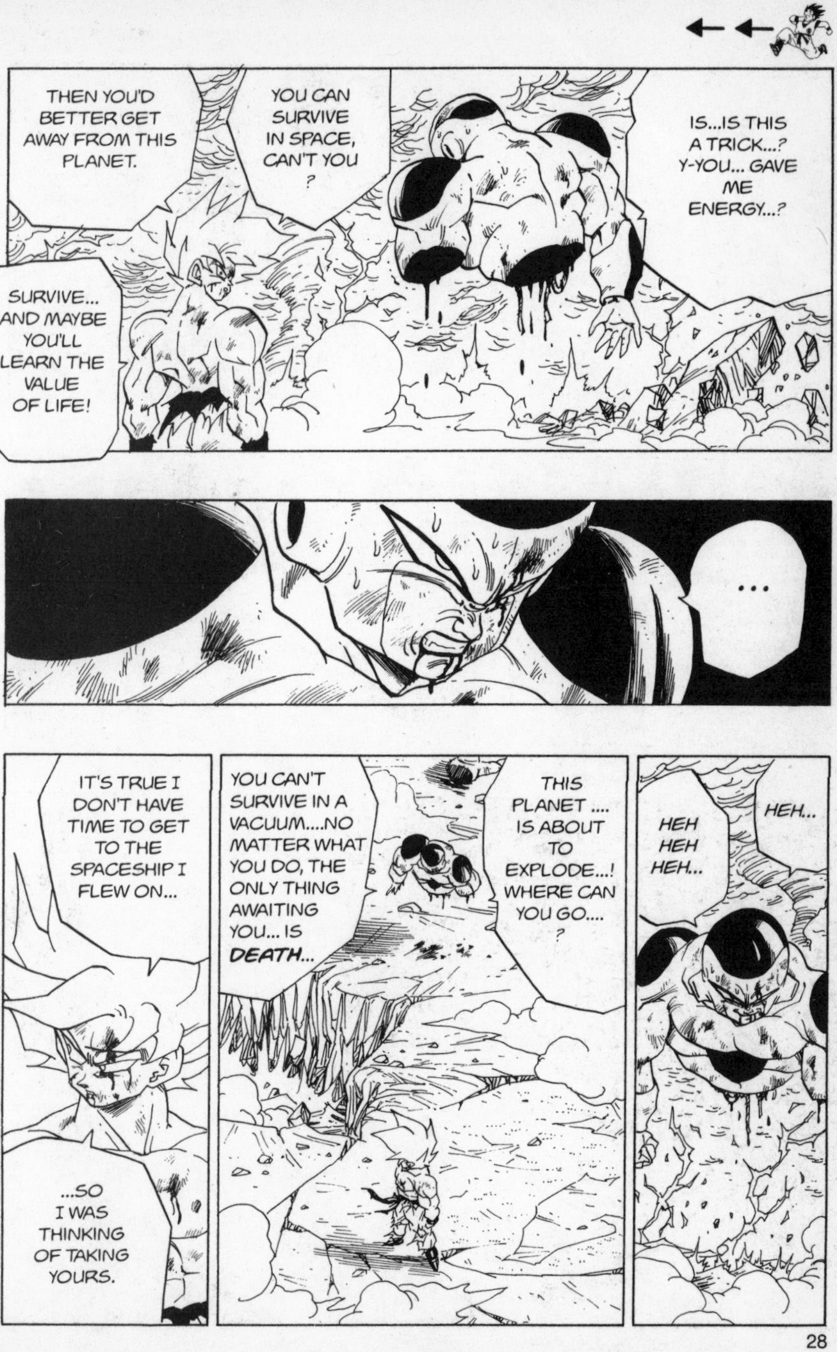
IS...IS THIS A TRICK...? Y-YOU... GAVE ME ENERGY...?
YOU CAN SURVIVE IN SPACE, CAN'T YOU ?
THEN YOU'D BETTER GET AWAY FROM THIS PLANET.
SURVIVE... AND MAYBE YOU'LL LEARN THE VALUE OF LIFE!
...
HEH...
HEH HEH HEH...
THIS PLANET .... IS ABOUT TO EXPLODE...! WHERE CAN YOU GO.... ?
YOU CAN'T SURVIVE IN A VACUUM....NO MATTER WHAT YOU DO, THE ONLY THING AWAITING YOU... IS DEATH...
IT'S TRUE I DON'T HAVE TIME TO GET TO THE SPACESHIP I FLEW ON...
...SO I WAS THINKING OF TAKING YOURS.

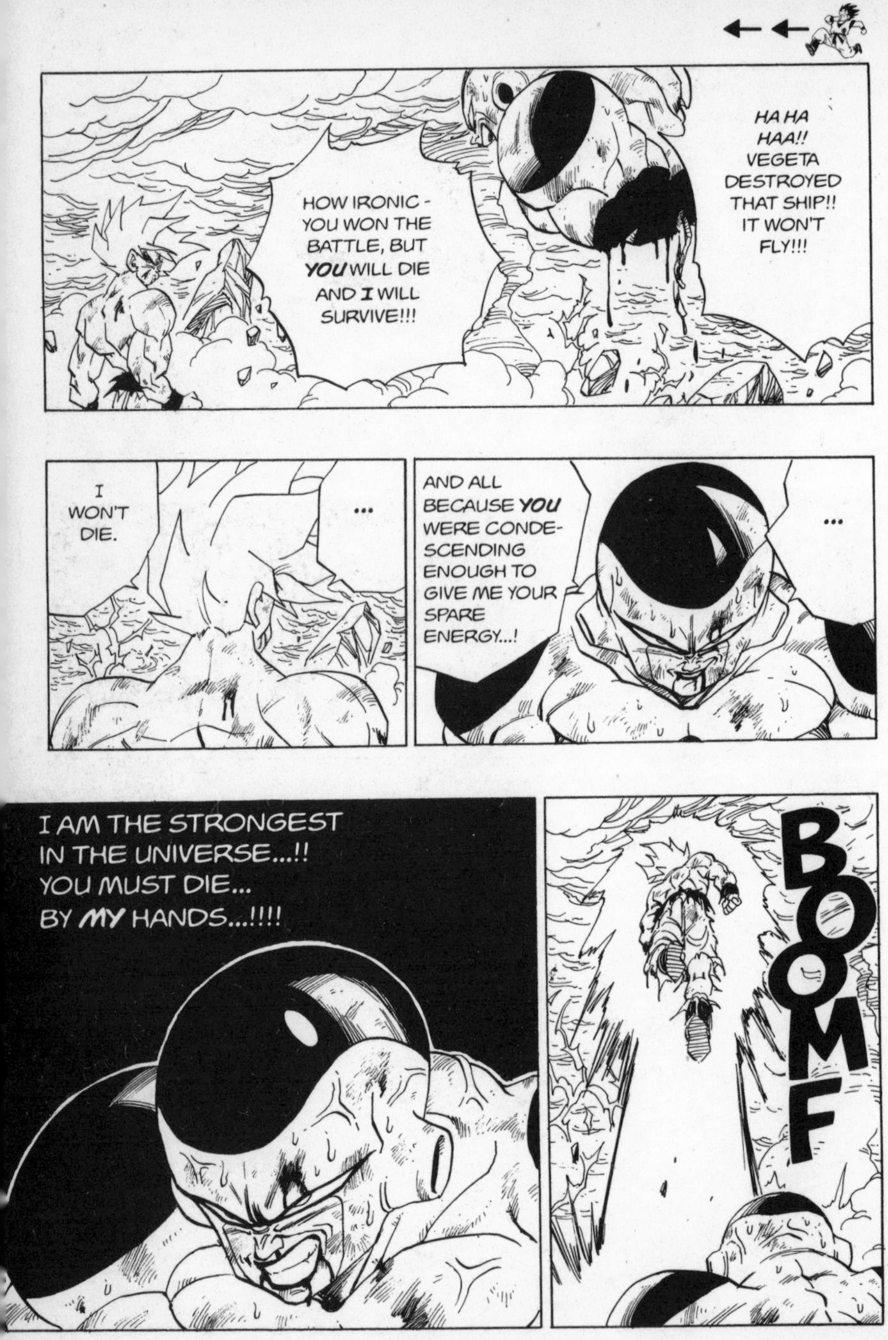
HA HA HAA!! VEGETA DESTROYED THAT SHIP!! IT WON'T FLY!!!
HOW IRONIC - YOU WON THE BATTLE, BUT YOU WILL DIE AND I WILL SURVIVE!!!
...
AND ALL BECAUSE YOU WERE CONDE-SCENDING ENOUGH TO GIVE ME YOUR SPARE ENERGY...!
...
I WON'T DIE.
BOOMF
I AM THE STRONGEST IN THE UNIVERSE...!! YOU MUST DIE... BY MY HANDS...!!!!

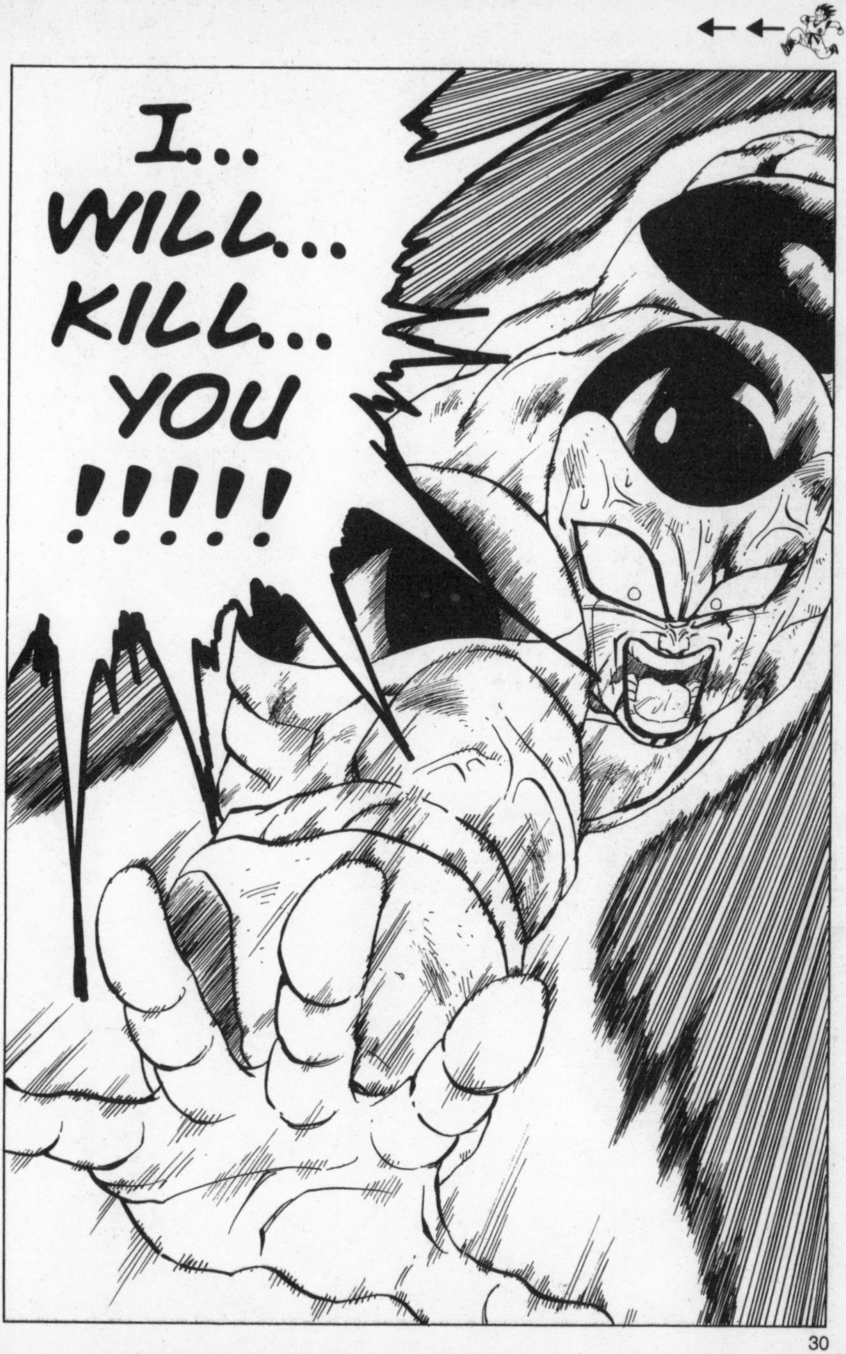
I... WILL... KILL... YOU !!!!!

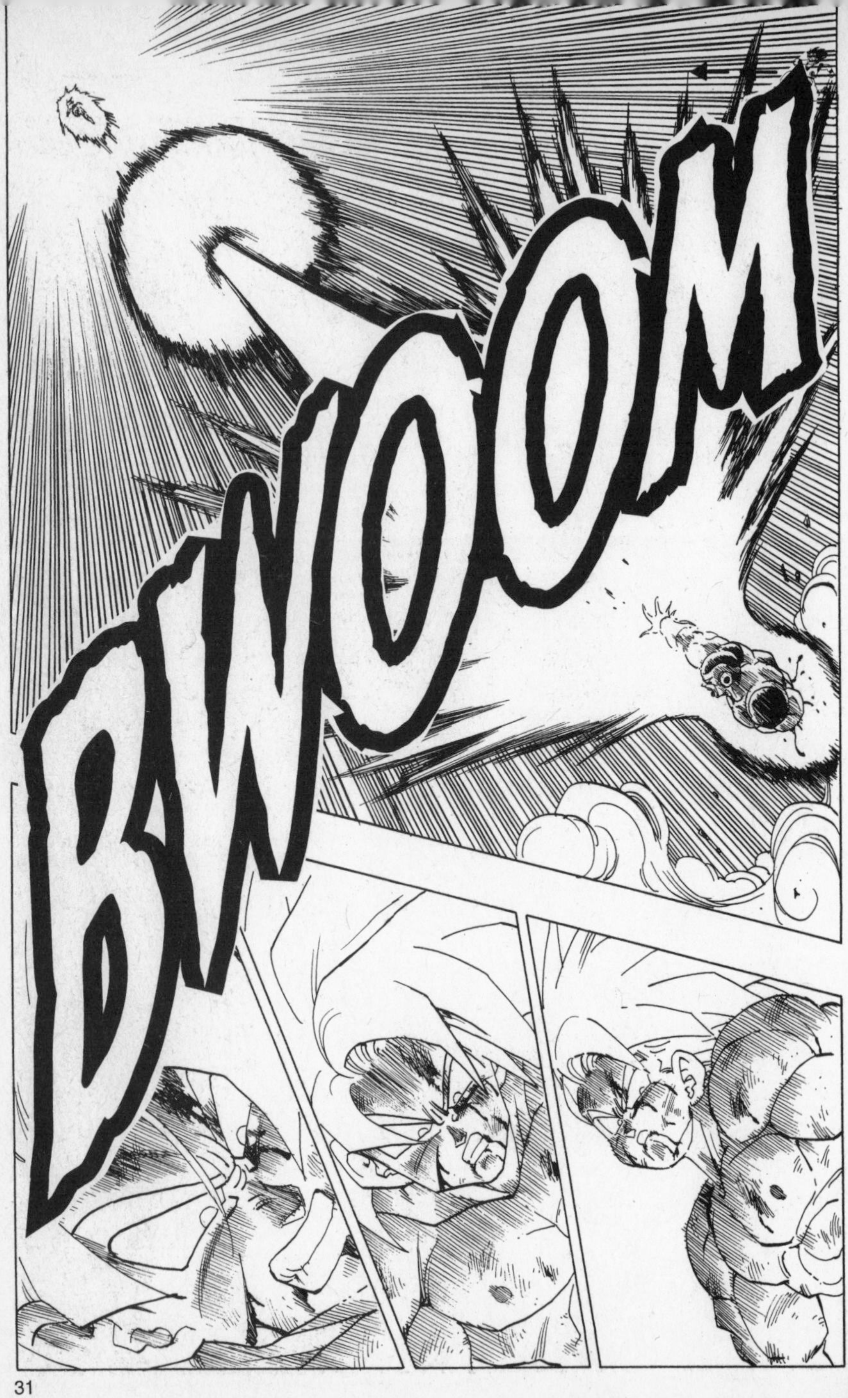
BWOOOM

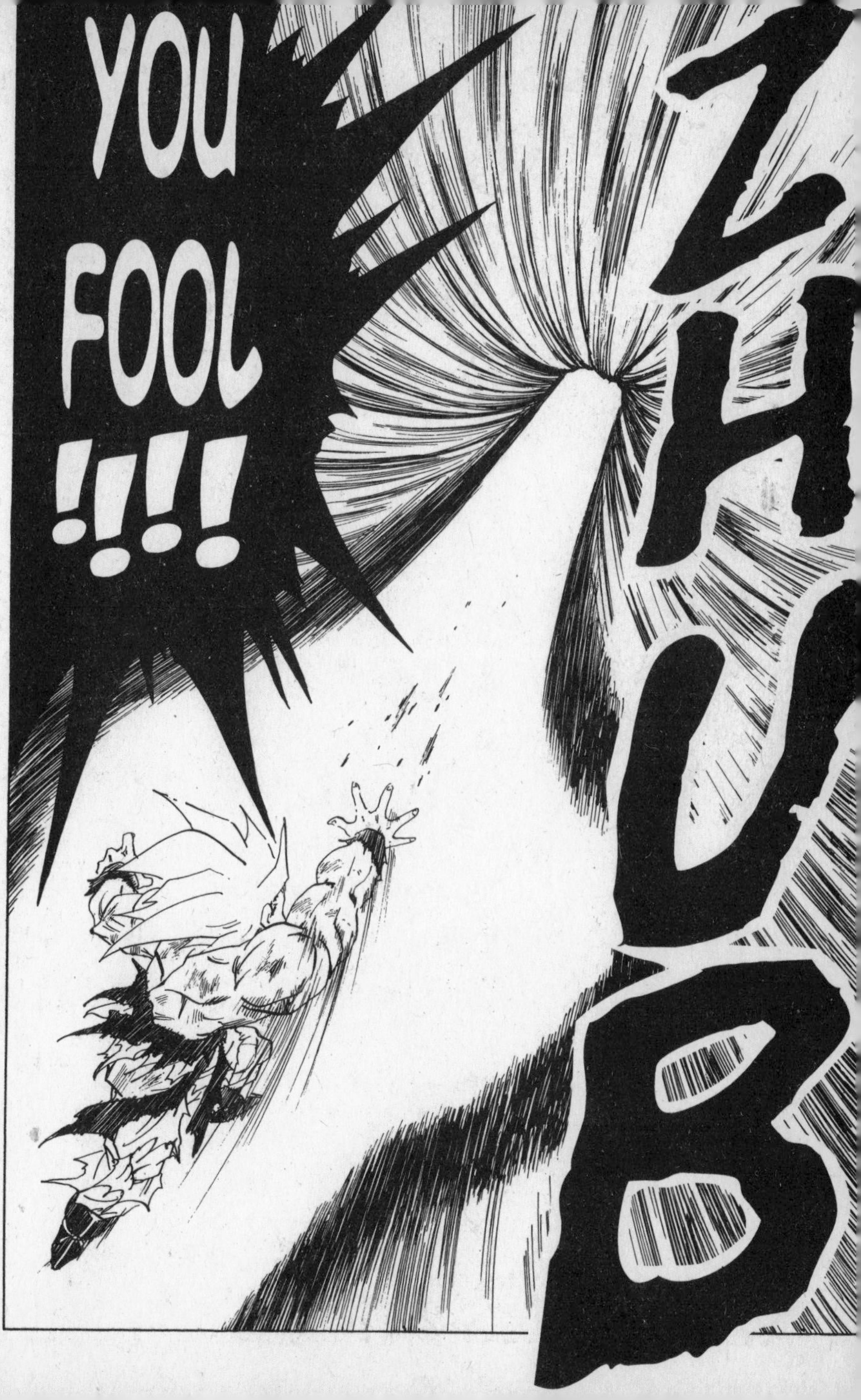
YOU FOOL !!!!

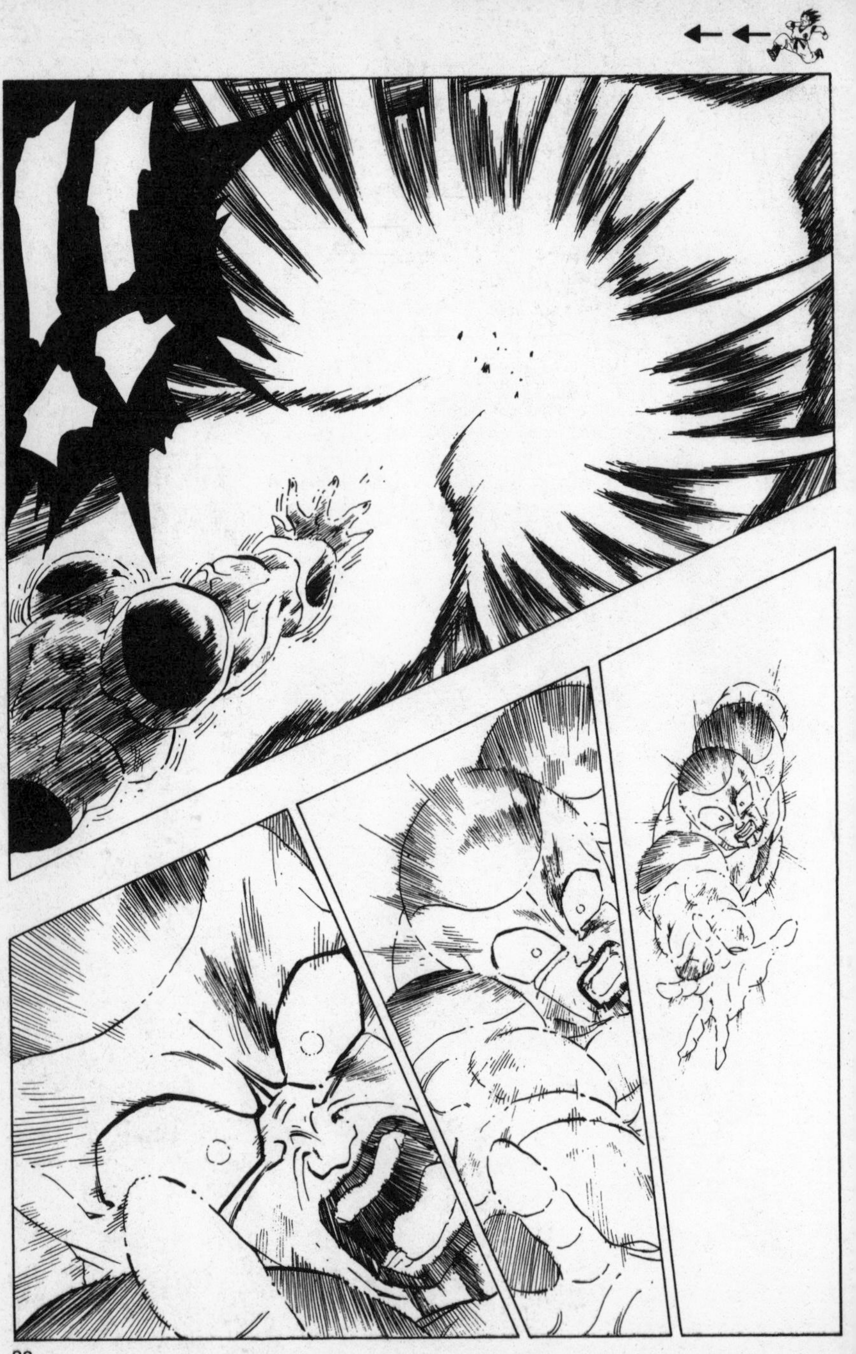

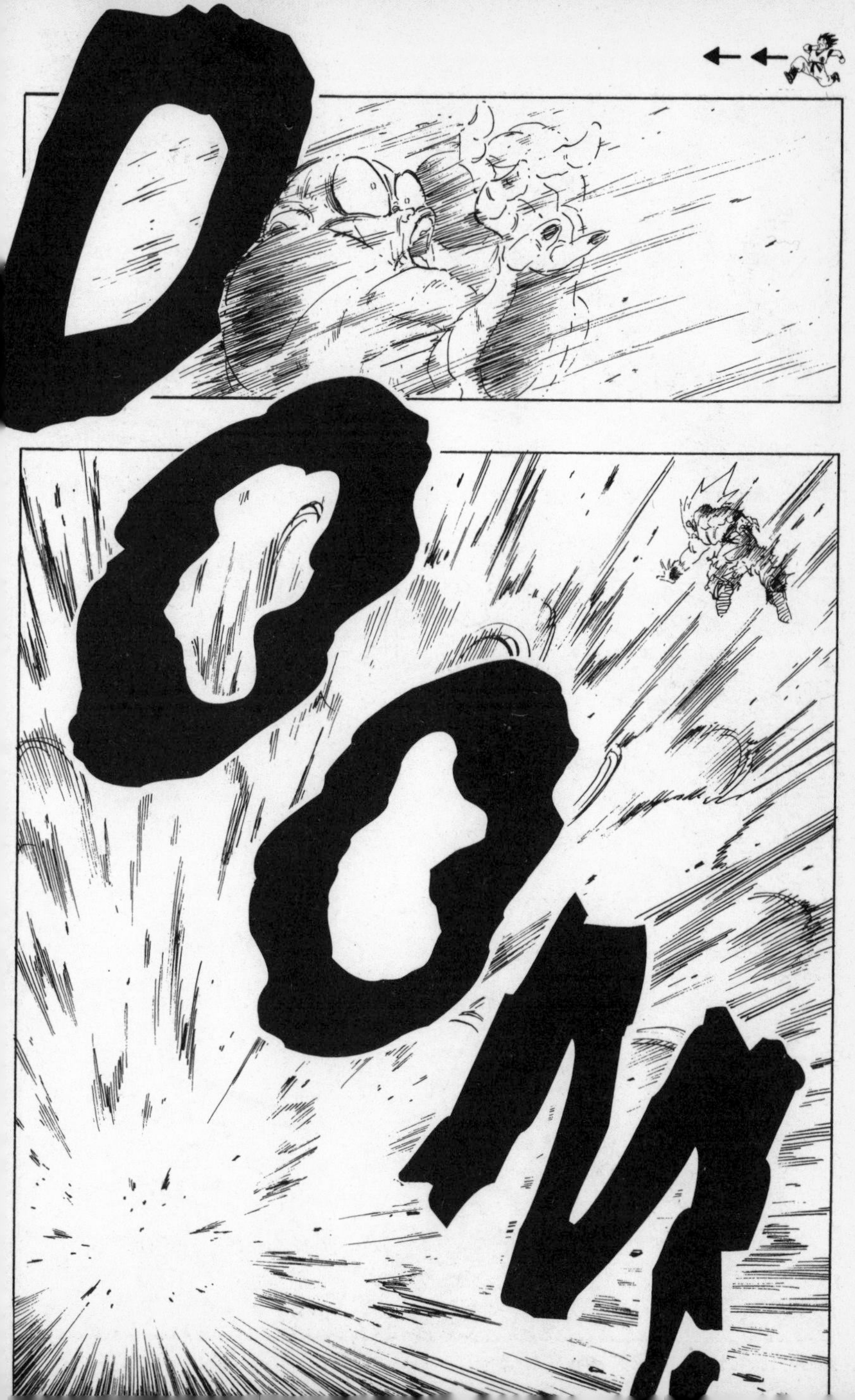
DOOOM!!

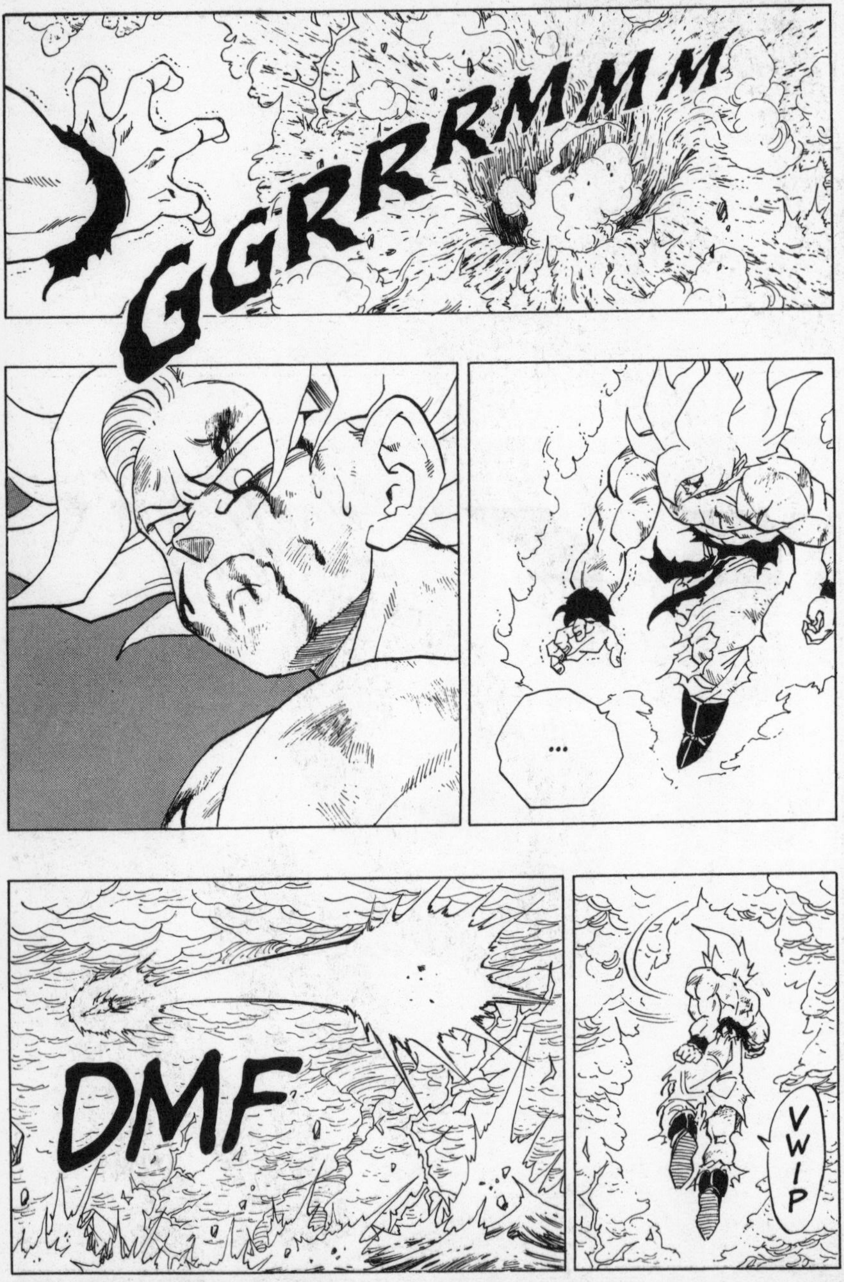
GGRRRMMMM
...
VWIP
DMF

NEXT: THE PLANET VANISHES

DBZ:134 • Namek's End

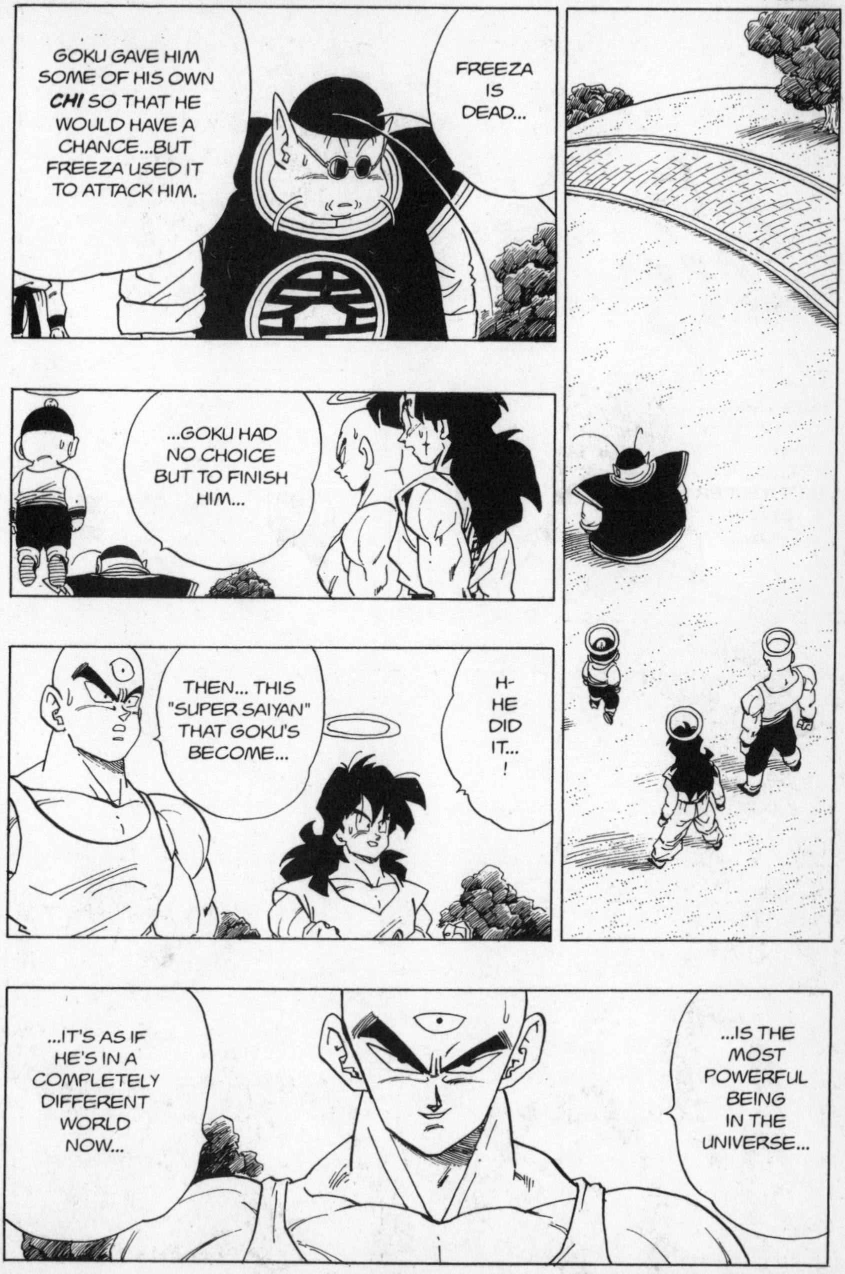
FREEZA IS DEAD...
GOKU GAVE HIM SOME OF HIS OWN *CHI* SO THAT HE WOULD HAVE A CHANCE...BUT FREEZA USED IT TO ATTACK HIM.
...GOKU HAD NO CHOICE BUT TO FINISH HIM...
H- HE DID IT... !
THEN... THIS "SUPER SAIYAN" THAT GOKU'S BECOME...
...IS THE MOST POWERFUL BEING IN THE UNIVERSE...
...IT'S AS IF HE'S IN A COMPLETELY DIFFERENT WORLD NOW...

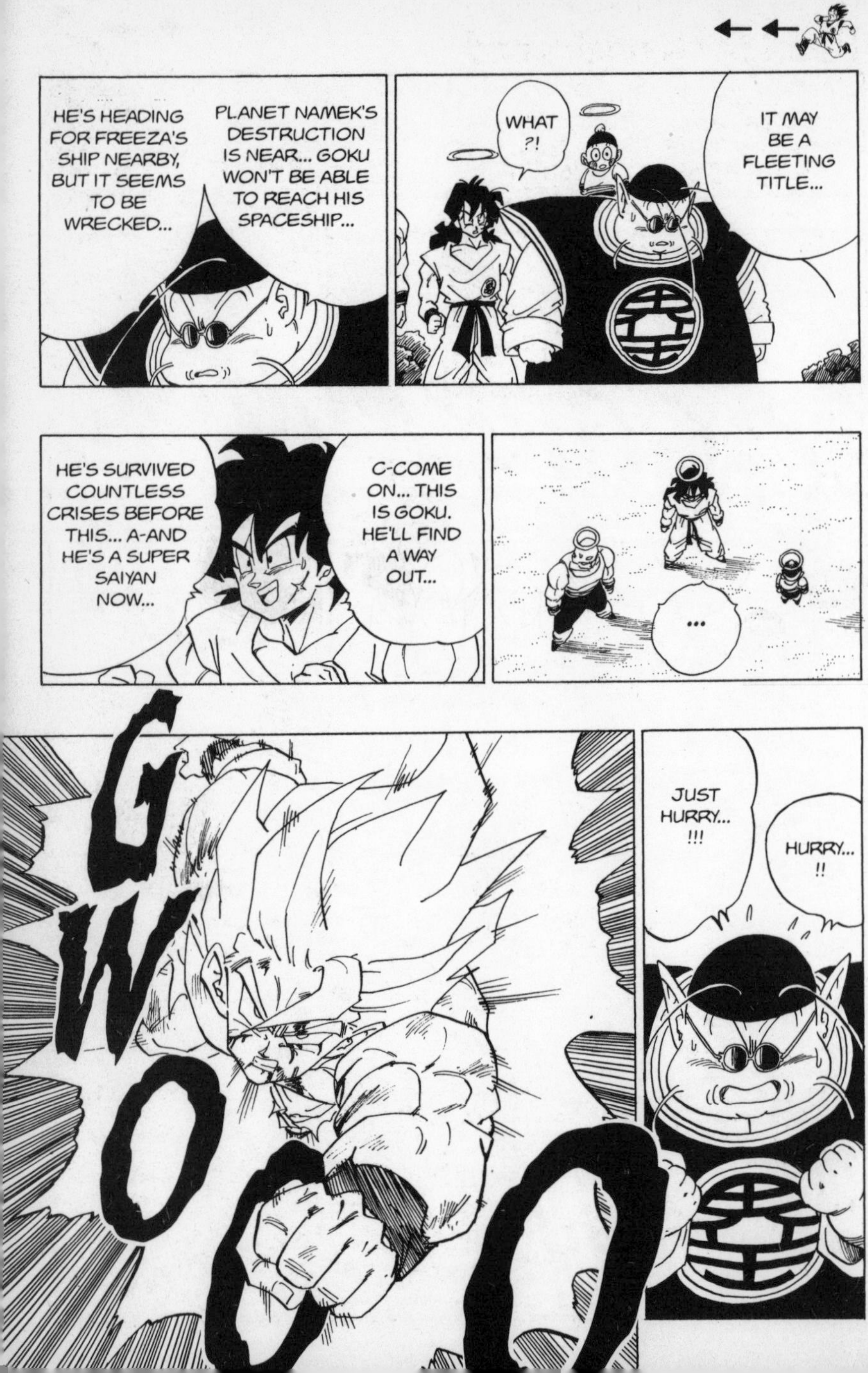
IT MAY BE A FLEETING TITLE...
WHAT ?!
PLANET NAMEK'S DESTRUCTION IS NEAR... GOKU WON'T BE ABLE TO REACH HIS SPACESHIP...
HE'S HEADING FOR FREEZA'S SHIP NEARBY, BUT IT SEEMS TO BE WRECKED...
...
C-COME ON... THIS IS GOKU. HE'LL FIND A WAY OUT...
HE'S SURVIVED COUNTLESS CRISES BEFORE THIS... A-AND HE'S A SUPER SAIYAN NOW...
HURRY... !!
JUST HURRY... !!!
GWOOOO

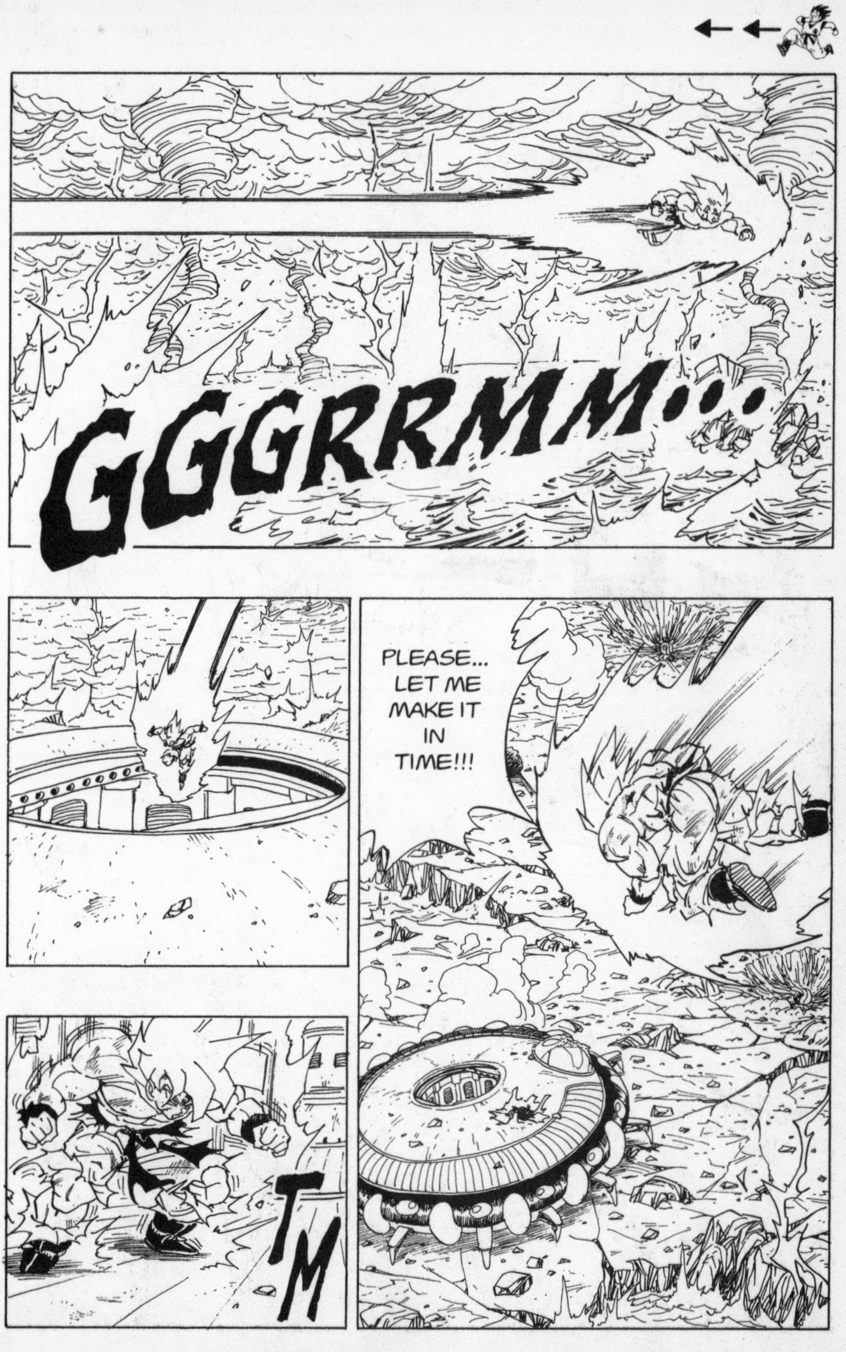
GGGRRMM...
PLEASE... LET ME MAKE IT IN TIME!!!
TM

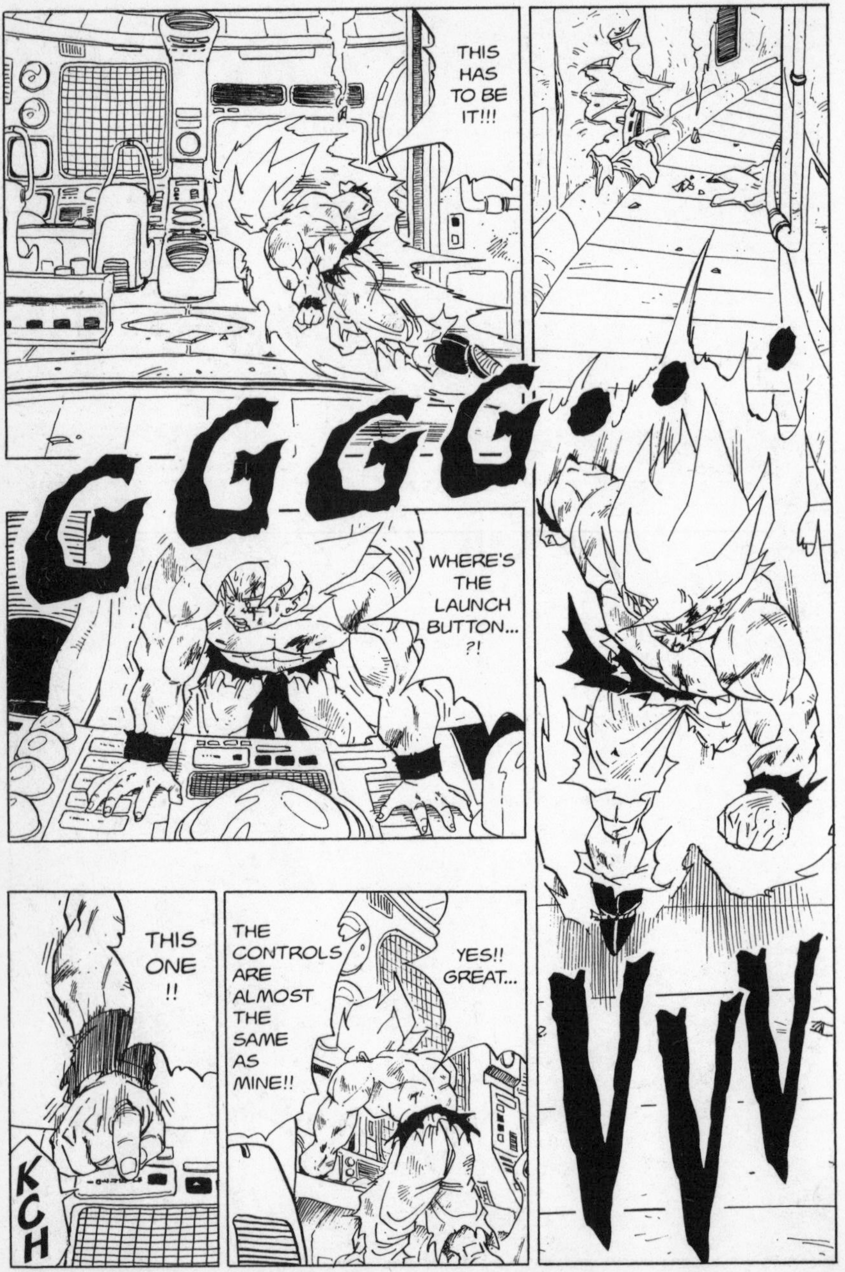
GGGG...
VVV
THIS HAS TO BE IT!!!
WHERE'S THE LAUNCH BUTTON...?!
YES!! GREAT...
THE CONTROLS ARE ALMOST THE SAME AS MINE!!
THIS ONE!!
KCH

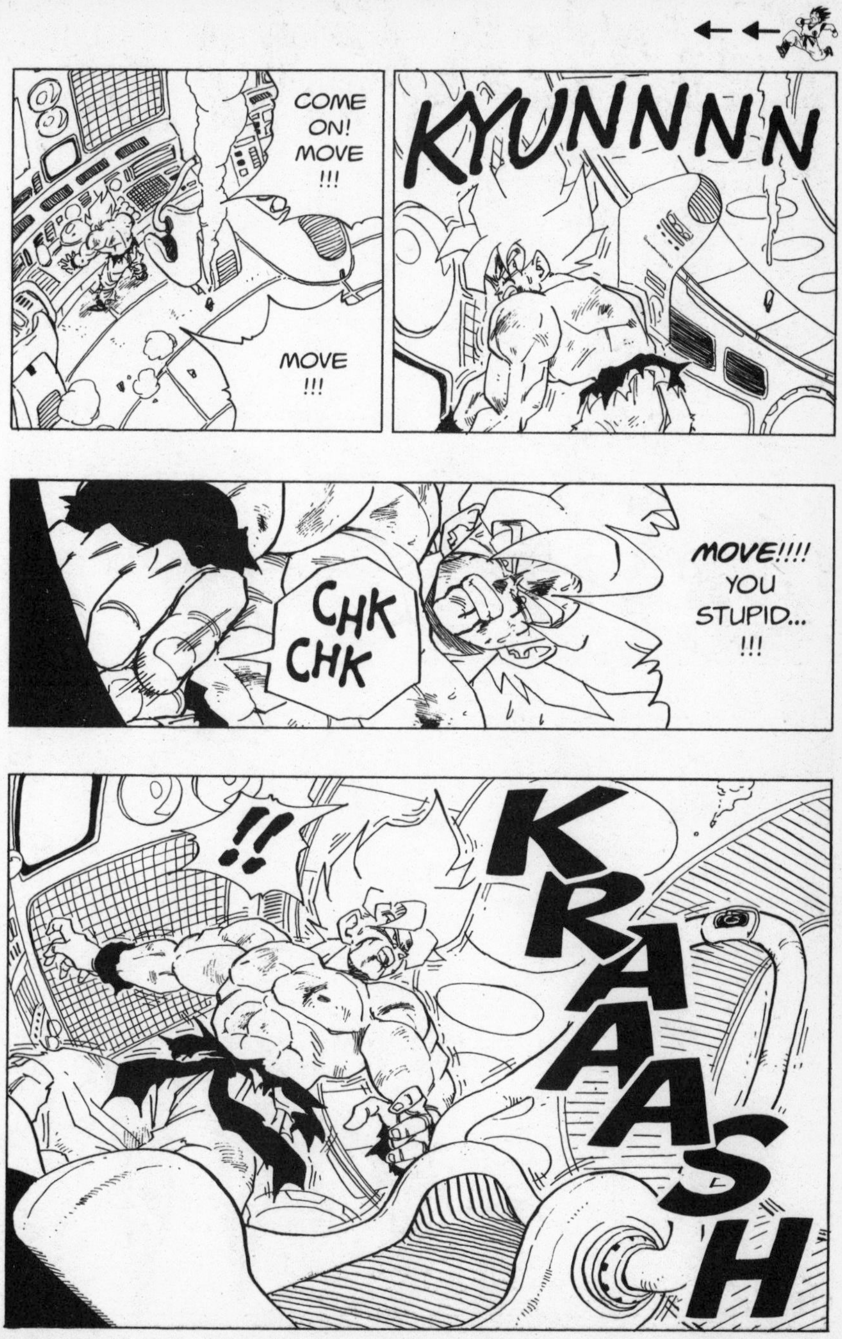
KYUNNNNN
COME ON! MOVE !!!
MOVE !!!
MOVE!!!! YOU STUPID... !!!
CHK CHK
KRAAASH
!!

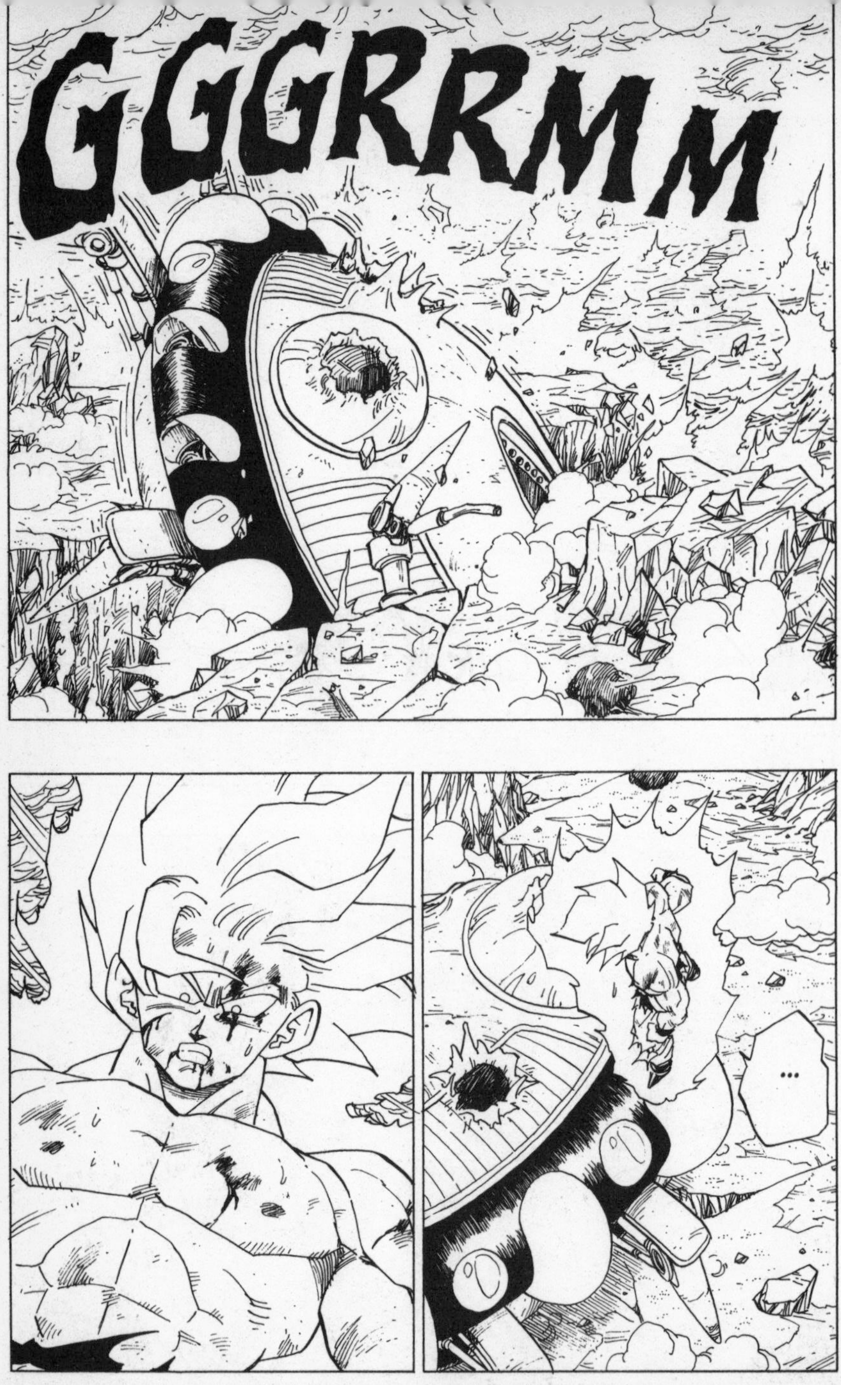
GGGRRMM
...

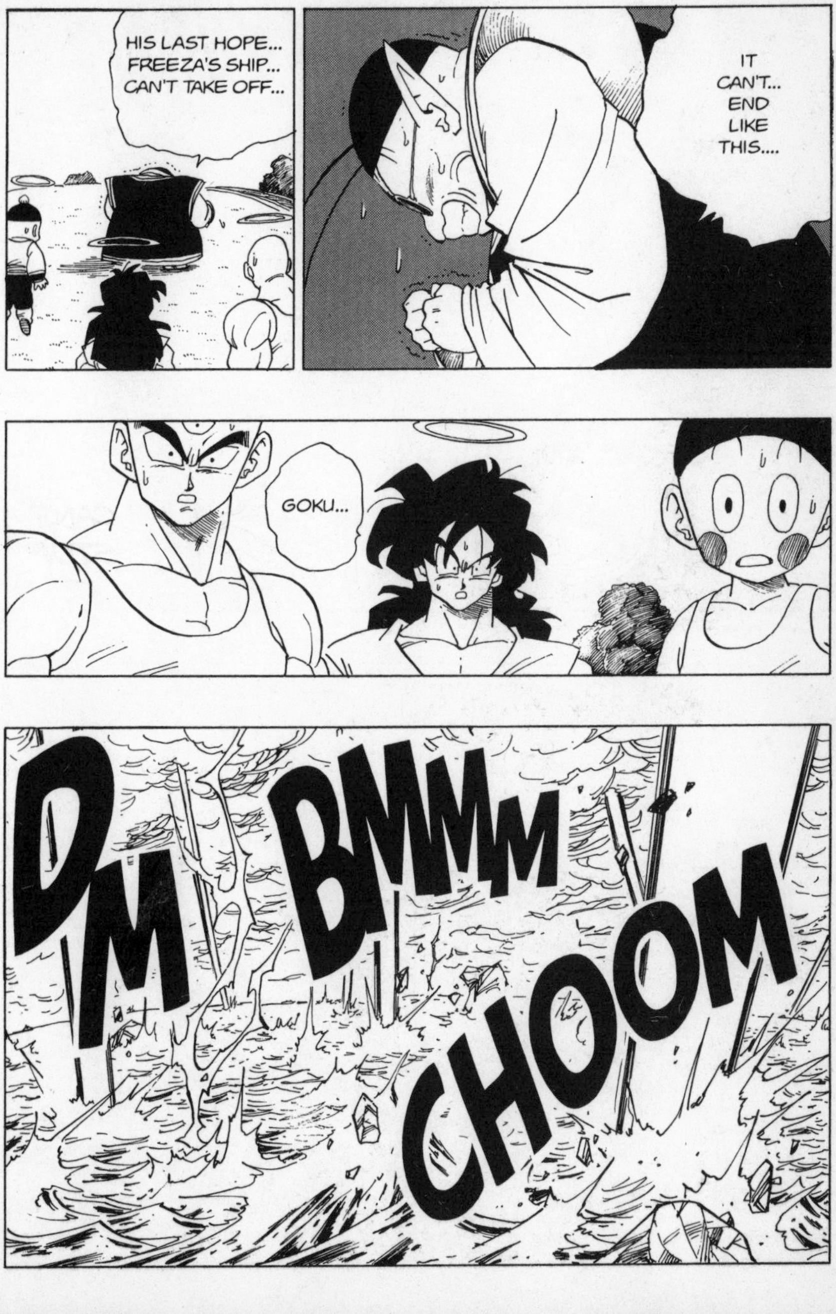
IT CAN'T... END LIKE THIS....
HIS LAST HOPE... FREEZA'S SHIP... CAN'T TAKE OFF...
GOKU...
DMBMMM CHOOM

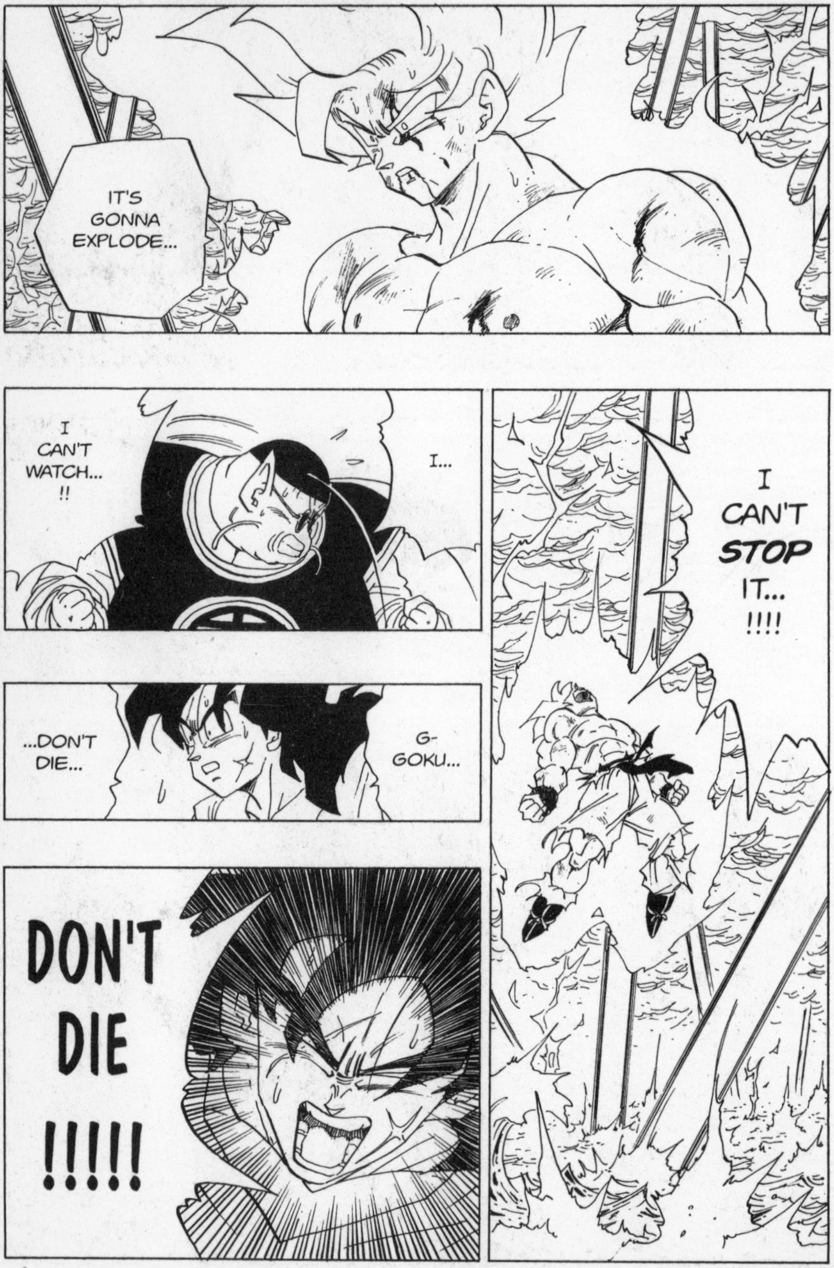
IT'S GONNA EXPLODE...
I CAN'T STOP IT... !!!!
I...
I CAN'T WATCH... !!
G-GOKU...
...DON'T DIE...
DON'T DIE !!!!!

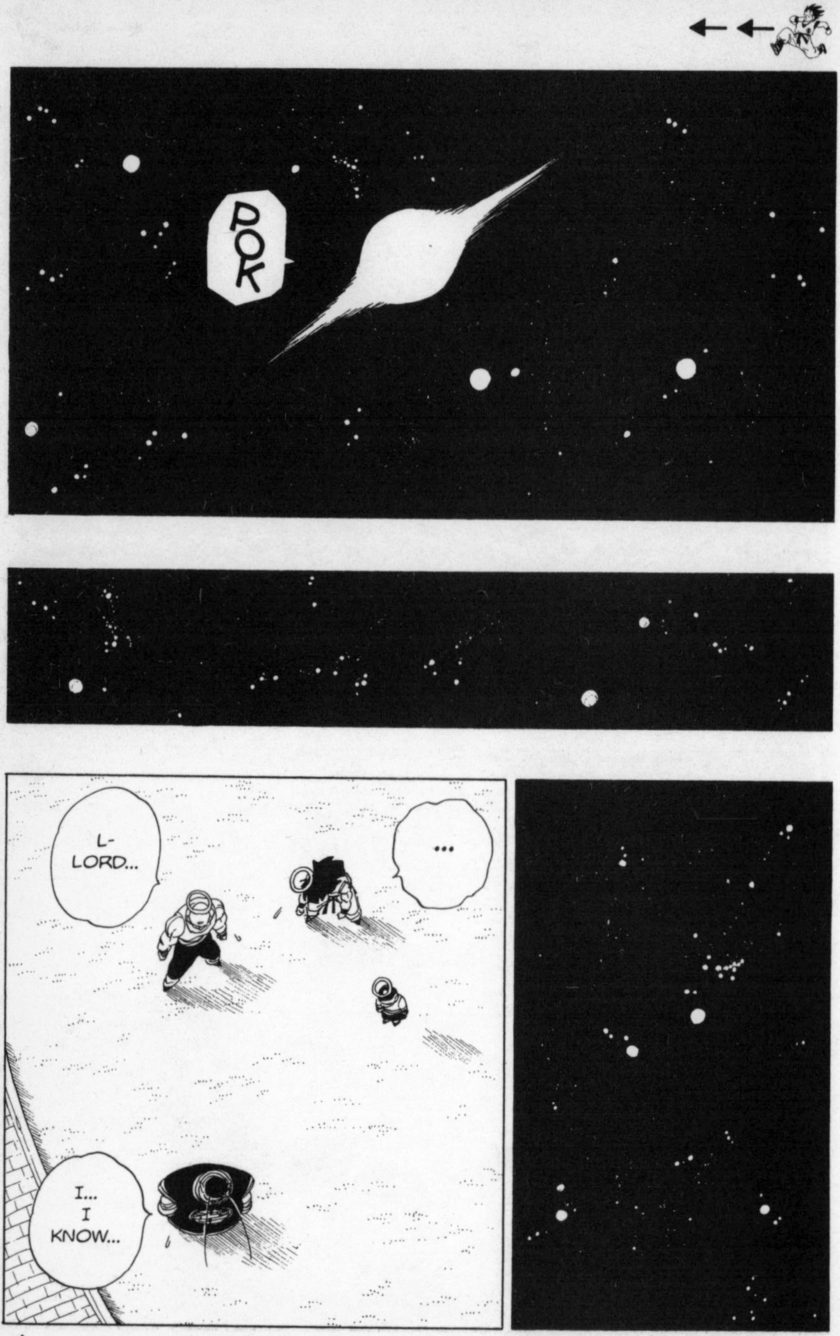
POK
...
L- LORD...
I... I KNOW...

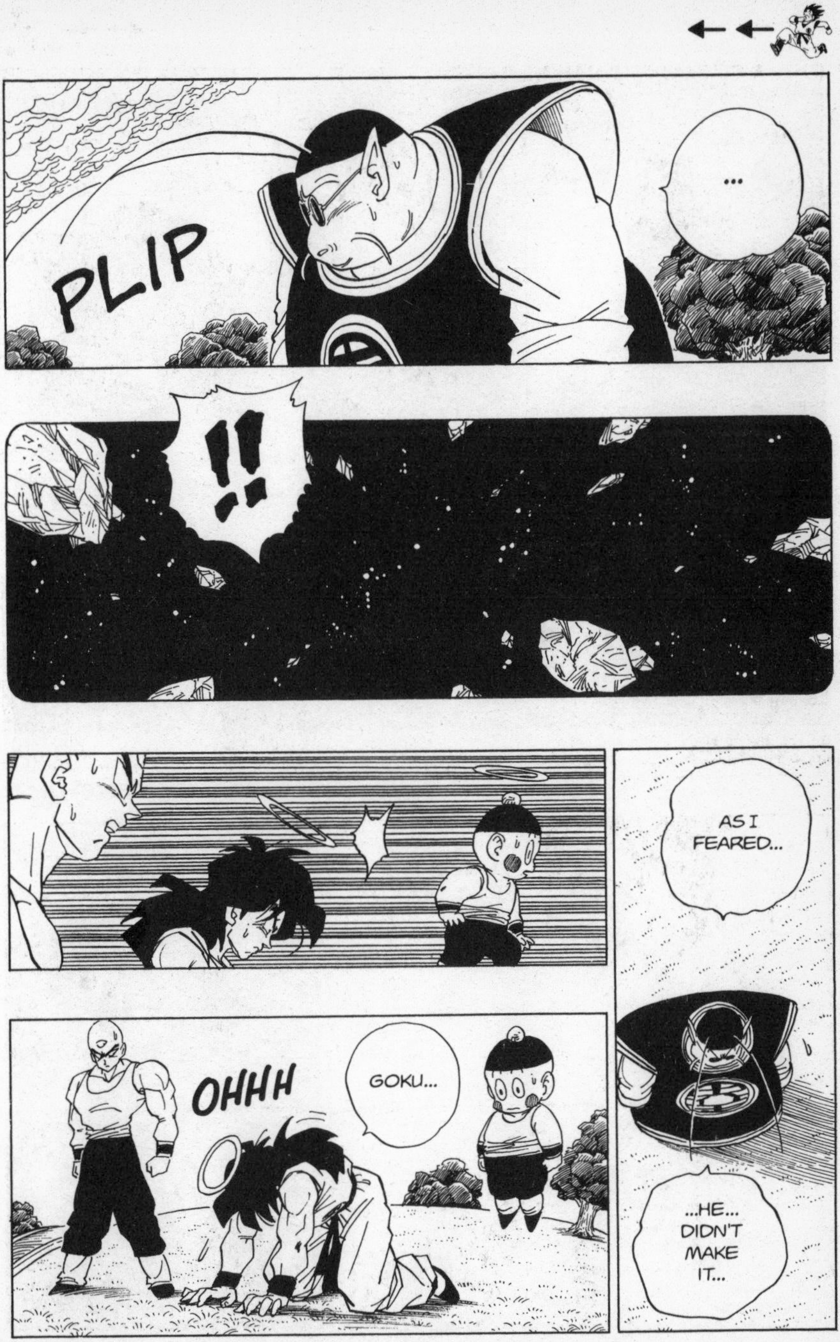

...
PLIP
!!
AS I FEARED...
...HE... DIDN'T MAKE IT...
GOKU...
OHHH

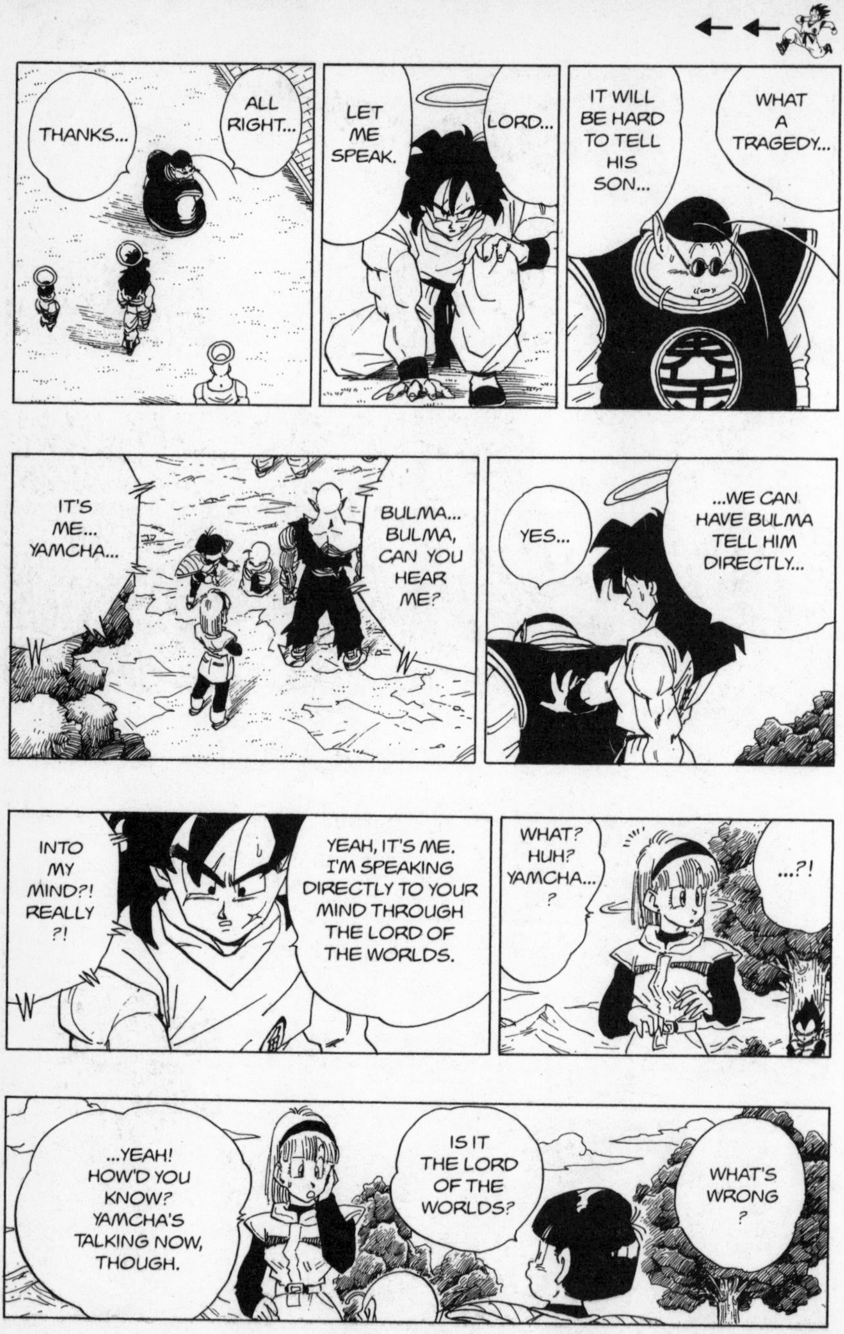
WHAT A TRAGEDY...
IT WILL BE HARD TO TELL HIS SON...
LORD...
LET ME SPEAK.
ALL RIGHT...
THANKS...
...WE CAN HAVE BULMA TELL HIM DIRECTLY...
YES...
BULMA... BULMA, CAN YOU HEAR ME?
IT'S ME... YAMCHA...
...?!
WHAT? HUH? YAMCHA...?
YEAH, IT'S ME. I'M SPEAKING DIRECTLY TO YOUR MIND THROUGH THE LORD OF THE WORLDS.
INTO MY MIND?! REALLY?!
WHAT'S WRONG?
IS IT THE LORD OF THE WORLDS?
...YEAH! HOW'D YOU KNOW? YAMCHA'S TALKING NOW, THOUGH.

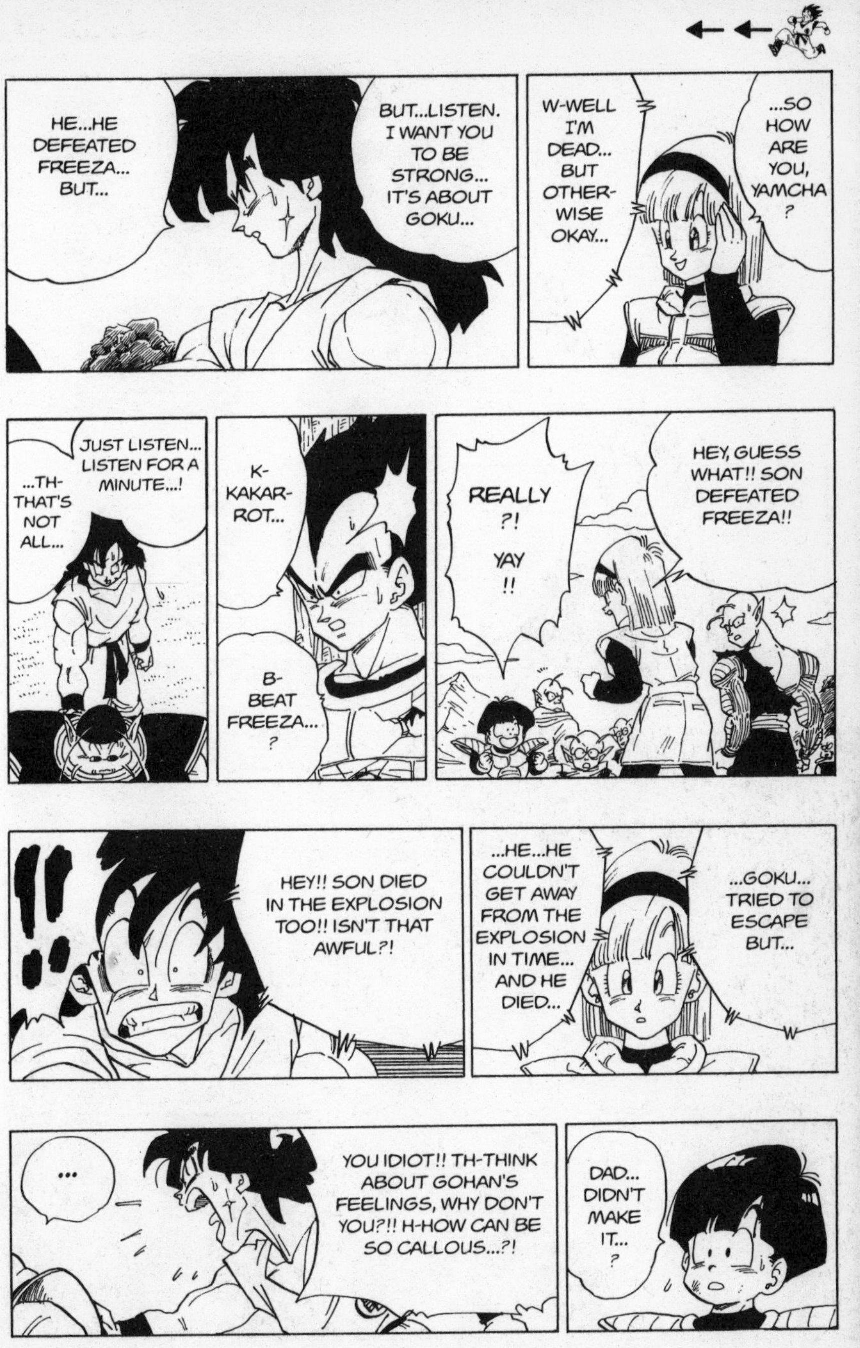
...SO HOW ARE YOU, YAMCHA?
W-WELL I'M DEAD... BUT OTHERWISE OKAY...
BUT...LISTEN. I WANT YOU TO BE STRONG... IT'S ABOUT GOKU...
HE...HE DEFEATED FREEZA... BUT...
HEY, GUESS WHAT!! SON DEFEATED FREEZA!!
REALLY?! YAY!!
K-KAKARROT...
B-BEAT FREEZA...?
JUST LISTEN... LISTEN FOR A MINUTE...!
...TH-THAT'S NOT ALL...
...GOKU... TRIED TO ESCAPE BUT...
...HE...HE COULDN'T GET AWAY FROM THE EXPLOSION IN TIME... AND HE DIED...
HEY!! SON DIED IN THE EXPLOSION TOO!! ISN'T THAT AWFUL?!
!!
DAD... DIDN'T MAKE IT...?
YOU IDIOT!! TH-THINK ABOUT GOHAN'S FEELINGS, WHY DON'T YOU?!! H-HOW CAN BE SO CALLOUS...?!
...

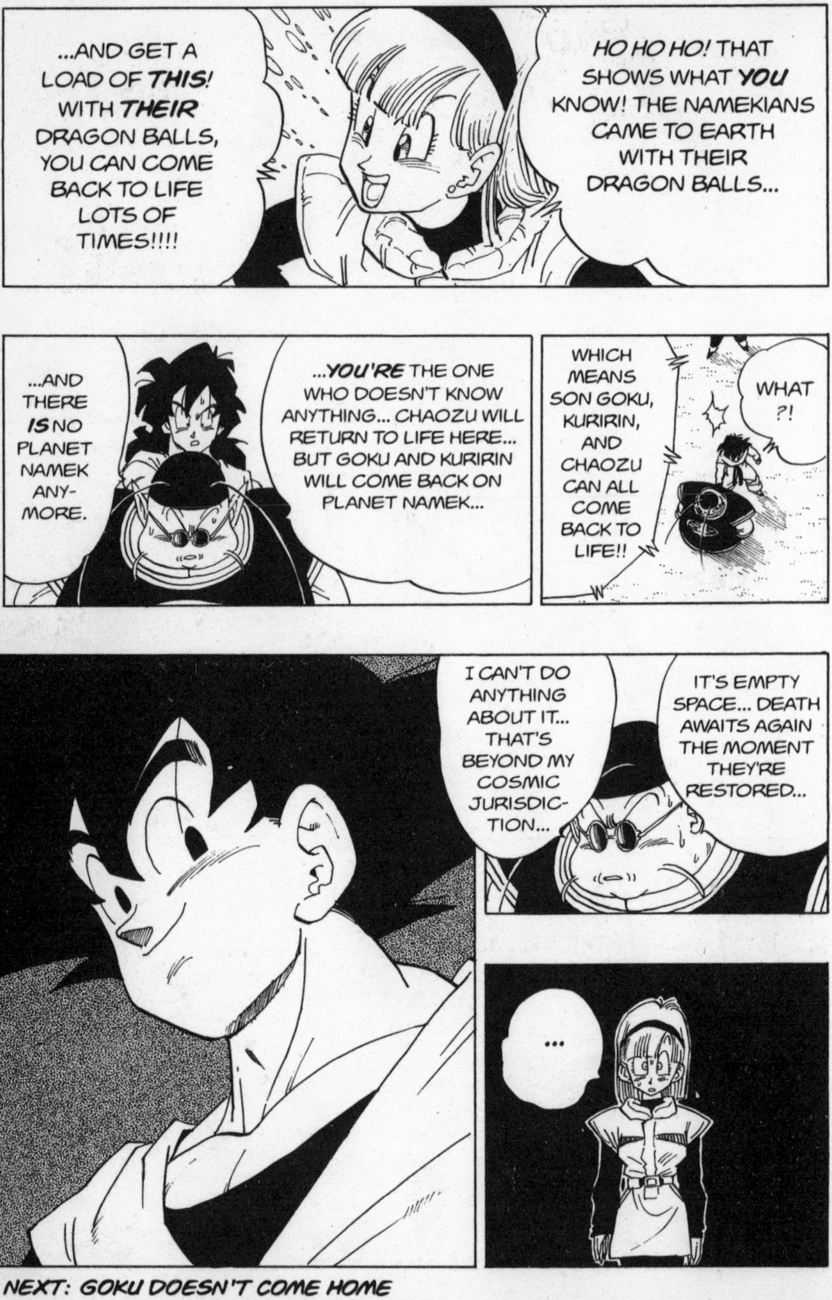
HO HO HO! THAT SHOWS WHAT YOU KNOW! THE NAMEKIANS CAME TO EARTH WITH THEIR DRAGON BALLS...
...AND GET A LOAD OF THIS! WITH THEIR DRAGON BALLS, YOU CAN COME BACK TO LIFE LOTS OF TIMES!!!!
WHICH MEANS SON GOKU, KURIRIN, AND CHAOZU CAN ALL COME BACK TO LIFE!!
WHAT ?!
...YOU'RE THE ONE WHO DOESN'T KNOW ANYTHING... CHAOZU WILL RETURN TO LIFE HERE... BUT GOKU AND KURIRIN WILL COME BACK ON PLANET NAMEK...
...AND THERE IS NO PLANET NAMEK ANY-MORE.
IT'S EMPTY SPACE... DEATH AWAITS AGAIN THE MOMENT THEY'RE RESTORED...
I CAN'T DO ANYTHING ABOUT IT... THAT'S BEYOND MY COSMIC JURISDIC-TION...
...

NEXT: GOKU DOESN'T COME HOME

DBZ:135 • Where is Goku?

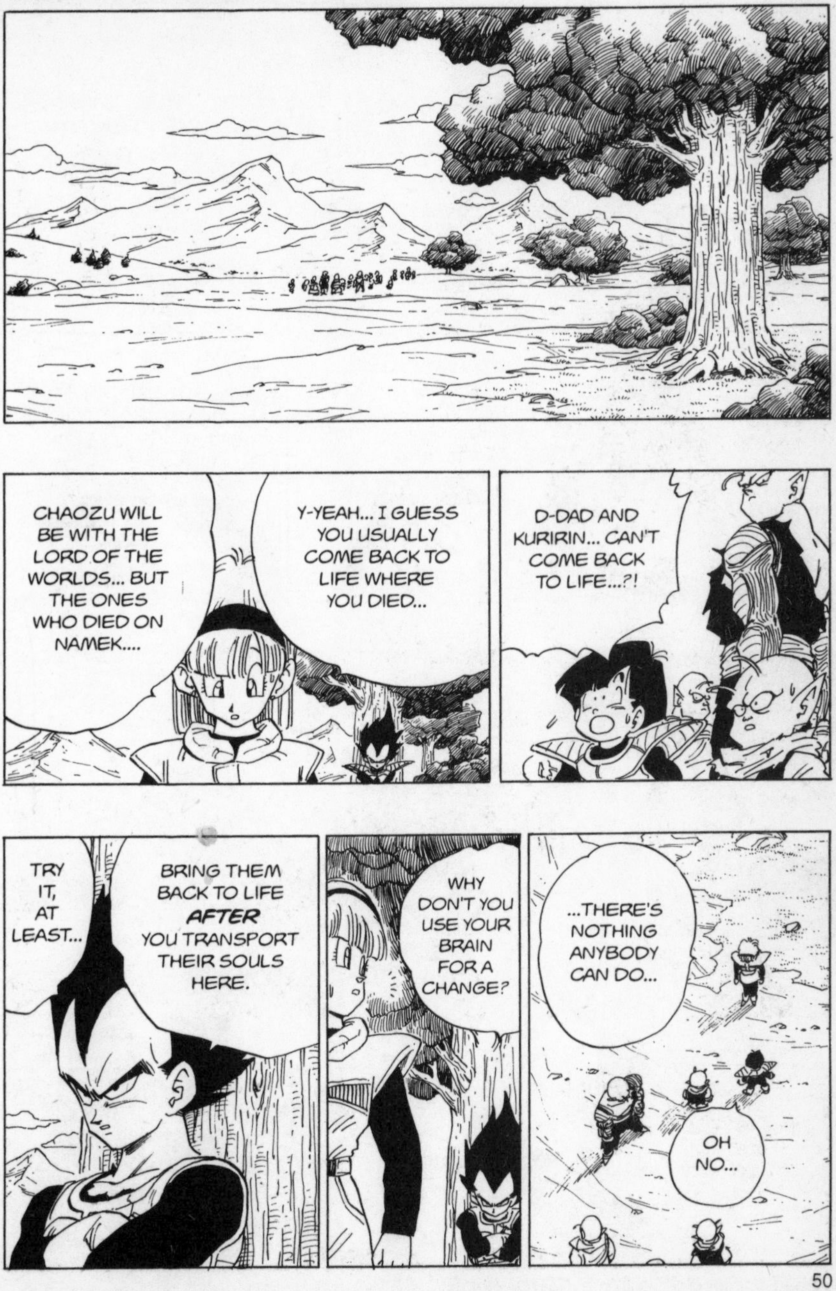

D-DAD AND KURIRIN... CAN'T COME BACK TO LIFE...?!
Y-YEAH... I GUESS YOU USUALLY COME BACK TO LIFE WHERE YOU DIED...
CHAOZU WILL BE WITH THE LORD OF THE WORLDS... BUT THE ONES WHO DIED ON NAMEK....
...THERE'S NOTHING ANYBODY CAN DO...
OH NO...
WHY DON'T YOU USE YOUR BRAIN FOR A CHANGE?
BRING THEM BACK TO LIFE ***AFTER*** YOU TRANSPORT THEIR SOULS HERE.
TRY IT, AT LEAST...

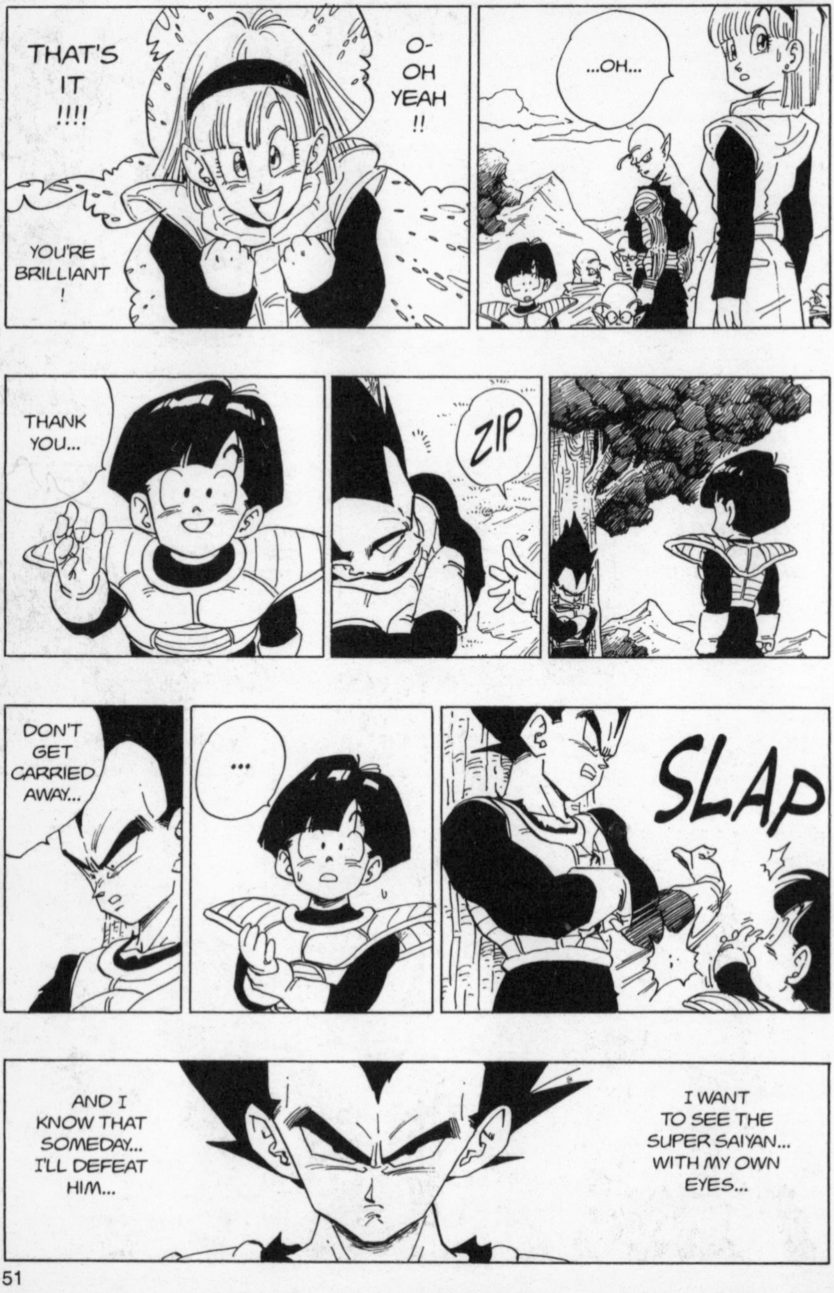
...OH...
O-OH YEAH !!
THAT'S IT !!!!
YOU'RE BRILLIANT !
ZIP
THANK YOU...
SLAP
...
DON'T GET CARRIED AWAY...
I WANT TO SEE THE SUPER SAIYAN... WITH MY OWN EYES...
AND I KNOW THAT SOMEDAY... I'LL DEFEAT HIM...

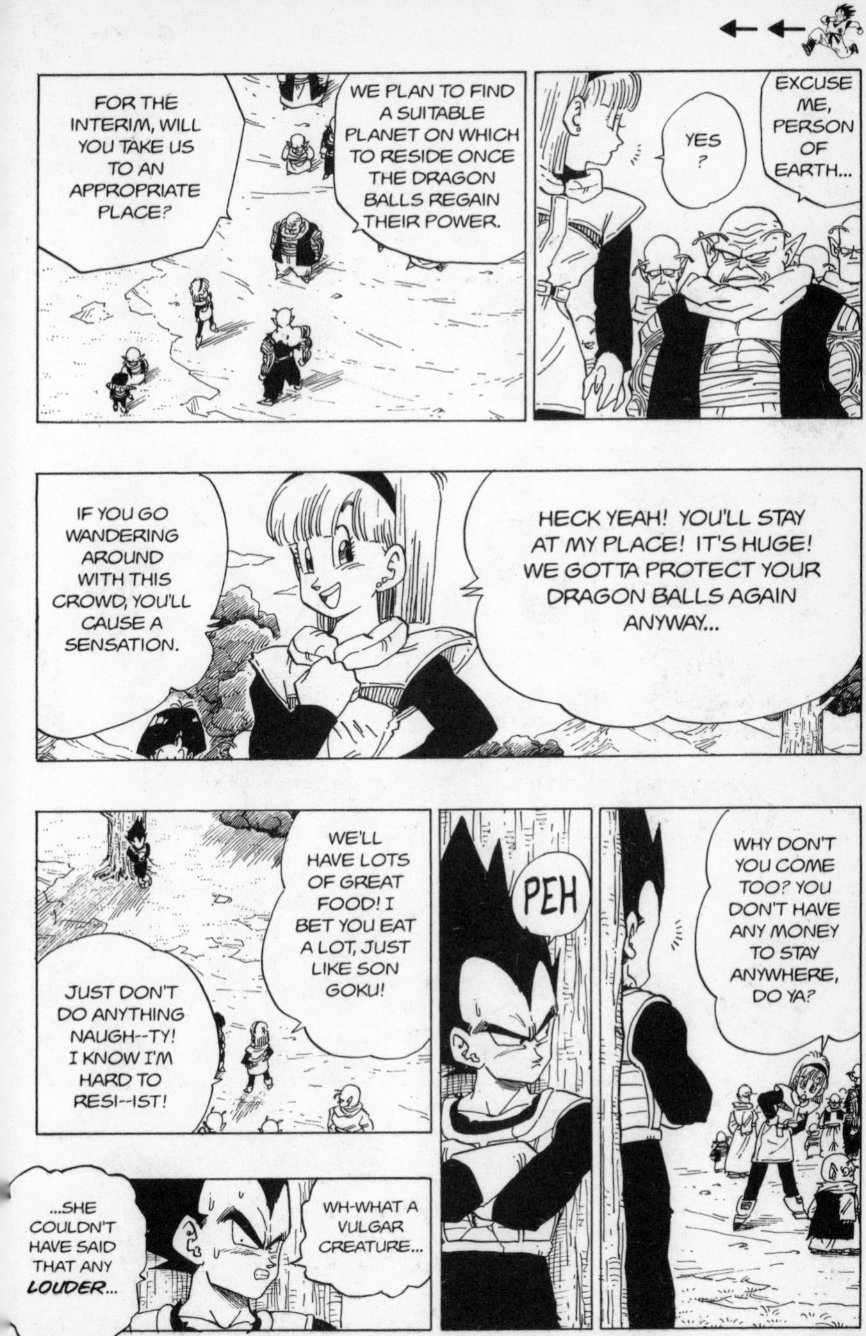
EXCUSE ME, PERSON OF EARTH...
YES ?
WE PLAN TO FIND A SUITABLE PLANET ON WHICH TO RESIDE ONCE THE DRAGON BALLS REGAIN THEIR POWER.
FOR THE INTERIM, WILL YOU TAKE US TO AN APPROPRIATE PLACE?
HECK YEAH! YOU'LL STAY AT MY PLACE! IT'S HUGE! WE GOTTA PROTECT YOUR DRAGON BALLS AGAIN ANYWAY...
IF YOU GO WANDERING AROUND WITH THIS CROWD, YOU'LL CAUSE A SENSATION.
WHY DON'T YOU COME TOO? YOU DON'T HAVE ANY MONEY TO STAY ANYWHERE, DO YA?
PEH
WE'LL HAVE LOTS OF GREAT FOOD! I BET YOU EAT A LOT, JUST LIKE SON GOKU!
JUST DON'T DO ANYTHING NAUGH--TY! I KNOW I'M HARD TO RESI--IST!
WH-WHAT A VULGAR CREATURE...
...SHE COULDN'T HAVE SAID THAT ANY ***LOUDER***...

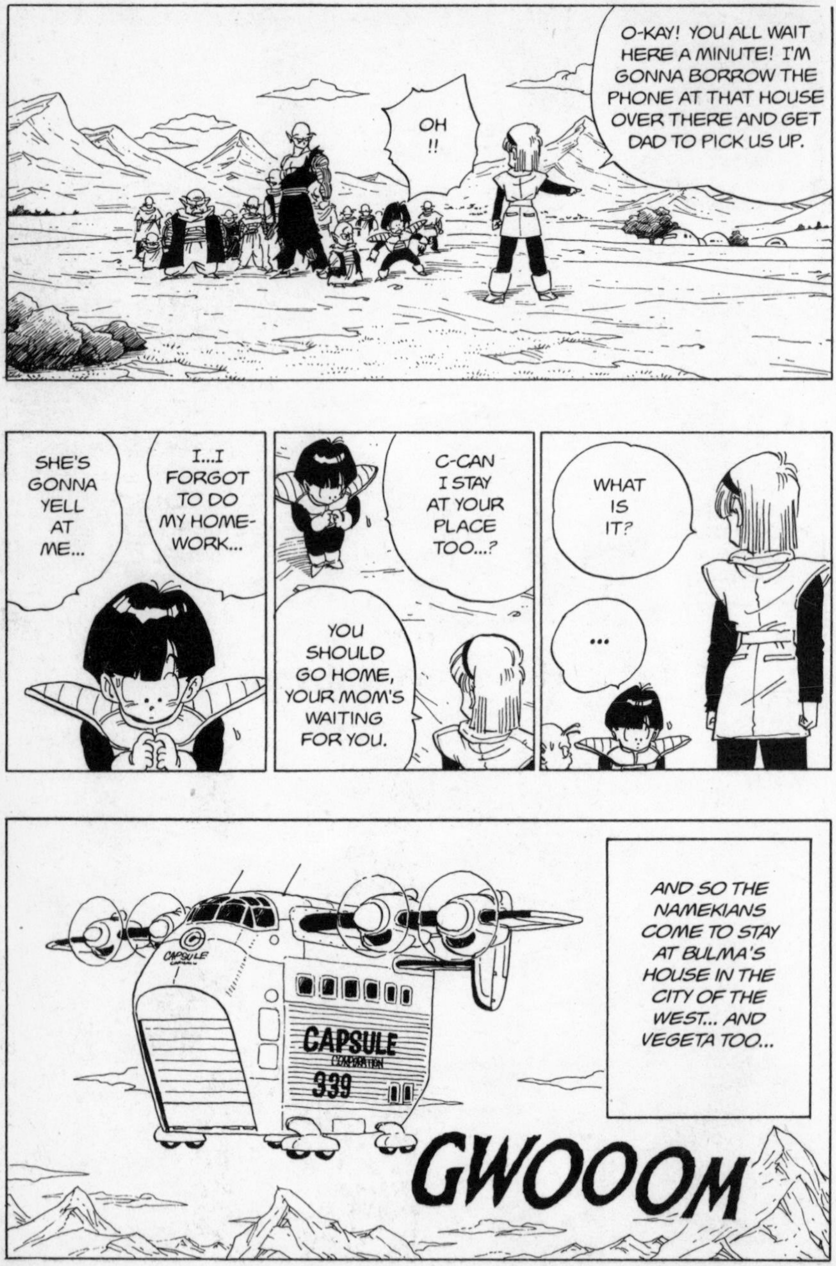
O-KAY! YOU ALL WAIT HERE A MINUTE! I'M GONNA BORROW THE PHONE AT THAT HOUSE OVER THERE AND GET DAD TO PICK US UP.
OH !!
WHAT IS IT?
...
C-CAN I STAY AT YOUR PLACE TOO...?
YOU SHOULD GO HOME, YOUR MOM'S WAITING FOR YOU.
I...I FORGOT TO DO MY HOME-WORK...
SHE'S GONNA YELL AT ME...
AND SO THE NAMEKIANS COME TO STAY AT BULMA'S HOUSE IN THE CITY OF THE WEST... AND VEGETA TOO...
CAPSULE CORPORATION
339
GWOOOM

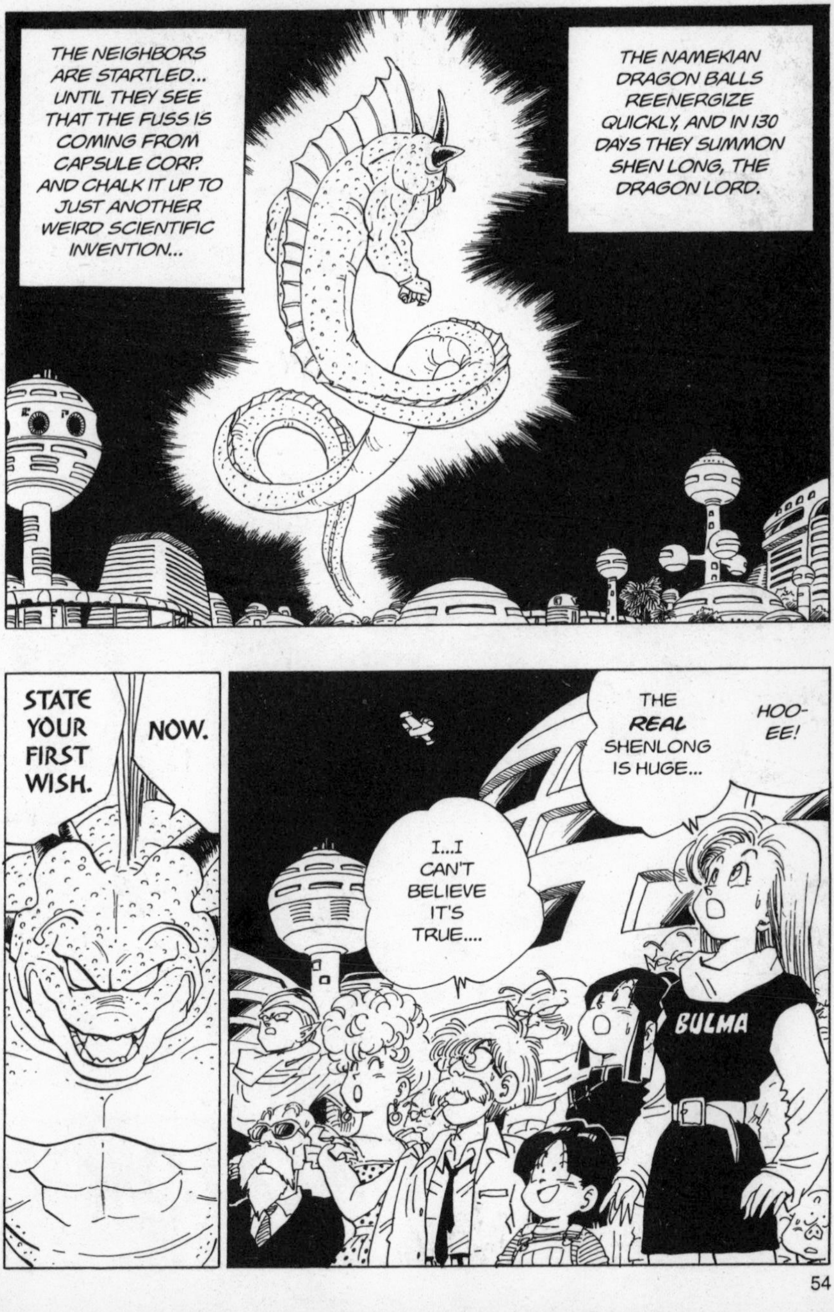
THE NAMEKIAN DRAGON BALLS REENERGIZE QUICKLY, AND IN 130 DAYS THEY SUMMON SHEN LONG, THE DRAGON LORD.
THE NEIGHBORS ARE STARTLED... UNTIL THEY SEE THAT THE FUSS IS COMING FROM CAPSULE CORP. AND CHALK IT UP TO JUST ANOTHER WEIRD SCIENTIFIC INVENTION...
HOO-EE!
THE REAL SHENLONG IS HUGE...
I...I CAN'T BELIEVE IT'S TRUE....
BULMA
STATE YOUR FIRST WISH.
NOW.

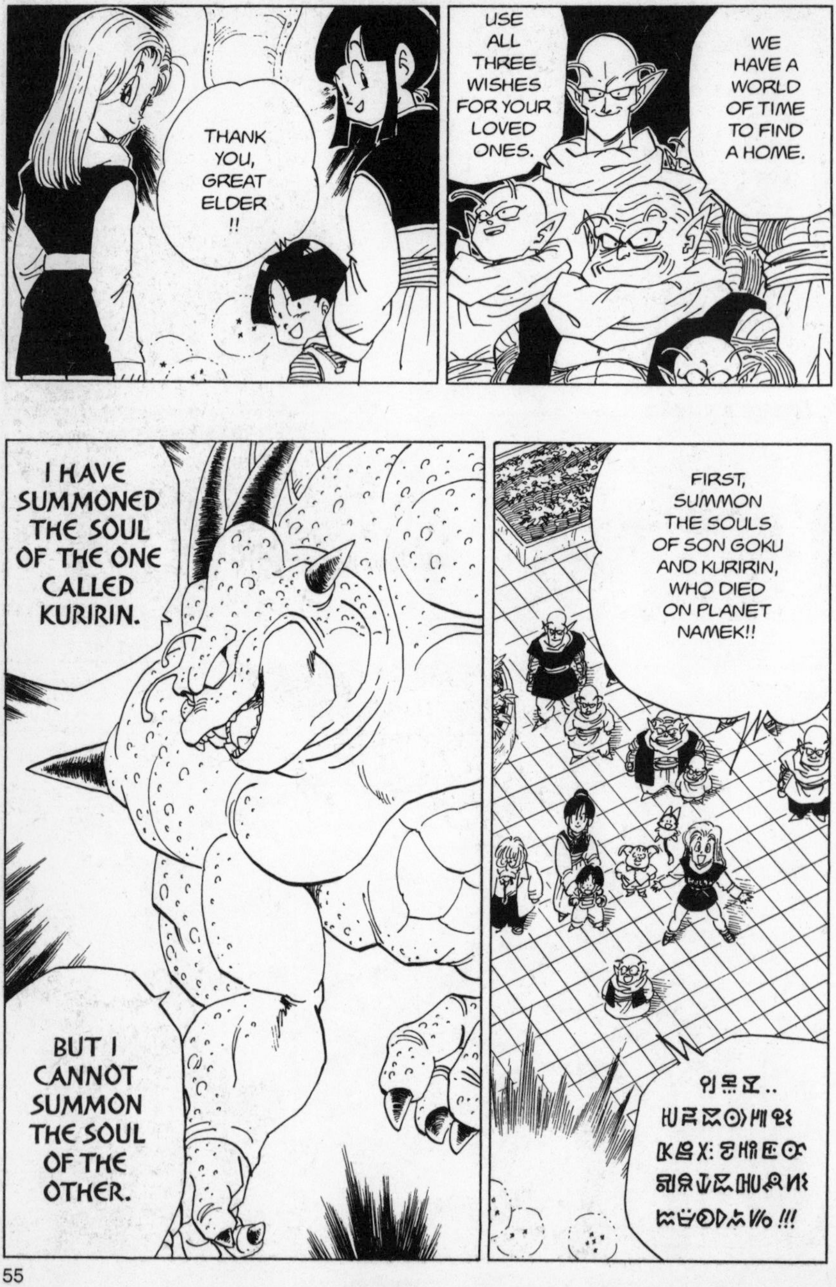
WE HAVE A WORLD OF TIME TO FIND A HOME.
USE ALL THREE WISHES FOR YOUR LOVED ONES.
THANK YOU, GREAT ELDER!!
FIRST, SUMMON THE SOULS OF SON GOKU AND KURIRIN, WHO DIED ON PLANET NAMEK!!
I HAVE SUMMONED THE SOUL OF THE ONE CALLED KURIRIN.
BUT I CANNOT SUMMON THE SOUL OF THE OTHER.

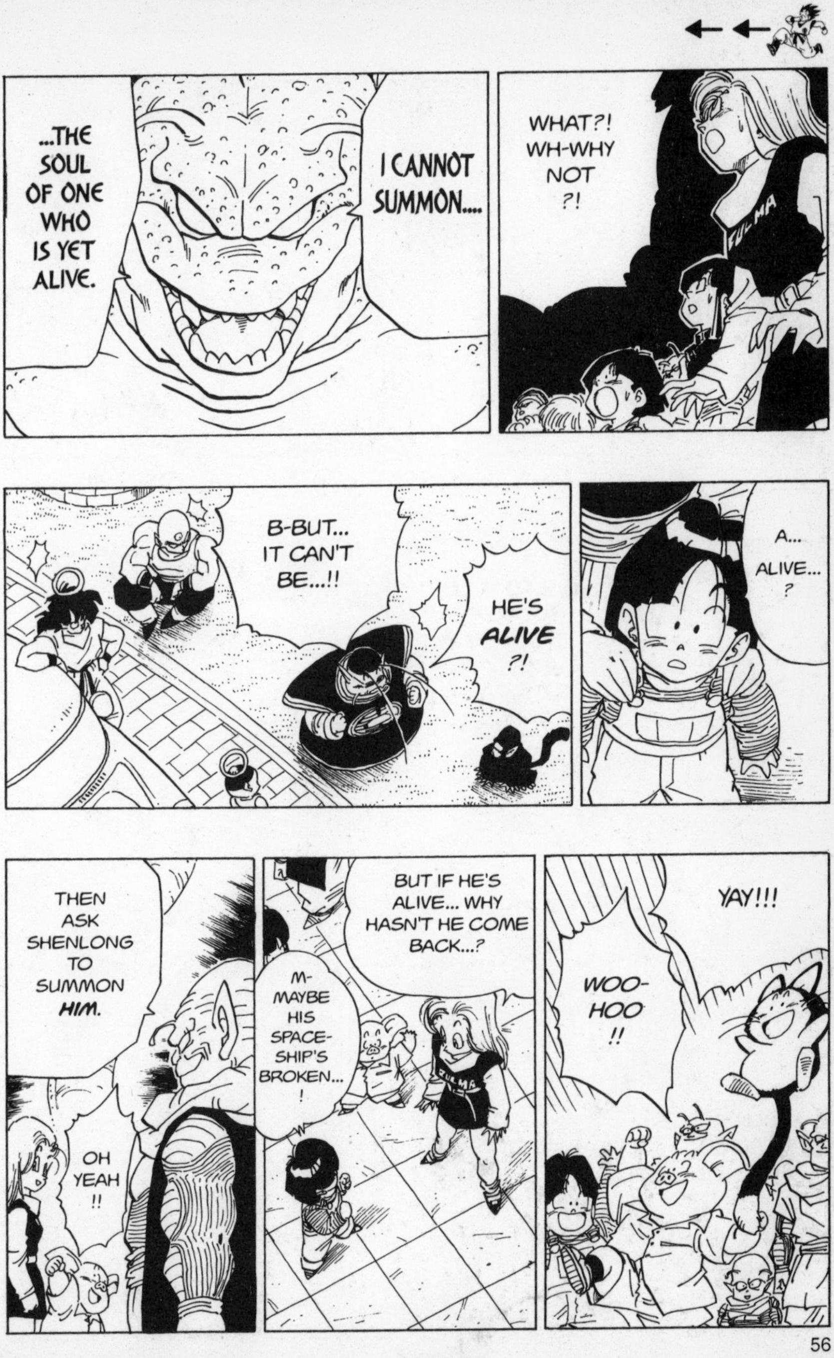
WHAT?! WH-WHY NOT ?!
I CANNOT SUMMON....
...THE SOUL OF ONE WHO IS YET ALIVE.
A... ALIVE... ?
B-BUT... IT CAN'T BE...!!
HE'S *ALIVE* ?!
YAY!!!
WOO-HOO !!
BUT IF HE'S ALIVE... WHY HASN'T HE COME BACK...?
M-MAYBE HIS SPACE-SHIP'S BROKEN... !
THEN ASK SHENLONG TO SUMMON *HIM*.
OH YEAH !!

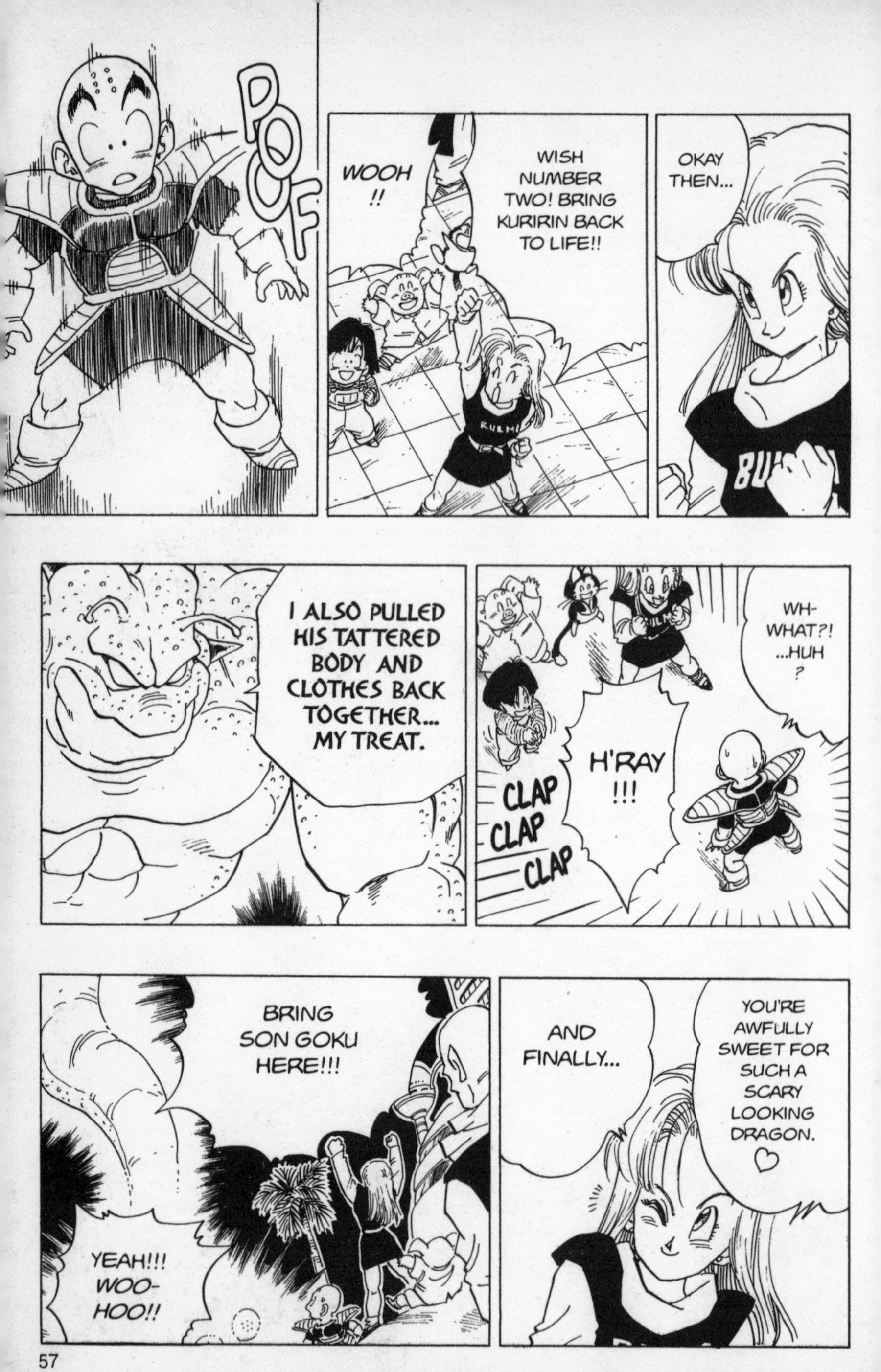
OKAY THEN...
WISH NUMBER TWO! BRING KURIRIN BACK TO LIFE!!
WOOH !!
POOF
WH- WHAT?! ...HUH ?
H'RAY !!!
CLAP CLAP CLAP
I ALSO PULLED HIS TATTERED BODY AND CLOTHES BACK TOGETHER... MY TREAT.
YOU'RE AWFULLY SWEET FOR SUCH A SCARY LOOKING DRAGON. ♡
AND FINALLY...
BRING SON GOKU HERE!!!
YEAH!!! WOO-HOO!!

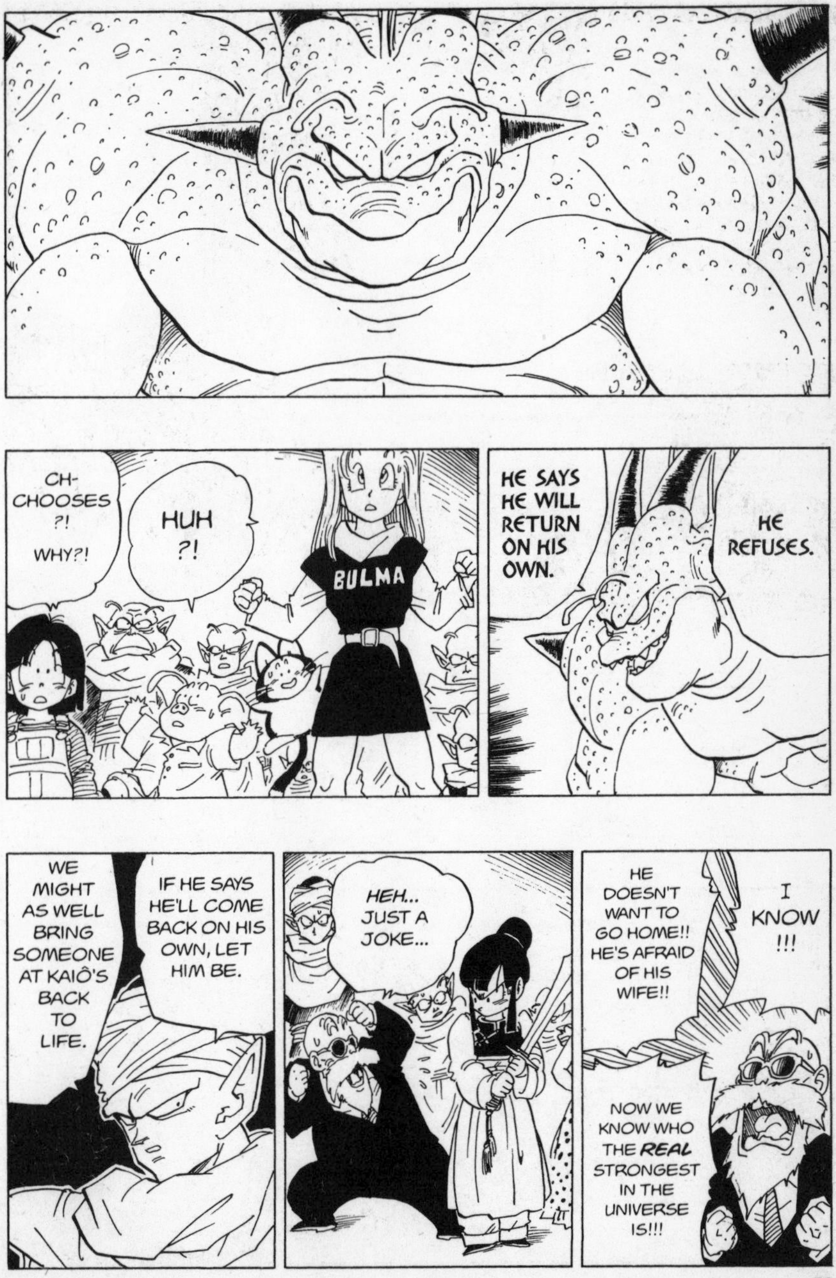
HE REFUSES.
HE SAYS HE WILL RETURN ON HIS OWN.
BULMA
HUH ?!
CH- CHOOSES ?! WHY?!
I KNOW !!!
HE DOESN'T WANT TO GO HOME!! HE'S AFRAID OF HIS WIFE!!
NOW WE KNOW WHO THE REAL STRONGEST IN THE UNIVERSE IS!!!
HEH... JUST A JOKE...
IF HE SAYS HE'LL COME BACK ON HIS OWN, LET HIM BE.
WE MIGHT AS WELL BRING SOMEONE AT KAIÔ'S BACK TO LIFE.

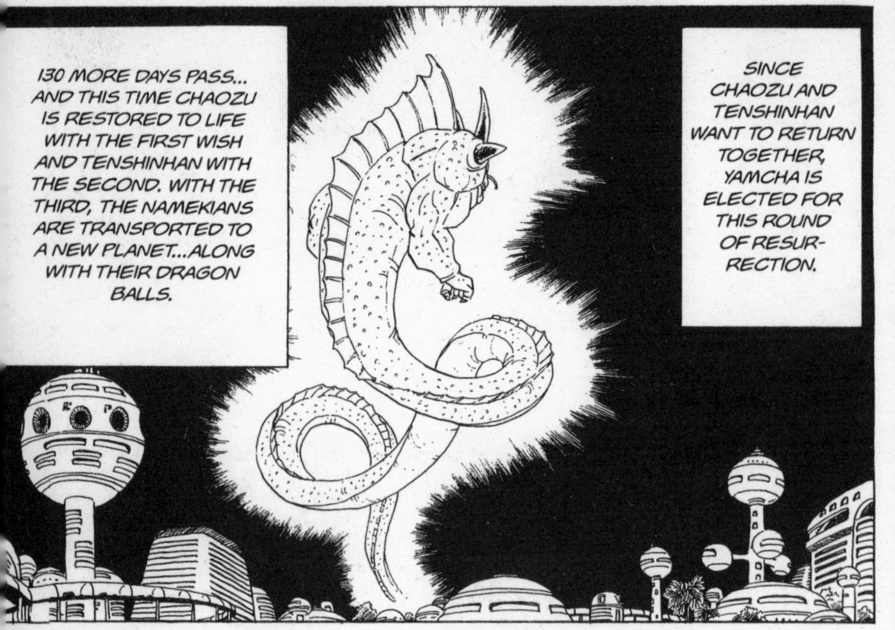
SINCE CHAOZU AND TENSHINHAN WANT TO RETURN TOGETHER, YAMCHA IS ELECTED FOR THIS ROUND OF RESUR-RECTION.
130 MORE DAYS PASS... AND THIS TIME CHAOZU IS RESTORED TO LIFE WITH THE FIRST WISH AND TENSHINHAN WITH THE SECOND. WITH THE THIRD, THE NAMEKIANS ARE TRANSPORTED TO A NEW PLANET...ALONG WITH THEIR DRAGON BALLS.

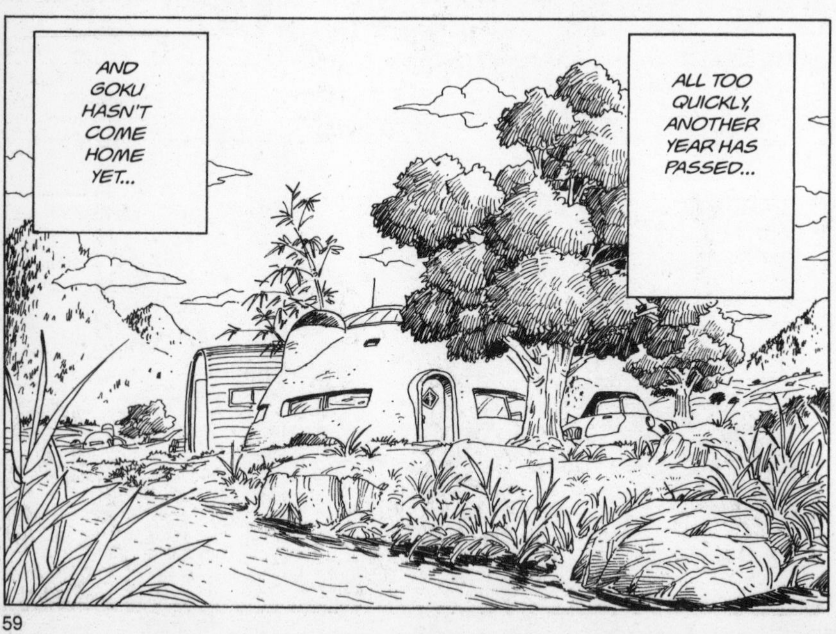
ALL TOO QUICKLY, ANOTHER YEAR HAS PASSED...
AND GOKU HASN'T COME HOME YET...

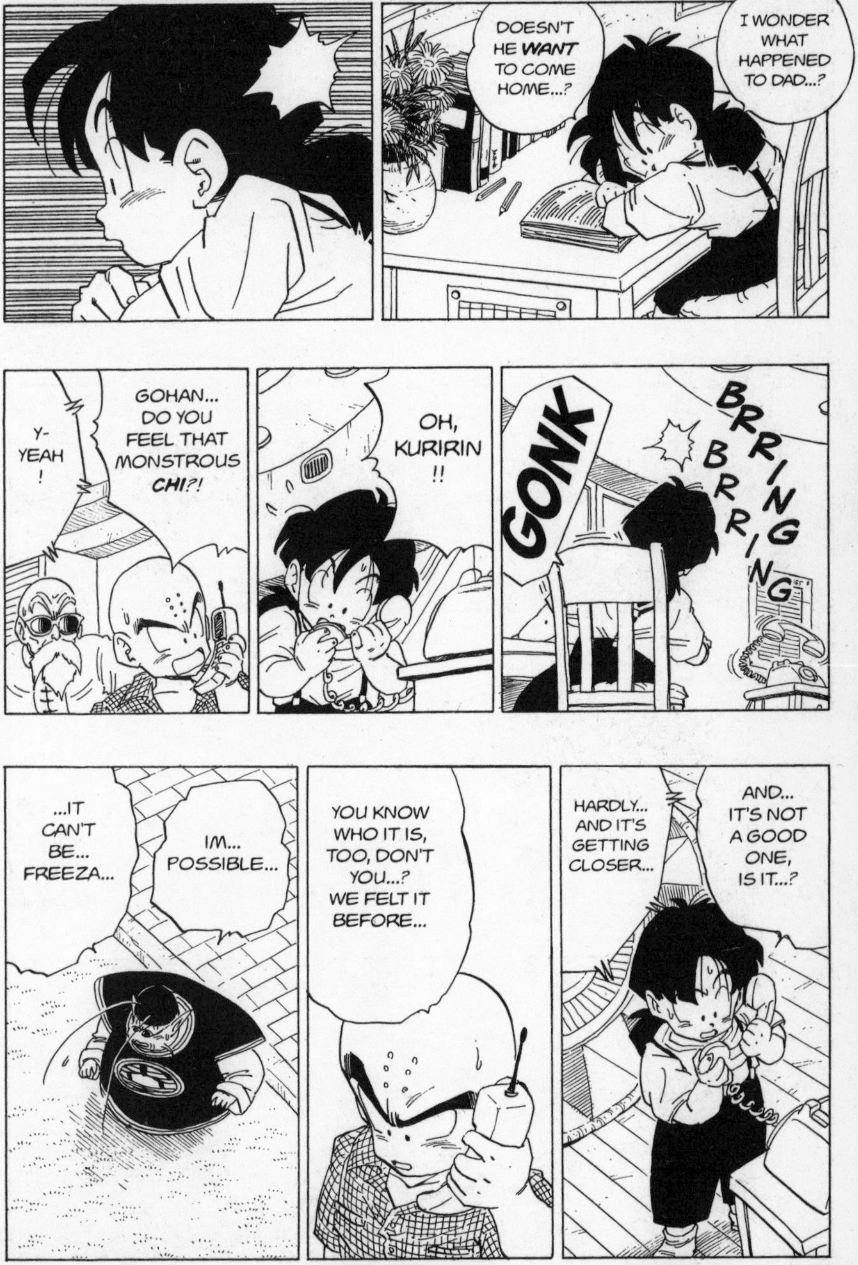
I WONDER WHAT HAPPENED TO DAD...?
DOESN'T HE **WANT** TO COME HOME...?
BRRRING
BRRRING
GONK
OH, KURIRIN!!
GOHAN... DO YOU FEEL THAT MONSTROUS **CHI**?!
Y-YEAH!
AND... IT'S NOT A GOOD ONE, IS IT...?
HARDLY... AND IT'S GETTING CLOSER...
YOU KNOW WHO IT IS, TOO, DON'T YOU...? WE FELT IT BEFORE...
...IT CAN'T BE... FREEZA...
IM... POSSIBLE...

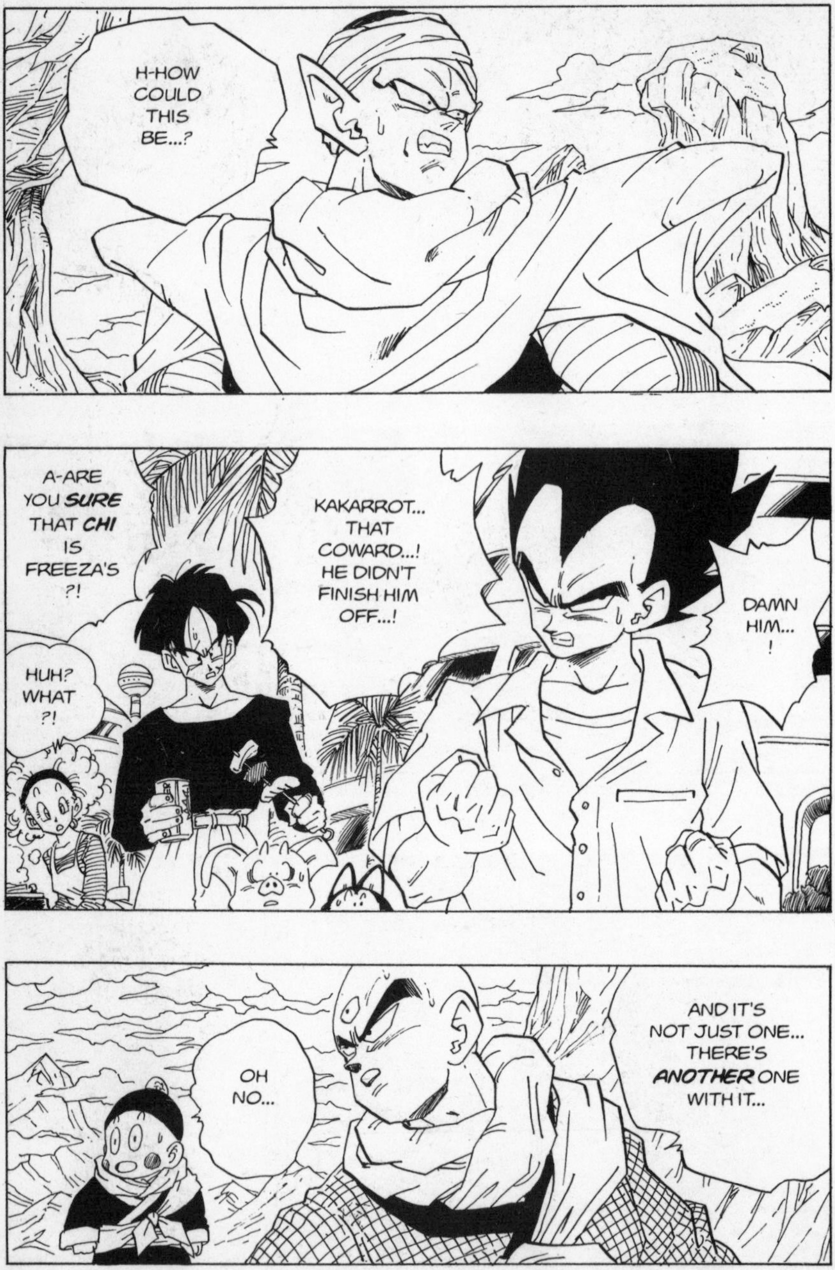
H-HOW COULD THIS BE...?
DAMN HIM...!
KAKARROT... THAT COWARD...! HE DIDN'T FINISH HIM OFF...!
A-ARE YOU **SURE** THAT **CHI** IS FREEZA'S ?!
HUH? WHAT ?!
AND IT'S NOT JUST ONE... THERE'S **ANOTHER** ONE WITH IT...
OH NO...

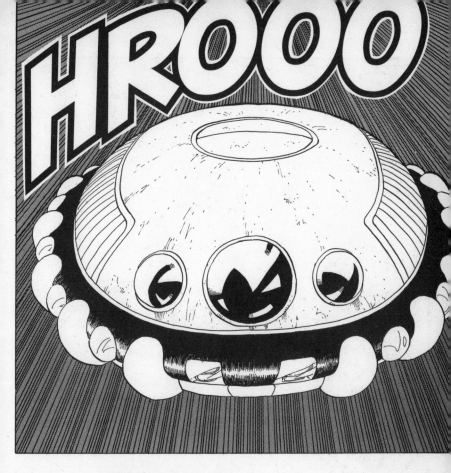

HROOO
THAT'S EARTH, DADDY...
IT SEEMS WE GOT HERE FASTER THAN THE SUPER SAIYAN WHO DID THIS TO ME.

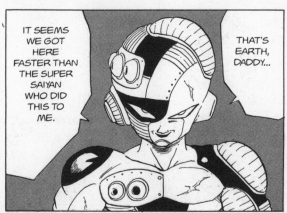

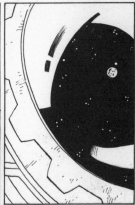

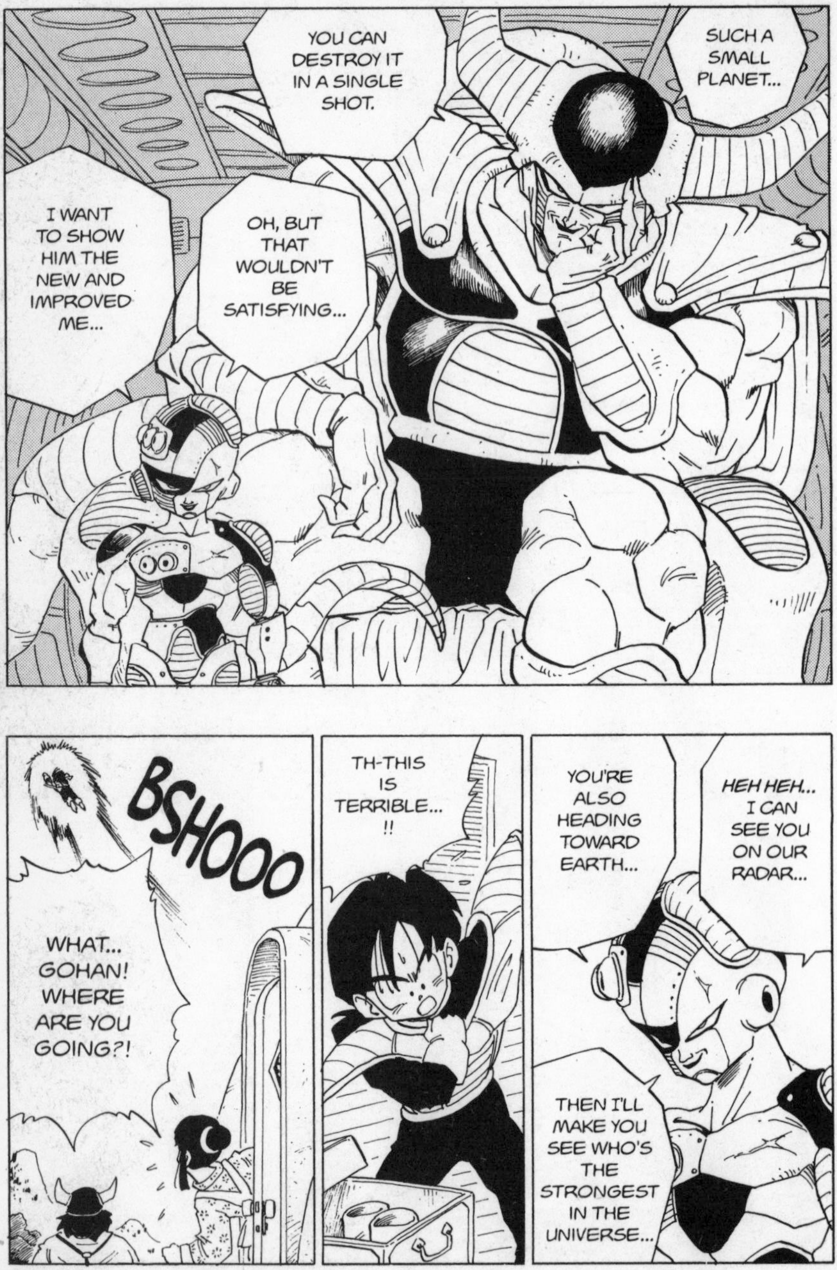
SUCH A SMALL PLANET...
YOU CAN DESTROY IT IN A SINGLE SHOT.
OH, BUT THAT WOULDN'T BE SATISFYING...
I WANT TO SHOW HIM THE NEW AND IMPROVED ME...
HEH HEH... I CAN SEE YOU ON OUR RADAR...
YOU'RE ALSO HEADING TOWARD EARTH...
THEN I'LL MAKE YOU SEE WHO'S THE STRONGEST IN THE UNIVERSE...
TH-THIS IS TERRIBLE... !!
BSHOOO
WHAT... GOHAN! WHERE ARE YOU GOING?!

NEXT: LIKE FATHER, LIKE SON

DBZ:136 • The Coming of King Cold

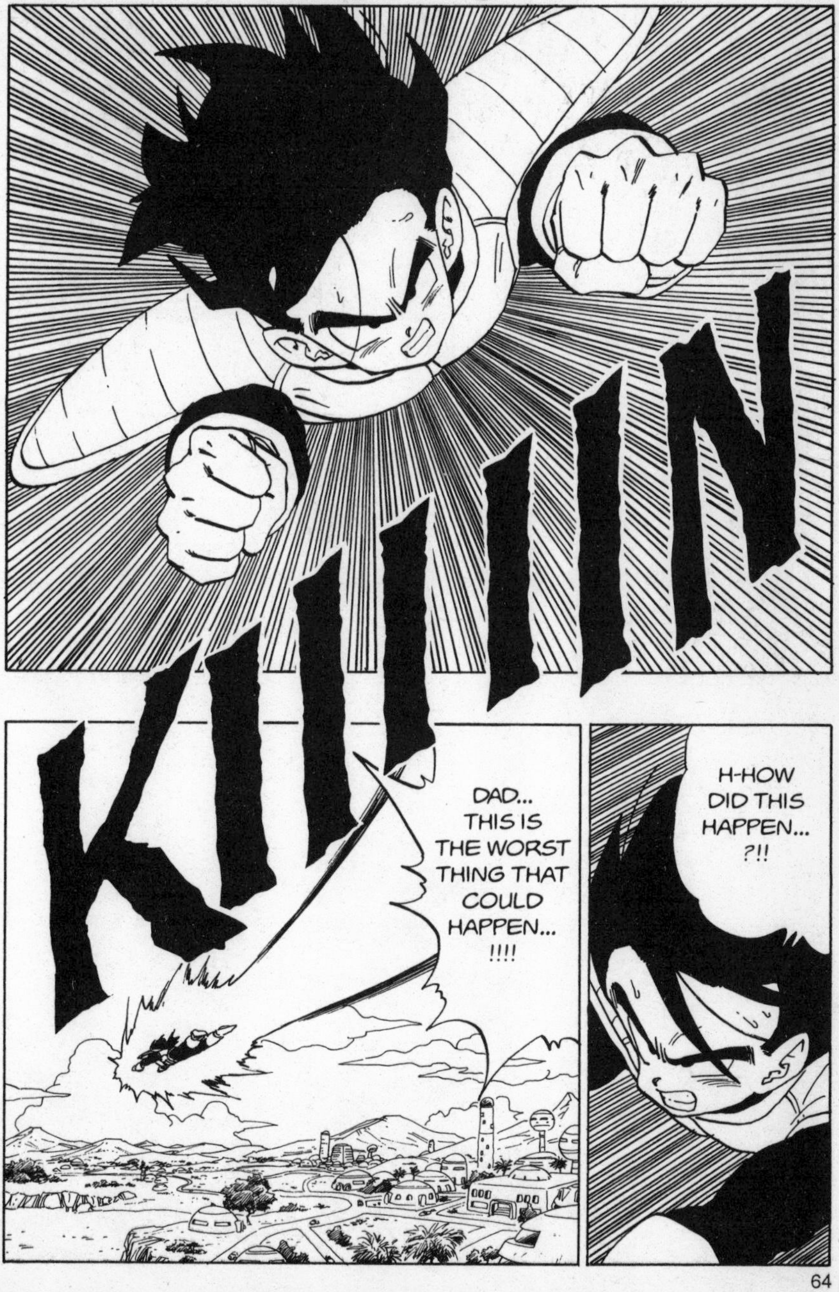
KIIIIIN
H-HOW DID THIS HAPPEN... ?!!
DAD... THIS IS THE WORST THING THAT COULD HAPPEN... !!!!

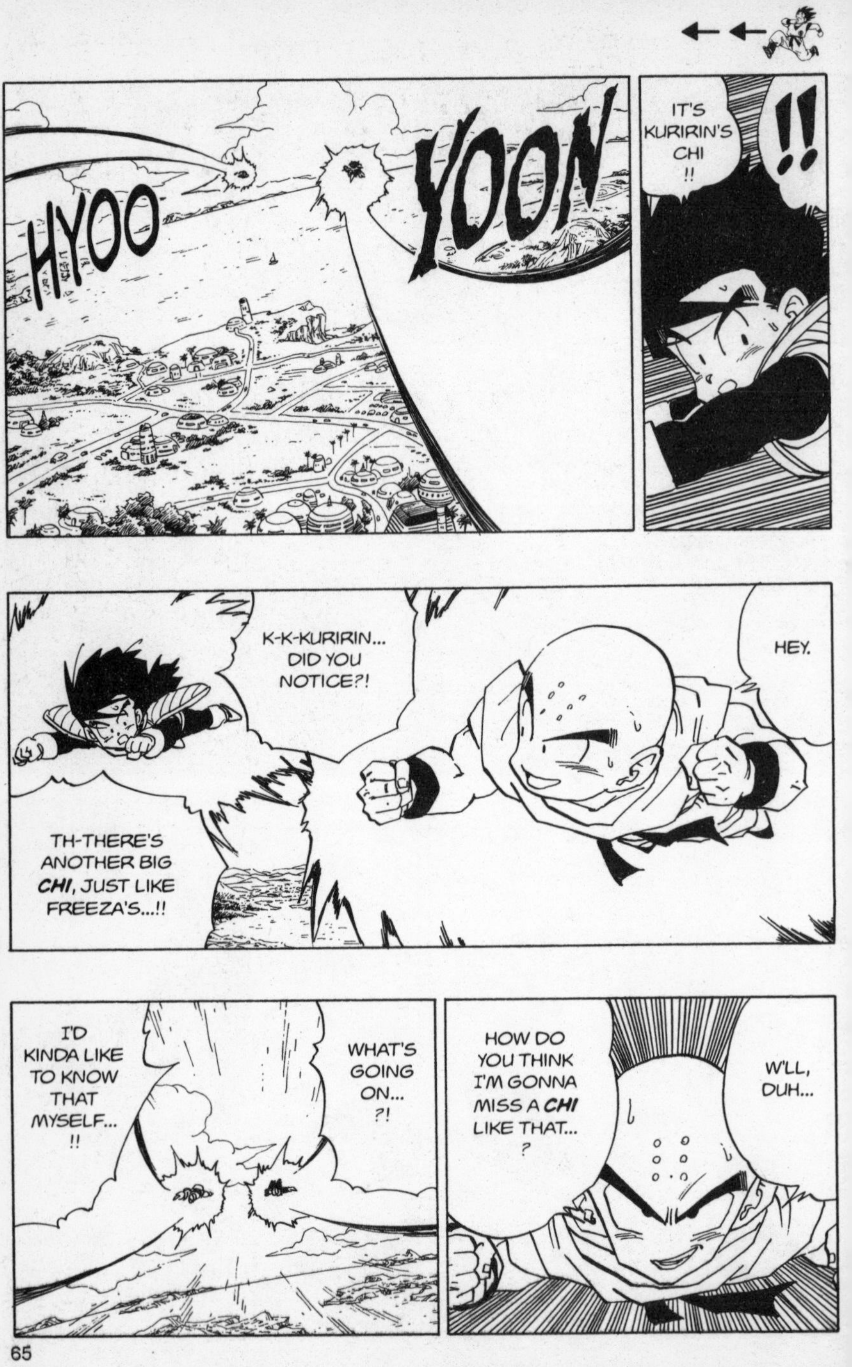
!!
IT'S KURIRIN'S CHI !!
YOON
HYOO
HEY.
K-K-KURIRIN... DID YOU NOTICE?!
TH-THERE'S ANOTHER BIG **CHI**, JUST LIKE FREEZA'S...!!
W'LL, DUH...
HOW DO YOU THINK I'M GONNA MISS A **CHI** LIKE THAT... ?
WHAT'S GOING ON... ?!
I'D KINDA LIKE TO KNOW THAT MYSELF... !!

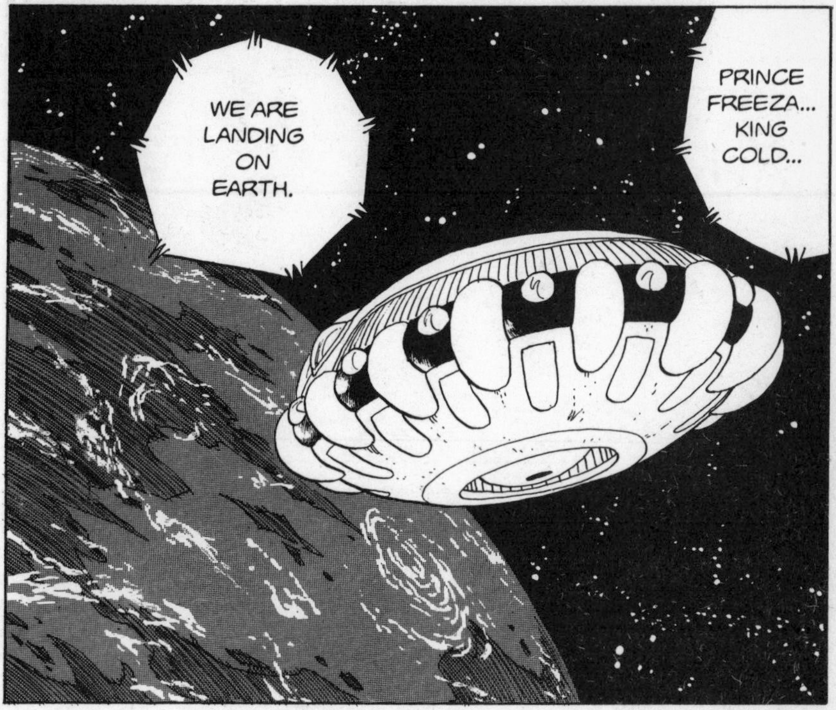
PRINCE FREEZA... KING COLD...
WE ARE LANDING ON EARTH.

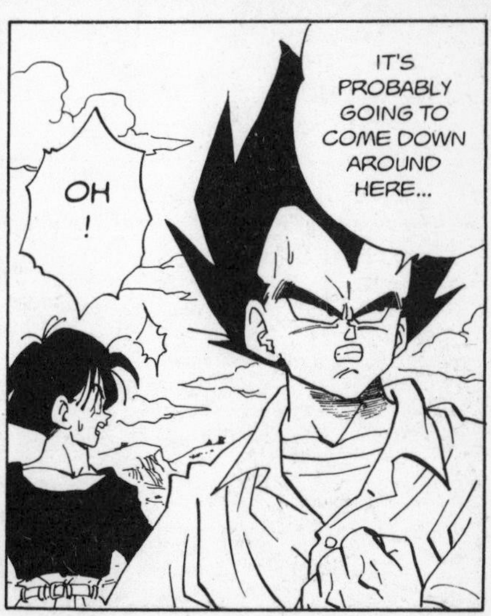
IT'S PROBABLY GOING TO COME DOWN AROUND HERE...
OH!

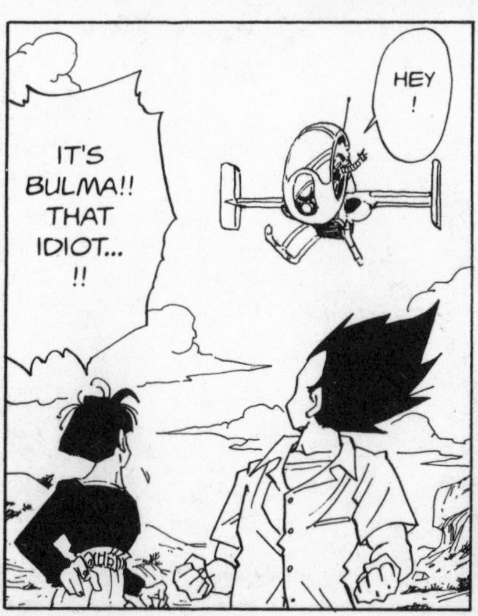
HEY!
IT'S BULMA!! THAT IDIOT... !!

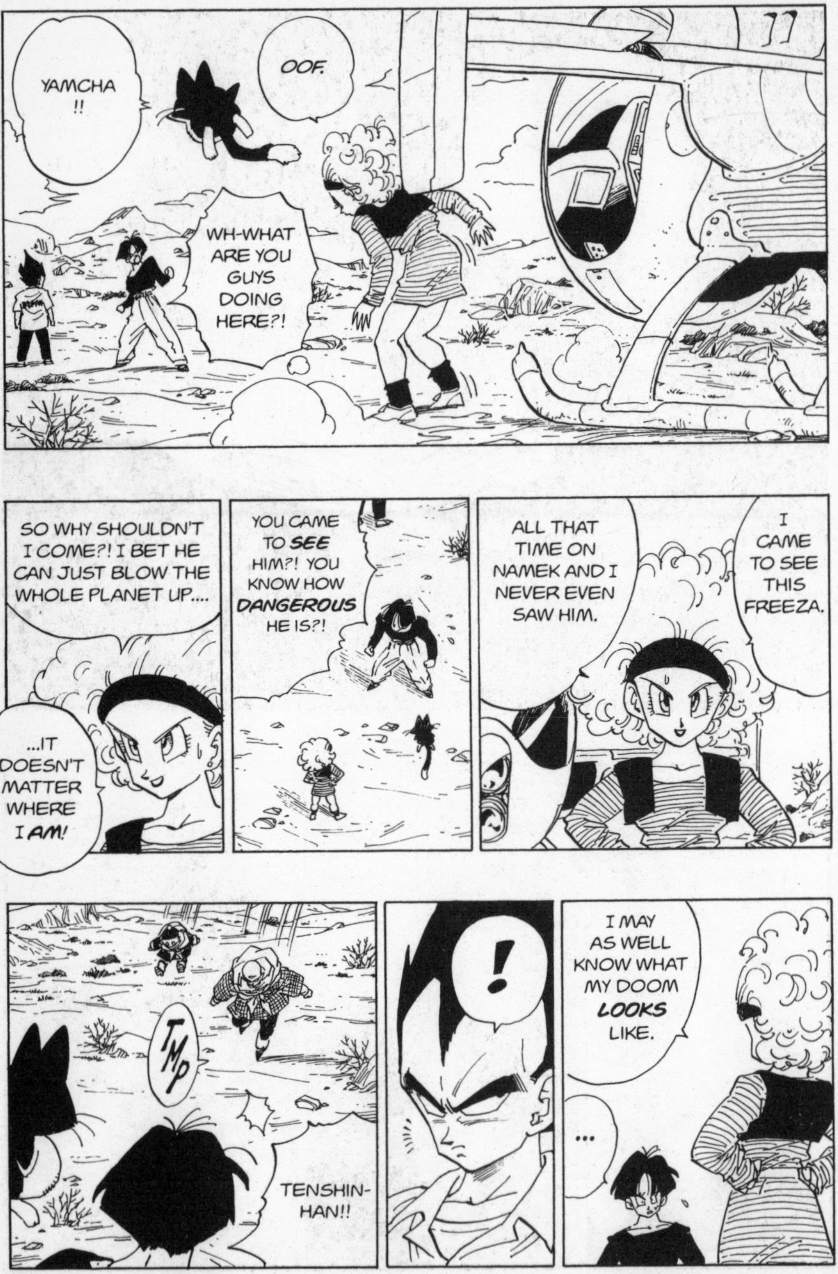
OOF.
YAMCHA !!
WH-WHAT ARE YOU GUYS DOING HERE?!
I CAME TO SEE THIS FREEZA.
ALL THAT TIME ON NAMEK AND I NEVER EVEN SAW HIM.
YOU CAME TO SEE HIM?! YOU KNOW HOW DANGEROUS HE IS?!
SO WHY SHOULDN'T I COME?! I BET HE CAN JUST BLOW THE WHOLE PLANET UP....
...IT DOESN'T MATTER WHERE I AM!
I MAY AS WELL KNOW WHAT MY DOOM LOOKS LIKE.
...
!
TMP
TENSHIN-HAN!!

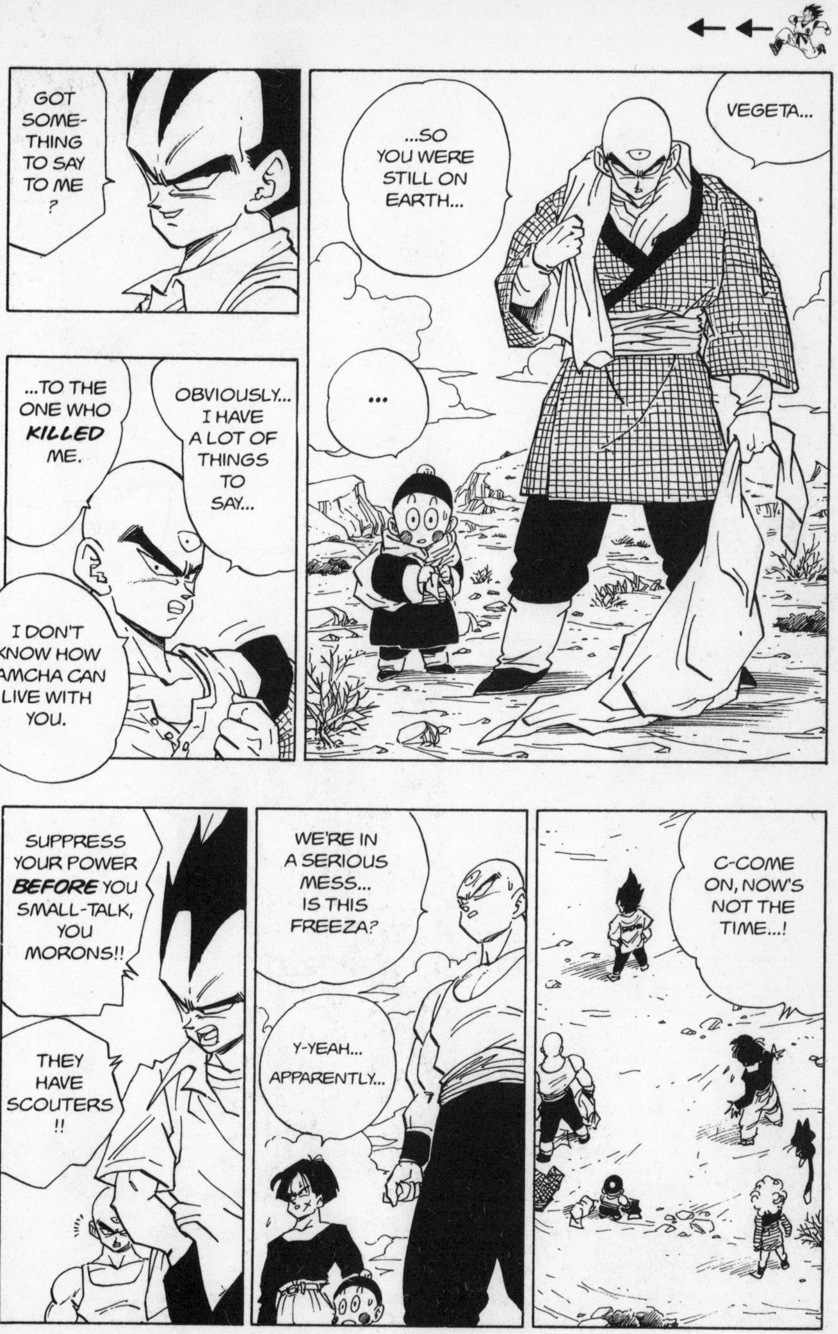
VEGETA...
...SO YOU WERE STILL ON EARTH...
...
GOT SOMETHING TO SAY TO ME?
OBVIOUSLY... I HAVE A LOT OF THINGS TO SAY...
...TO THE ONE WHO **KILLED** ME.
I DON'T KNOW HOW YAMCHA CAN LIVE WITH YOU.
C-COME ON, NOW'S NOT THE TIME...!
WE'RE IN A SERIOUS MESS... IS THIS FREEZA?
Y-YEAH... APPARENTLY...
SUPPRESS YOUR POWER **BEFORE** YOU SMALL-TALK, YOU MORONS!!
THEY HAVE SCOUTERS!!

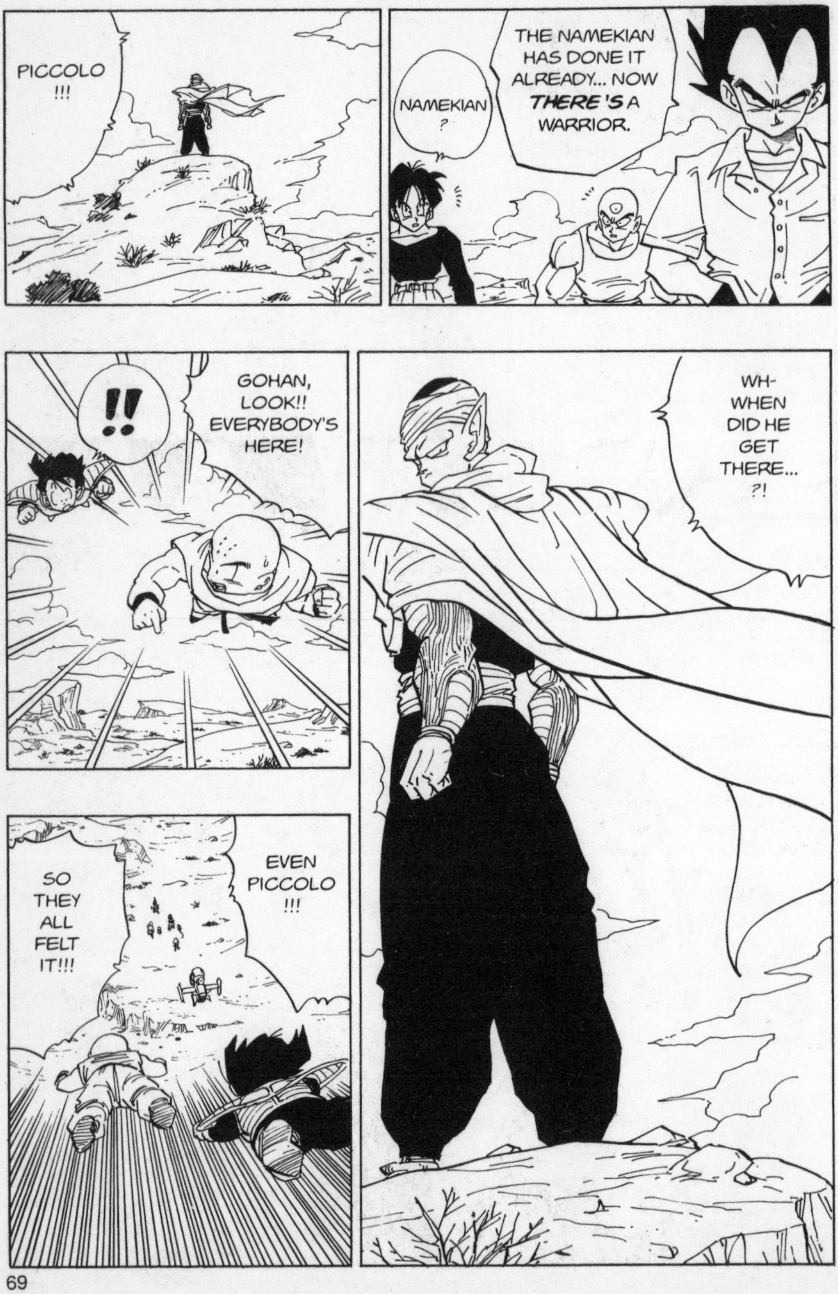
THE NAMEKIAN HAS DONE IT ALREADY... NOW *THERE'S* A WARRIOR.
NAMEKIAN ?
PICCOLO !!!
WH- WHEN DID HE GET THERE... ?!
GOHAN, LOOK!! EVERYBODY'S HERE!
!!
EVEN PICCOLO !!!
SO THEY ALL FELT IT!!!

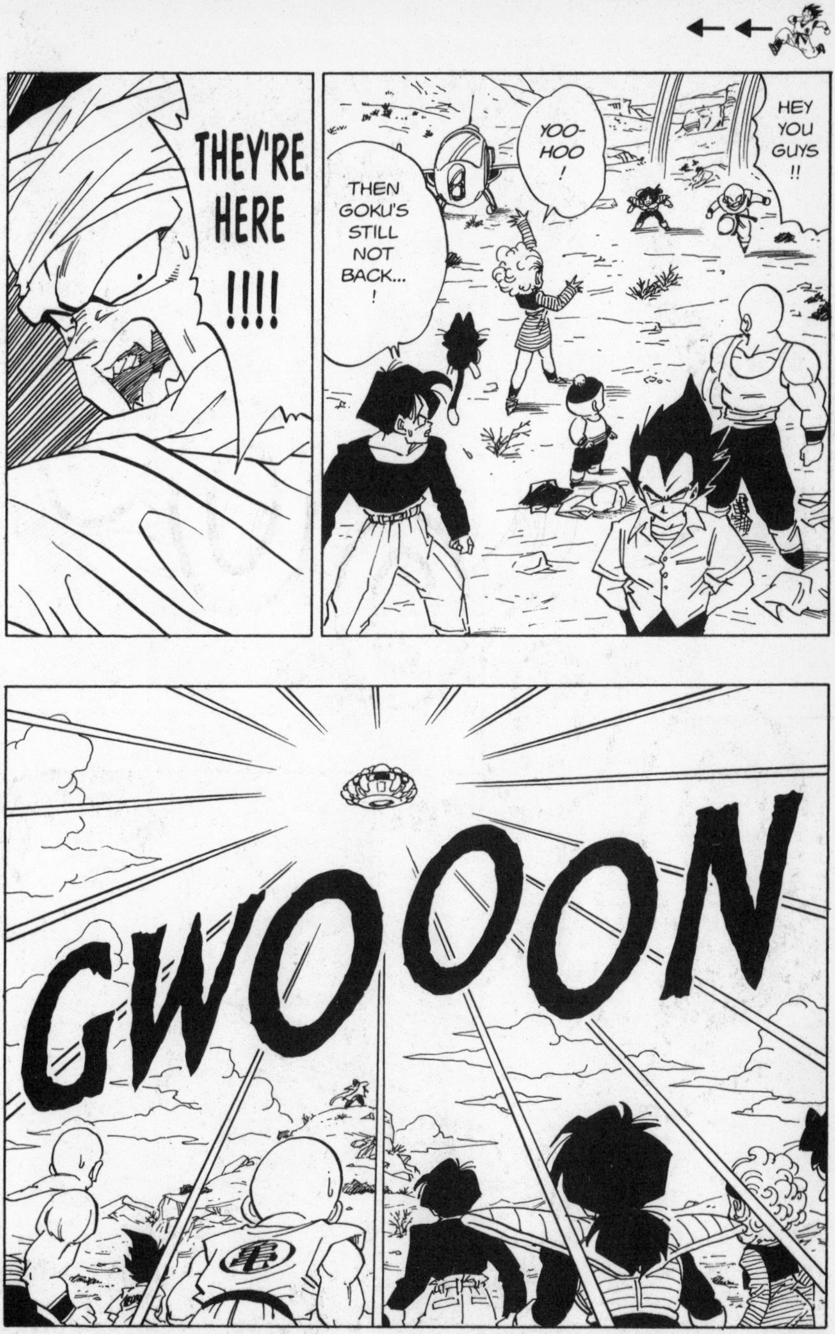
HEY YOU GUYS !!
YOO-HOO !
THEN GOKU'S STILL NOT BACK... !
THEY'RE HERE !!!!
GWOOON

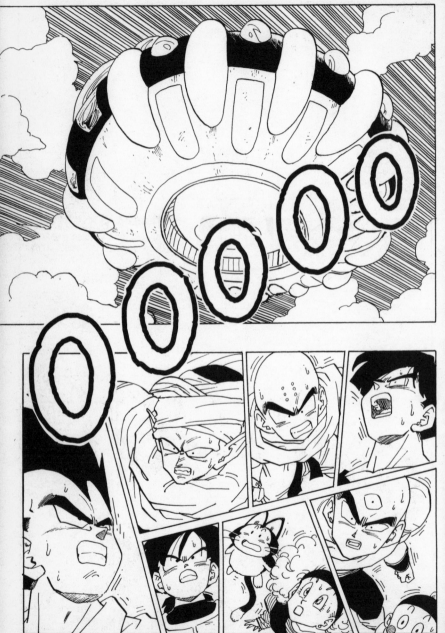

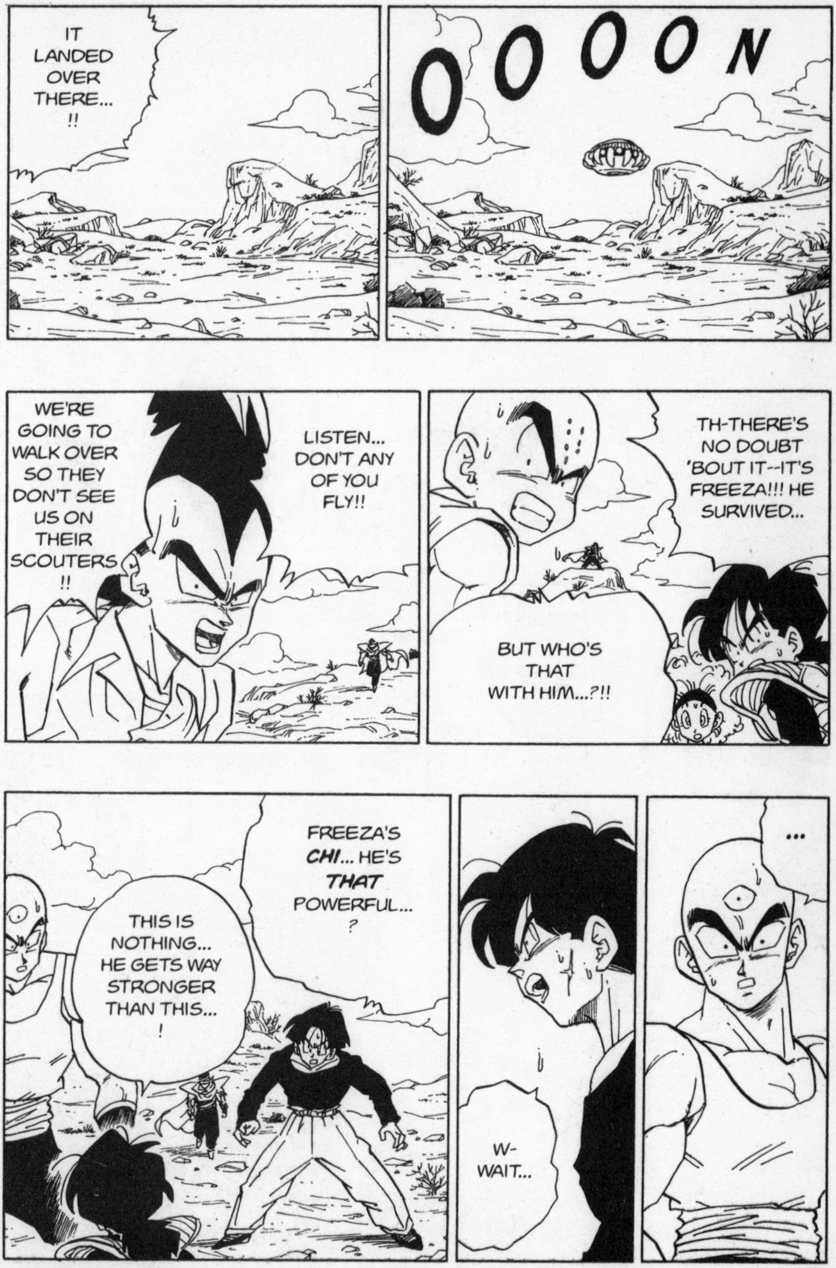

OOOON
IT LANDED OVER THERE... !!
TH-THERE'S NO DOUBT 'BOUT IT--IT'S FREEZA!!! HE SURVIVED...
BUT WHO'S THAT WITH HIM...?!!
LISTEN... DON'T ANY OF YOU FLY!!
WE'RE GOING TO WALK OVER SO THEY DON'T SEE US ON THEIR SCOUTERS !!
...
W-WAIT...
FREEZA'S CHI... HE'S THAT POWERFUL... ?
THIS IS NOTHING... HE GETS WAY STRONGER THAN THIS... !

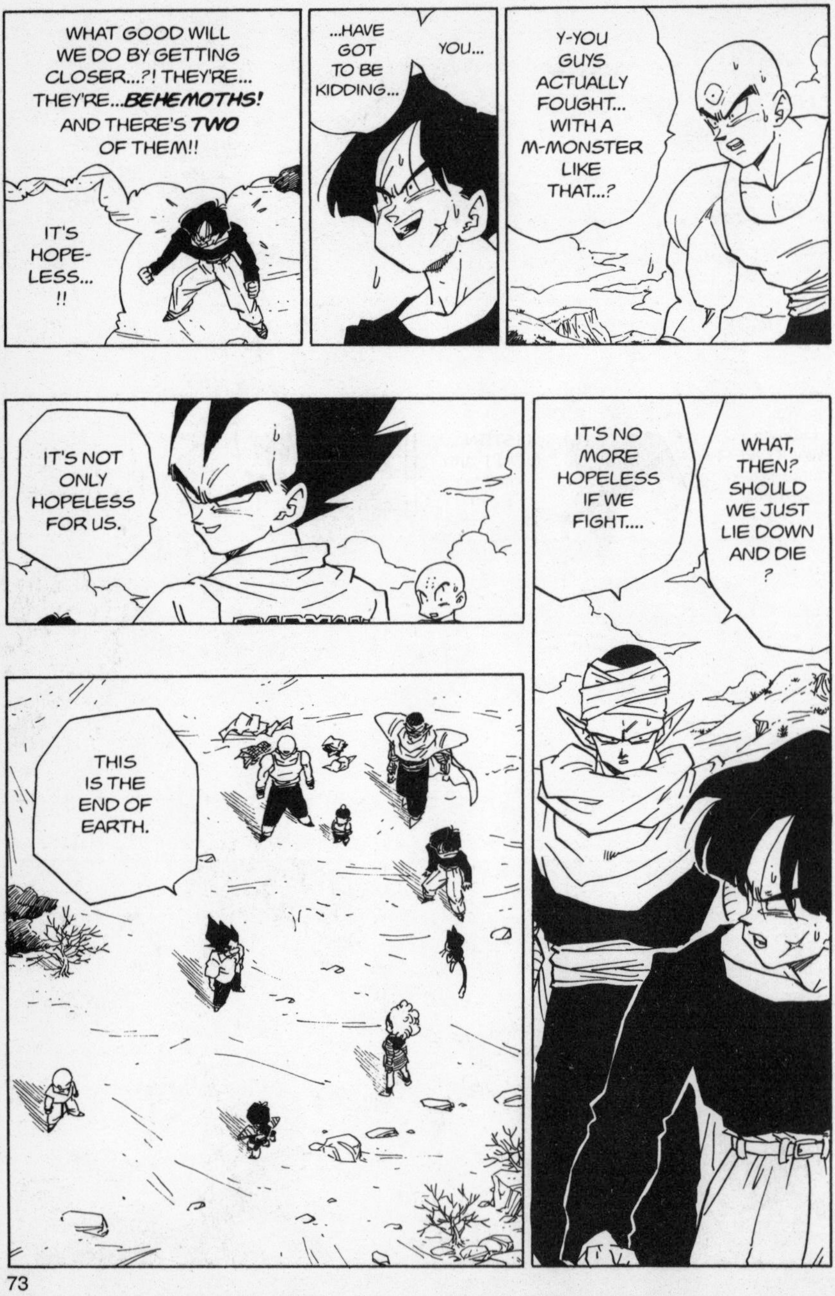
Y-YOU GUYS ACTUALLY FOUGHT... WITH A M-MONSTER LIKE THAT...?
YOU...
...HAVE GOT TO BE KIDDING...
WHAT GOOD WILL WE DO BY GETTING CLOSER...?! THEY'RE... THEY'RE...**BEHEMOTHS!** AND THERE'S **TWO** OF THEM!!
IT'S HOPE-LESS... !!
WHAT, THEN? SHOULD WE JUST LIE DOWN AND DIE?
IT'S NO MORE HOPELESS IF WE FIGHT....
IT'S NOT ONLY HOPELESS FOR US.
THIS IS THE END OF EARTH.

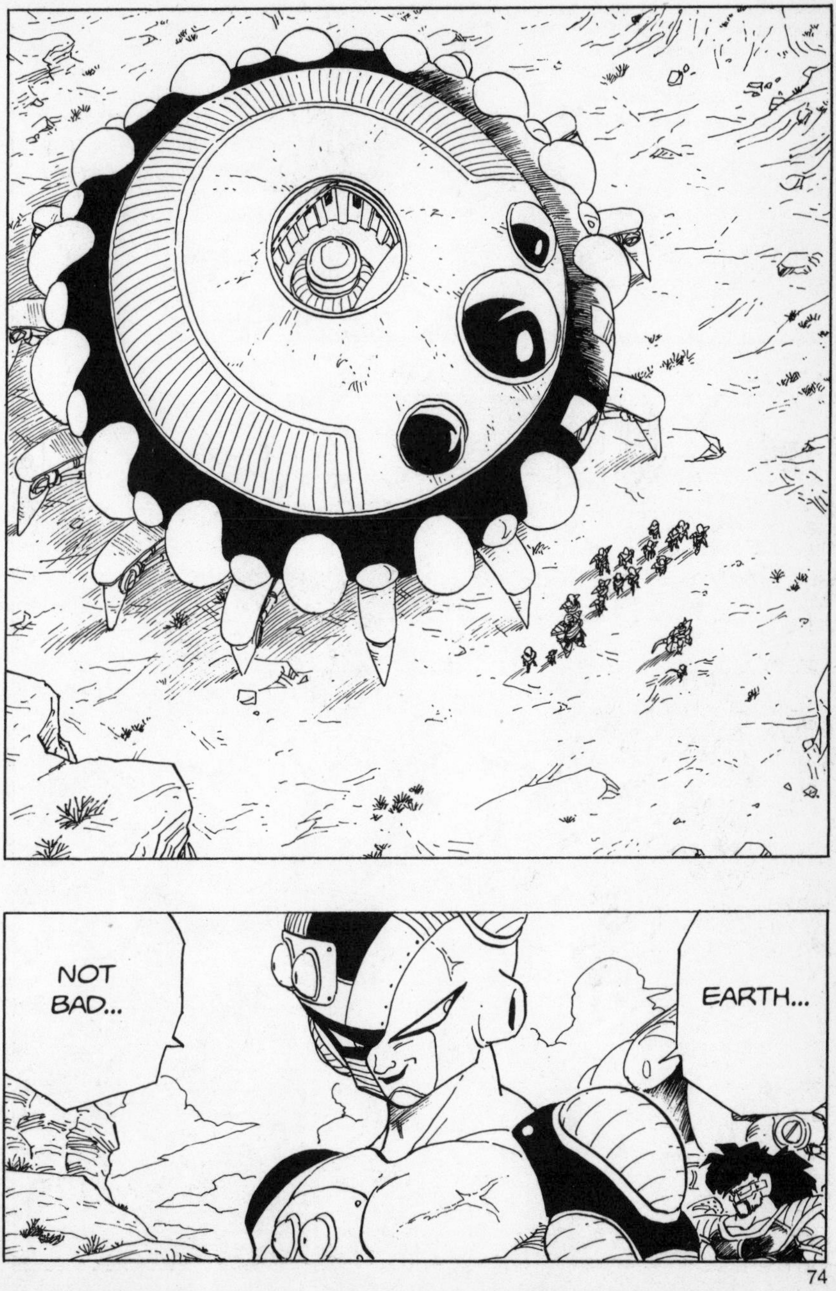
EARTH...
NOT BAD...

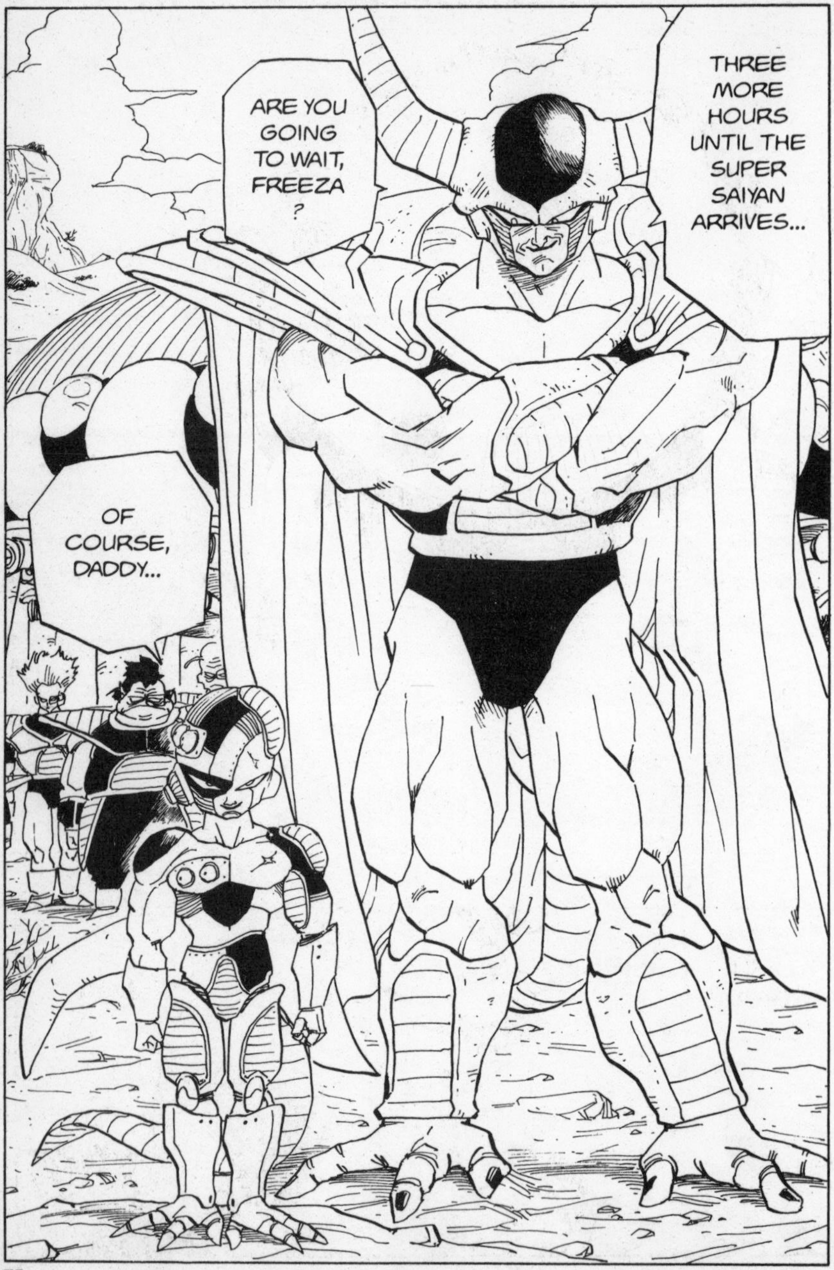
THREE MORE HOURS UNTIL THE SUPER SAIYAN ARRIVES...
ARE YOU GOING TO WAIT, FREEZA ?
OF COURSE, DADDY...

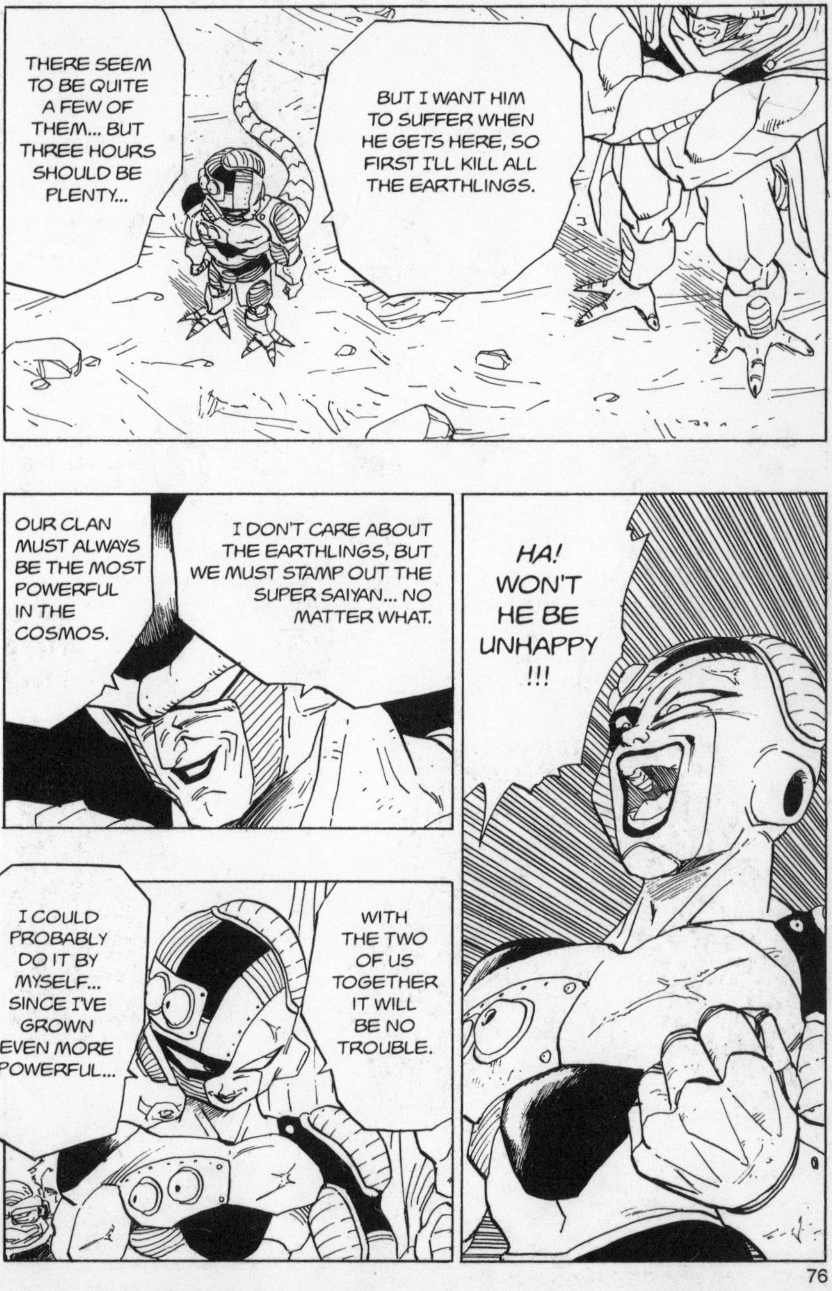

BUT I WANT HIM TO SUFFER WHEN HE GETS HERE, SO FIRST I'LL KILL ALL THE EARTHLINGS.
THERE SEEM TO BE QUITE A FEW OF THEM... BUT THREE HOURS SHOULD BE PLENTY...
HA! WON'T HE BE UNHAPPY!!!
I DON'T CARE ABOUT THE EARTHLINGS, BUT WE MUST STAMP OUT THE SUPER SAIYAN... NO MATTER WHAT.
OUR CLAN MUST ALWAYS BE THE MOST POWERFUL IN THE COSMOS.
WITH THE TWO OF US TOGETHER IT WILL BE NO TROUBLE.
I COULD PROBABLY DO IT BY MYSELF... SINCE I'VE GROWN EVEN MORE POWERFUL...

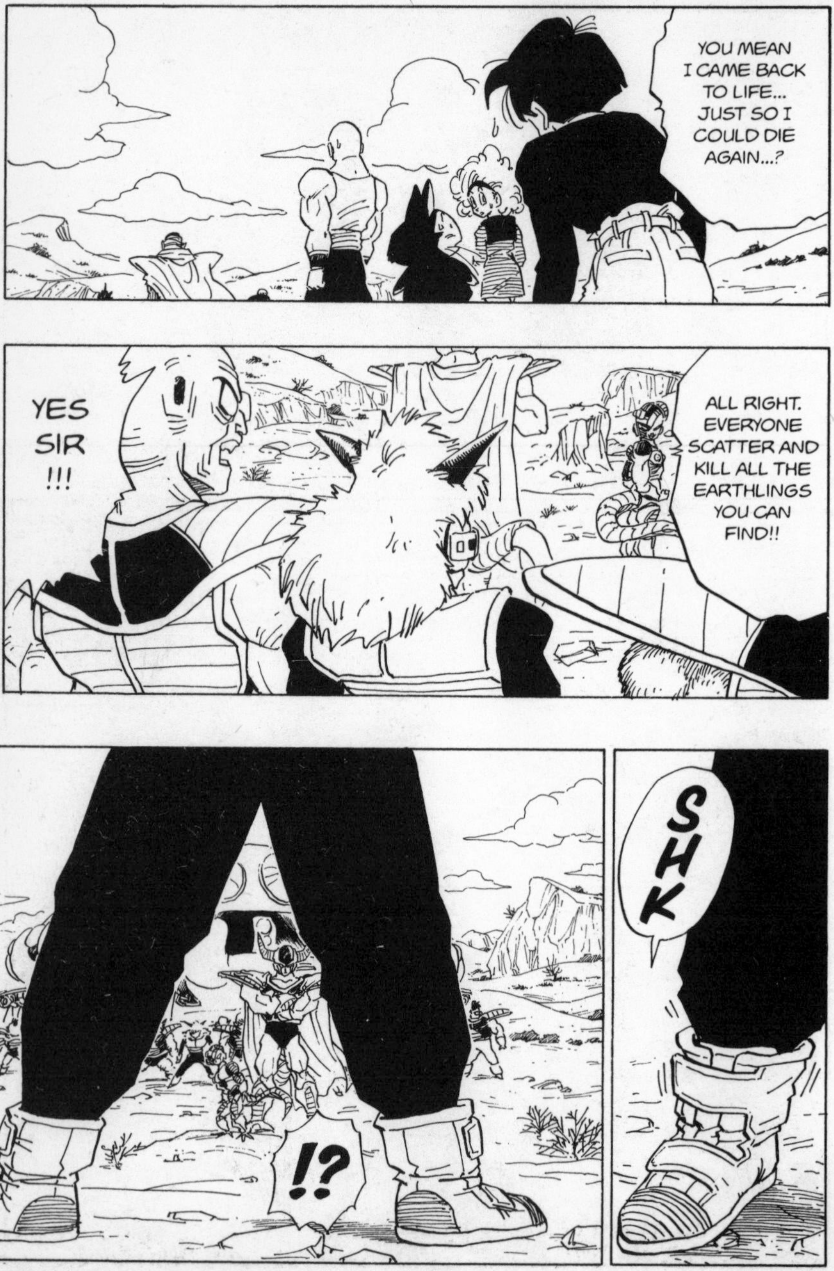
YOU MEAN I CAME BACK TO LIFE... JUST SO I COULD DIE AGAIN...?
ALL RIGHT. EVERYONE SCATTER AND KILL ALL THE EARTHLINGS YOU CAN FIND!!
YES SIR !!!
SHK
!?

NEXT: THE MYSTERIOUS YOUTH

DBZ: 137 • The Young Man of Mystery

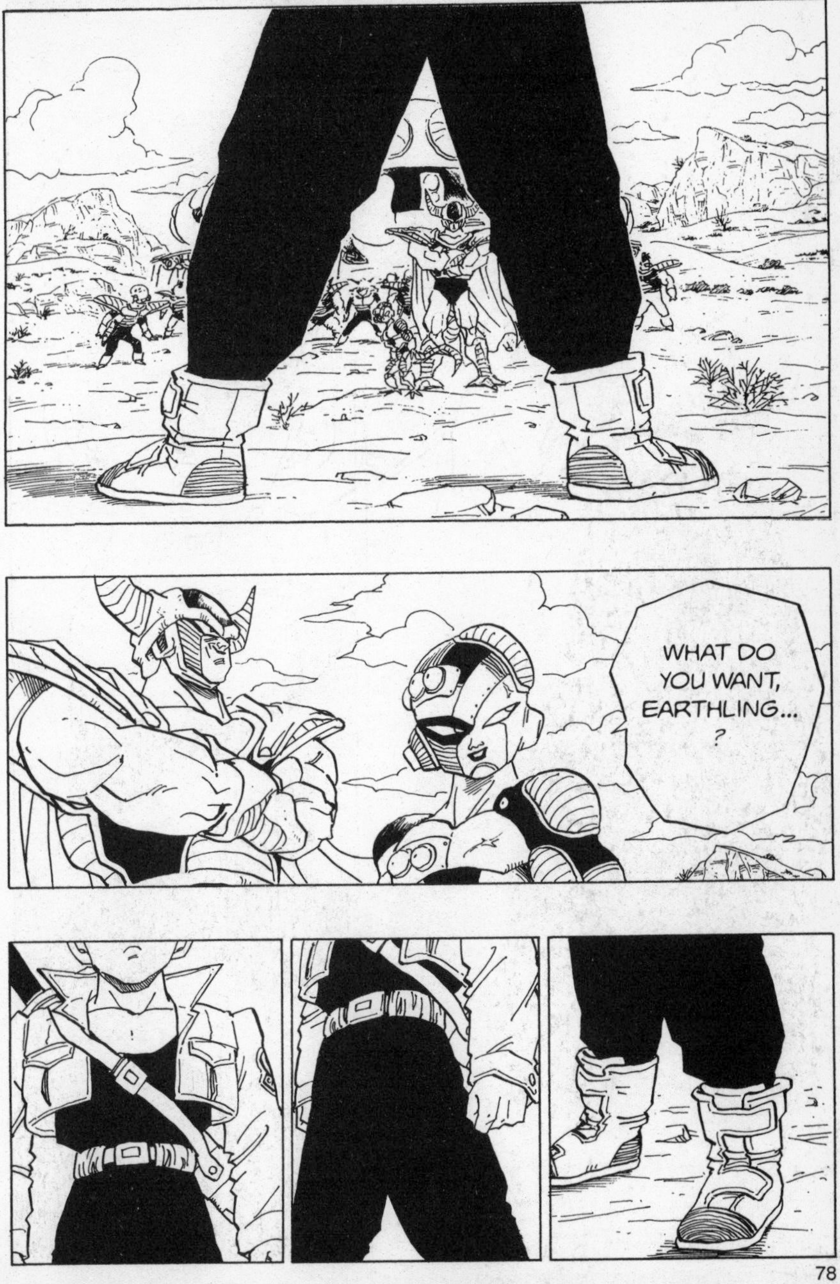
WHAT DO YOU WANT, EARTHLING...?

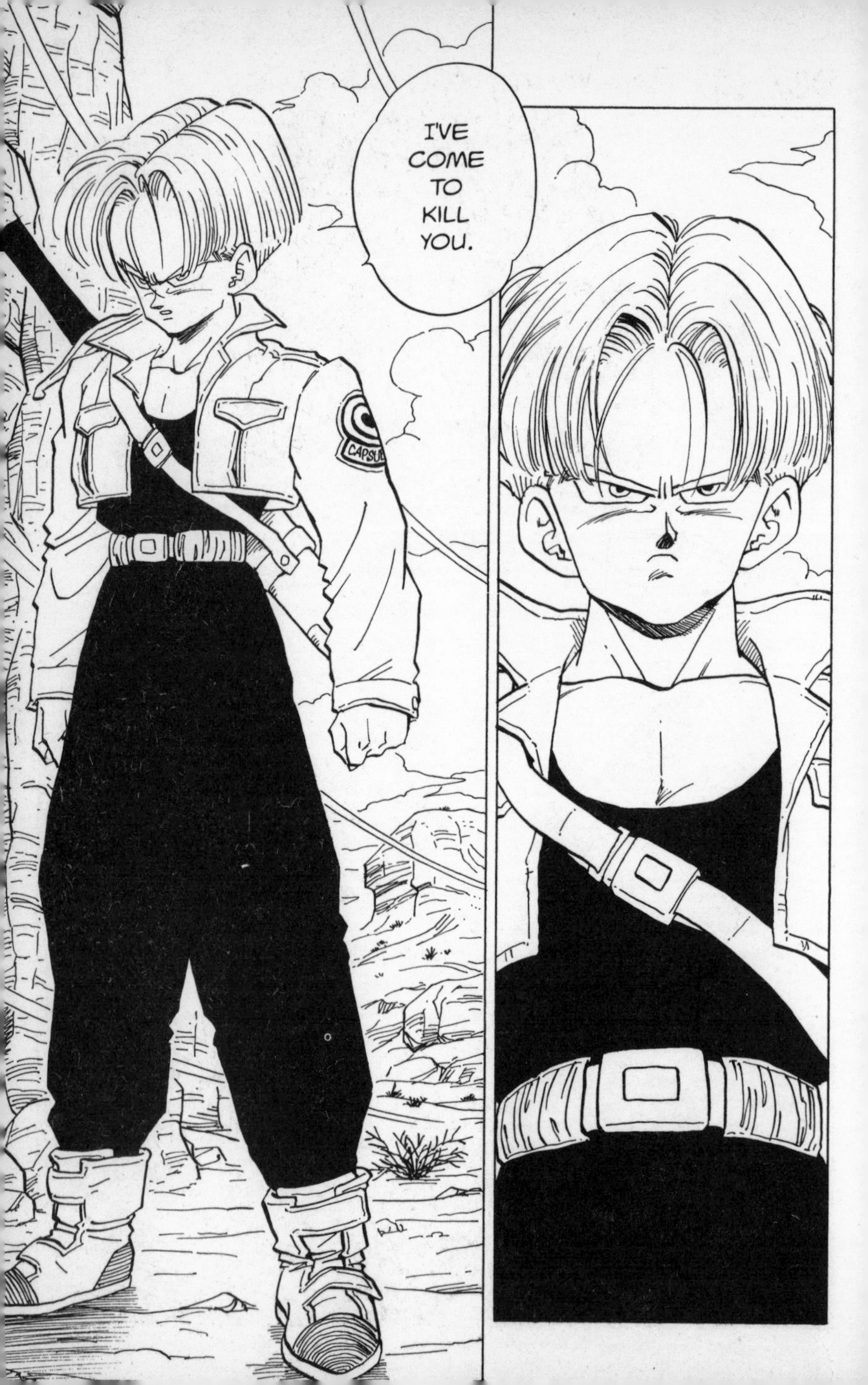
I'VE COME TO KILL YOU.

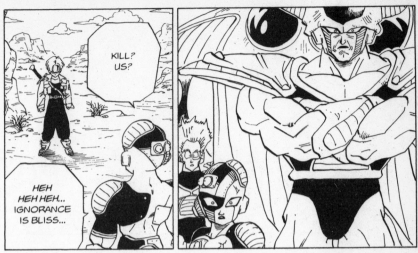

KILL? US?
HEH HEH HEH... IGNORANCE IS BLISS...
WHO'S IGNORANT?
FREEZA... RIGHT?
!
I'M HONORED THAT MY NAME IS KNOWN EVEN IN THE JERKWATER OUTSKIRTS OF THE GALAXY.
A PITY THAT YOU APPARENTLY DON'T ALSO KNOW THAT I AM THE MOST POWERFUL BEING IN THE UNIVERSE...
GET RID OF HIM.
YES, SIR!

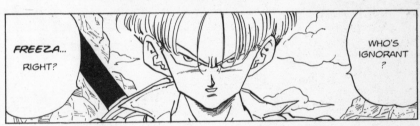

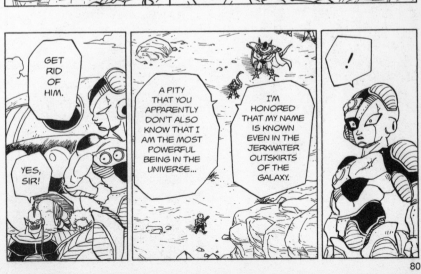

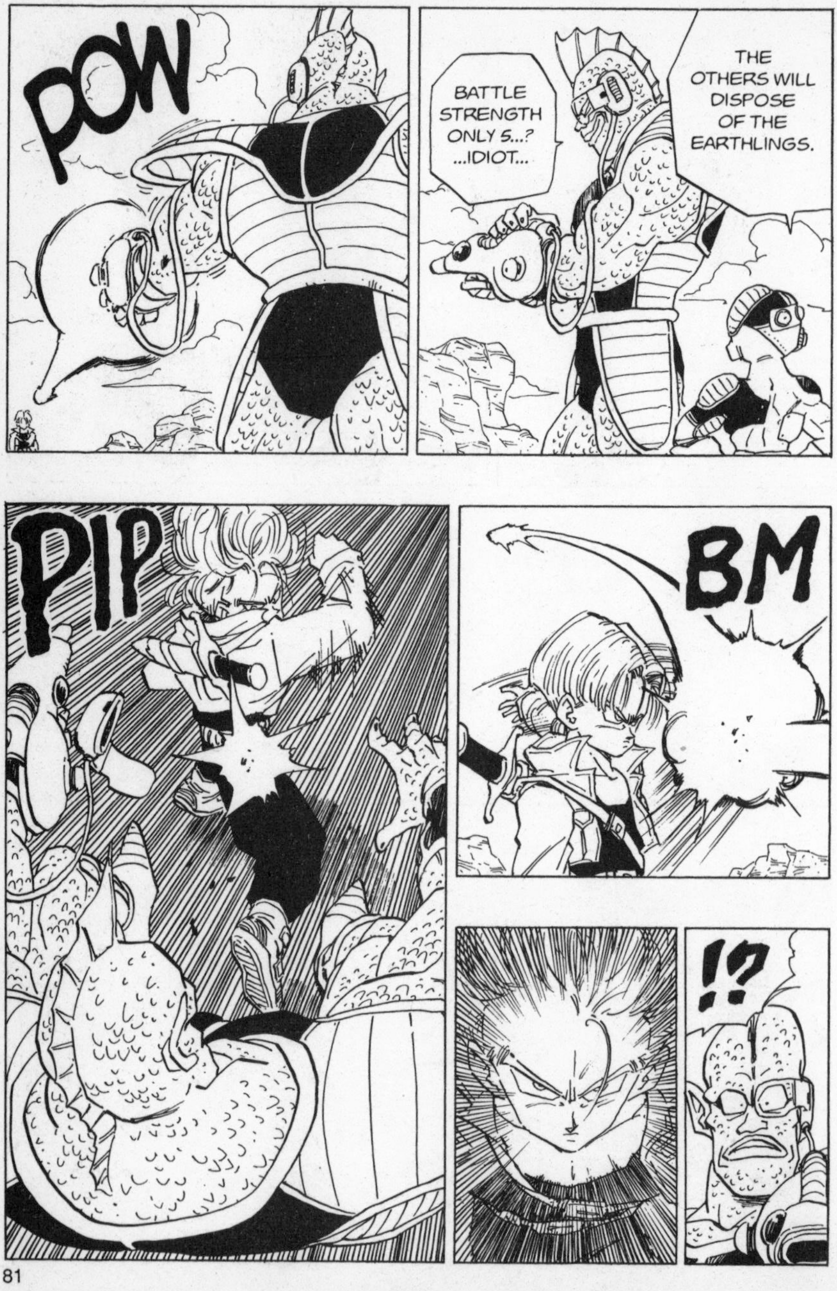
THE OTHERS WILL DISPOSE OF THE EARTHLINGS.
BATTLE STRENGTH ONLY 5...? ...IDIOT...
POW
BM
!?
PIP

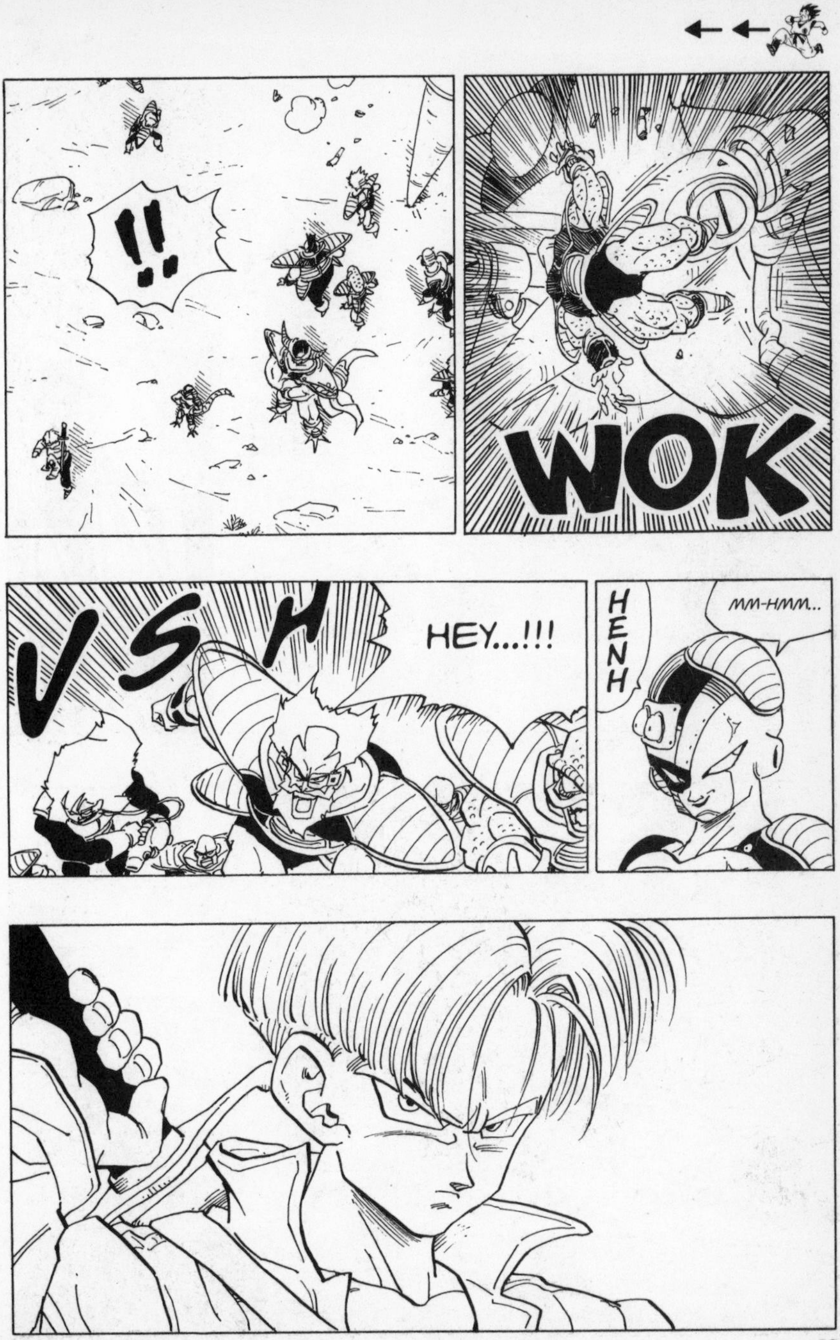
WOK
!!
MM-HMM...
HENH
HEY...!!!
VSH

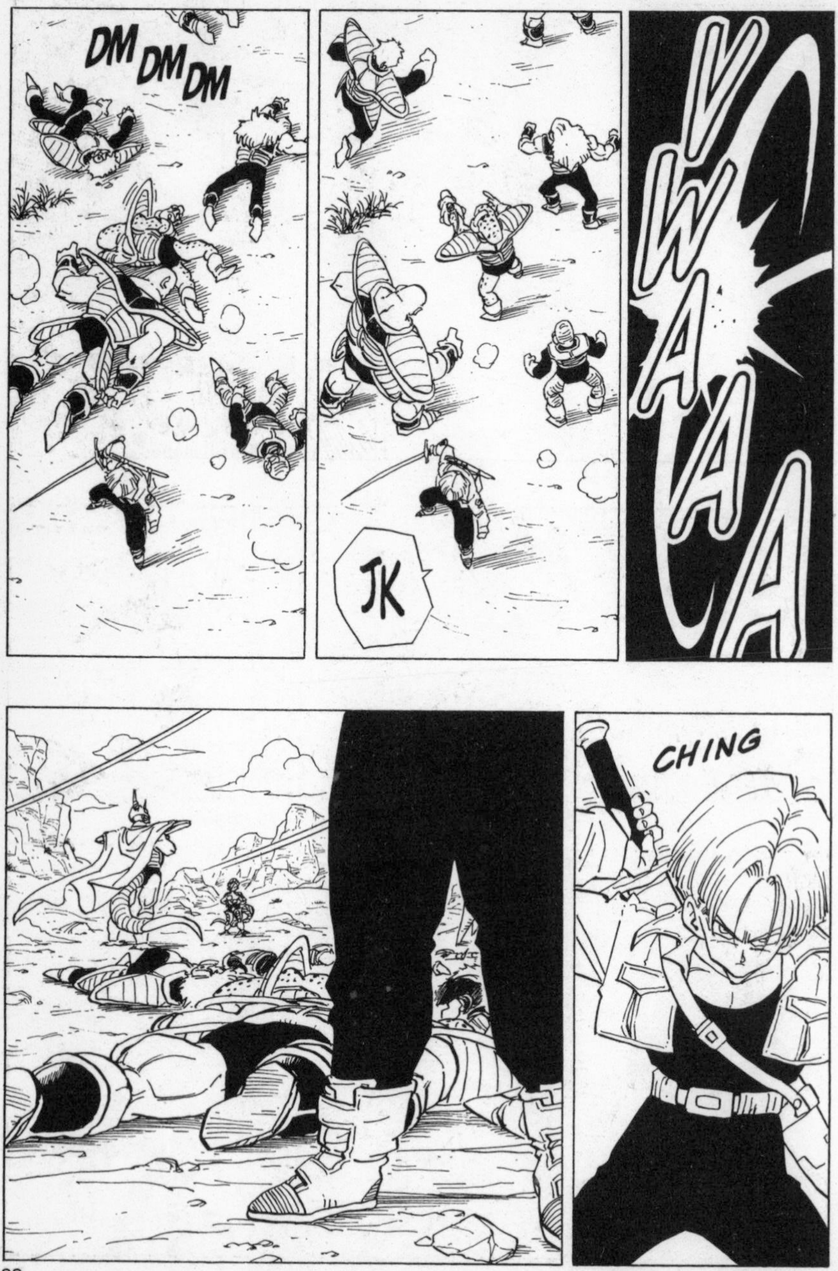
WWAAAA
JK
DM DM DM
CHING

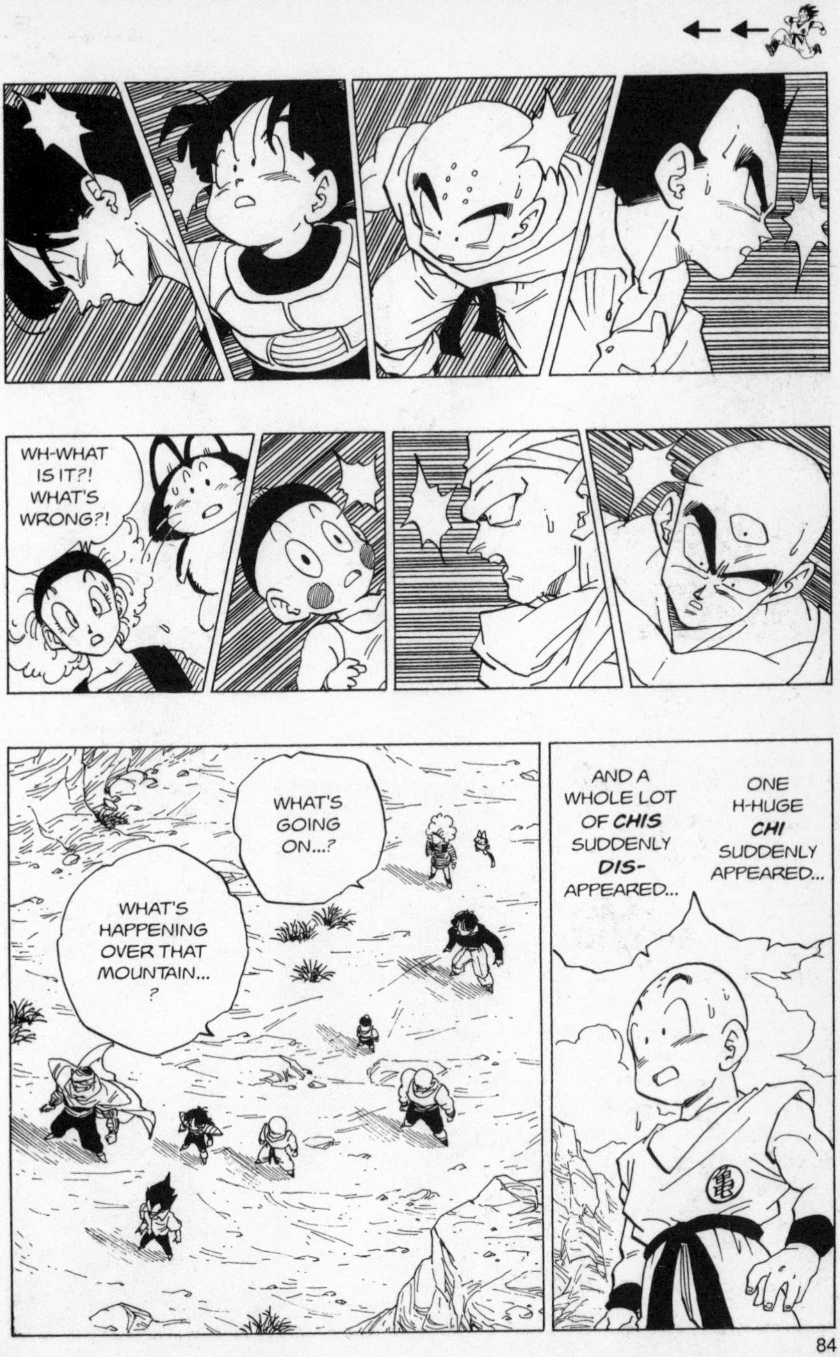
WH-WHAT IS IT?! WHAT'S WRONG?!
ONE H-HUGE ***CHI*** SUDDENLY APPEARED...
AND A WHOLE LOT OF ***CHIS*** SUDDENLY ***DIS-***APPEARED...
WHAT'S GOING ON...?
WHAT'S HAPPENING OVER THAT MOUNTAIN...?

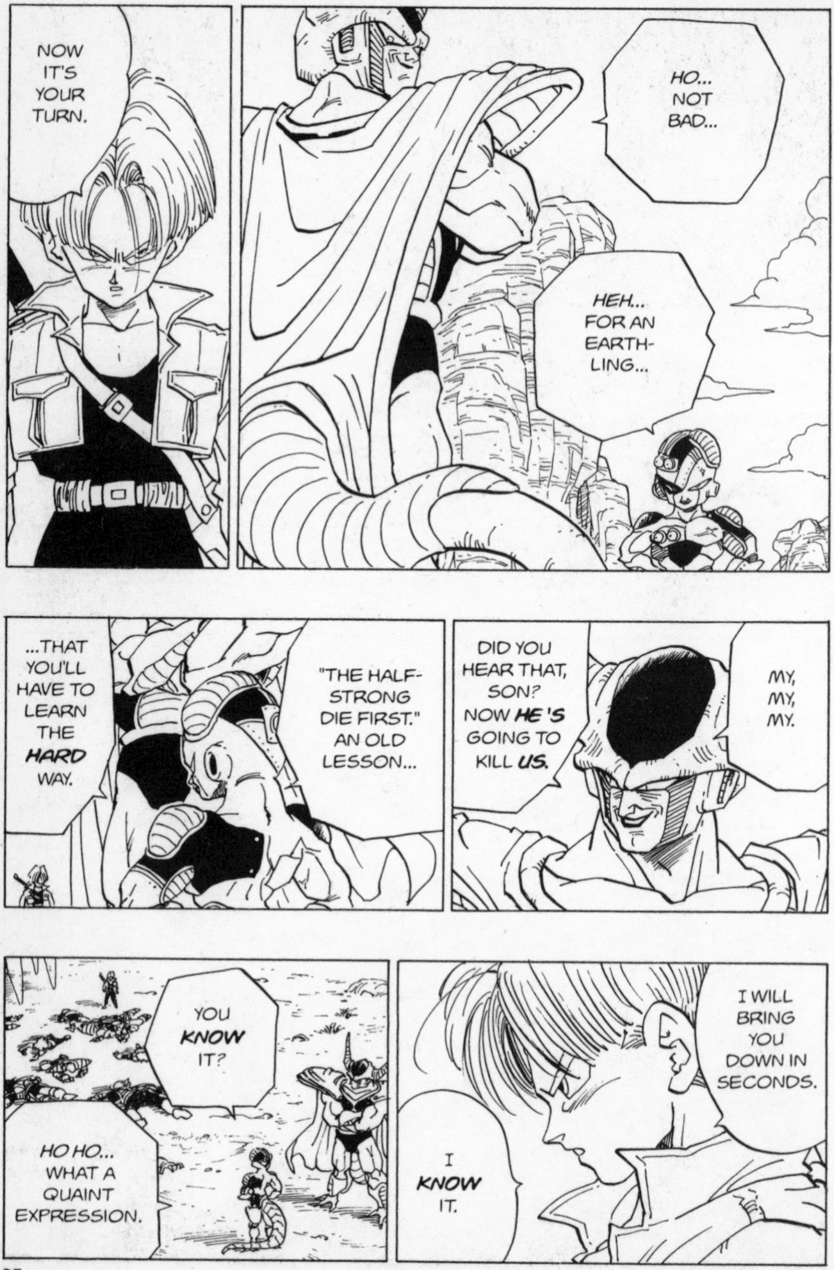
HO... NOT BAD...
HEH... FOR AN EARTHLING...
NOW IT'S YOUR TURN.
MY, MY, MY.
DID YOU HEAR THAT, SON? NOW **HE'S** GOING TO KILL **US**.
"THE HALF-STRONG DIE FIRST." AN OLD LESSON...
...THAT YOU'LL HAVE TO LEARN THE **HARD** WAY.
I WILL BRING YOU DOWN IN SECONDS.
I **KNOW** IT.
YOU **KNOW** IT?
HO HO... WHAT A QUAINT EXPRESSION.

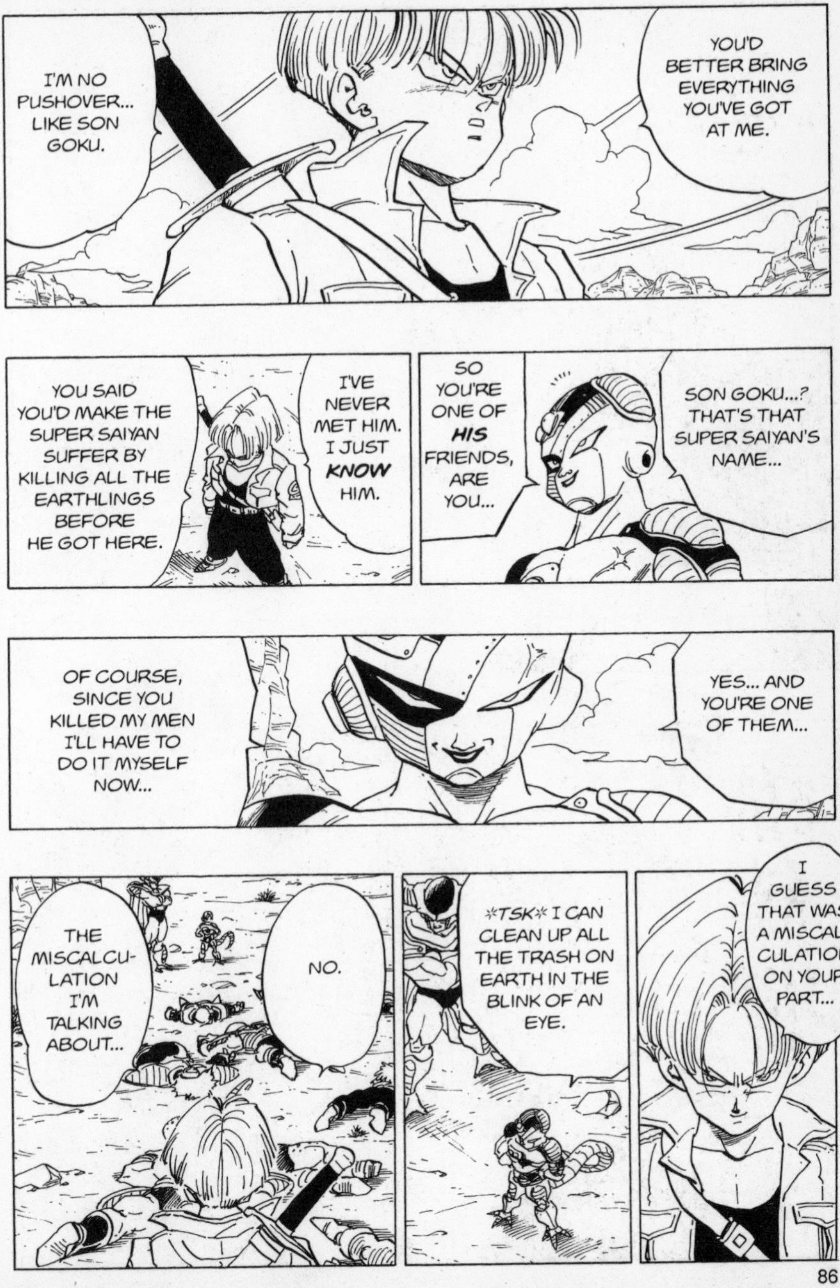
YOU'D BETTER BRING EVERYTHING YOU'VE GOT AT ME.
I'M NO PUSHOVER... LIKE SON GOKU.
SON GOKU...? THAT'S THAT SUPER SAIYAN'S NAME...
SO YOU'RE ONE OF HIS FRIENDS, ARE YOU...
I'VE NEVER MET HIM. I JUST KNOW HIM.
YOU SAID YOU'D MAKE THE SUPER SAIYAN SUFFER BY KILLING ALL THE EARTHLINGS BEFORE HE GOT HERE.
YES... AND YOU'RE ONE OF THEM...
OF COURSE, SINCE YOU KILLED MY MEN I'LL HAVE TO DO IT MYSELF NOW...
I GUESS THAT WAS A MISCAL-CULATION ON YOUR PART...
TSK I CAN CLEAN UP ALL THE TRASH ON EARTH IN THE BLINK OF AN EYE.
NO.
THE MISCALCU-LATION I'M TALKING ABOUT...

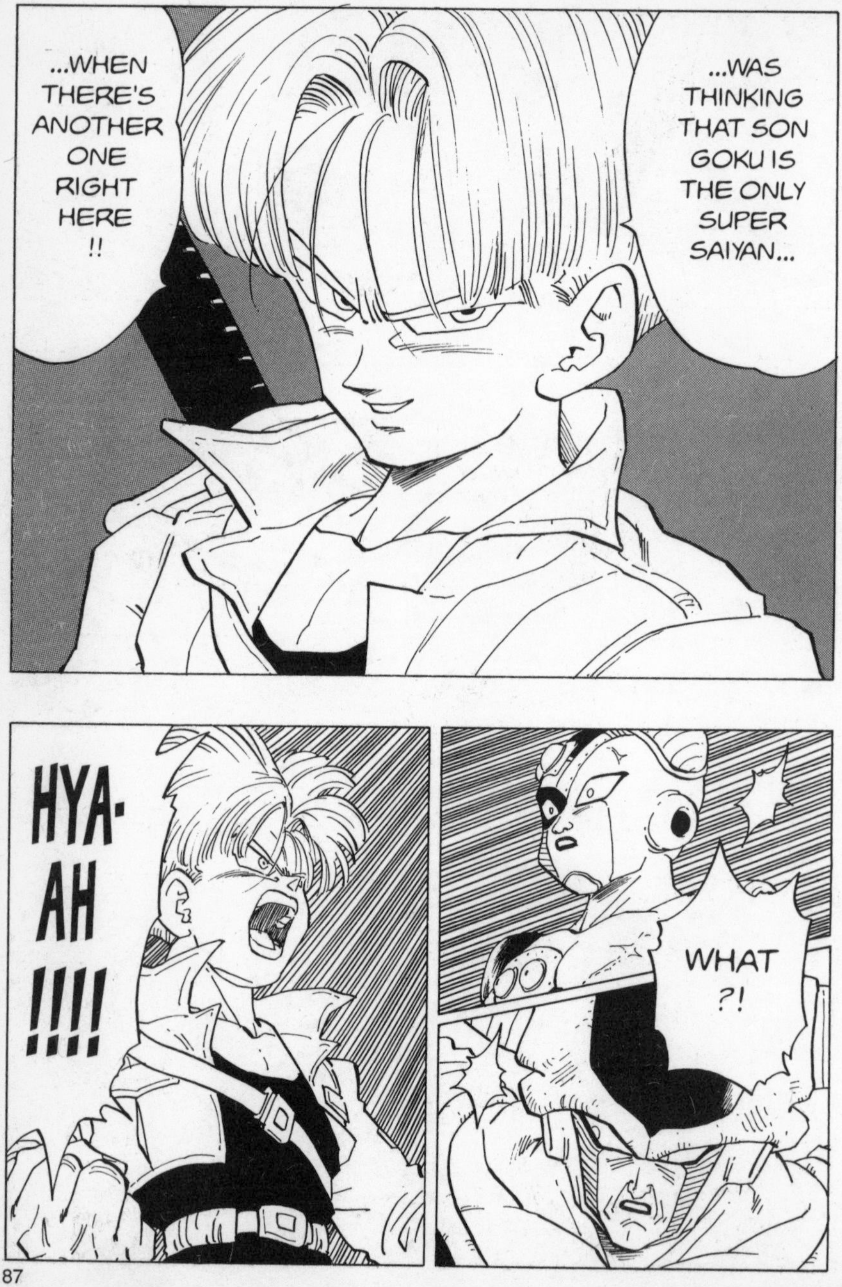
...WAS THINKING THAT SON GOKU IS THE ONLY SUPER SAIYAN...
...WHEN THERE'S ANOTHER ONE RIGHT HERE !!
WHAT ?!
HYA-AH !!!!

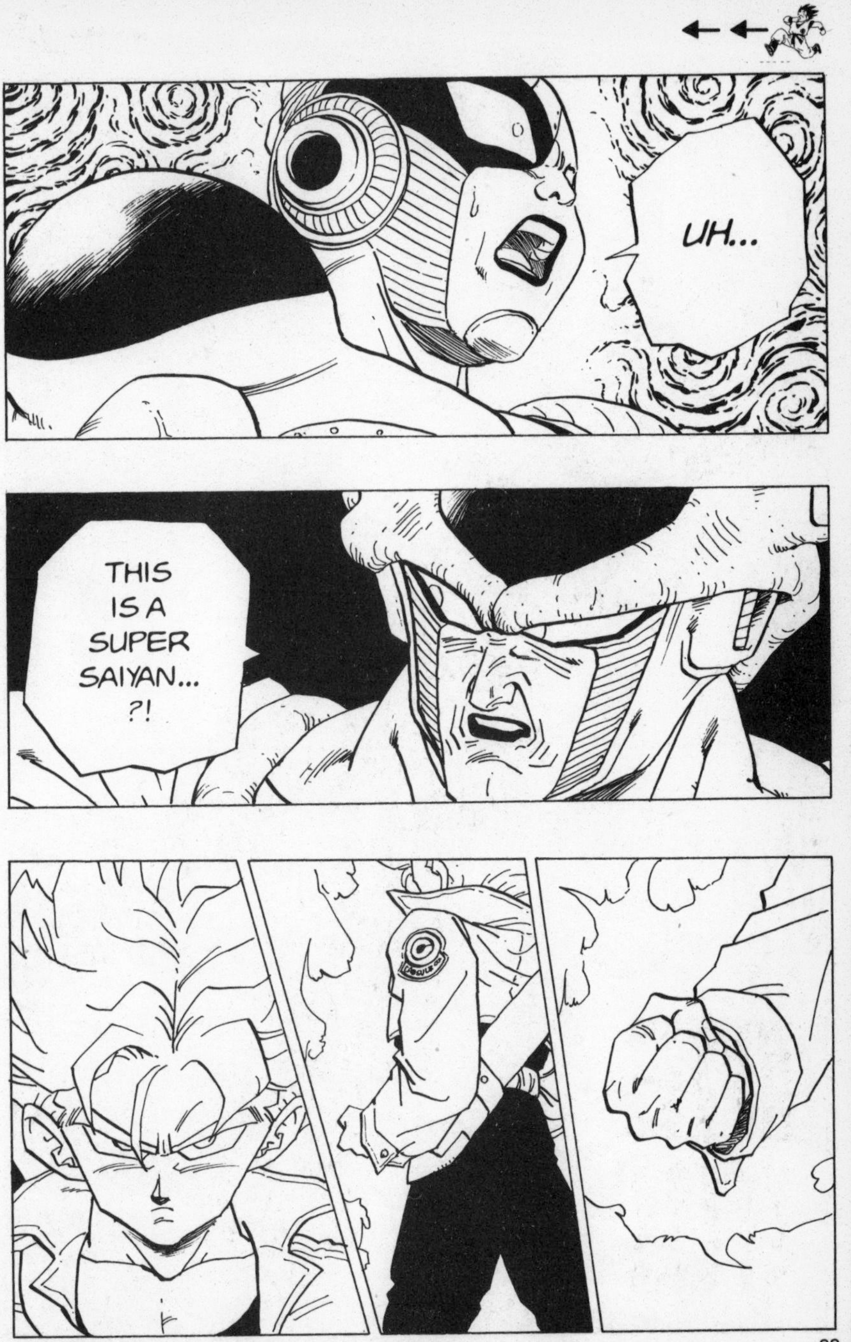
UH...
THIS IS A SUPER SAIYAN... ?!

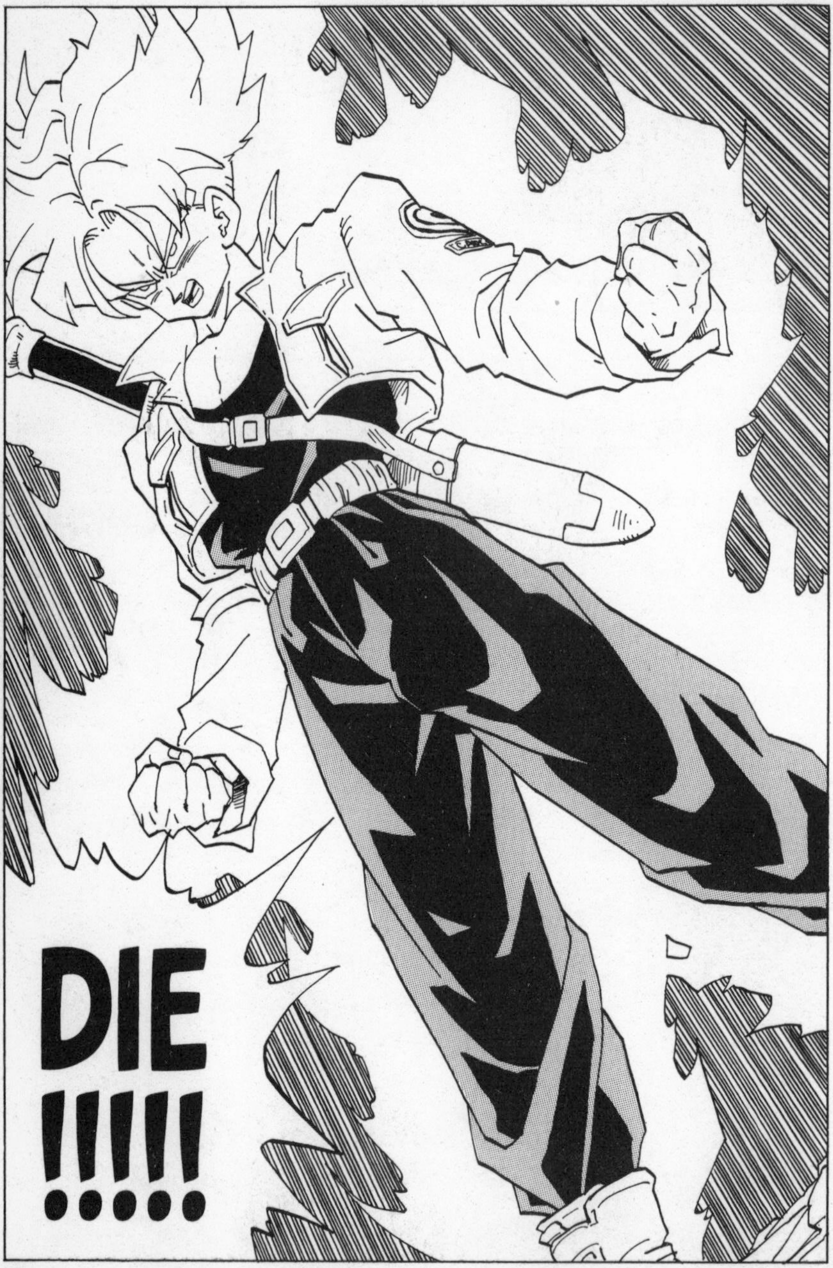
DIE!!!!!!

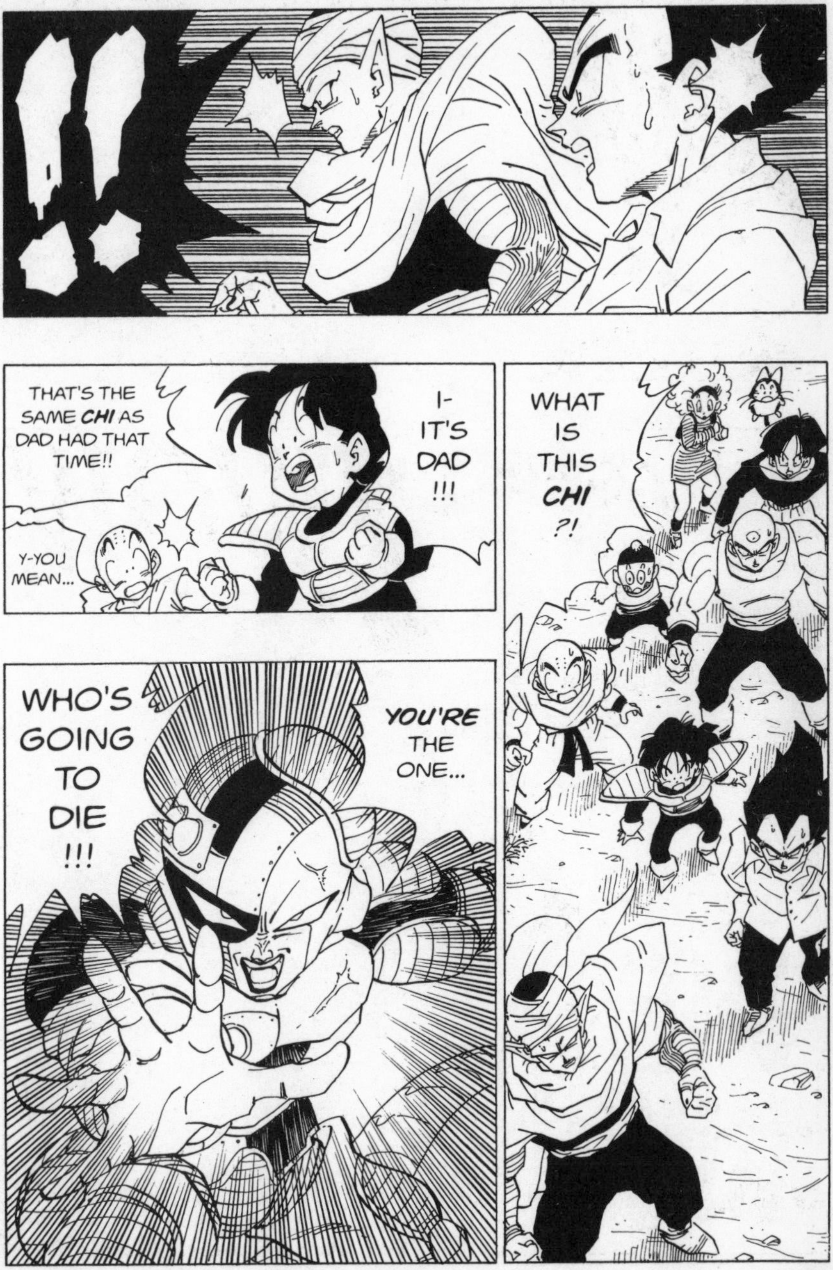
!!
WHAT IS THIS CHI?!
I- IT'S DAD!!!
THAT'S THE SAME CHI AS DAD HAD THAT TIME!!
Y-YOU MEAN...
YOU'RE THE ONE...
WHO'S GOING TO DIE!!!

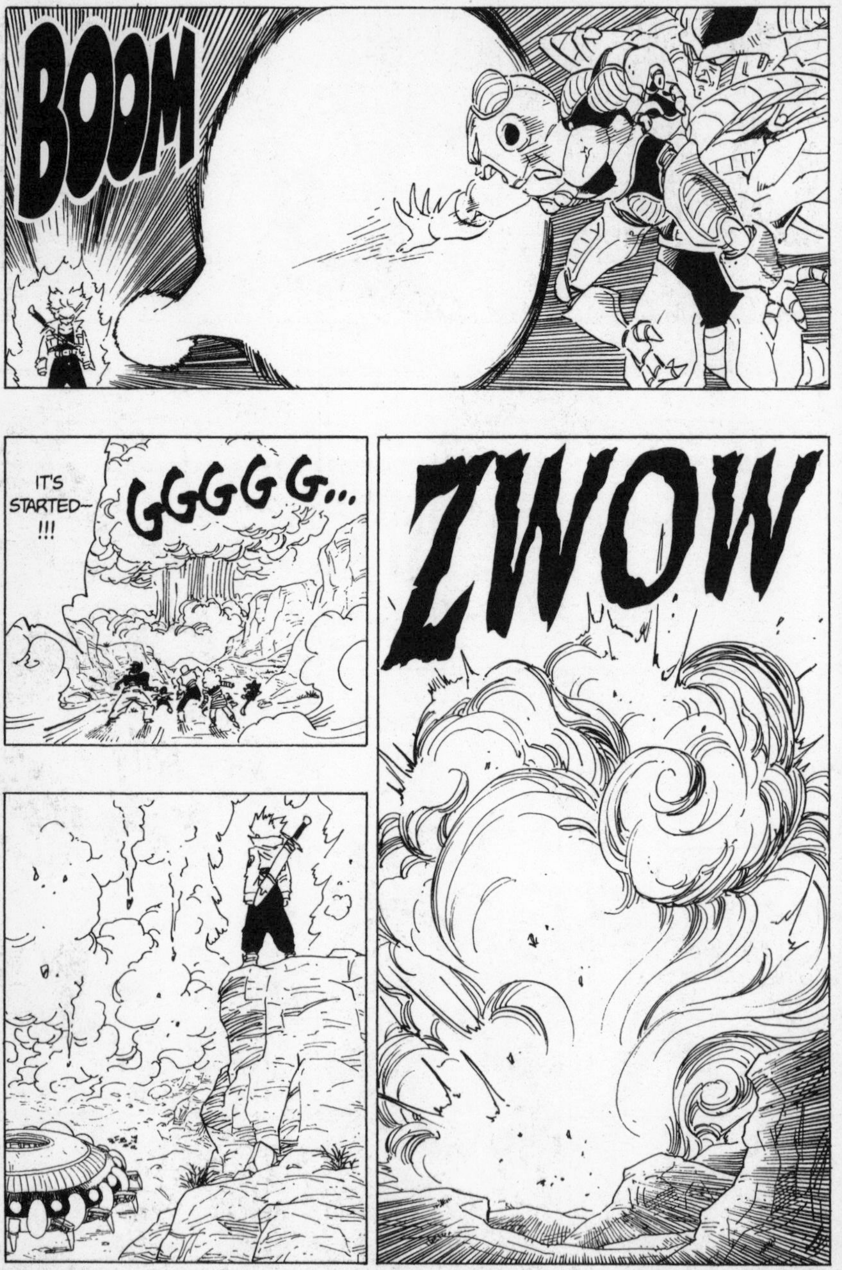
BOOM
ZWOW
GGGGG...
IT'S STARTED--!!!

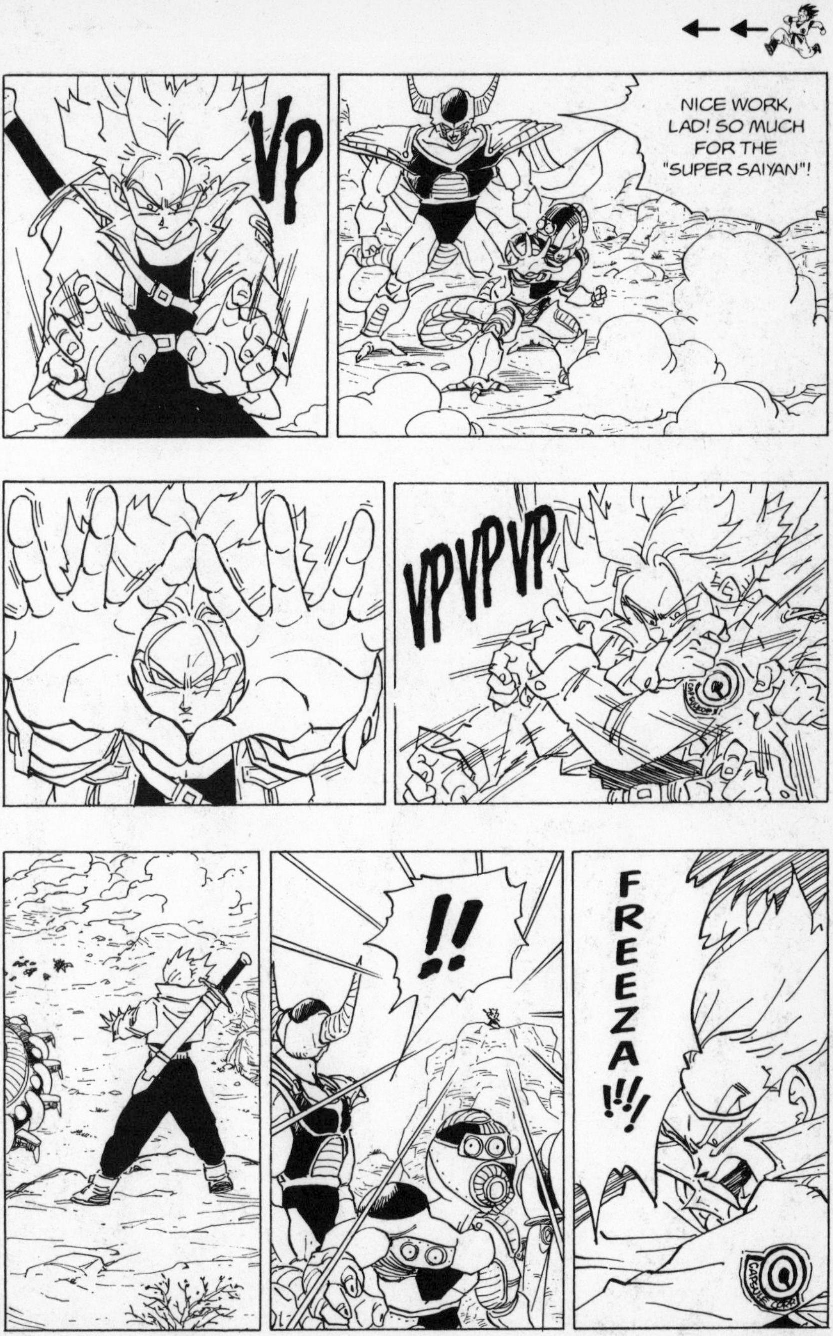
NICE WORK, LAD! SO MUCH FOR THE "SUPER SAIYAN"!
VP
VPVPVP
FREEZA!!!!
!!

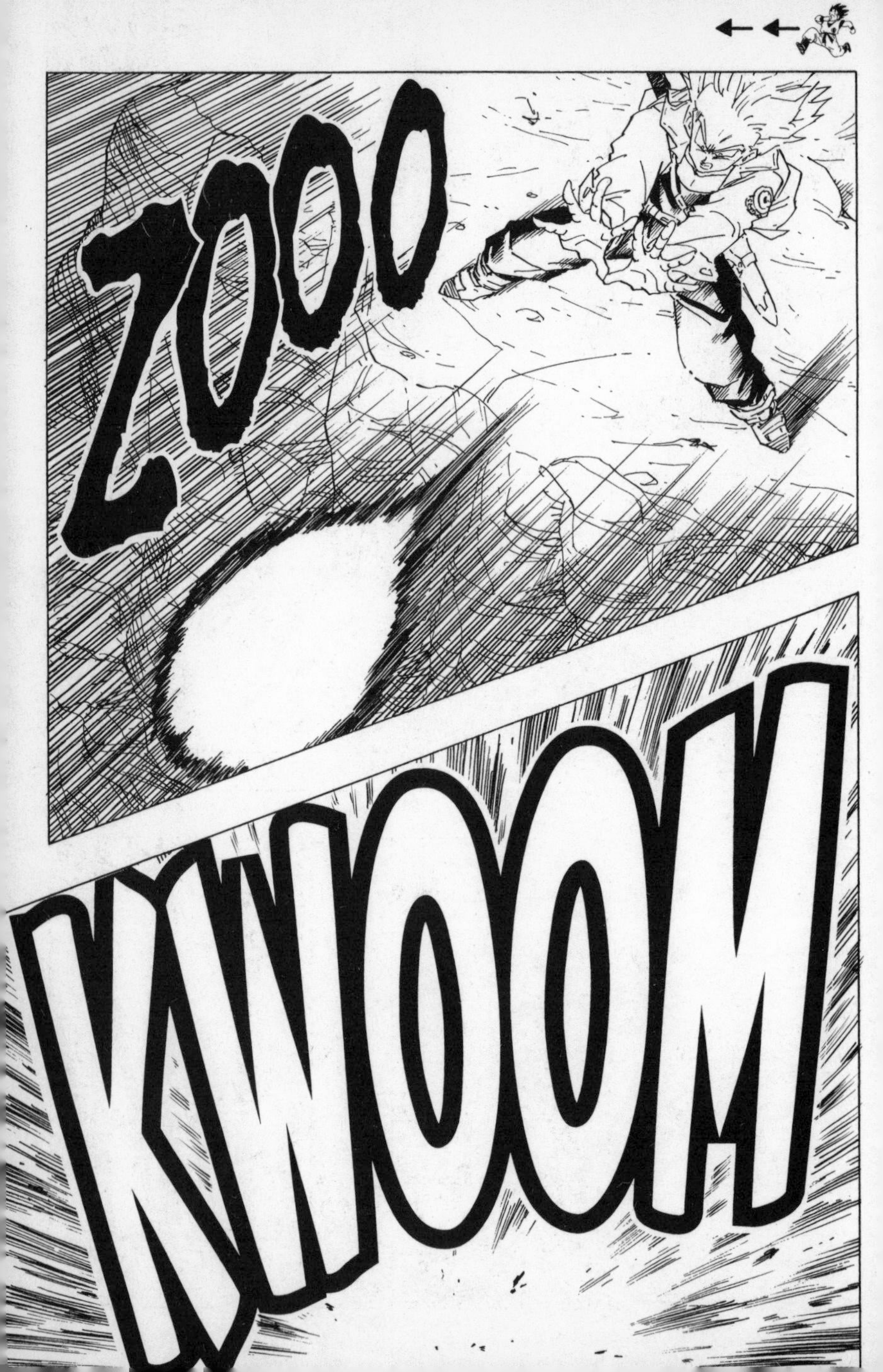
ZOOO
KWOOM

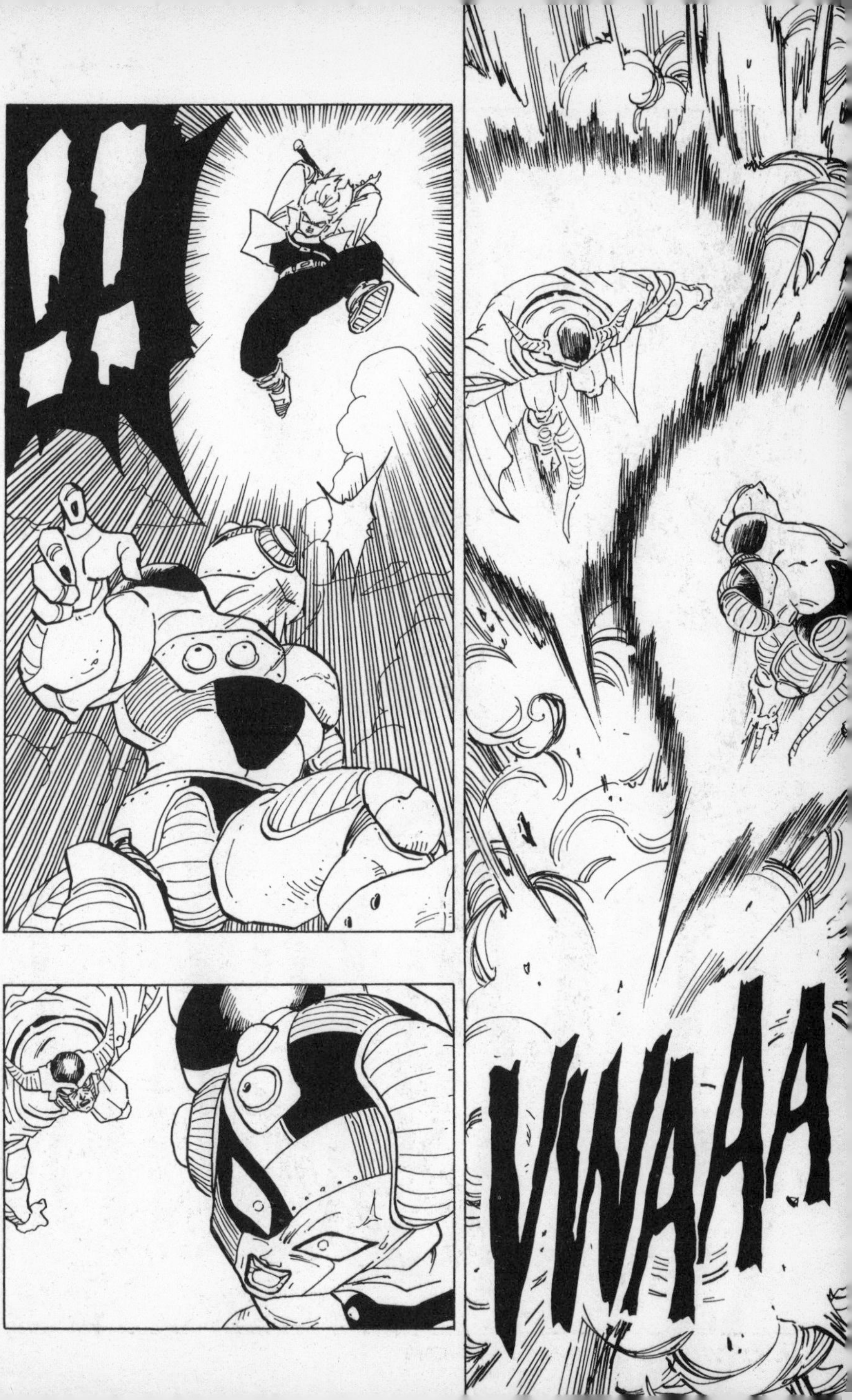
VWAAA
!!

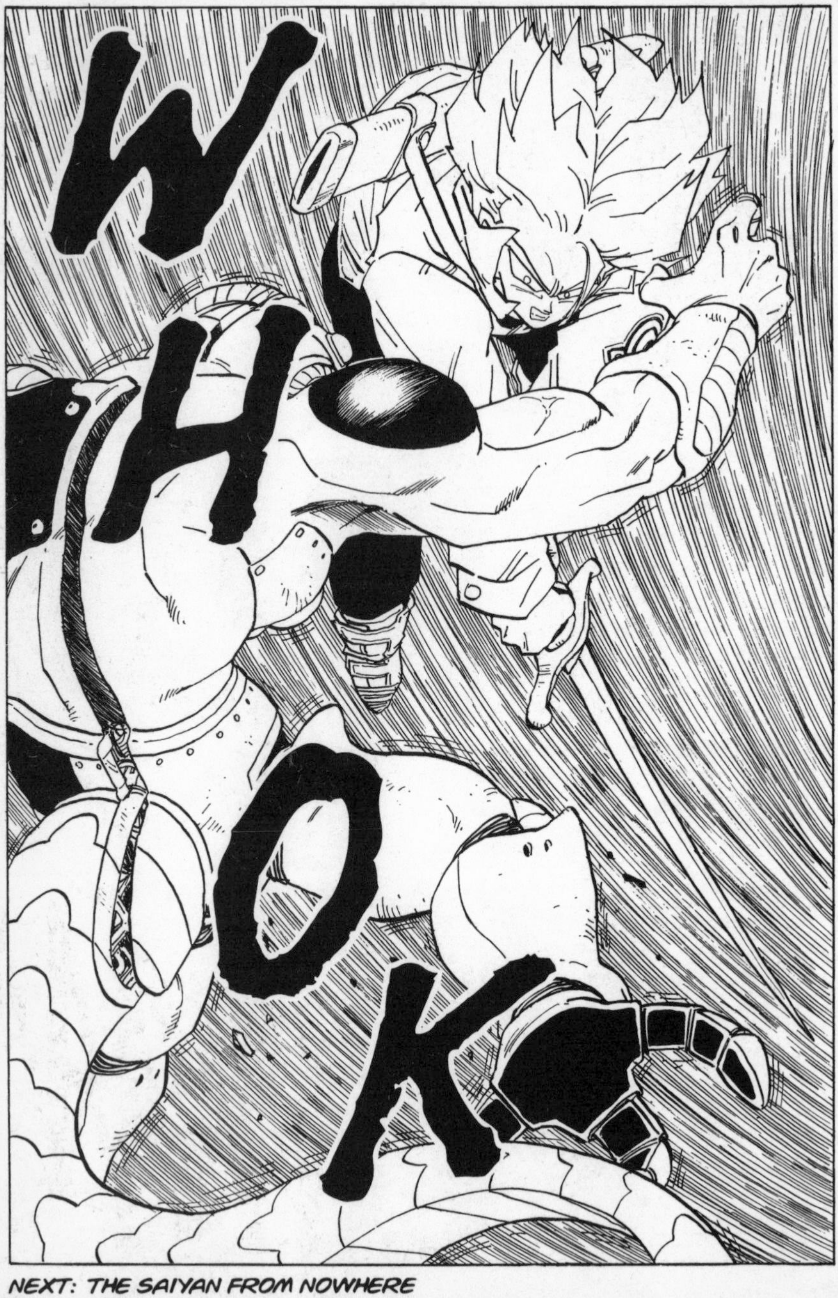
WHOK

NEXT: THE SAIYAN FROM NOWHERE

DBZ:138 • The Second Super Saiyan

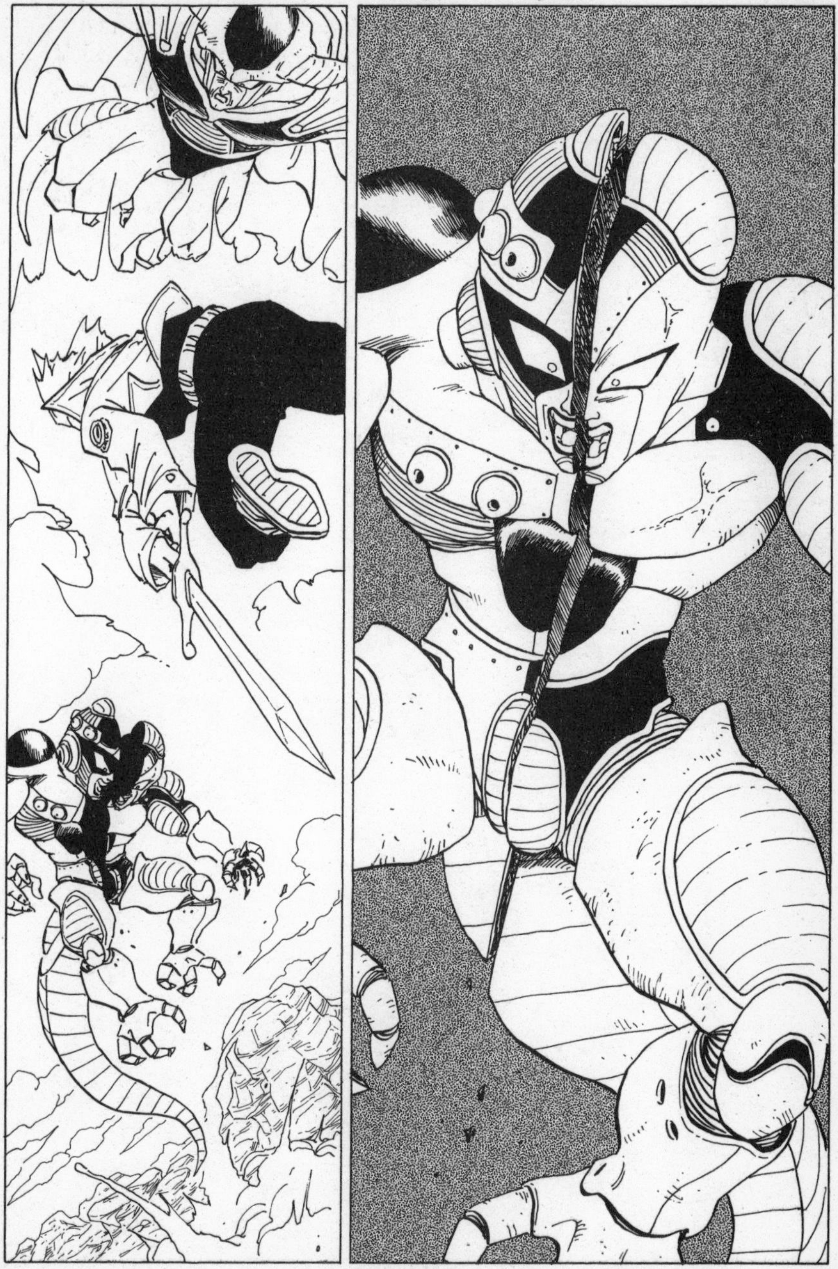

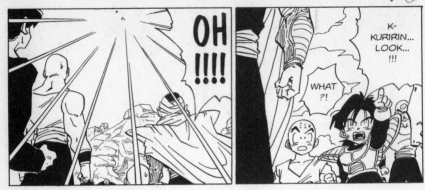

OH
!!!!

K-
KURIRIN...
LOOK...
!!!

WHAT
?!

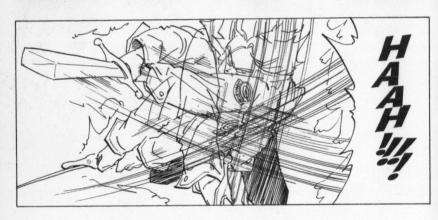

H
A
A
H
!!!
!!!
!

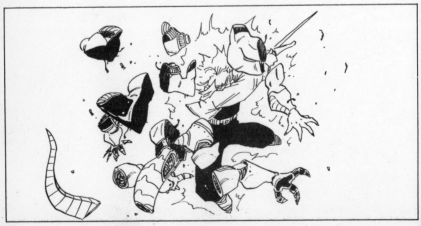

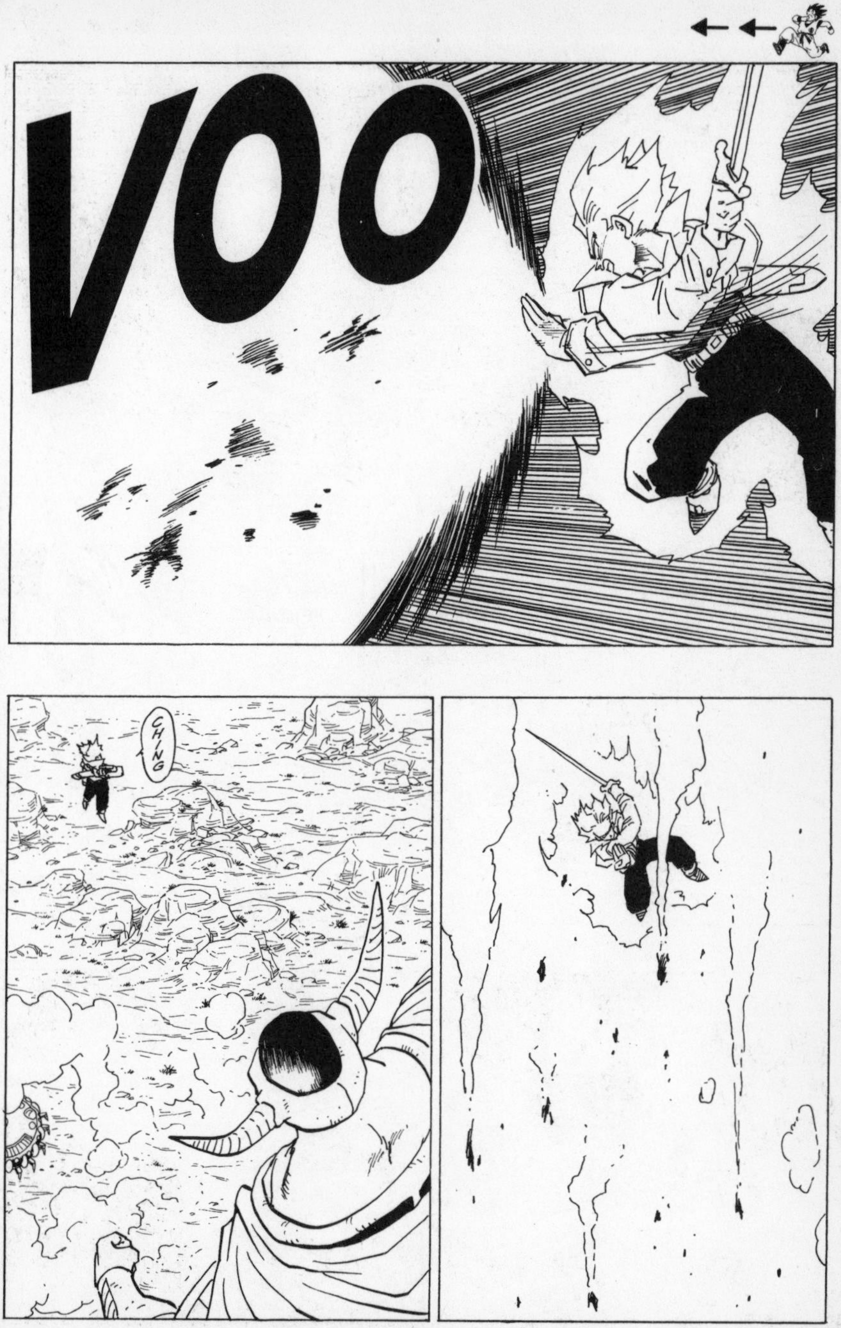
VOO
CHING

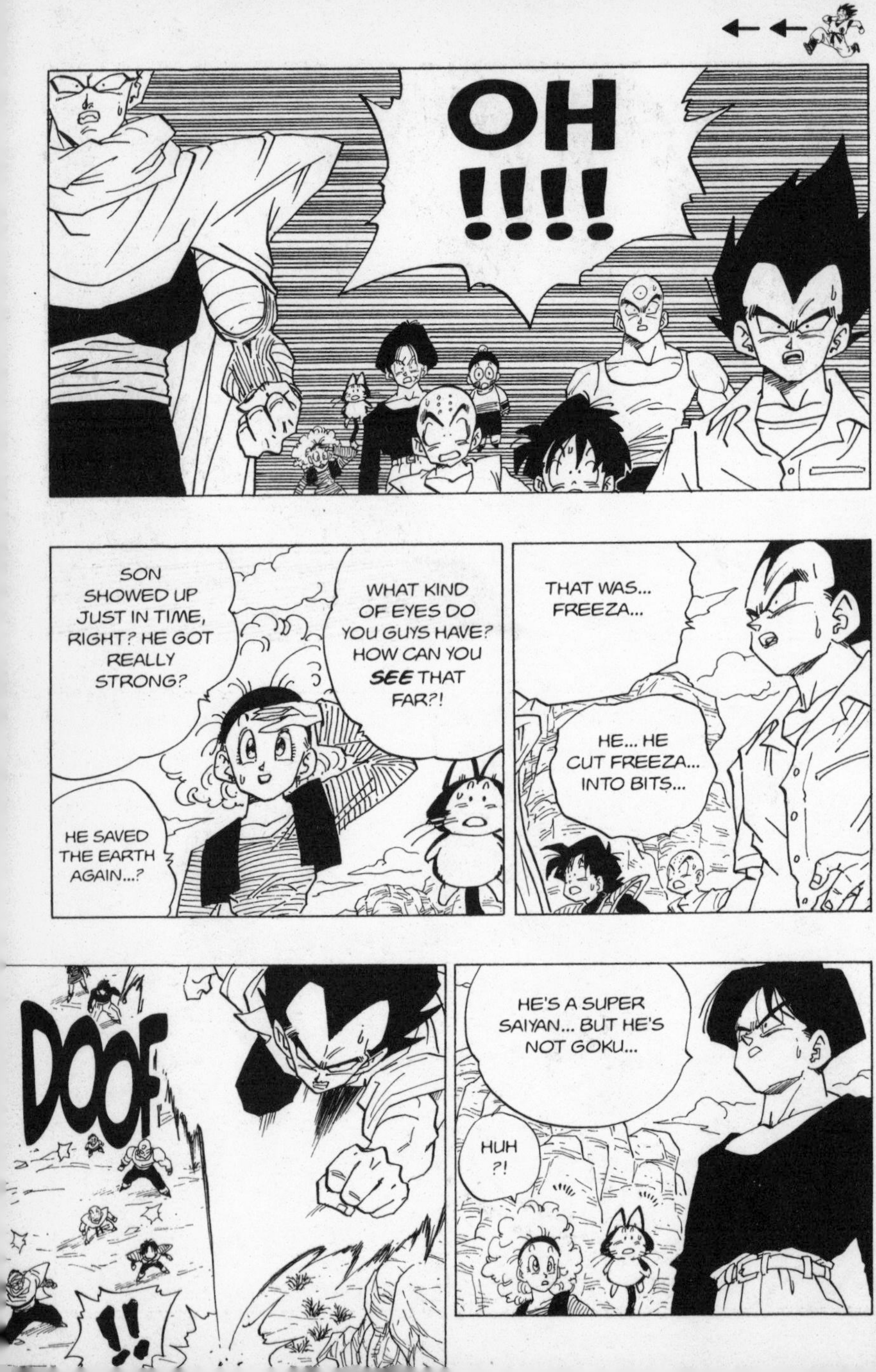
OH !!!!
THAT WAS... FREEZA...
HE... HE CUT FREEZA... INTO BITS...
WHAT KIND OF EYES DO YOU GUYS HAVE? HOW CAN YOU SEE THAT FAR?!
SON SHOWED UP JUST IN TIME, RIGHT? HE GOT REALLY STRONG?
HE SAVED THE EARTH AGAIN...?
HE'S A SUPER SAIYAN... BUT HE'S NOT GOKU...
HUH ?!
DOOF
!!

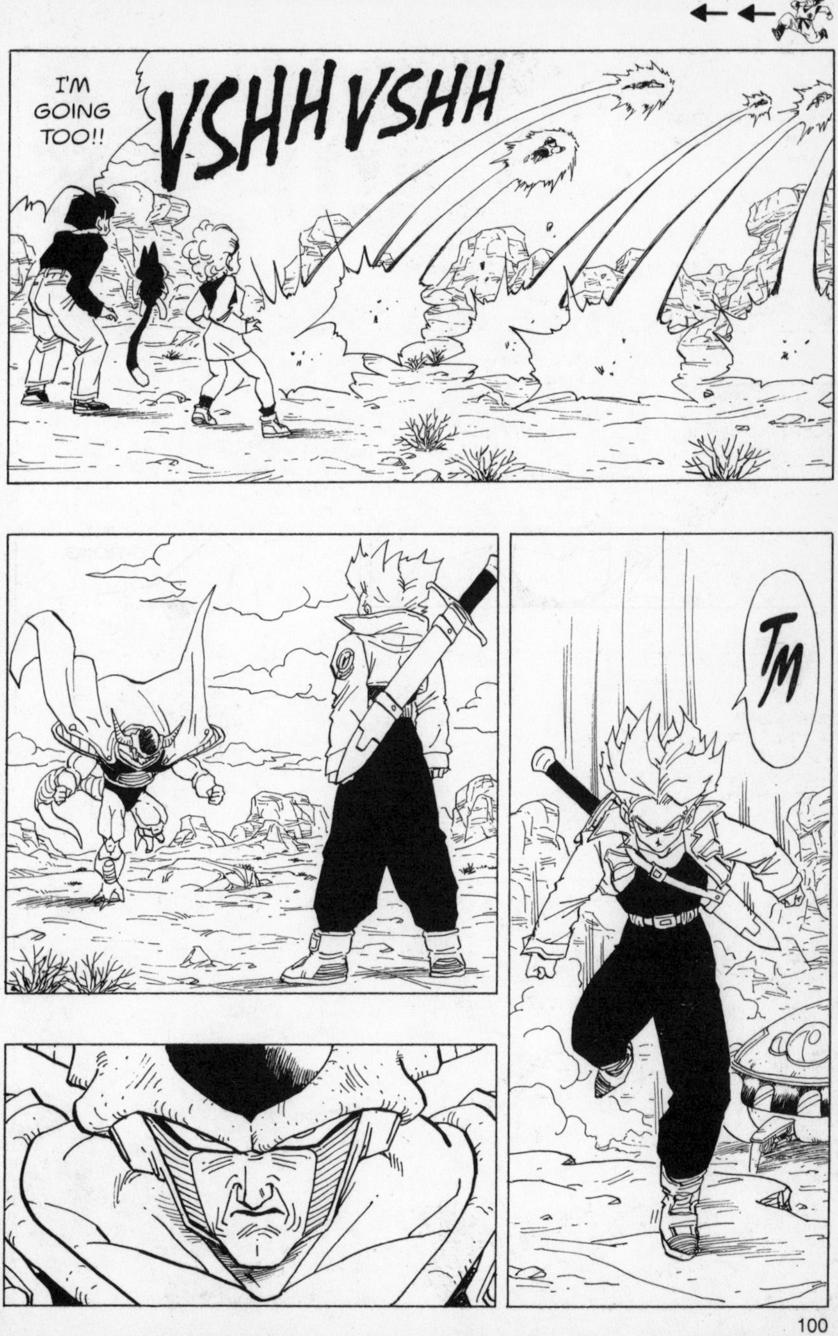
I'M GOING TOO!!
VSHH VSHH
TM

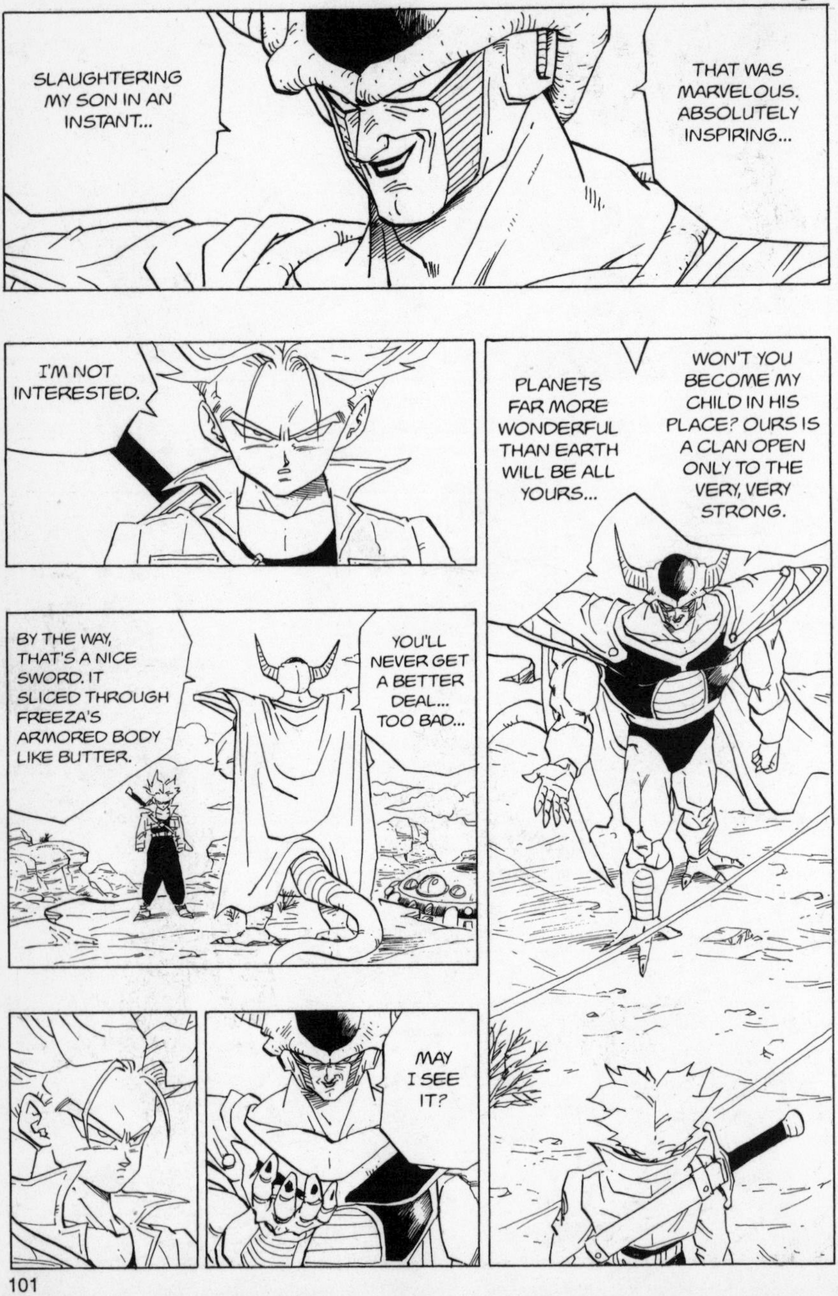
THAT WAS MARVELOUS. ABSOLUTELY INSPIRING...
SLAUGHTERING MY SON IN AN INSTANT...
WON'T YOU BECOME MY CHILD IN HIS PLACE? OURS IS A CLAN OPEN ONLY TO THE VERY, VERY STRONG.
PLANETS FAR MORE WONDERFUL THAN EARTH WILL BE ALL YOURS...
I'M NOT INTERESTED.
YOU'LL NEVER GET A BETTER DEAL... TOO BAD...
BY THE WAY, THAT'S A NICE SWORD. IT SLICED THROUGH FREEZA'S ARMORED BODY LIKE BUTTER.
MAY I SEE IT?

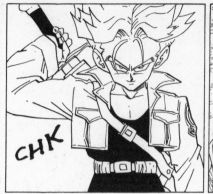

CHK

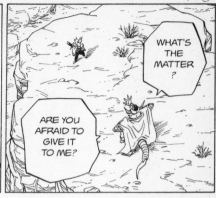

WHAT'S THE MATTER?

ARE YOU AFRAID TO GIVE IT TO ME?

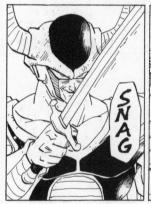

SNAG

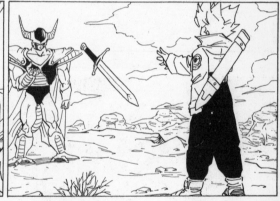

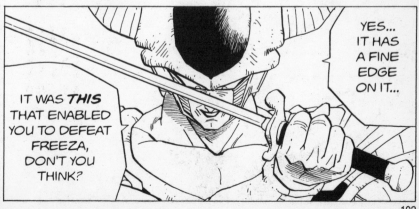

YES... IT HAS A FINE EDGE ON IT...

IT WAS **THIS** THAT ENABLED YOU TO DEFEAT FREEZA, DON'T YOU THINK?

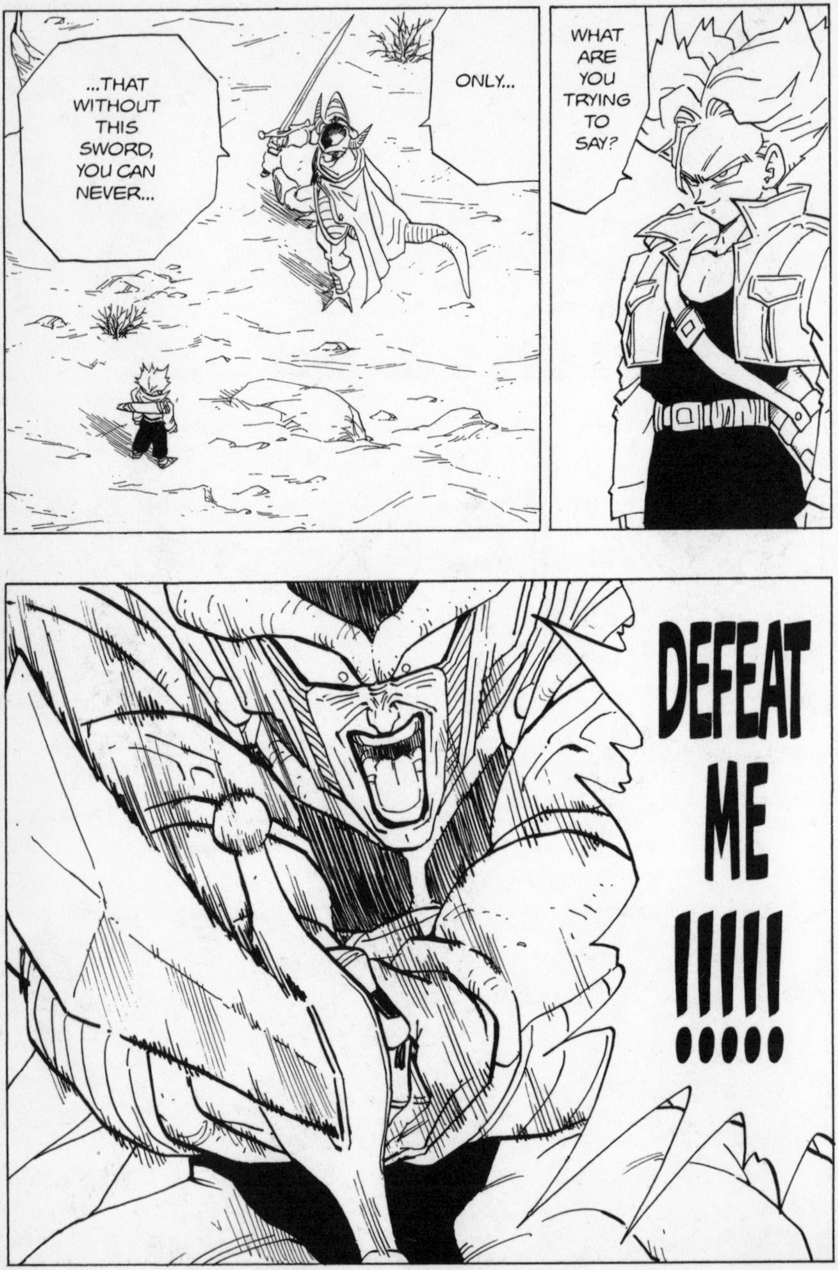
WHAT ARE YOU TRYING TO SAY?
ONLY...
...THAT WITHOUT THIS SWORD, YOU CAN NEVER...
DEFEAT ME!!!!!

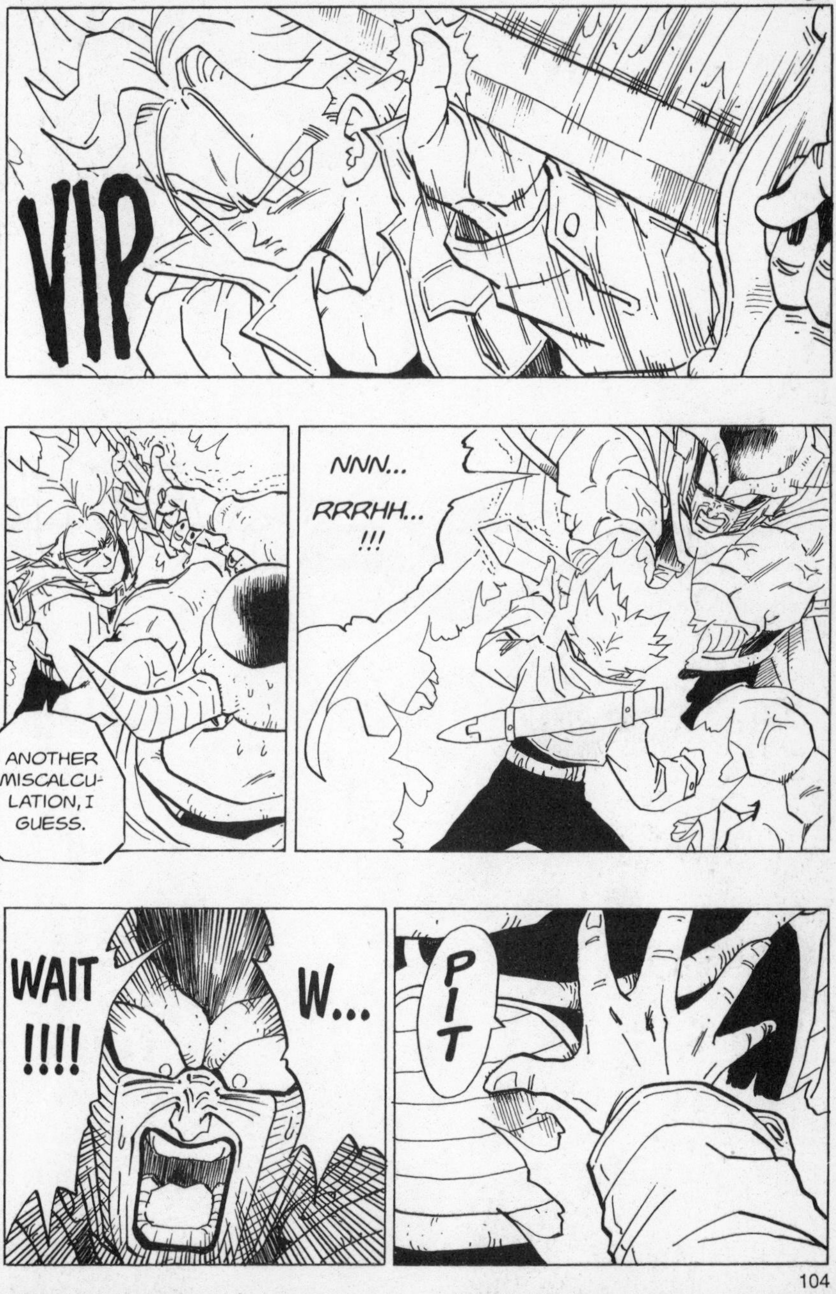
VIP
NNN...
RRRHH... !!!
ANOTHER MISCALCU-LATION, I GUESS.
PIT
W...
WAIT !!!!

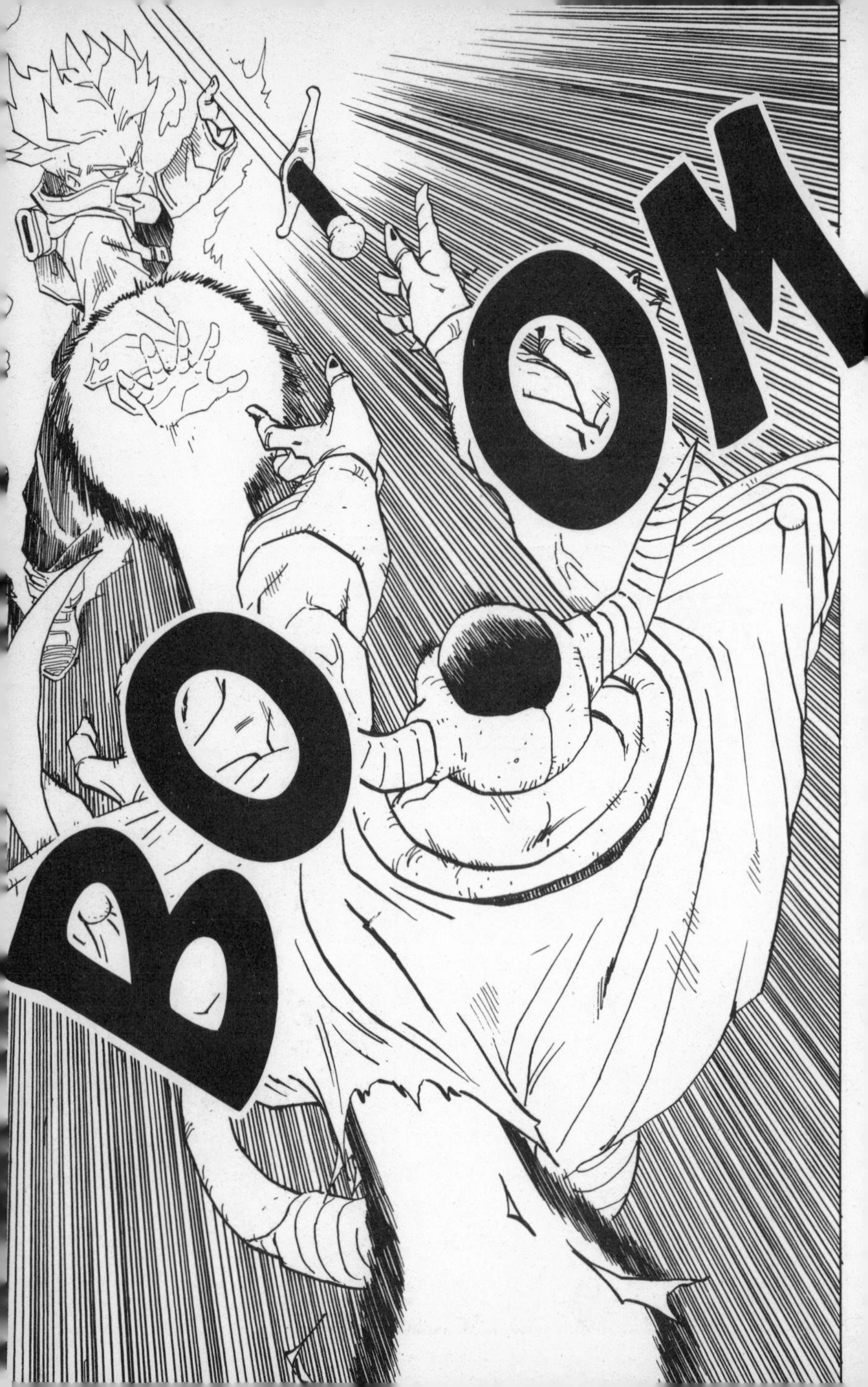
BOOOM

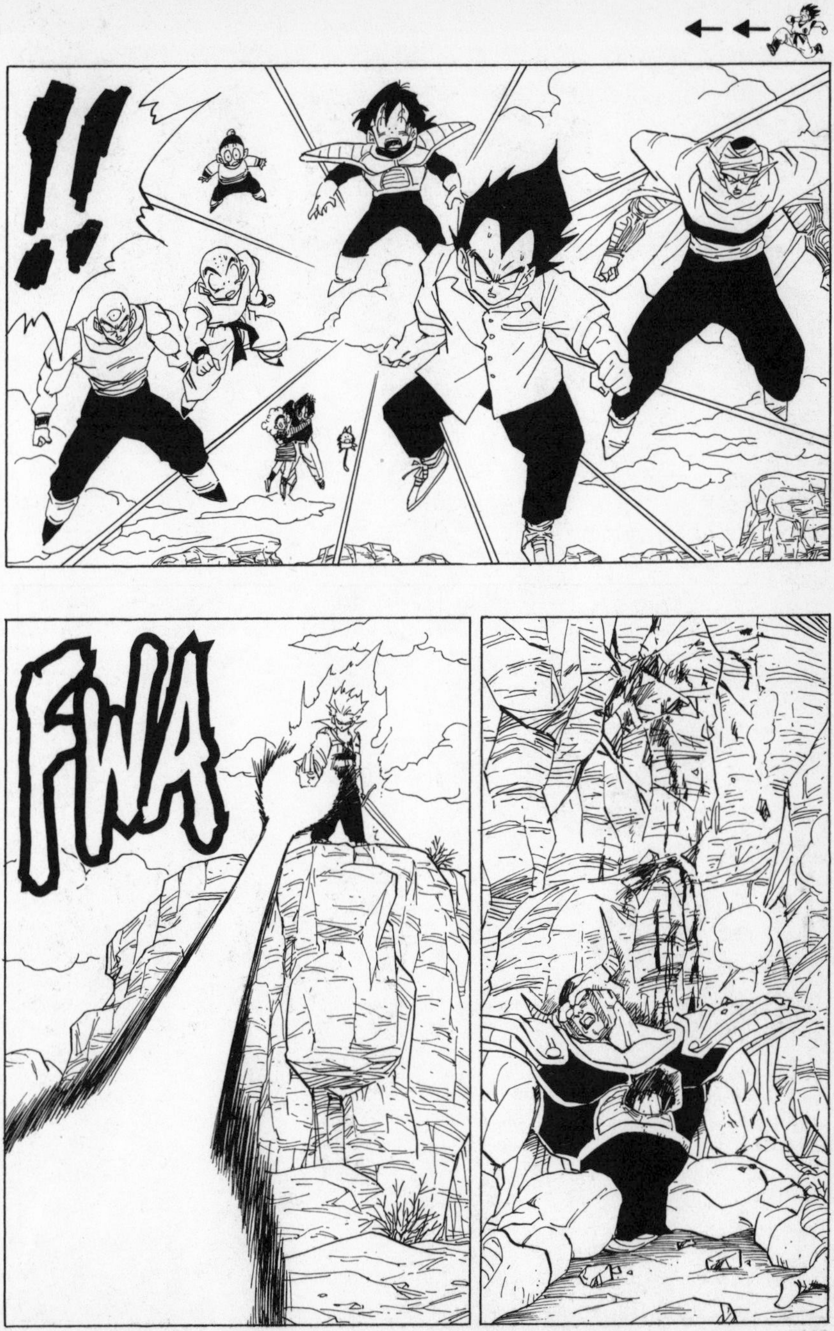
!!
FWA

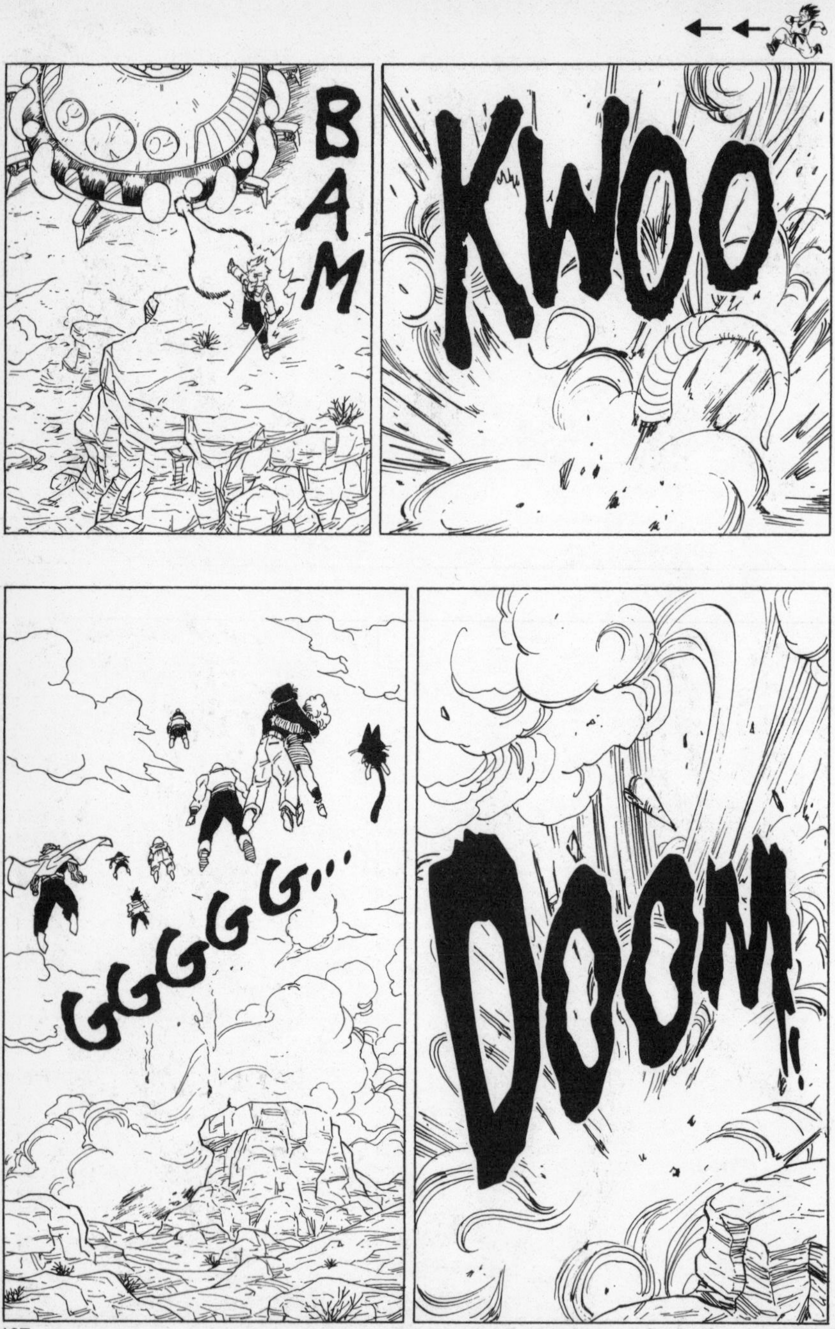
KWOO
BAM
DOOM!!
GGGGG...

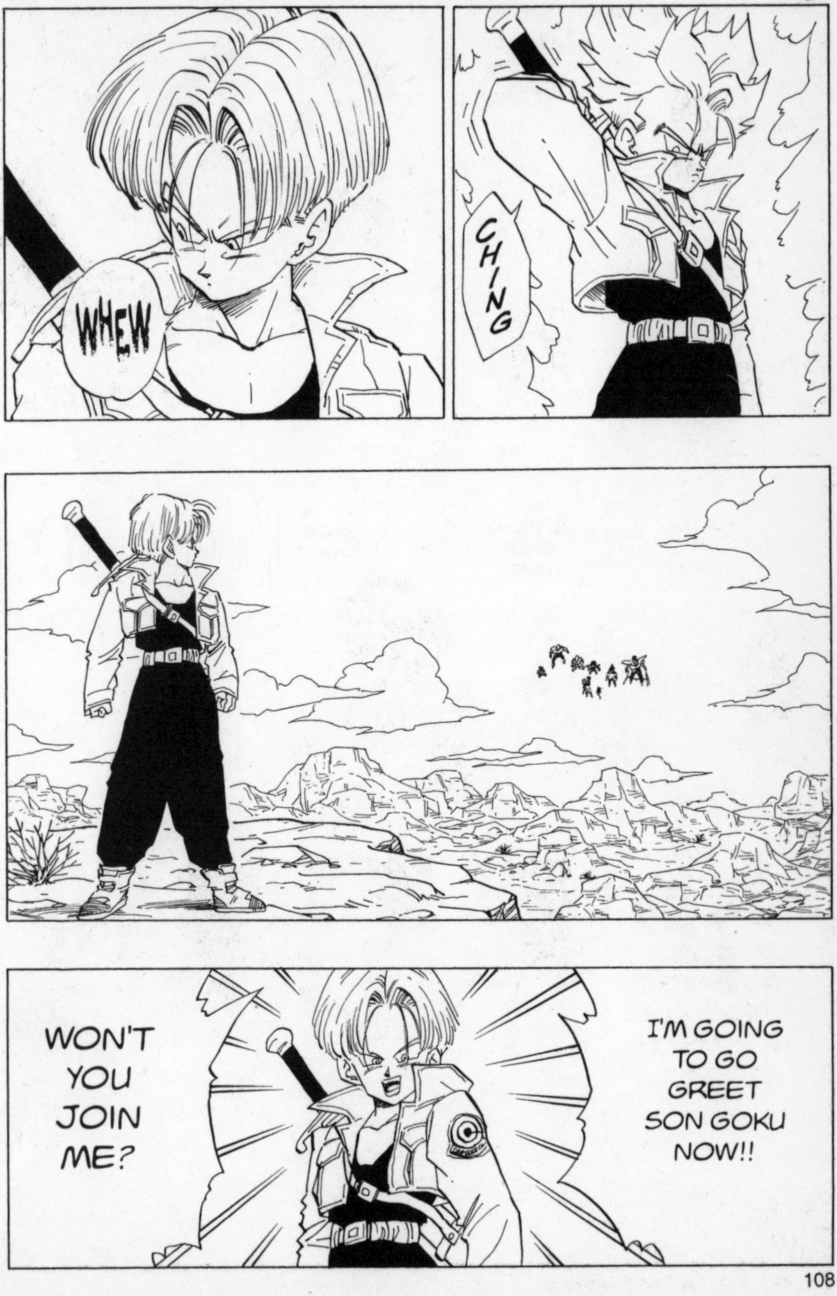
CHING
WHEW
I'M GOING TO GO GREET SON GOKU NOW!!
WON'T YOU JOIN ME?

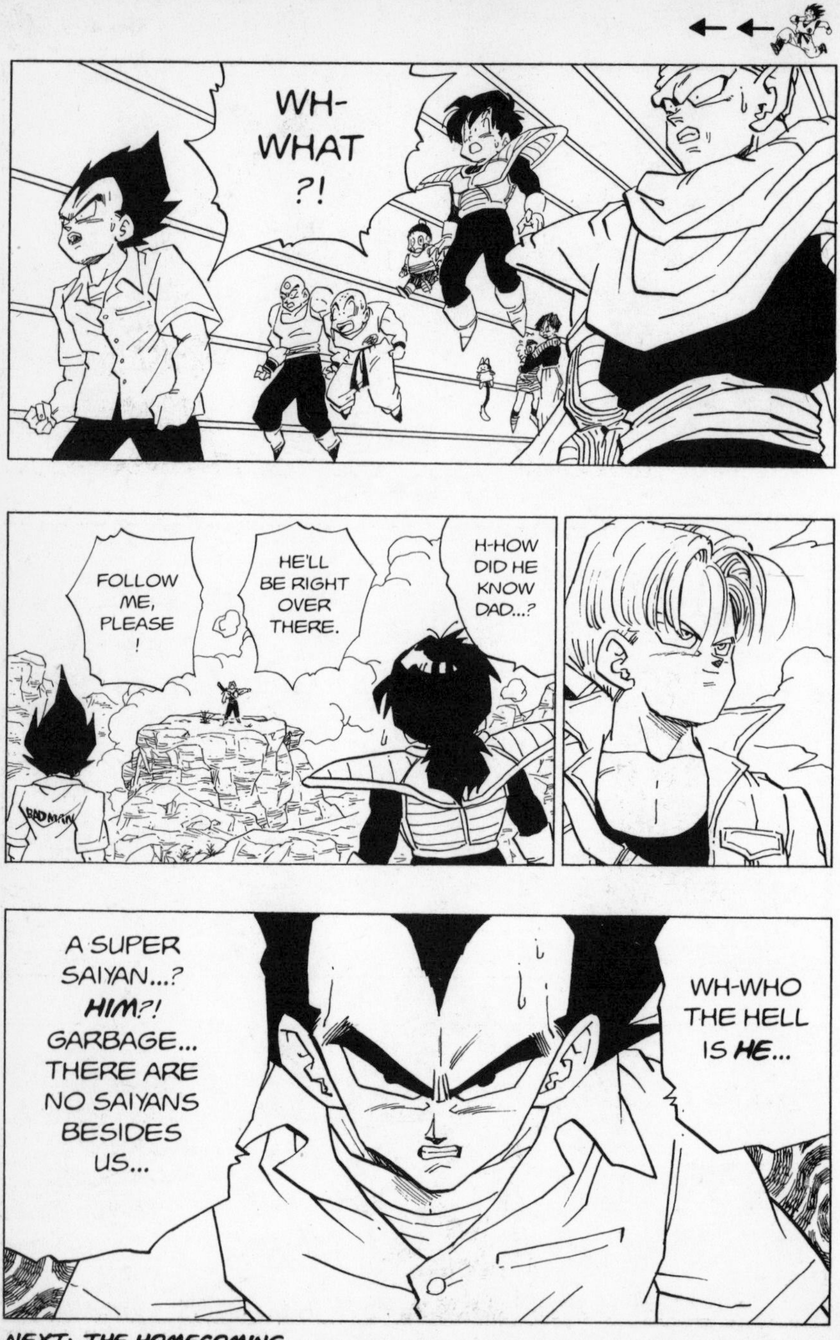
WH- WHAT ?!
H-HOW DID HE KNOW DAD...?
HE'LL BE RIGHT OVER THERE.
FOLLOW ME, PLEASE !
BAD MAN
WH-WHO THE HELL IS **HE**...
A SUPER SAIYAN...? **HIM**?! GARBAGE... THERE ARE NO SAIYANS BESIDES US...

NEXT: THE HOMECOMING

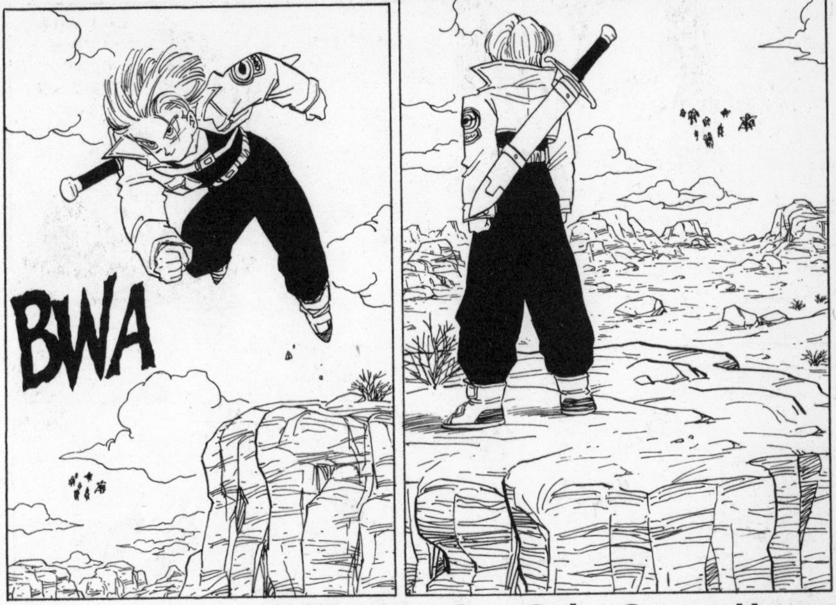
BWA

DBZ:139 • Son Goku Comes Home

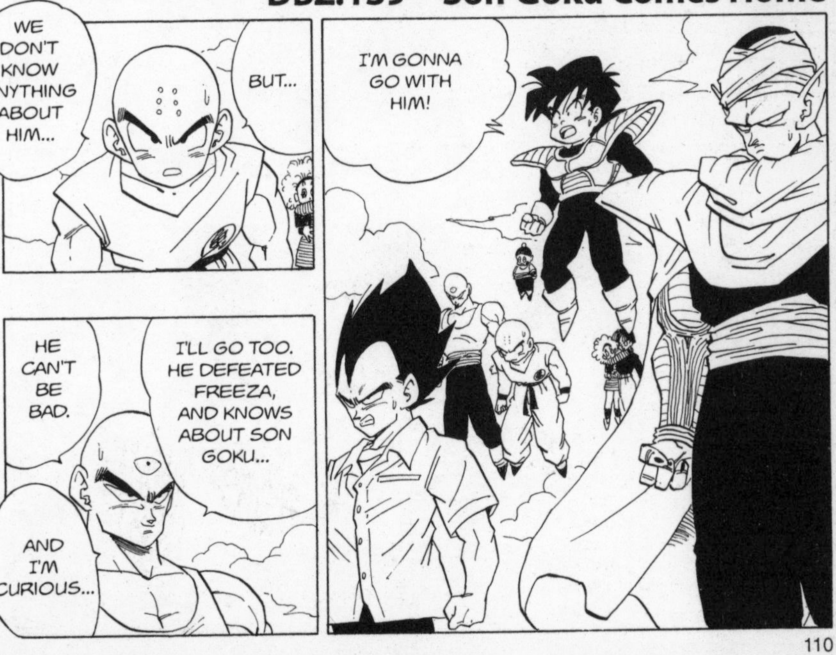
I'M GONNA GO WITH HIM!
BUT...
WE DON'T KNOW ANYTHING ABOUT HIM...
I'LL GO TOO. HE DEFEATED FREEZA, AND KNOWS ABOUT SON GOKU...
HE CAN'T BE BAD.
AND I'M CURIOUS...

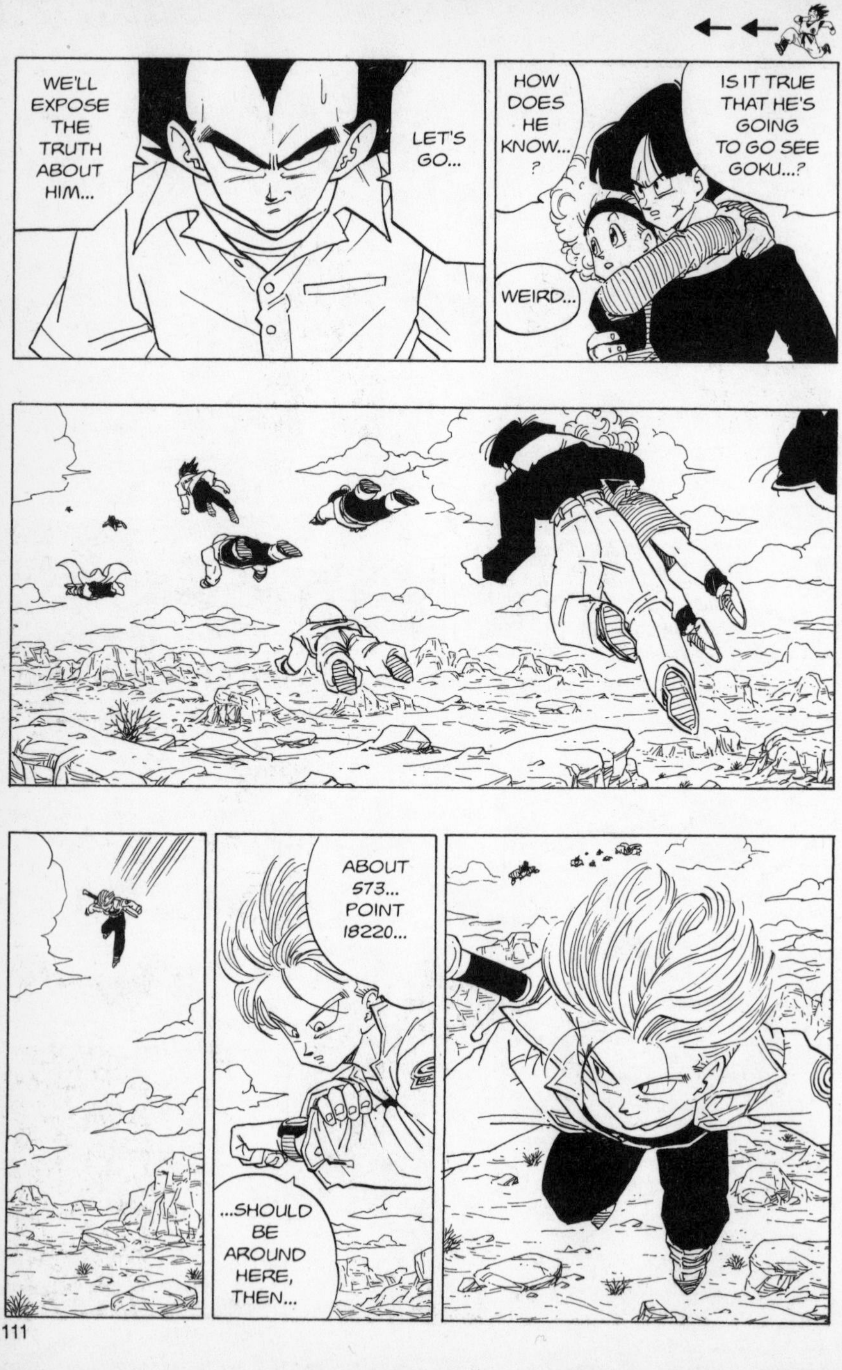
IS IT TRUE THAT HE'S GOING TO GO SEE GOKU...?
HOW DOES HE KNOW...?
WEIRD...
LET'S GO...
WE'LL EXPOSE THE TRUTH ABOUT HIM...
ABOUT 573... POINT 18220...
...SHOULD BE AROUND HERE, THEN...

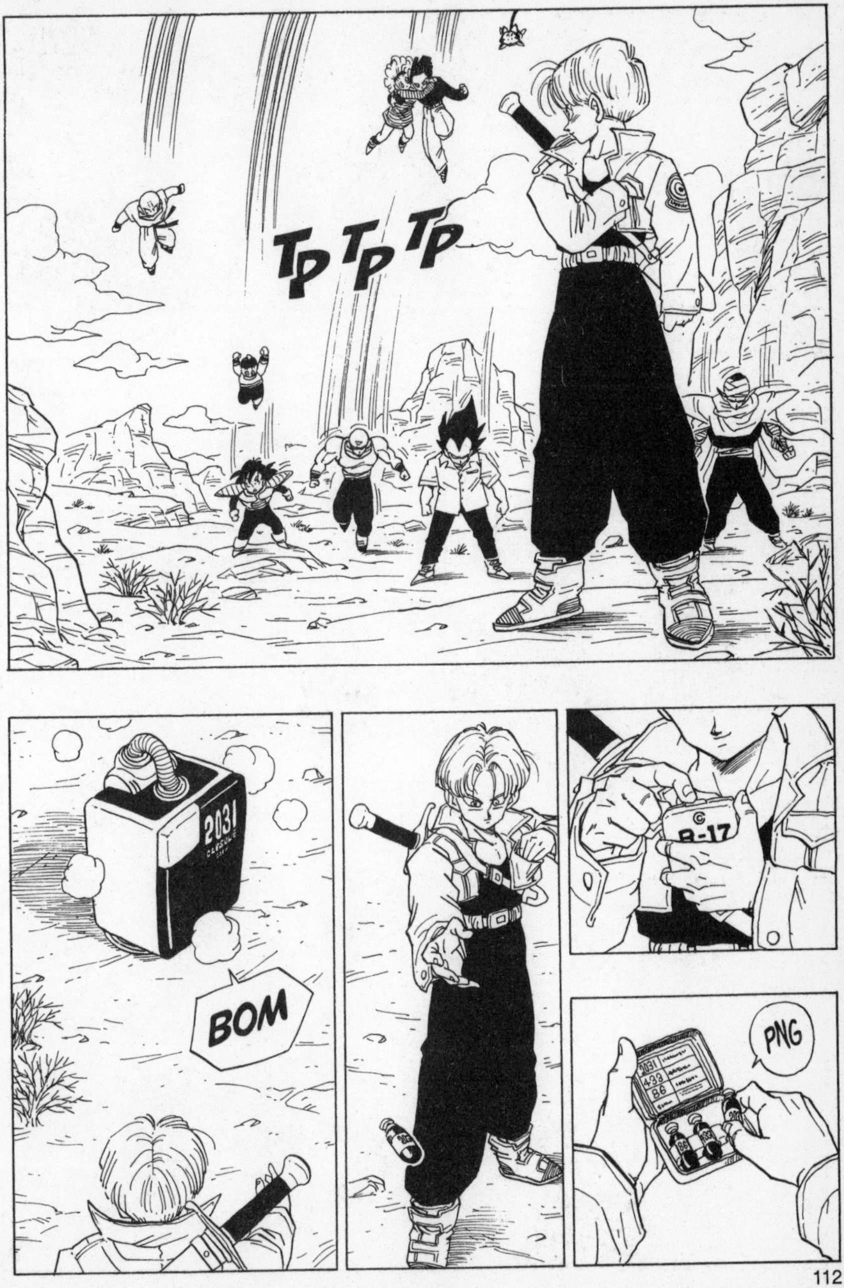
TP TP TP
B-17
PNG
2031
BOM

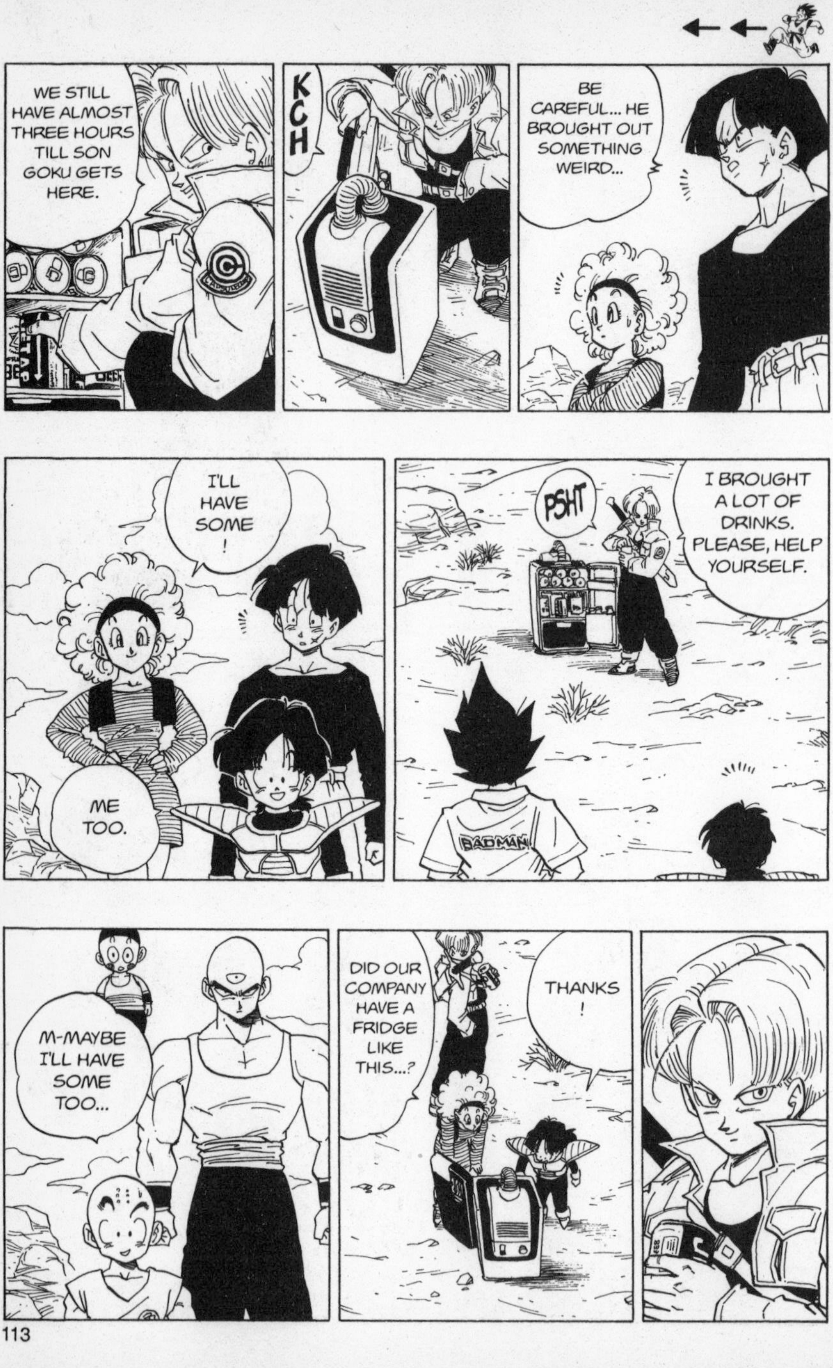
BE CAREFUL... HE BROUGHT OUT SOMETHING WEIRD...
KCH
WE STILL HAVE ALMOST THREE HOURS TILL SON GOKU GETS HERE.
I BROUGHT A LOT OF DRINKS. PLEASE, HELP YOURSELF.
PSHT
BADMAN
I'LL HAVE SOME!
ME TOO.
THANKS!
DID OUR COMPANY HAVE A FRIDGE LIKE THIS...?
M-MAYBE I'LL HAVE SOME TOO...

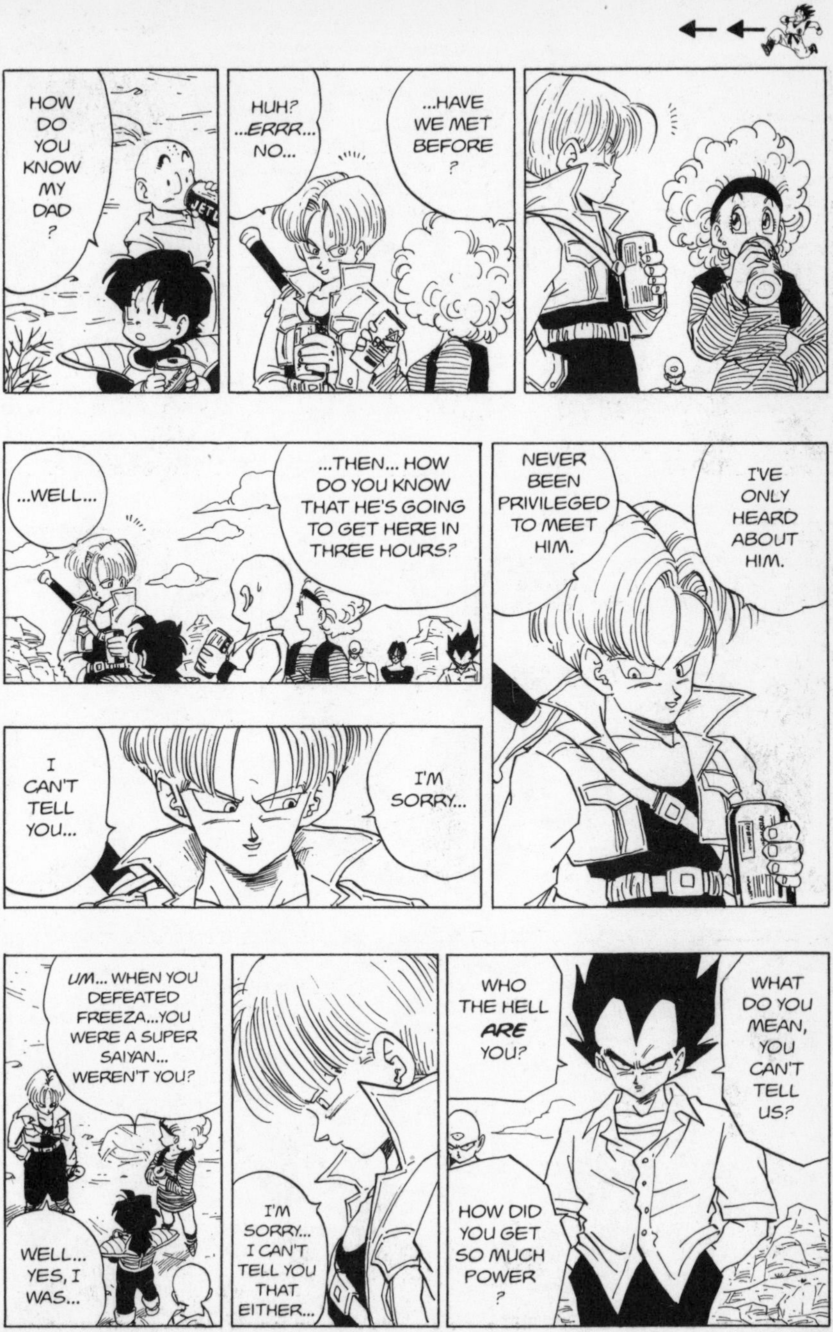
...HAVE WE MET BEFORE?
HUH? ...ERRR... NO...
HOW DO YOU KNOW MY DAD?
I'VE ONLY HEARD ABOUT HIM.
NEVER BEEN PRIVILEGED TO MEET HIM.
...THEN... HOW DO YOU KNOW THAT HE'S GOING TO GET HERE IN THREE HOURS?
...WELL...
I'M SORRY...
I CAN'T TELL YOU...
WHAT DO YOU MEAN, YOU CAN'T TELL US?
WHO THE HELL ARE YOU?
HOW DID YOU GET SO MUCH POWER?
I'M SORRY... I CAN'T TELL YOU THAT EITHER...
UM... WHEN YOU DEFEATED FREEZA...YOU WERE A SUPER SAIYAN... WEREN'T YOU?
WELL... YES, I WAS...

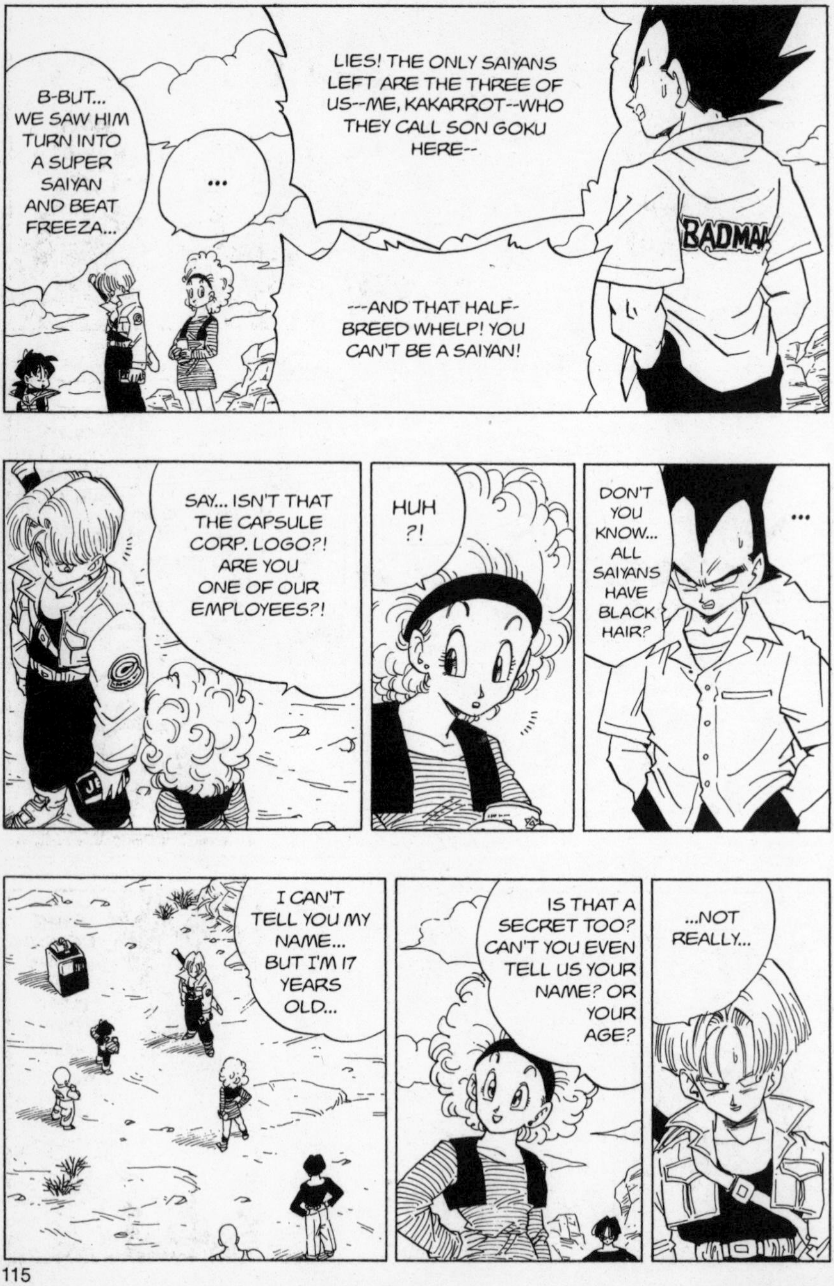
LIES! THE ONLY SAIYANS LEFT ARE THE THREE OF US--ME, KAKARROT--WHO THEY CALL SON GOKU HERE--
---AND THAT HALF-BREED WHELP! YOU CAN'T BE A SAIYAN!
...
B-BUT... WE SAW HIM TURN INTO A SUPER SAIYAN AND BEAT FREEZA...
...
DON'T YOU KNOW... ALL SAIYANS HAVE BLACK HAIR?
HUH ?!
SAY... ISN'T THAT THE CAPSULE CORP. LOGO?! ARE YOU ONE OF OUR EMPLOYEES?!
...NOT REALLY...
IS THAT A SECRET TOO? CAN'T YOU EVEN TELL US YOUR NAME? OR YOUR AGE?
I CAN'T TELL YOU MY NAME... BUT I'M 17 YEARS OLD...

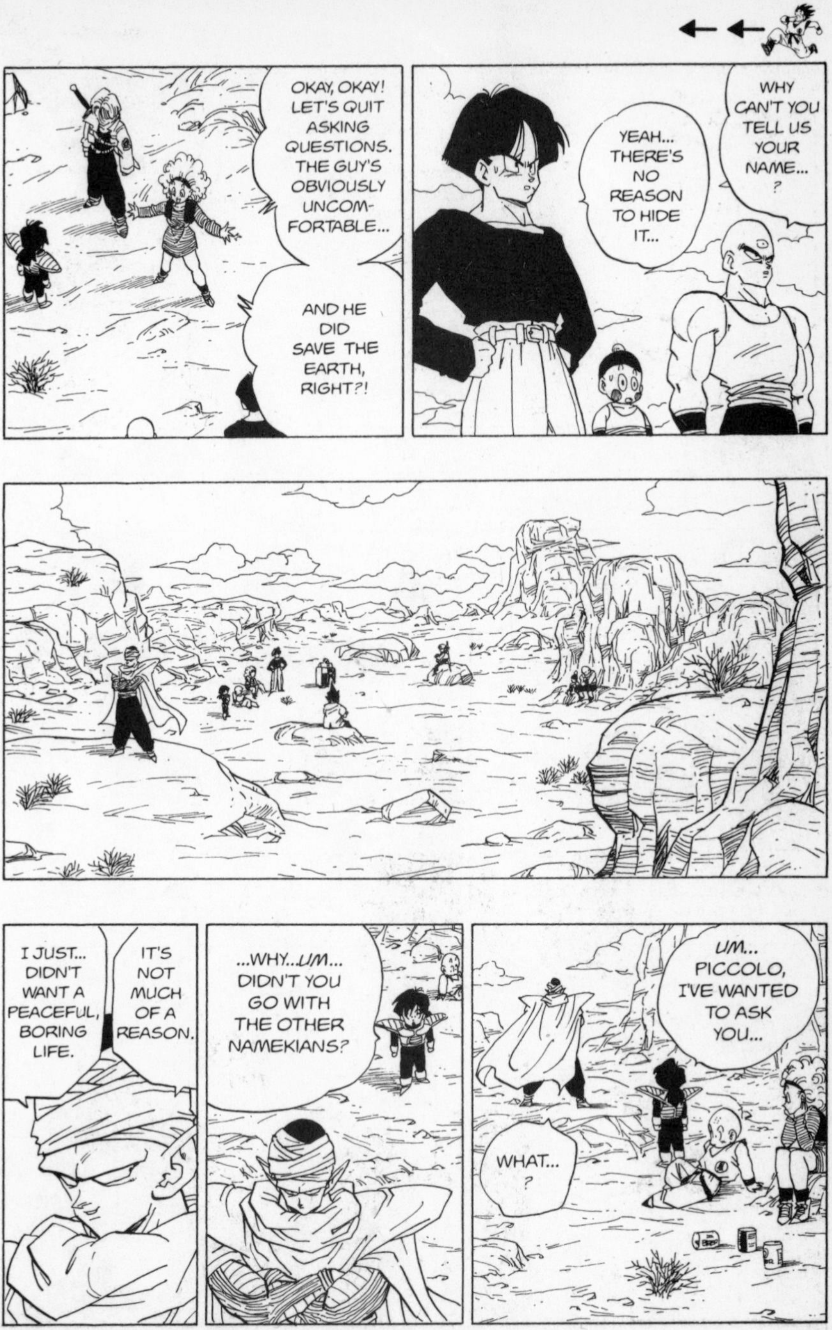
WHY CAN'T YOU TELL US YOUR NAME...?
YEAH... THERE'S NO REASON TO HIDE IT...
OKAY, OKAY! LET'S QUIT ASKING QUESTIONS. THE GUY'S OBVIOUSLY UNCOMFORTABLE...
AND HE DID SAVE THE EARTH, RIGHT?!
UM... PICCOLO, I'VE WANTED TO ASK YOU...
WHAT...?
...WHY...UM... DIDN'T YOU GO WITH THE OTHER NAMEKIANS?
IT'S NOT MUCH OF A REASON.
I JUST... DIDN'T WANT A PEACEFUL, BORING LIFE.

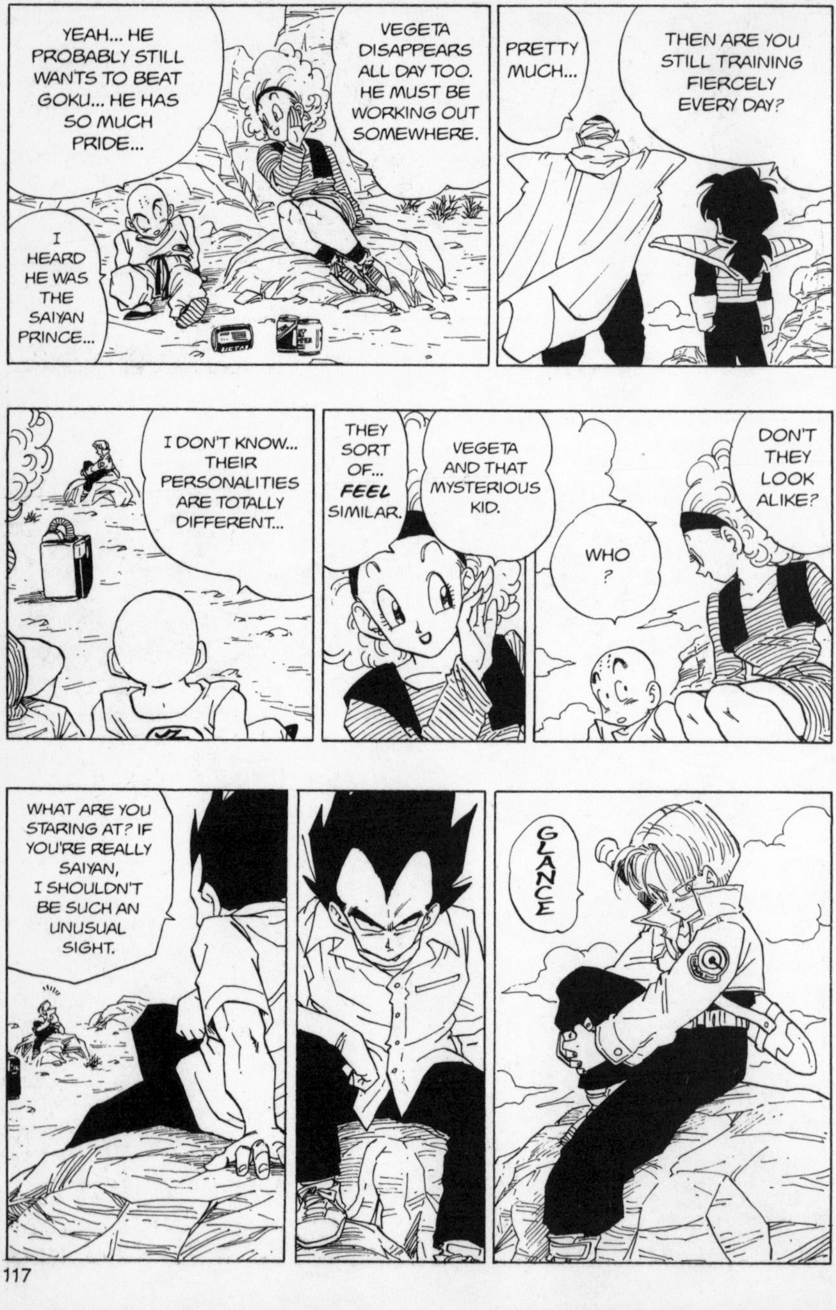
THEN ARE YOU STILL TRAINING FIERCELY EVERY DAY?
PRETTY MUCH...
VEGETA DISAPPEARS ALL DAY TOO. HE MUST BE WORKING OUT SOMEWHERE.
I HEARD HE WAS THE SAIYAN PRINCE...
YEAH... HE PROBABLY STILL WANTS TO BEAT GOKU... HE HAS SO MUCH PRIDE...
DON'T THEY LOOK ALIKE?
WHO?
VEGETA AND THAT MYSTERIOUS KID.
THEY SORT OF... FEEL SIMILAR.
I DON'T KNOW... THEIR PERSONALITIES ARE TOTALLY DIFFERENT...
GLANCE
WHAT ARE YOU STARING AT? IF YOU'RE REALLY SAIYAN, I SHOULDN'T BE SUCH AN UNUSUAL SIGHT.

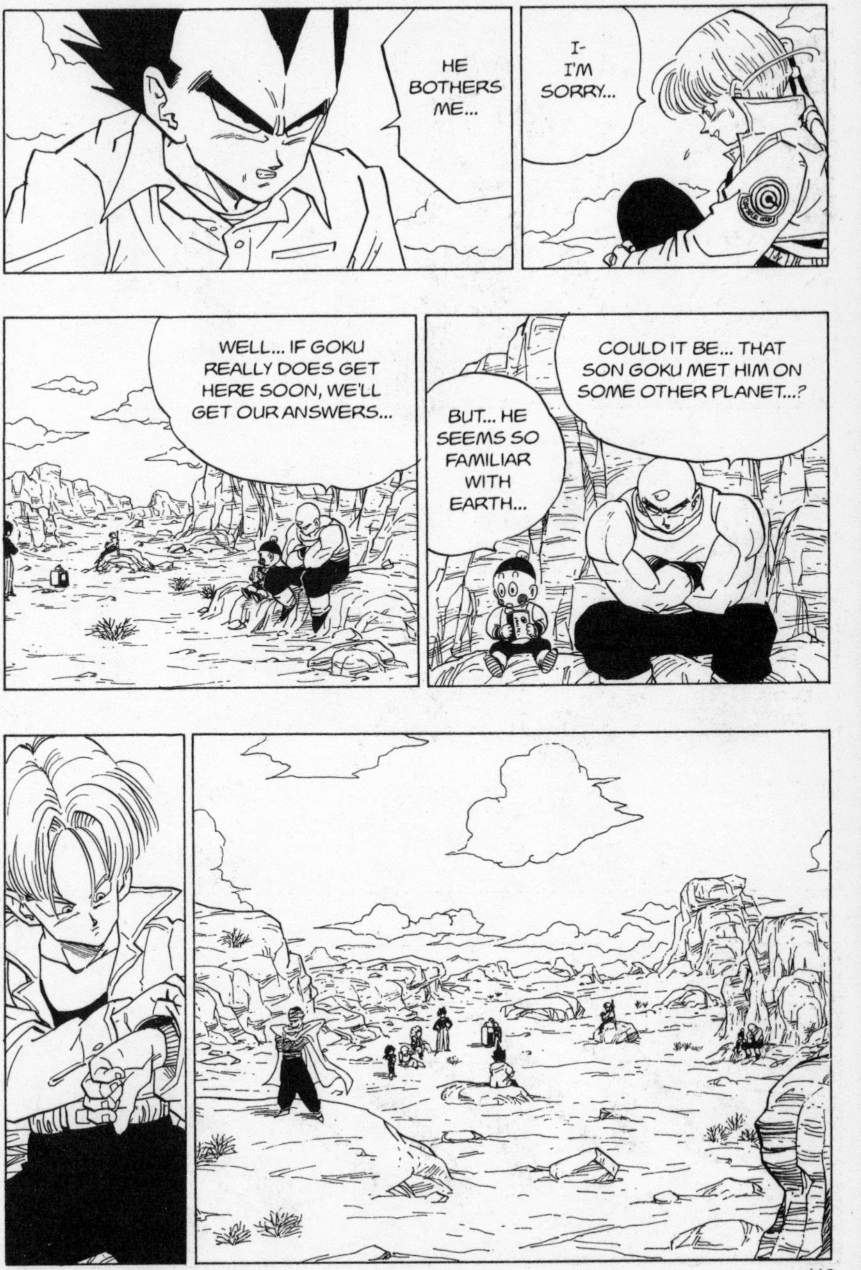
I- I'M SORRY...
HE BOTHERS ME...
COULD IT BE... THAT SON GOKU MET HIM ON SOME OTHER PLANET...?
BUT... HE SEEMS SO FAMILIAR WITH EARTH...
WELL... IF GOKU REALLY DOES GET HERE SOON, WE'LL GET OUR ANSWERS...

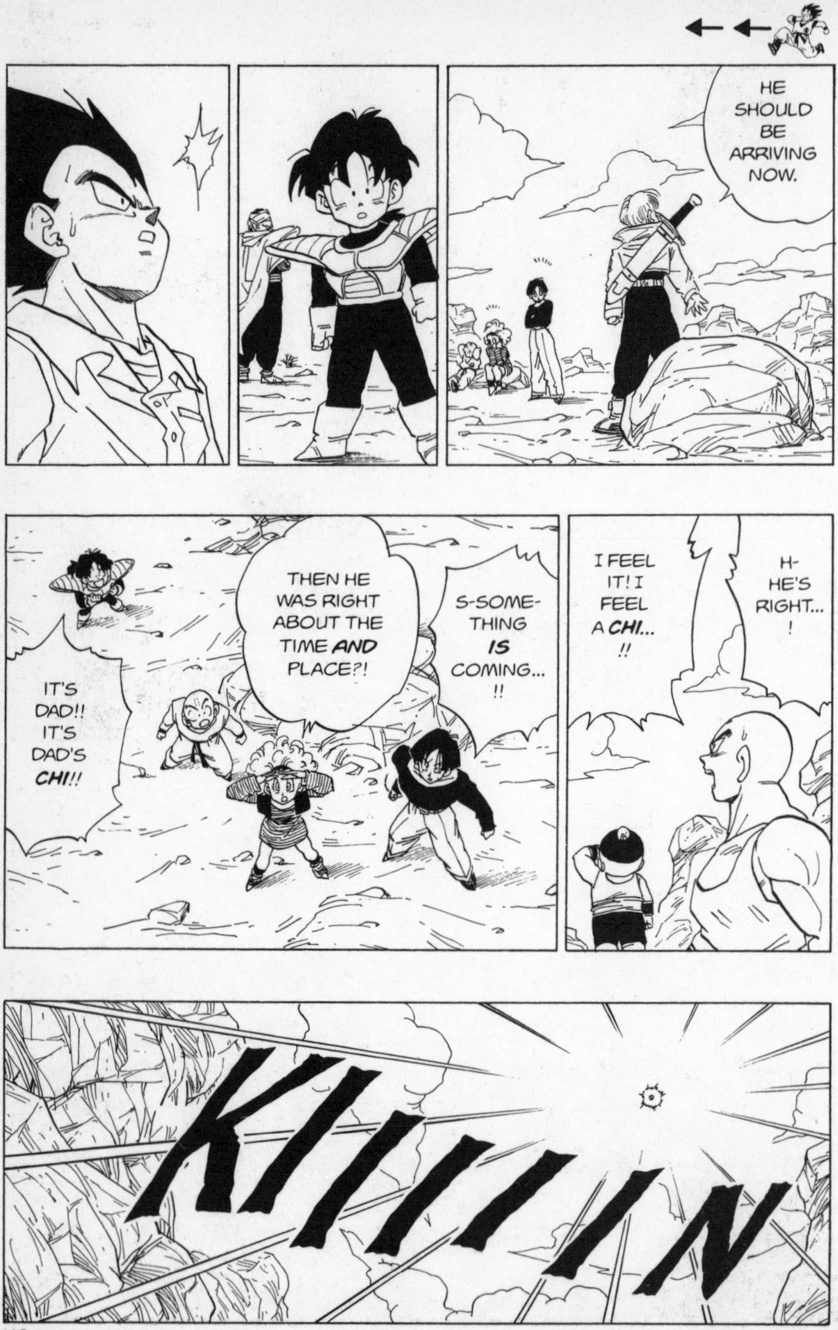
HE SHOULD BE ARRIVING NOW.
H-HE'S RIGHT...!
I FEEL IT! I FEEL A **CHI**...!!
S-SOMETHING **IS** COMING...!!
THEN HE WAS RIGHT ABOUT THE TIME **AND** PLACE?!
IT'S DAD!! IT'S DAD'S **CHI**!!
KIIIIN

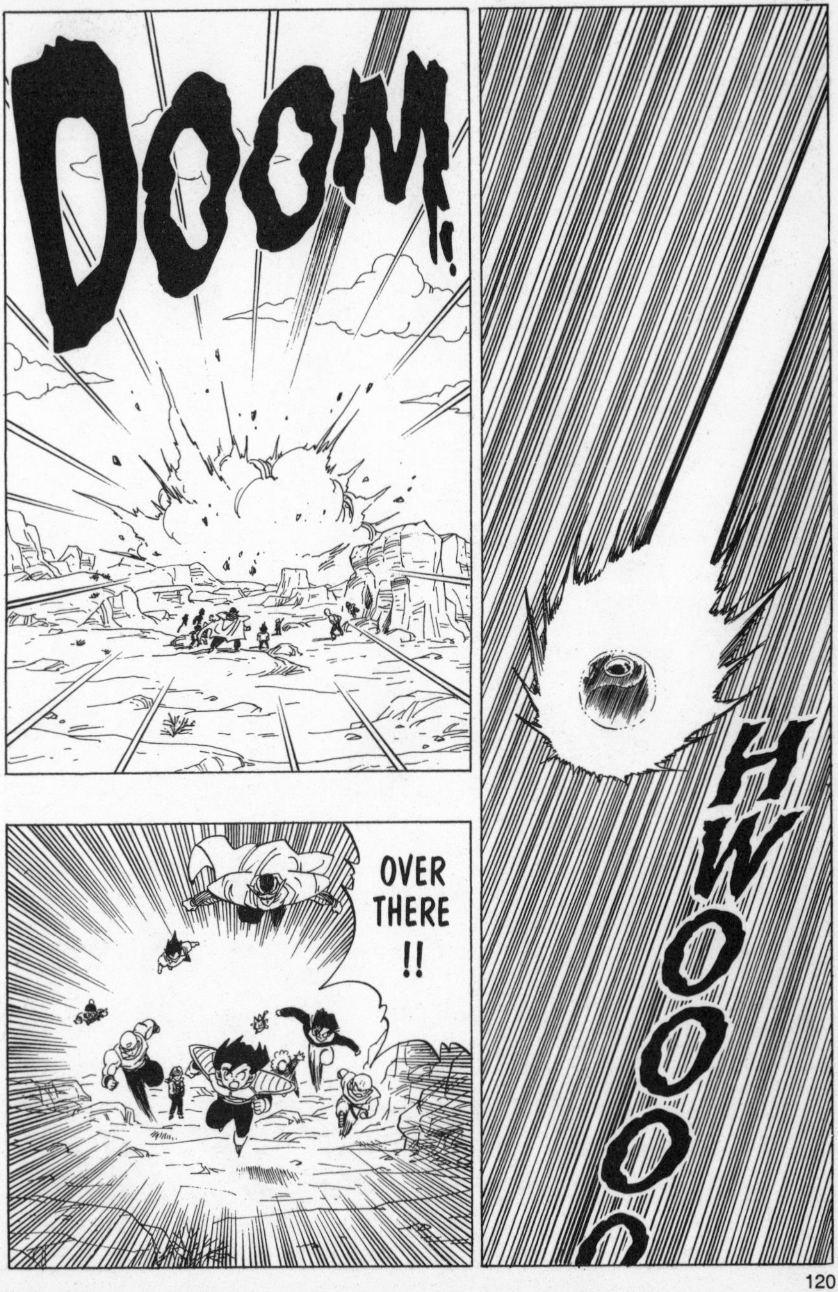
HWOOOOO
DOOM!!
OVER THERE !!

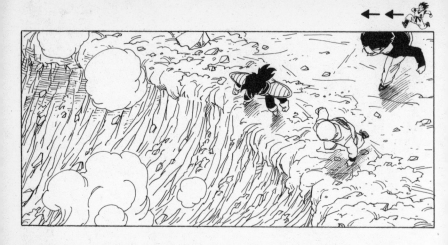

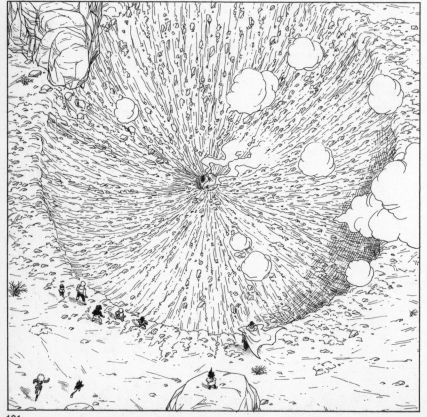

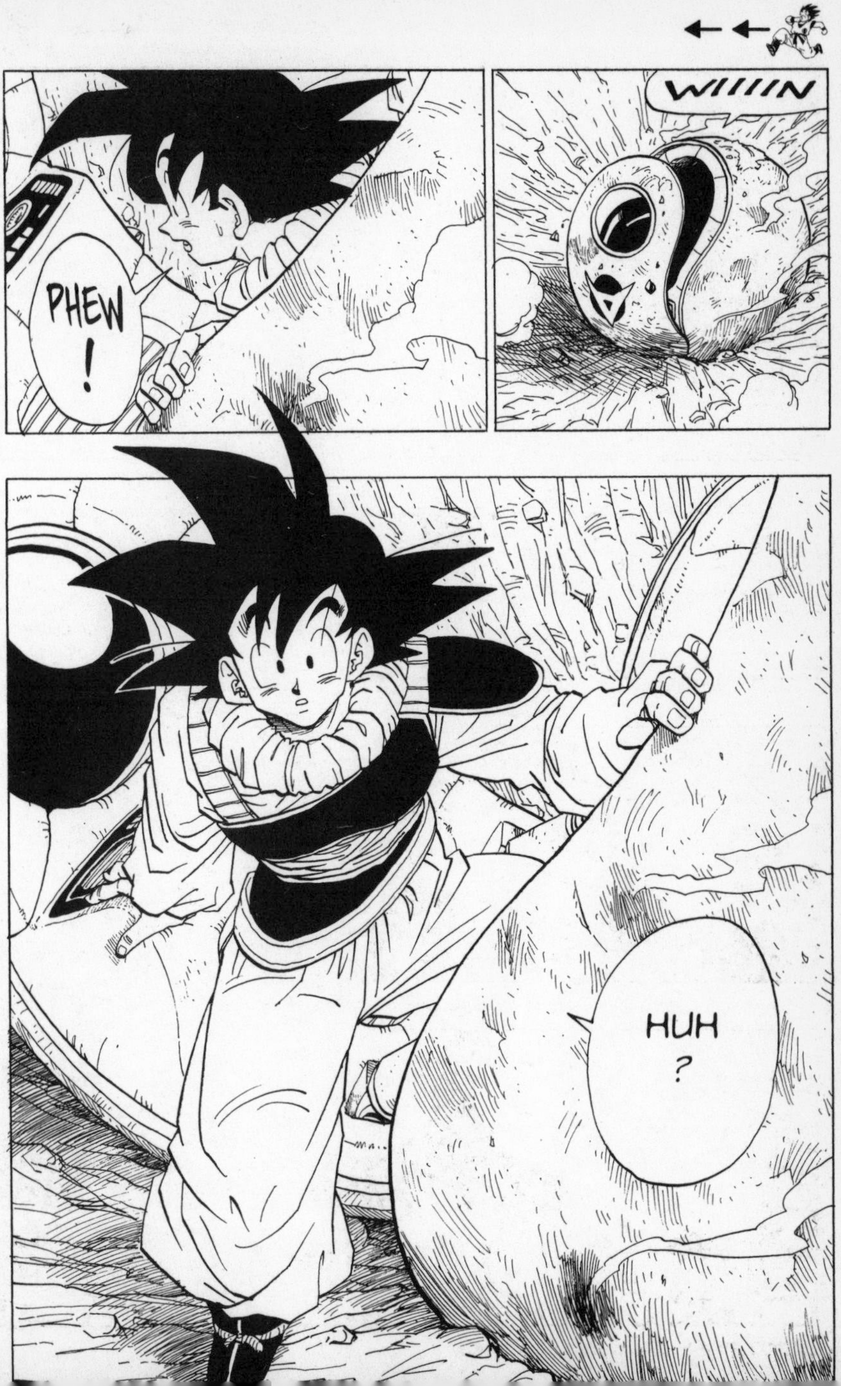
WIIIIN
PHEW!
HUH?

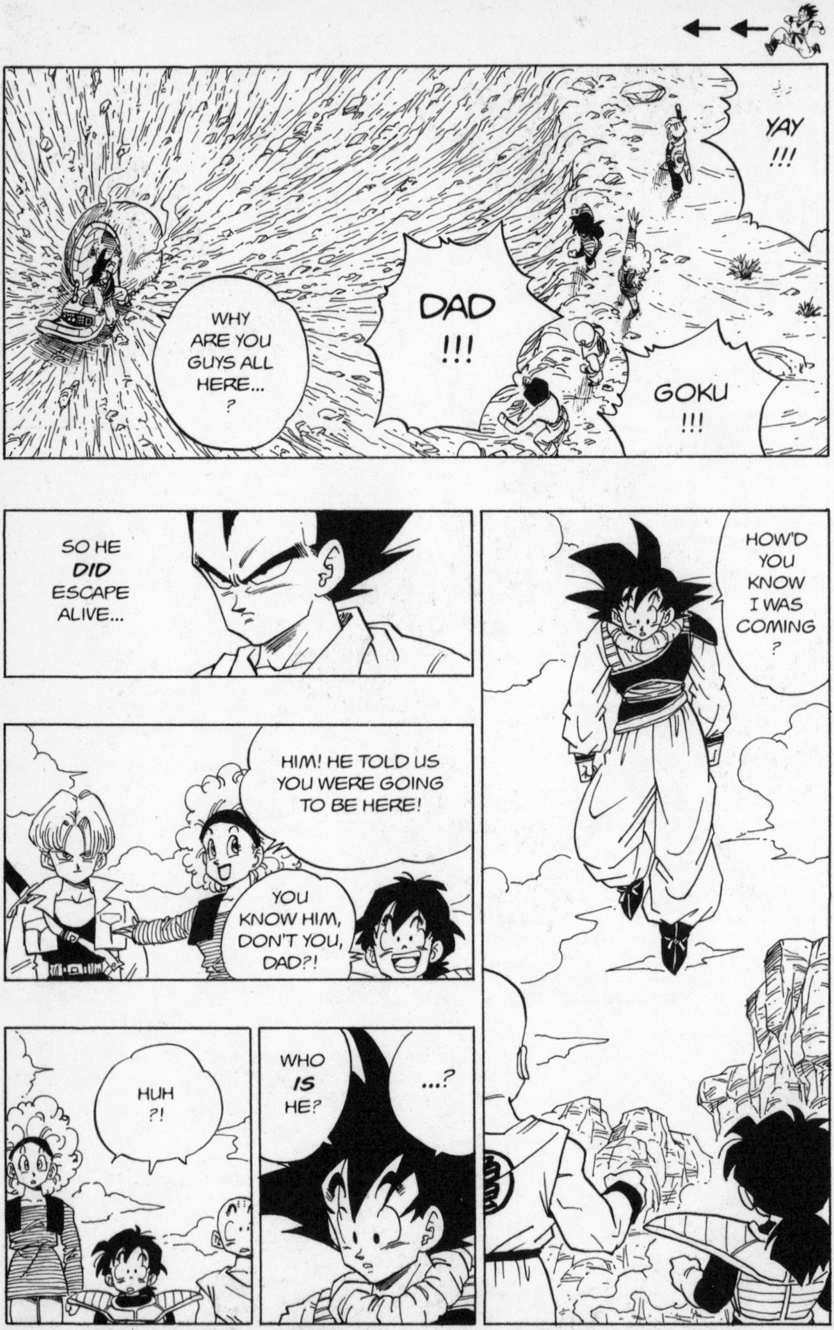
YAY !!!
GOKU !!!
DAD !!!
WHY ARE YOU GUYS ALL HERE... ?
HOW'D YOU KNOW I WAS COMING ?
SO HE **DID** ESCAPE ALIVE...
HIM! HE TOLD US YOU WERE GOING TO BE HERE!
YOU KNOW HIM, DON'T YOU, DAD?!
...?
WHO **IS** HE?
HUH ?!

NEXT: THEY CALL HIM...TRUNKS

DBZ:140 • The Boy from the Future

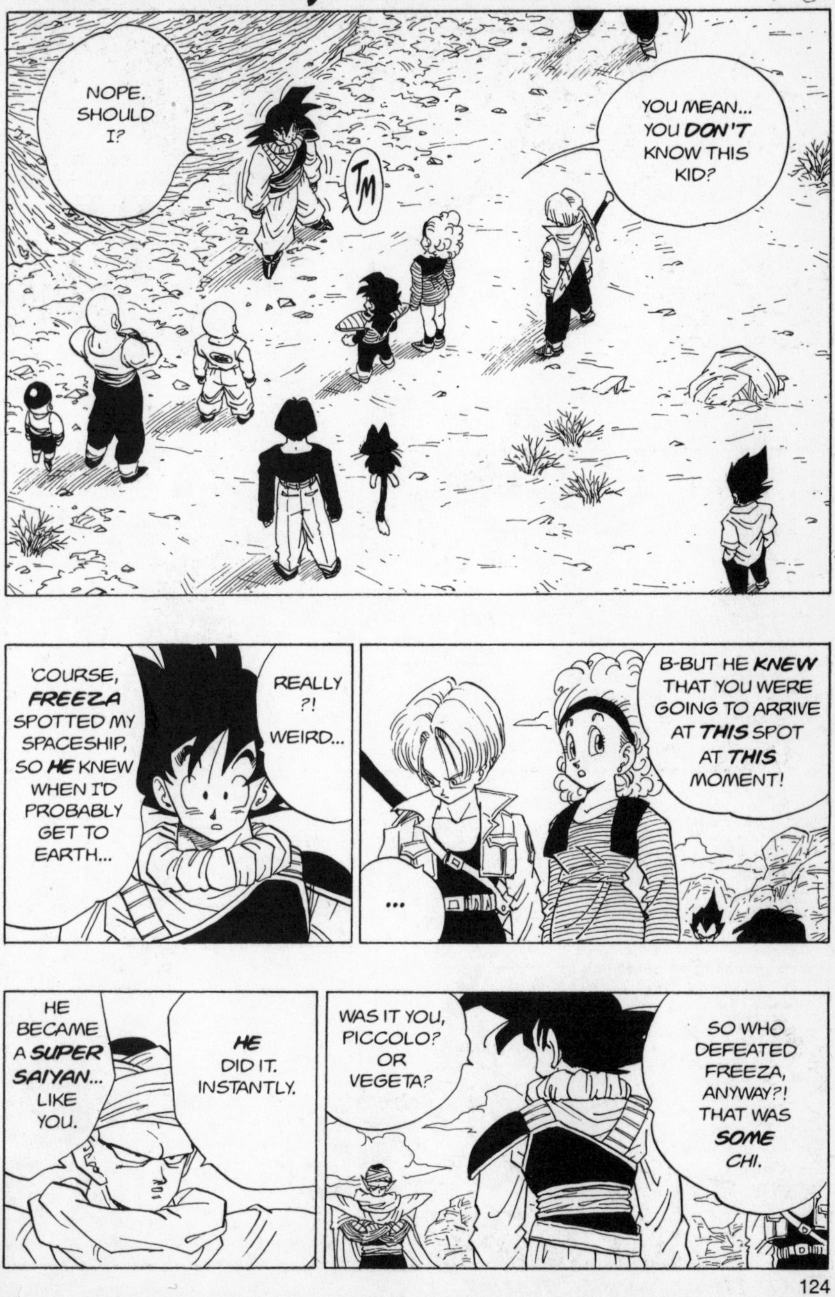
YOU MEAN... YOU **DON'T** KNOW THIS KID?
NOPE. SHOULD I?
B-BUT HE **KNEW** THAT YOU WERE GOING TO ARRIVE AT **THIS** SPOT AT **THIS** MOMENT!
...
REALLY?! WEIRD...
'COURSE, **FREEZA** SPOTTED MY SPACESHIP, SO **HE** KNEW WHEN I'D PROBABLY GET TO EARTH...
SO WHO DEFEATED FREEZA, ANYWAY?! THAT WAS **SOME** CHI.
WAS IT YOU, PICCOLO? OR VEGETA?
HE DID IT. INSTANTLY.
HE BECAME A **SUPER SAIYAN**... LIKE YOU.

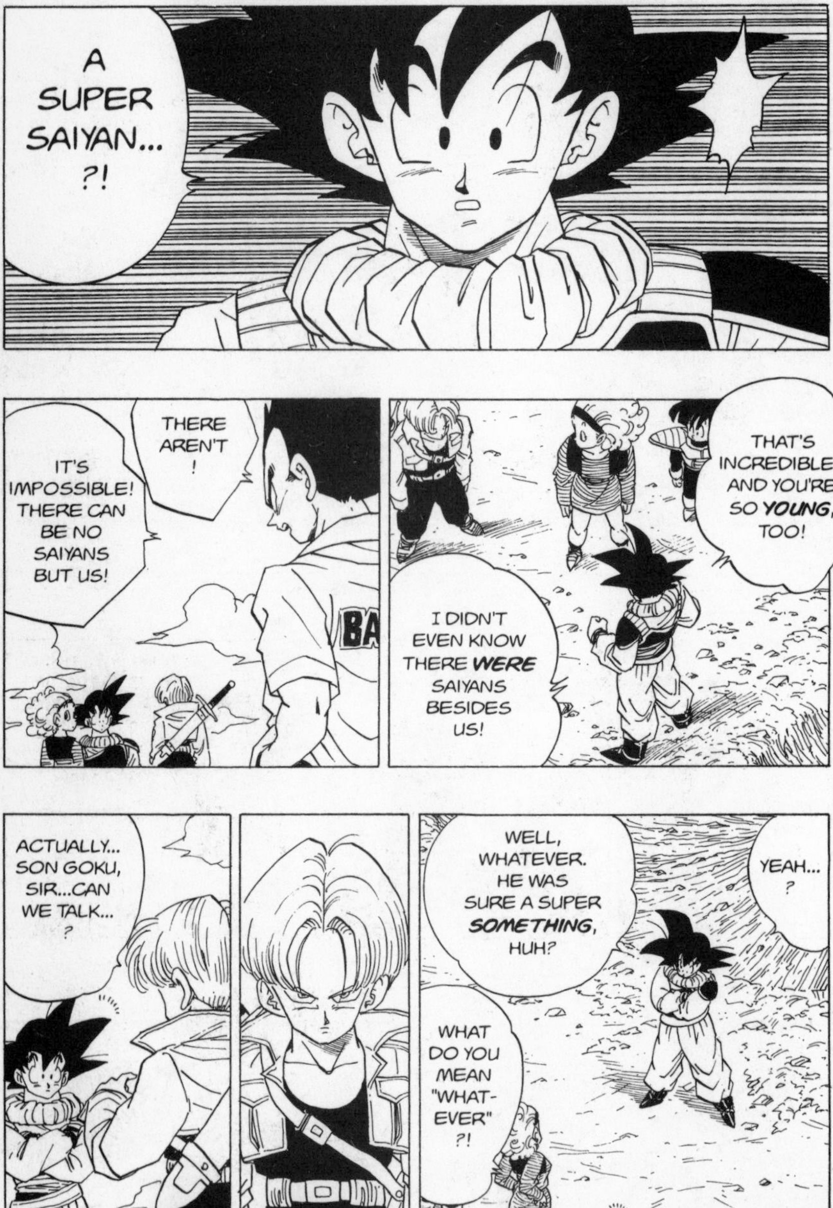
A SUPER SAIYAN...?!
THAT'S INCREDIBLE!! AND YOU'RE SO YOUNG, TOO!
I DIDN'T EVEN KNOW THERE WERE SAIYANS BESIDES US!
THERE AREN'T!
IT'S IMPOSSIBLE! THERE CAN BE NO SAIYANS BUT US!
BA
YEAH...?
WELL, WHATEVER. HE WAS SURE A SUPER SOMETHING, HUH?
WHAT DO YOU MEAN "WHAT-EVER"?!
ACTUALLY... SON GOKU, SIR...CAN WE TALK...?

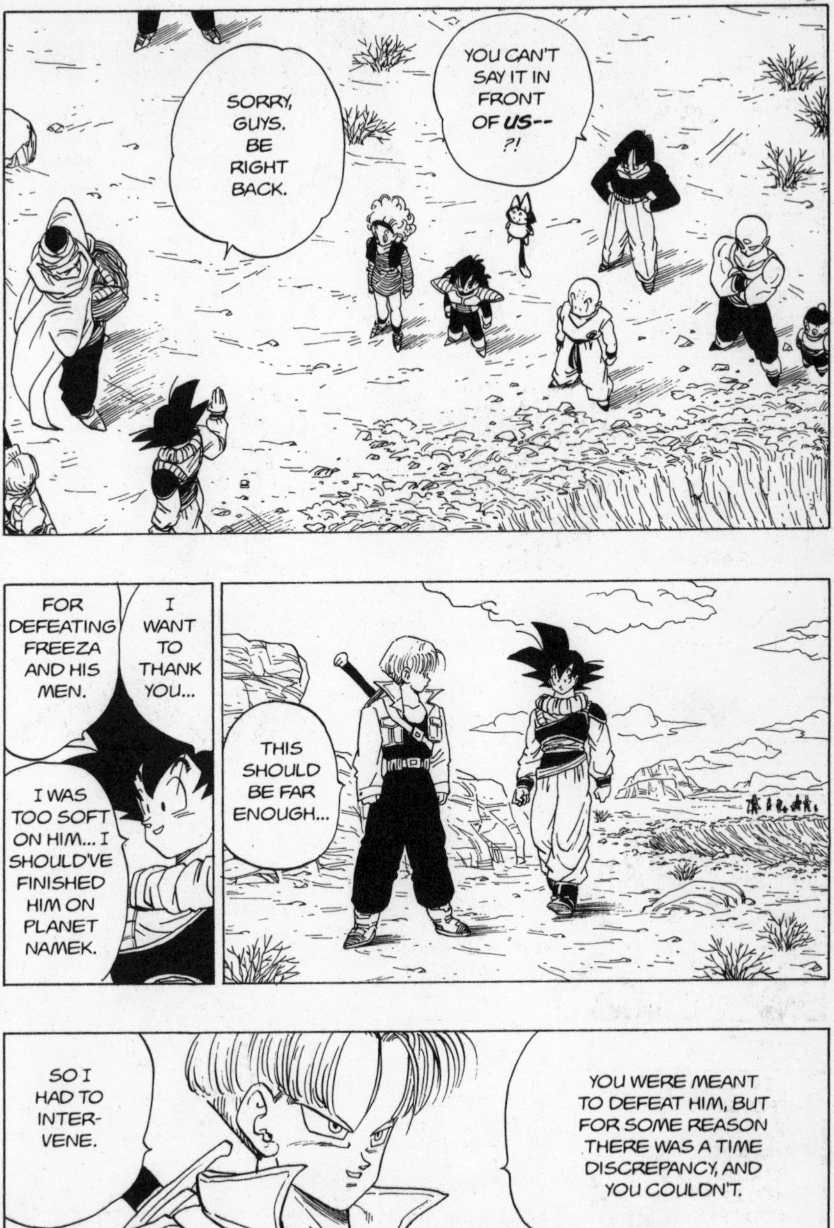
YOU CAN'T SAY IT IN FRONT OF US-- ?!
SORRY, GUYS. BE RIGHT BACK.
THIS SHOULD BE FAR ENOUGH...
I WANT TO THANK YOU...
FOR DEFEATING FREEZA AND HIS MEN.
I WAS TOO SOFT ON HIM... I SHOULD'VE FINISHED HIM ON PLANET NAMEK.
YOU WERE MEANT TO DEFEAT HIM, BUT FOR SOME REASON THERE WAS A TIME DISCREPANCY, AND YOU COULDN'T.
SO I HAD TO INTER-VENE.

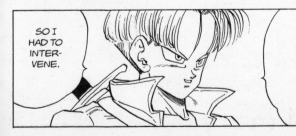

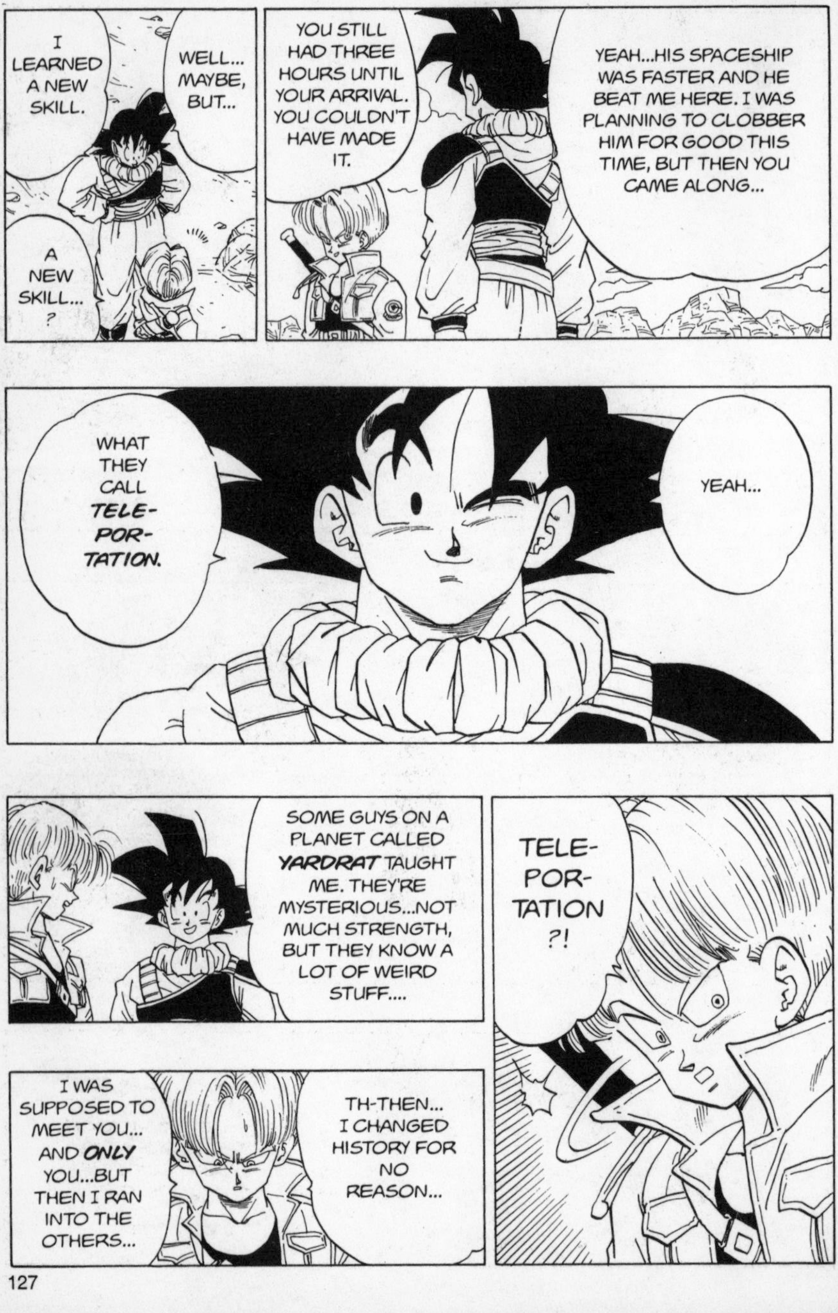
YEAH...HIS SPACESHIP WAS FASTER AND HE BEAT ME HERE. I WAS PLANNING TO CLOBBER HIM FOR GOOD THIS TIME, BUT THEN YOU CAME ALONG...
YOU STILL HAD THREE HOURS UNTIL YOUR ARRIVAL. YOU COULDN'T HAVE MADE IT.
WELL... MAYBE, BUT...
I LEARNED A NEW SKILL.
A NEW SKILL...?
YEAH...
WHAT THEY CALL *TELE-PORTATION.*
TELE-PORTATION?!
SOME GUYS ON A PLANET CALLED *YARDRAT* TAUGHT ME. THEY'RE MYSTERIOUS...NOT MUCH STRENGTH, BUT THEY KNOW A LOT OF WEIRD STUFF....
TH-THEN... I CHANGED HISTORY FOR NO REASON...
I WAS SUPPOSED TO MEET YOU... AND *ONLY* YOU...BUT THEN I RAN INTO THE OTHERS...

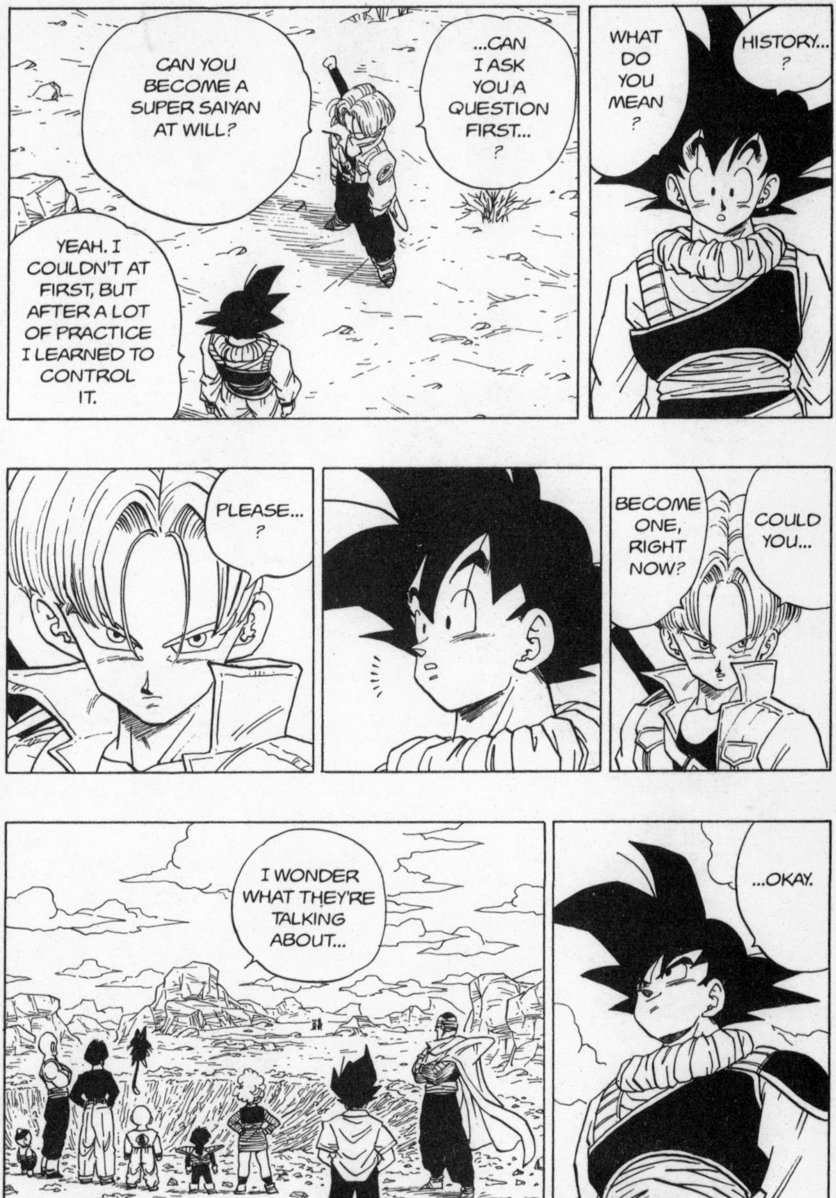
HISTORY...?
WHAT DO YOU MEAN?
...CAN I ASK YOU A QUESTION FIRST...?
CAN YOU BECOME A SUPER SAIYAN AT WILL?
YEAH. I COULDN'T AT FIRST, BUT AFTER A LOT OF PRACTICE I LEARNED TO CONTROL IT.
COULD YOU...
BECOME ONE, RIGHT NOW?
PLEASE...?
...OKAY.
I WONDER WHAT THEY'RE TALKING ABOUT...

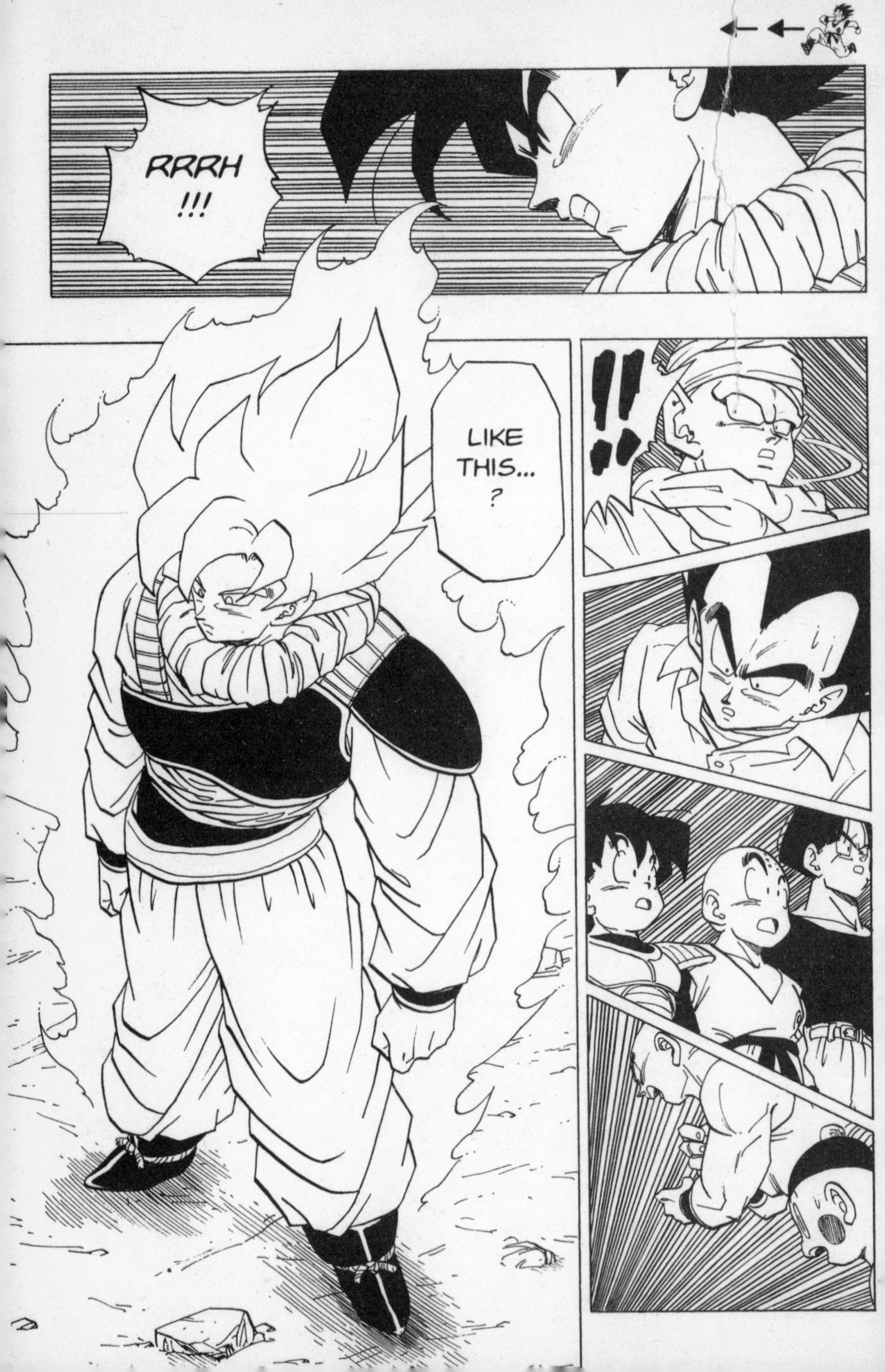
RRRH !!!
!!
LIKE THIS... ?

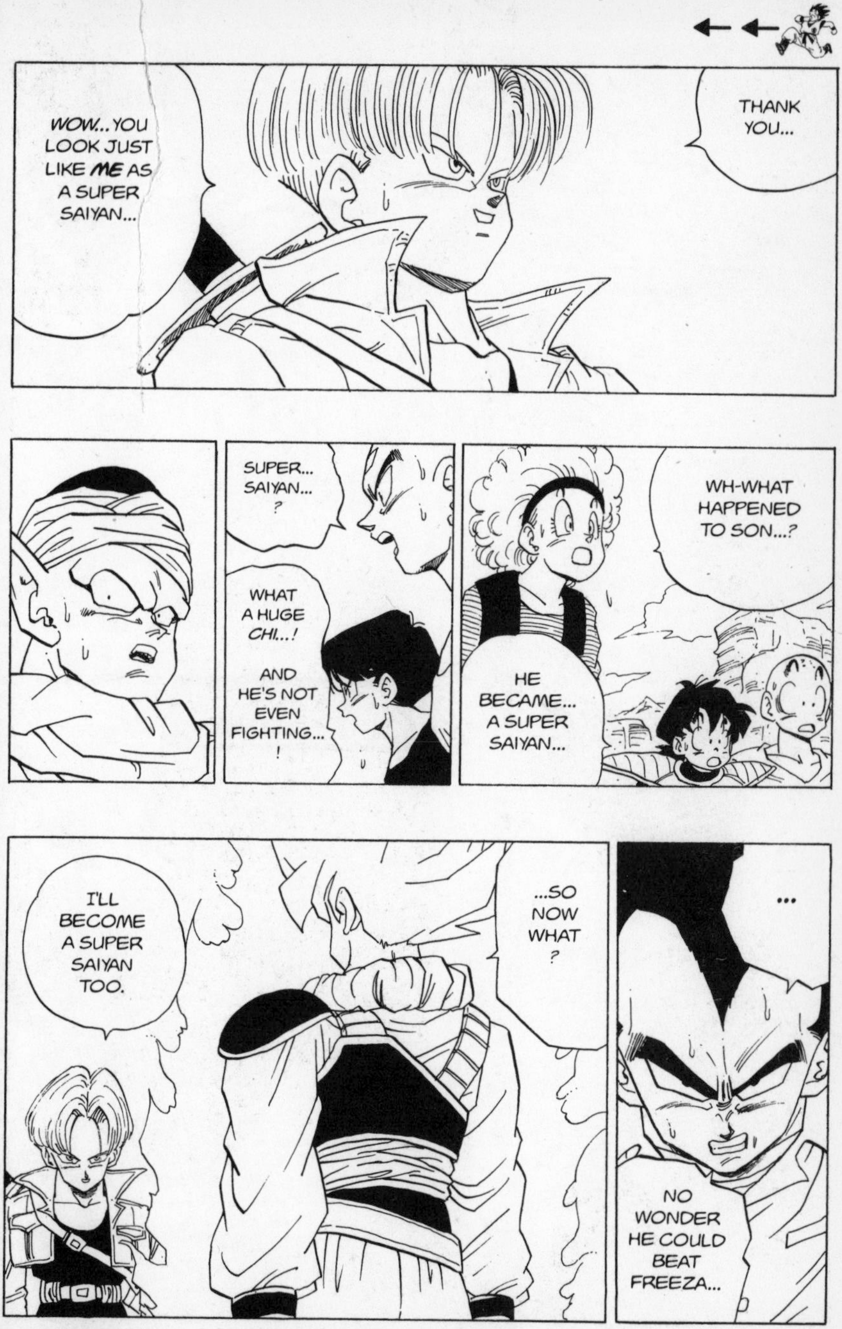
THANK YOU...
WOW... YOU LOOK JUST LIKE ME AS A SUPER SAIYAN...
WH-WHAT HAPPENED TO SON...?
HE BECAME... A SUPER SAIYAN...
SUPER... SAIYAN...?
WHAT A HUGE CHI...!
AND HE'S NOT EVEN FIGHTING...!
...
NO WONDER HE COULD BEAT FREEZA...
...SO NOW WHAT?
I'LL BECOME A SUPER SAIYAN TOO.

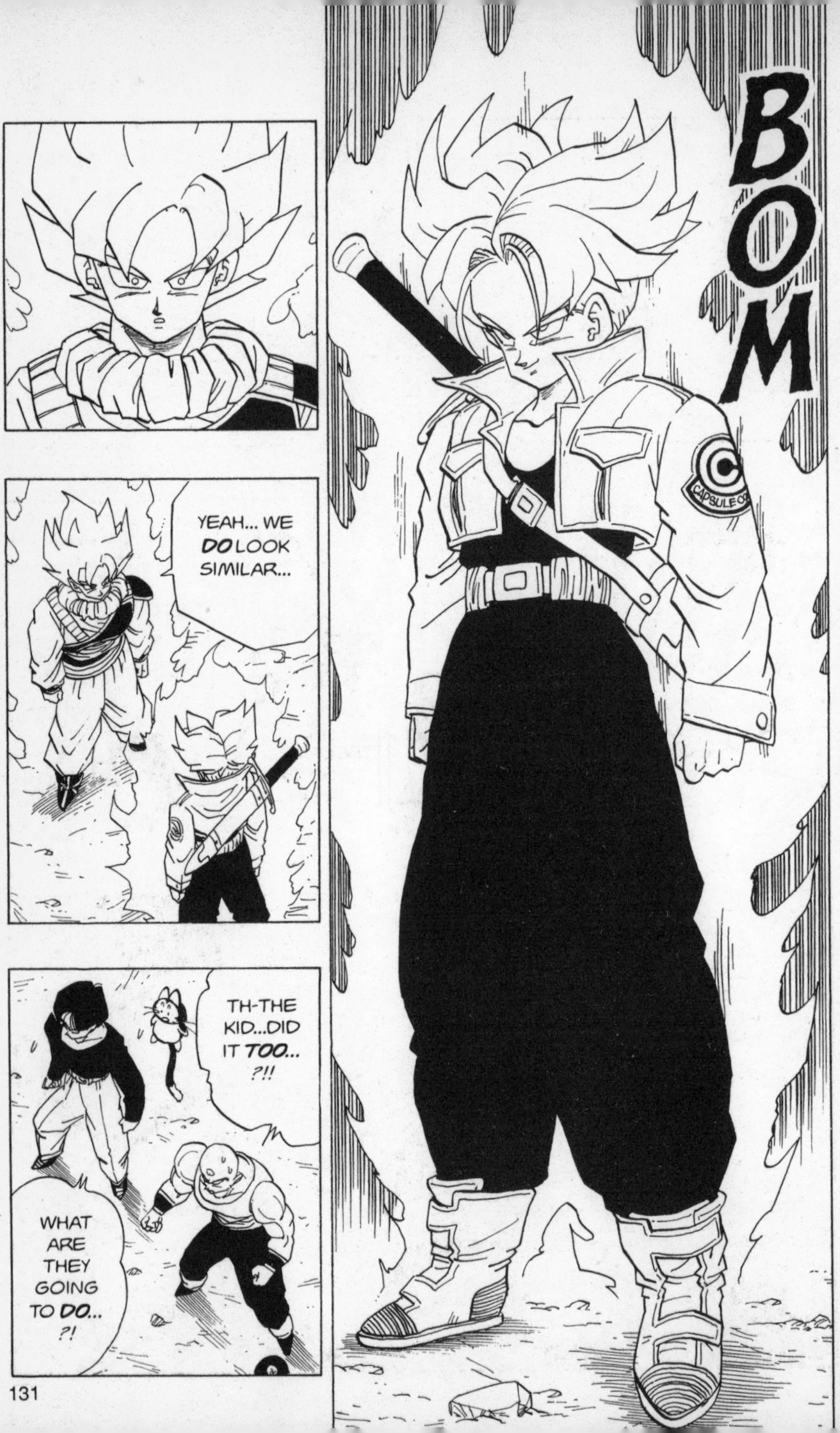
BOM
YEAH... WE DO LOOK SIMILAR...
TH-THE KID...DID IT TOO...?!!
WHAT ARE THEY GOING TO DO...?!

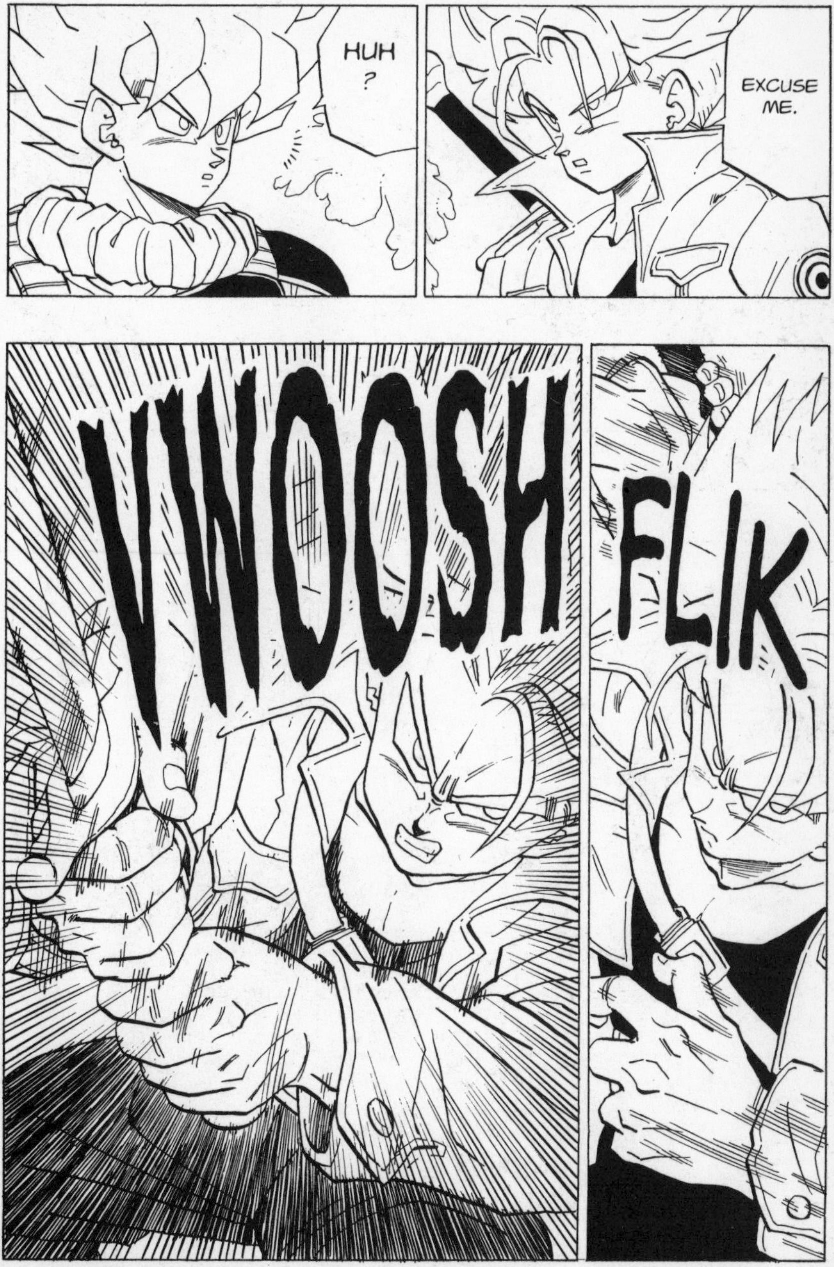
EXCUSE ME.
HUH ?
FLIK
VWOOSH

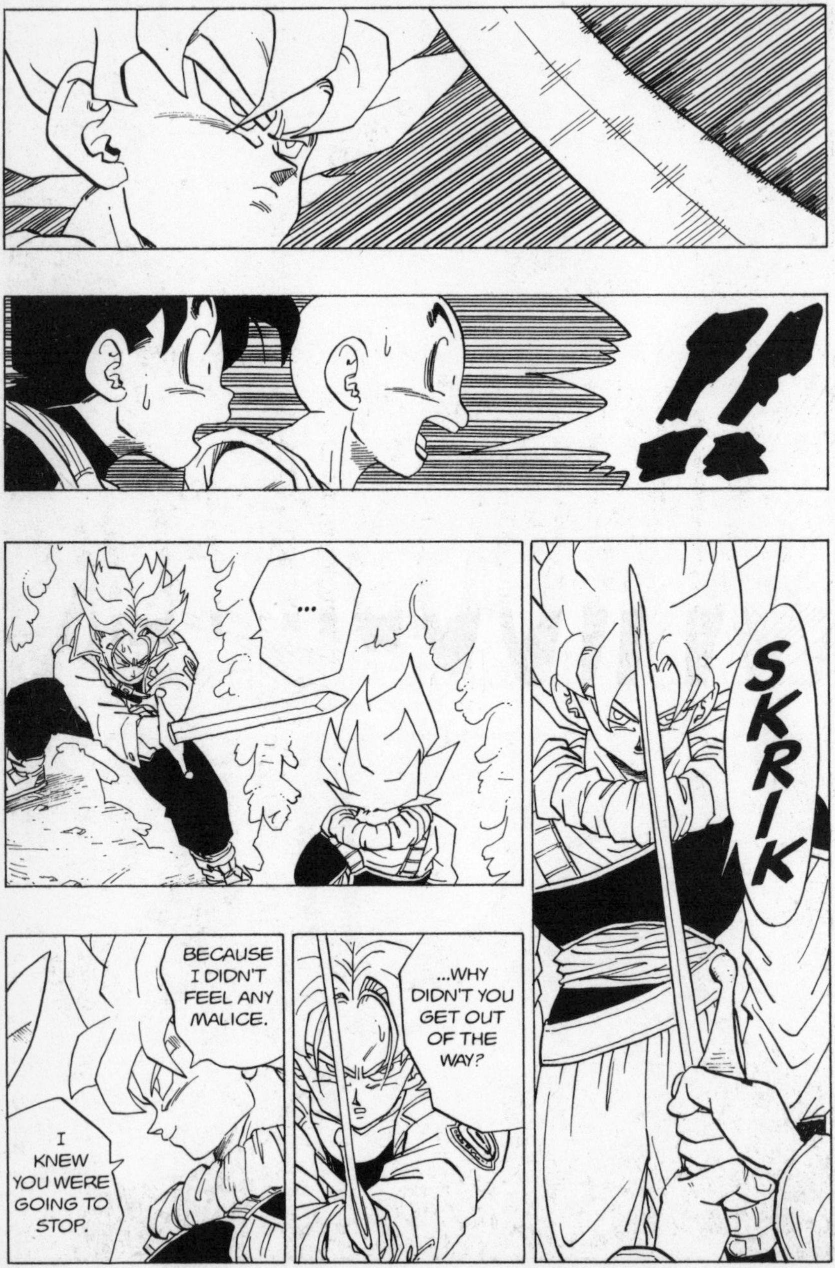
!!
SKRIK
...
...WHY DIDN'T YOU GET OUT OF THE WAY?
BECAUSE I DIDN'T FEEL ANY MALICE.
I KNEW YOU WERE GOING TO STOP.

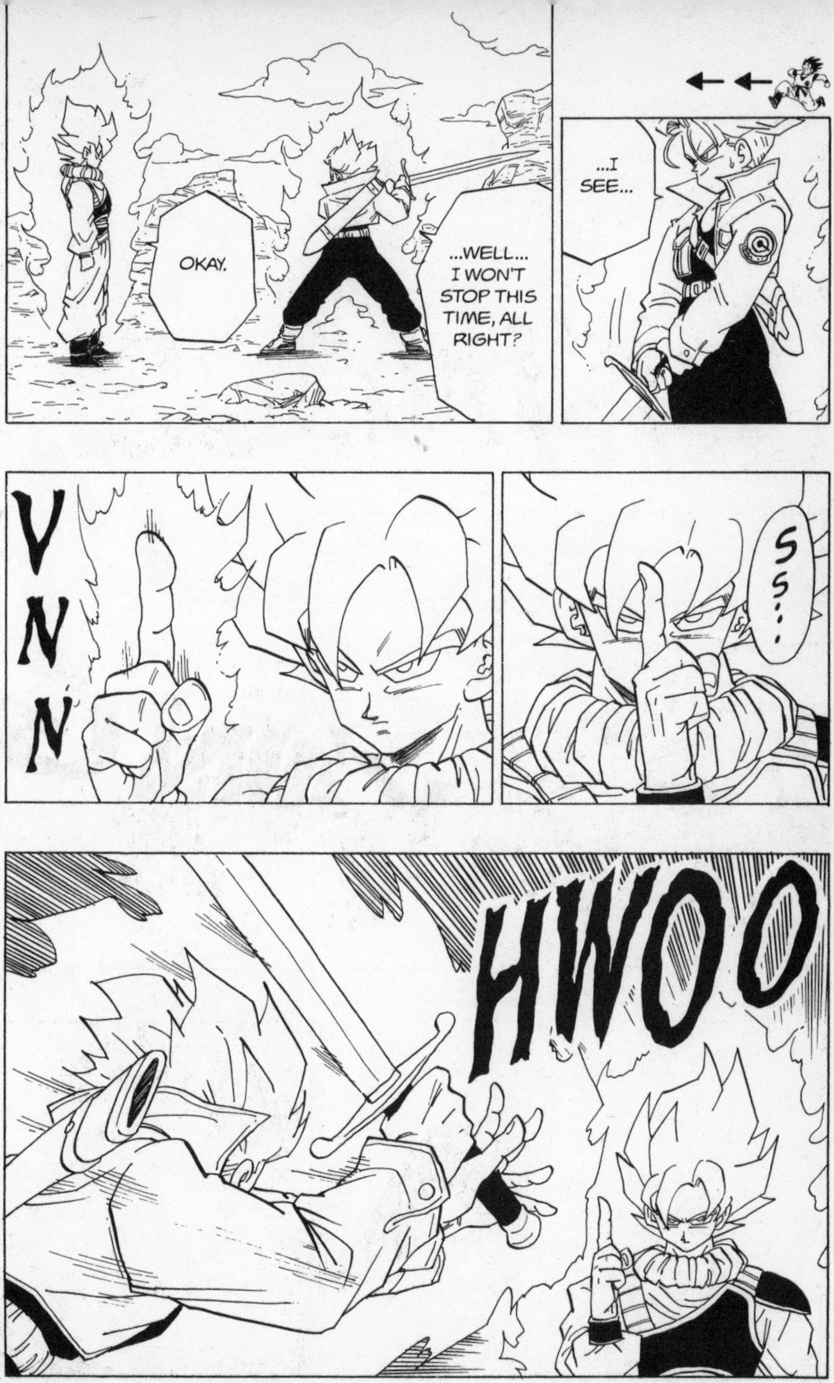
...I SEE...
...WELL... I WON'T STOP THIS TIME, ALL RIGHT?
OKAY.
SS...
VNN
HWOO

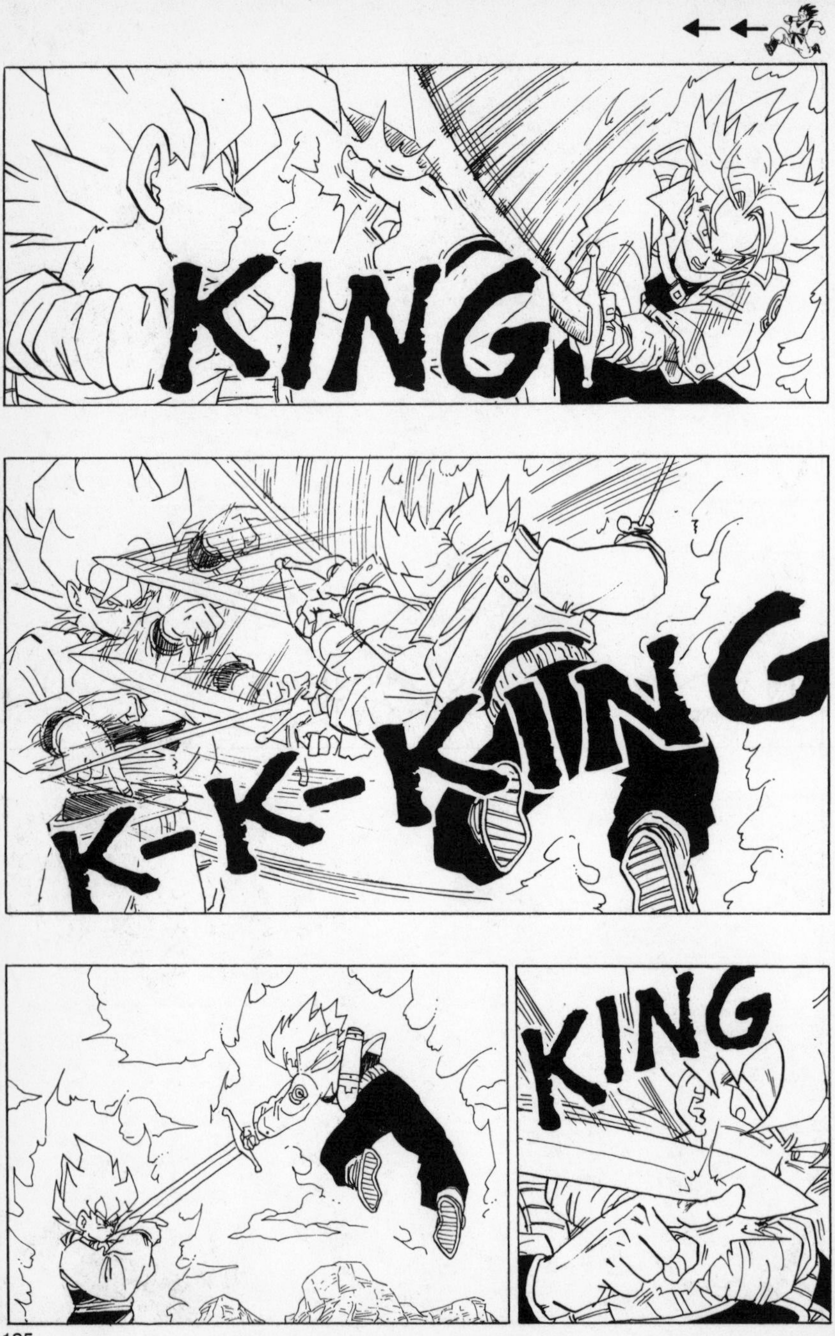
KING
K-K-KIIING
KING

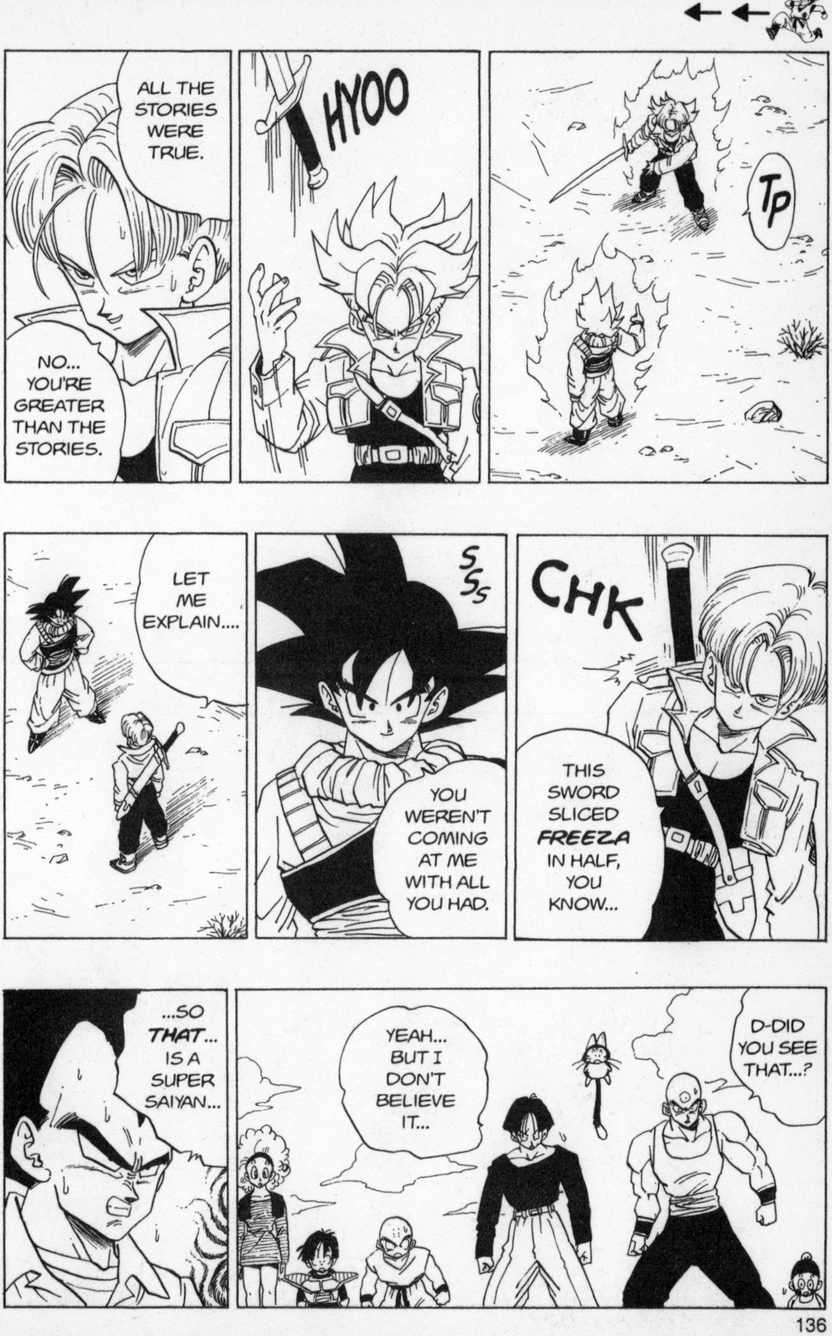

TP
HYOO
ALL THE STORIES WERE TRUE.
NO... YOU'RE GREATER THAN THE STORIES.
CHK
THIS SWORD SLICED *FREEZA* IN HALF, YOU KNOW...
SSS
YOU WEREN'T COMING AT ME WITH ALL YOU HAD.
LET ME EXPLAIN....
D-DID YOU SEE THAT...?
YEAH... BUT I DON'T BELIEVE IT...
...SO *THAT*... IS A SUPER SAIYAN...

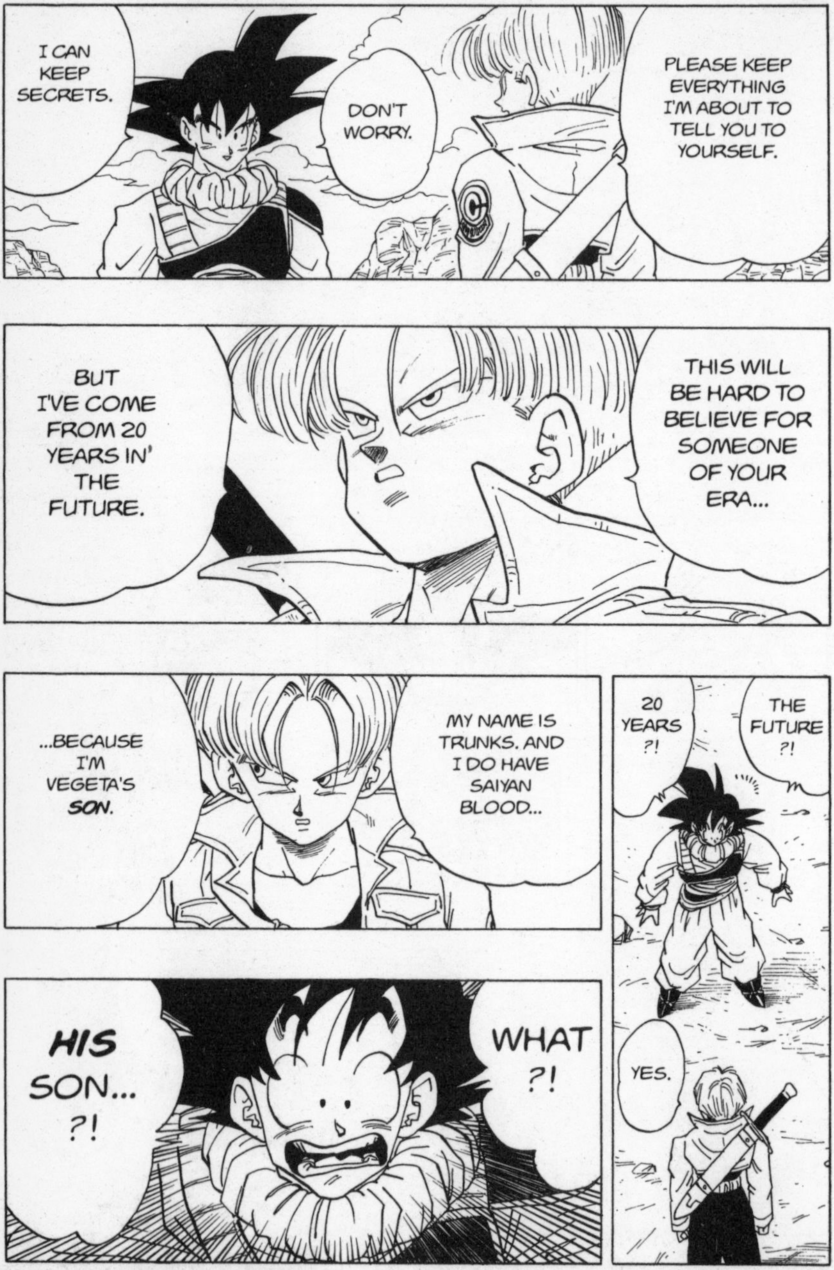
PLEASE KEEP EVERYTHING I'M ABOUT TO TELL YOU TO YOURSELF.
DON'T WORRY.
I CAN KEEP SECRETS.
THIS WILL BE HARD TO BELIEVE FOR SOMEONE OF YOUR ERA...
BUT I'VE COME FROM 20 YEARS IN' THE FUTURE.
THE FUTURE ?!
20 YEARS ?!
YES.
MY NAME IS TRUNKS. AND I DO HAVE SAIYAN BLOOD...
...BECAUSE I'M VEGETA'S *SON*.
WHAT ?!
HIS SON... ?!

NEXT: CHANGING HISTORY

DBZ:141 • The Terrifying Message

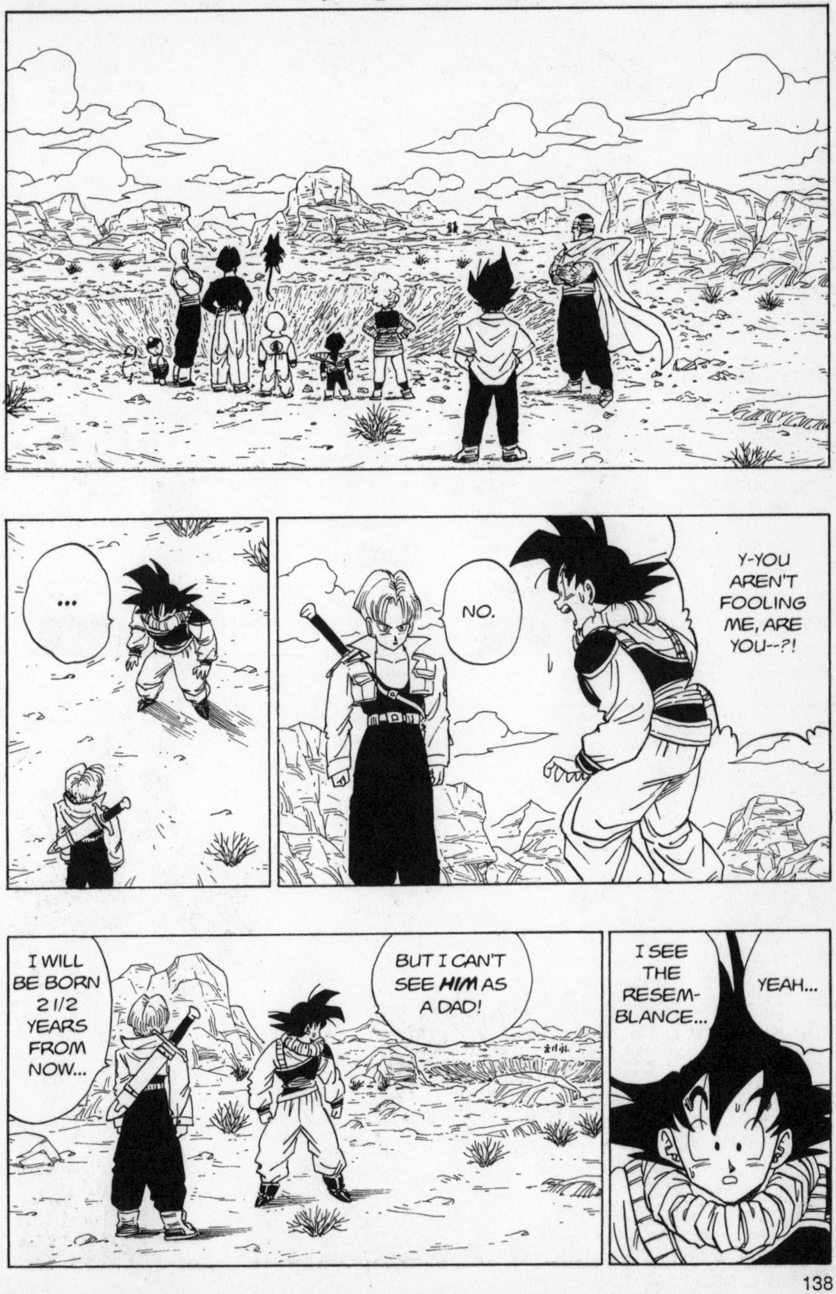
Y-YOU AREN'T FOOLING ME, ARE YOU--?!
NO.
...
YEAH...
I SEE THE RESEM-BLANCE...
BUT I CAN'T SEE ***HIM*** AS A DAD!
I WILL BE BORN 2 1/2 YEARS FROM NOW...

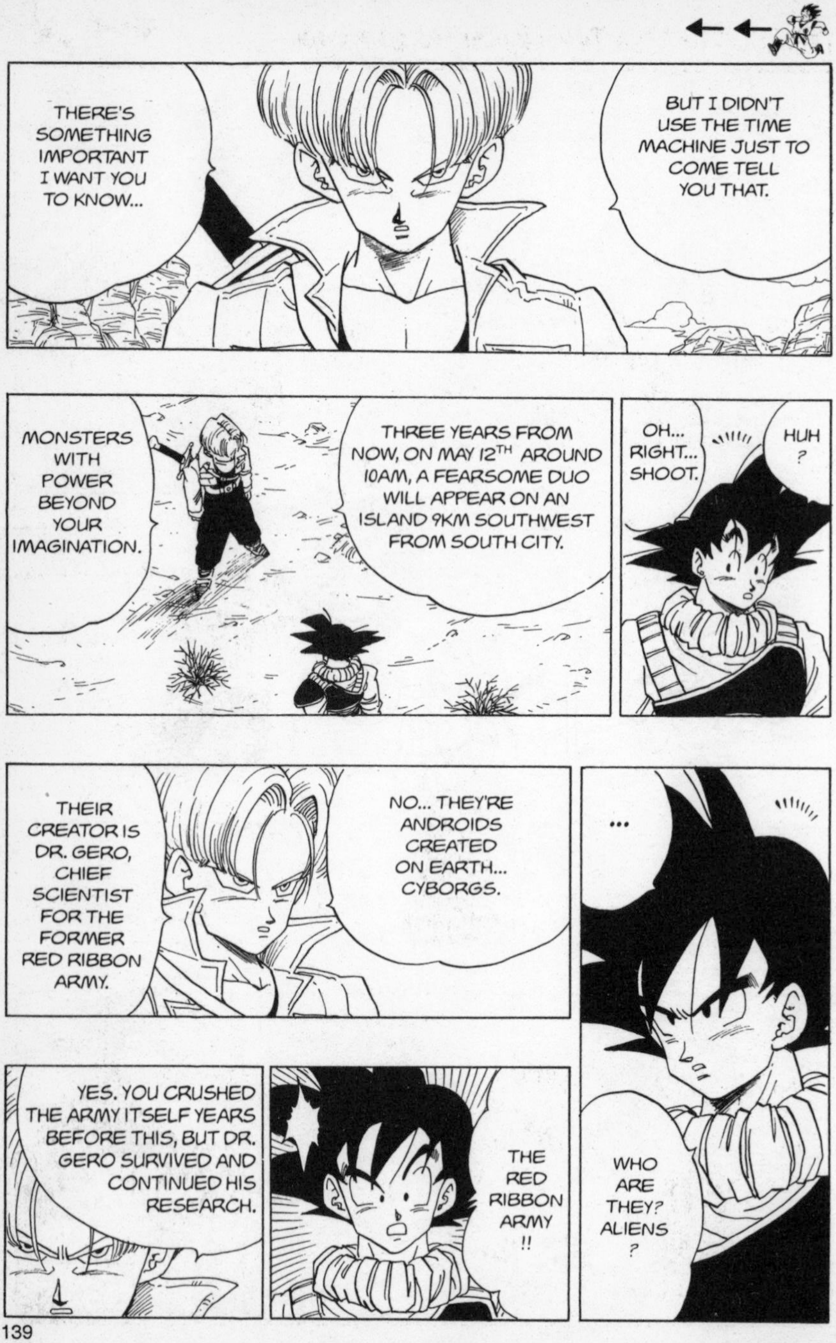

BUT I DIDN'T USE THE TIME MACHINE JUST TO COME TELL YOU THAT.
THERE'S SOMETHING IMPORTANT I WANT YOU TO KNOW...
HUH ?
OH... RIGHT... SHOOT.
THREE YEARS FROM NOW, ON MAY 12TH AROUND 10AM, A FEARSOME DUO WILL APPEAR ON AN ISLAND 9KM SOUTHWEST FROM SOUTH CITY.
MONSTERS WITH POWER BEYOND YOUR IMAGINATION.
...
WHO ARE THEY? ALIENS ?
NO... THEY'RE ANDROIDS CREATED ON EARTH... CYBORGS.
THEIR CREATOR IS DR. GERO, CHIEF SCIENTIST FOR THE FORMER RED RIBBON ARMY.
THE RED RIBBON ARMY !!
YES. YOU CRUSHED THE ARMY ITSELF YEARS BEFORE THIS, BUT DR. GERO SURVIVED AND CONTINUED HIS RESEARCH.

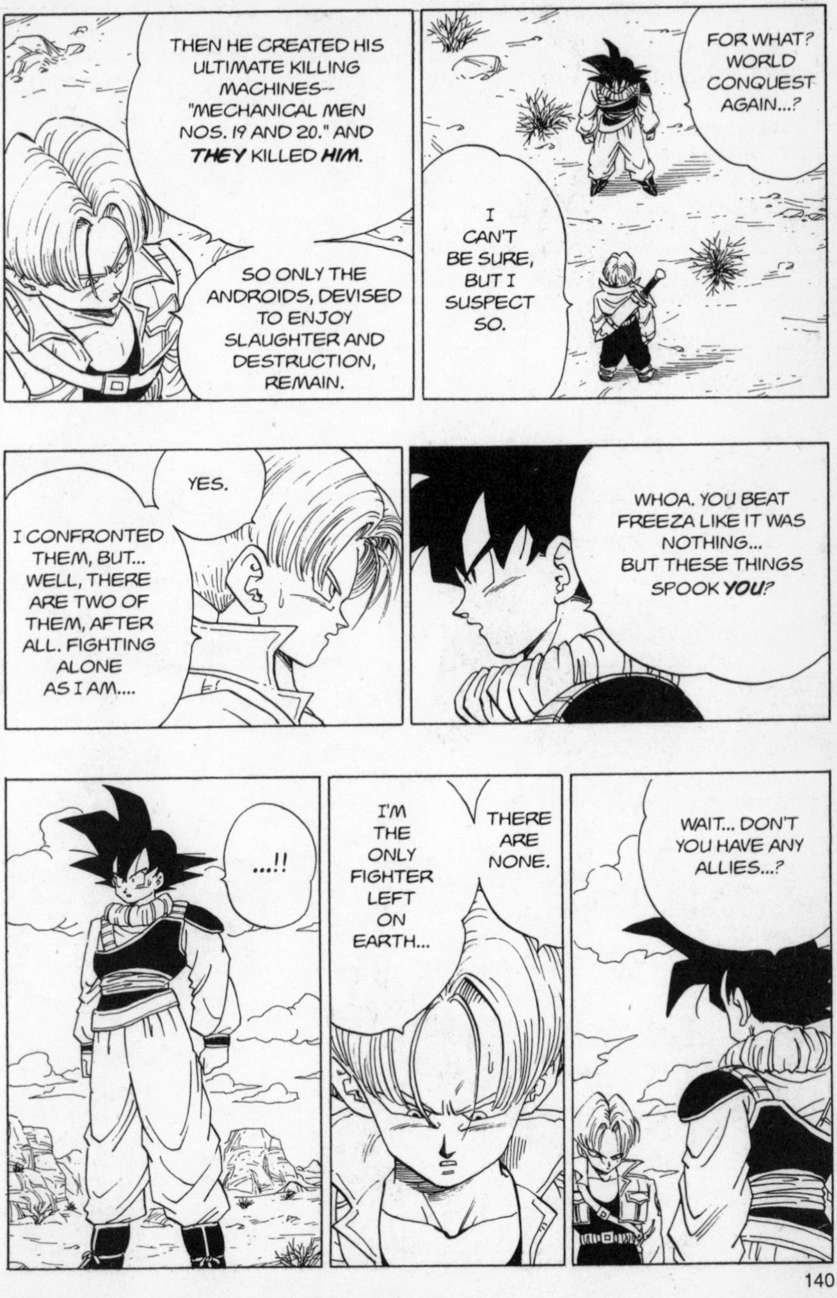

FOR WHAT? WORLD CONQUEST AGAIN...?
I CAN'T BE SURE, BUT I SUSPECT SO.
THEN HE CREATED HIS ULTIMATE KILLING MACHINES-- "MECHANICAL MEN NOS. 19 AND 20." AND **THEY** KILLED **HIM**.
SO ONLY THE ANDROIDS, DEVISED TO ENJOY SLAUGHTER AND DESTRUCTION, REMAIN.
WHOA. YOU BEAT FREEZA LIKE IT WAS NOTHING... BUT THESE THINGS SPOOK **YOU**?
YES.
I CONFRONTED THEM, BUT... WELL, THERE ARE TWO OF THEM, AFTER ALL. FIGHTING ALONE AS I AM....
WAIT... DON'T YOU HAVE ANY ALLIES...?
THERE ARE NONE.
I'M THE ONLY FIGHTER LEFT ON EARTH...
...!!

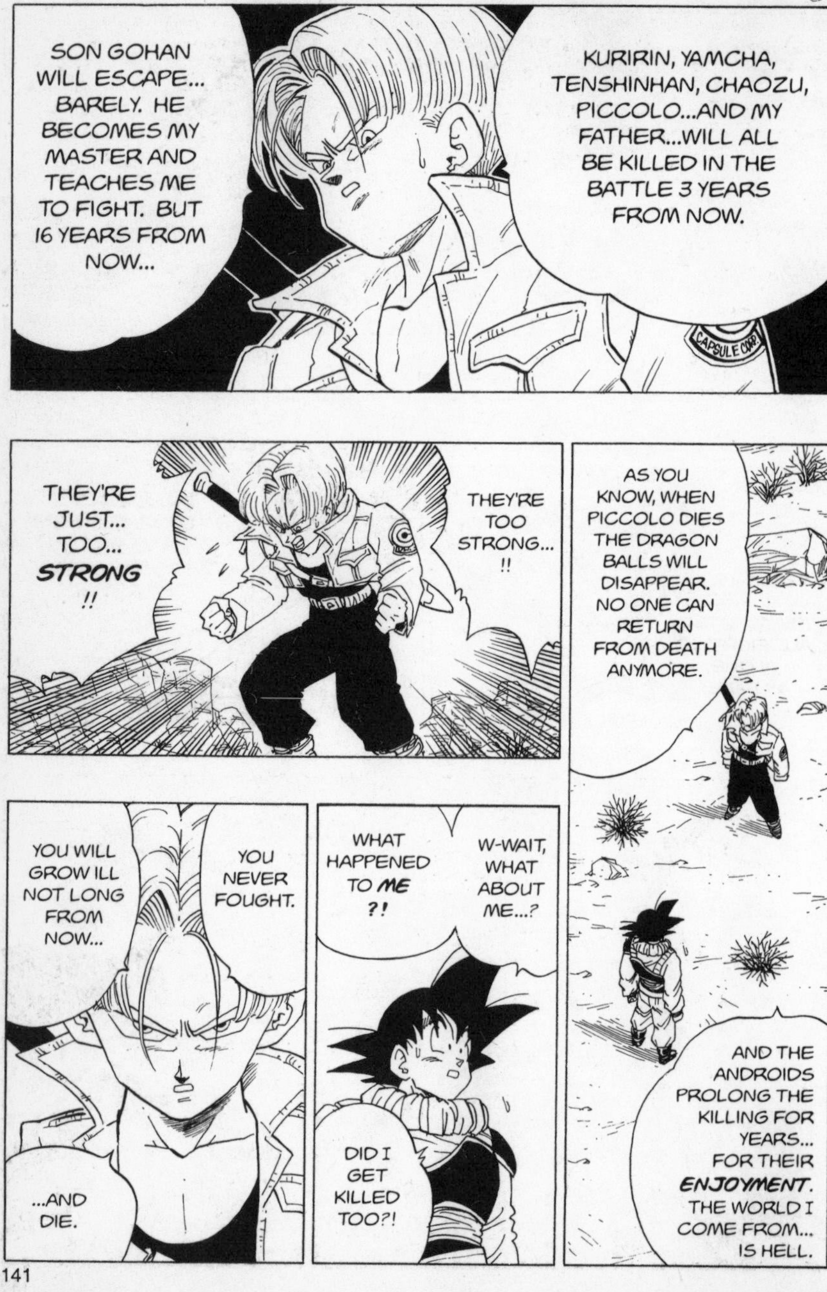
KURIRIN, YAMCHA, TENSHINHAN, CHAOZU, PICCOLO...AND MY FATHER...WILL ALL BE KILLED IN THE BATTLE 3 YEARS FROM NOW.
SON GOHAN WILL ESCAPE... BARELY. HE BECOMES MY MASTER AND TEACHES ME TO FIGHT. BUT 16 YEARS FROM NOW...
CAPSULE CORP.
AS YOU KNOW, WHEN PICCOLO DIES THE DRAGON BALLS WILL DISAPPEAR. NO ONE CAN RETURN FROM DEATH ANYMORE.
AND THE ANDROIDS PROLONG THE KILLING FOR YEARS... FOR THEIR *ENJOYMENT*. THE WORLD I COME FROM... IS HELL.
THEY'RE TOO STRONG... !!
THEY'RE JUST... TOO... *STRONG* !!
W-WAIT, WHAT ABOUT ME...?
WHAT HAPPENED TO *ME* ?!
DID I GET KILLED TOO?!
YOU NEVER FOUGHT.
YOU WILL GROW ILL NOT LONG FROM NOW...
...AND DIE.

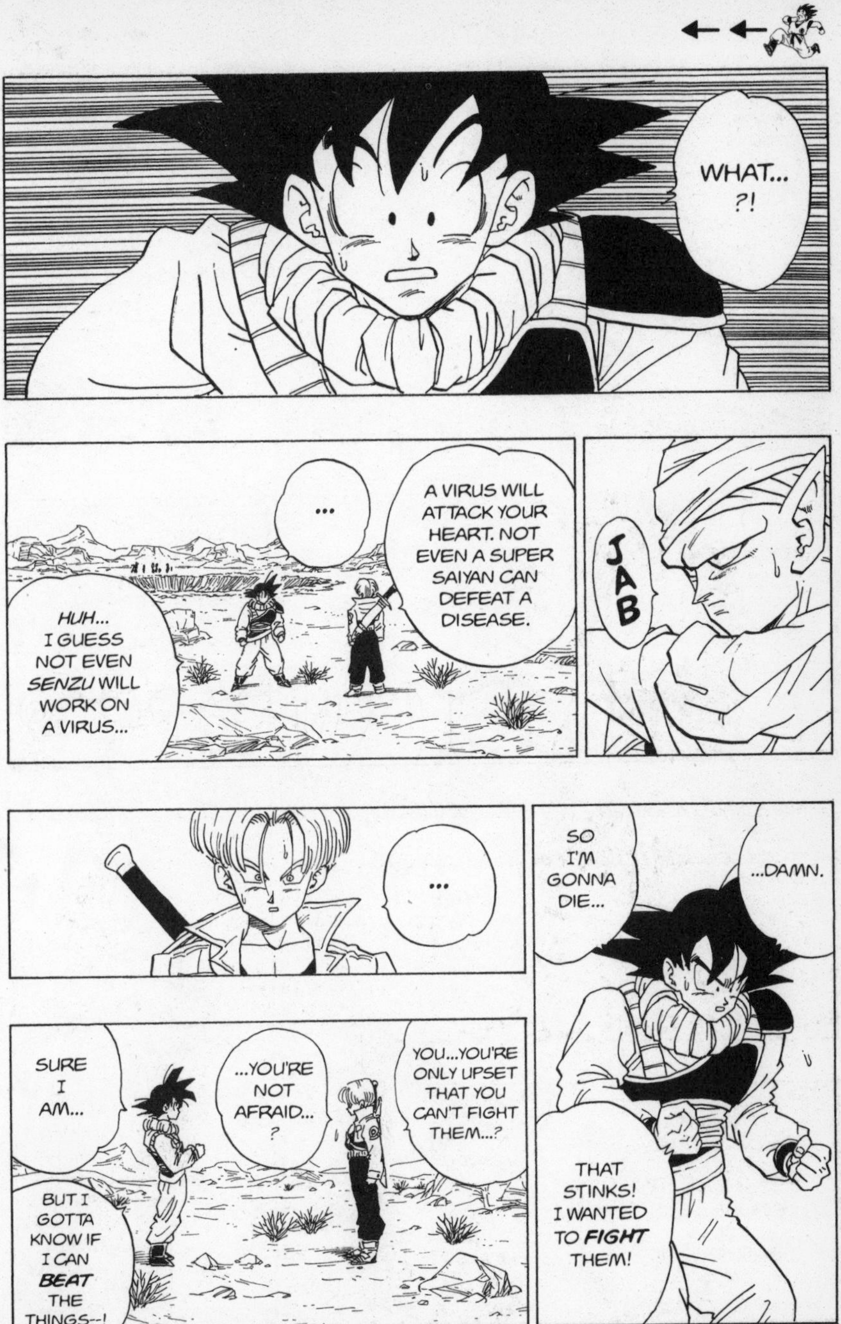
WHAT... ?!
JAB
A VIRUS WILL ATTACK YOUR HEART. NOT EVEN A SUPER SAIYAN CAN DEFEAT A DISEASE.
...
HUH... I GUESS NOT EVEN *SENZU* WILL WORK ON A VIRUS...
...DAMN.
SO I'M GONNA DIE...
THAT STINKS! I WANTED TO ***FIGHT*** THEM!
...
YOU...YOU'RE ONLY UPSET THAT YOU CAN'T FIGHT THEM...?
...YOU'RE NOT AFRAID... ?
SURE I AM...
BUT I GOTTA KNOW IF I CAN ***BEAT*** THE THINGS--!

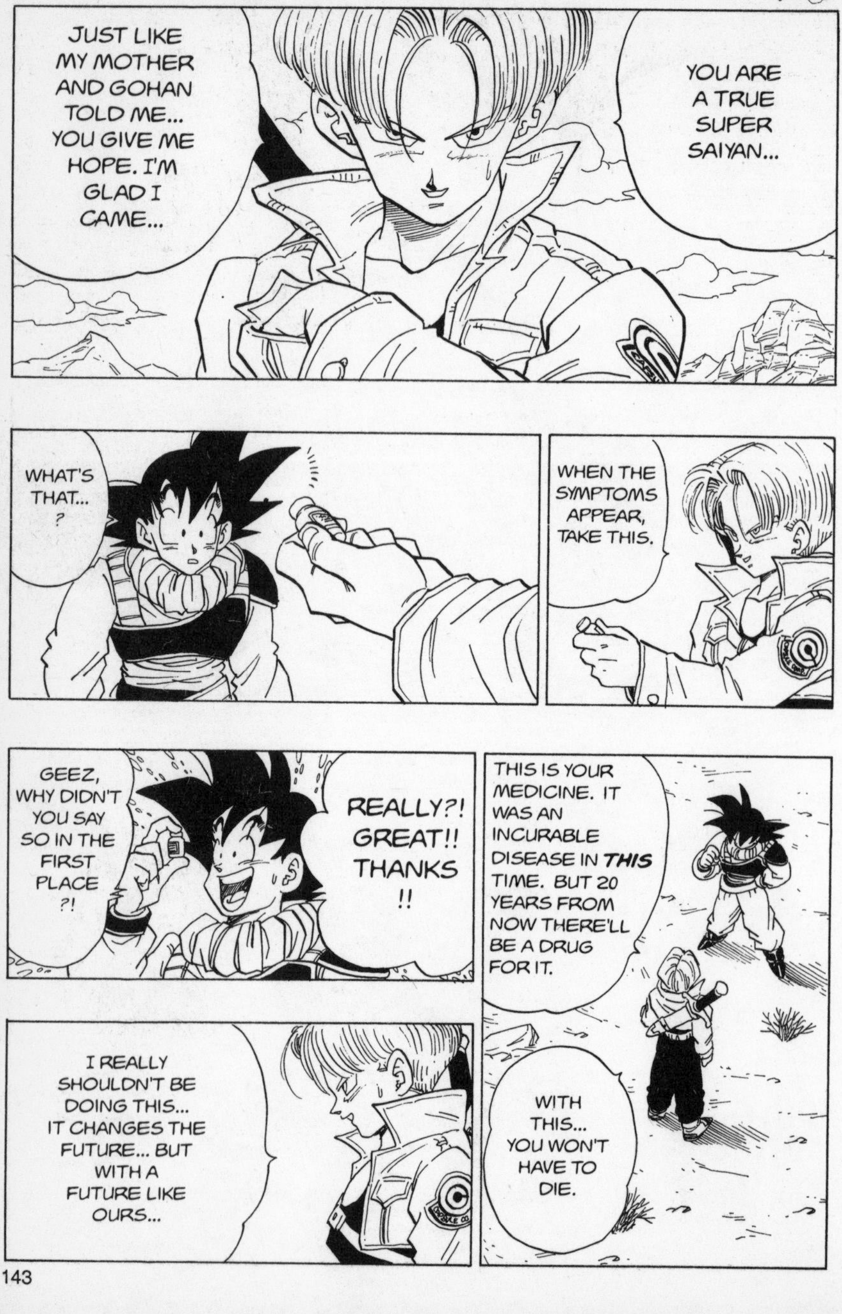
YOU ARE A TRUE SUPER SAIYAN...
JUST LIKE MY MOTHER AND GOHAN TOLD ME... YOU GIVE ME HOPE. I'M GLAD I CAME...
WHEN THE SYMPTOMS APPEAR, TAKE THIS.
WHAT'S THAT... ?
THIS IS YOUR MEDICINE. IT WAS AN INCURABLE DISEASE IN ***THIS*** TIME. BUT 20 YEARS FROM NOW THERE'LL BE A DRUG FOR IT.
WITH THIS... YOU WON'T HAVE TO DIE.
REALLY?! GREAT!! THANKS !!
GEEZ, WHY DIDN'T YOU SAY SO IN THE FIRST PLACE ?!
I REALLY SHOULDN'T BE DOING THIS... IT CHANGES THE FUTURE... BUT WITH A FUTURE LIKE OURS...

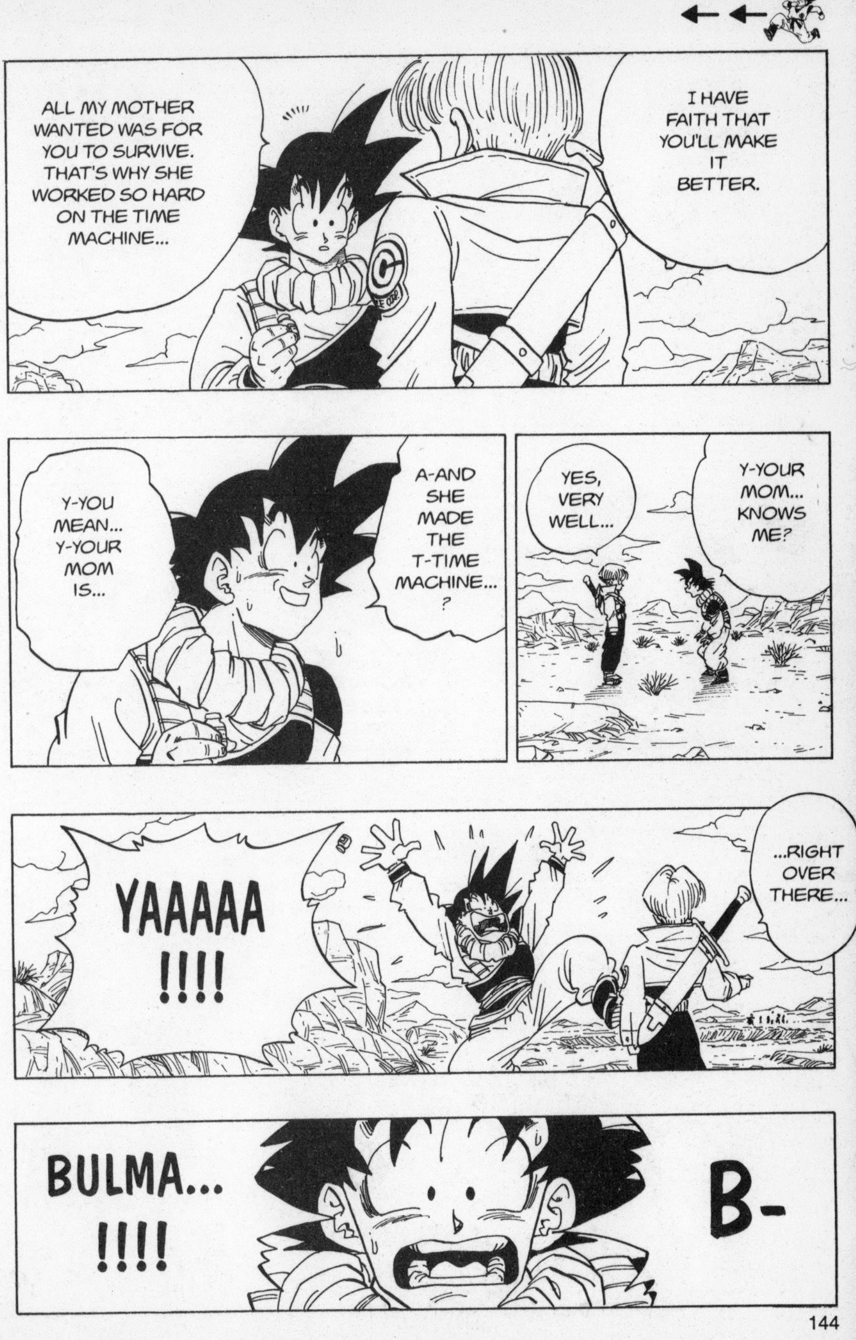
I HAVE FAITH THAT YOU'LL MAKE IT BETTER.
ALL MY MOTHER WANTED WAS FOR YOU TO SURVIVE. THAT'S WHY SHE WORKED SO HARD ON THE TIME MACHINE...
Y-YOUR MOM... KNOWS ME?
YES, VERY WELL...
A-AND SHE MADE THE T-TIME MACHINE...?
Y-YOU MEAN... Y-YOUR MOM IS...
...RIGHT OVER THERE...
YAAAAA !!!!
B-
BULMA... !!!!

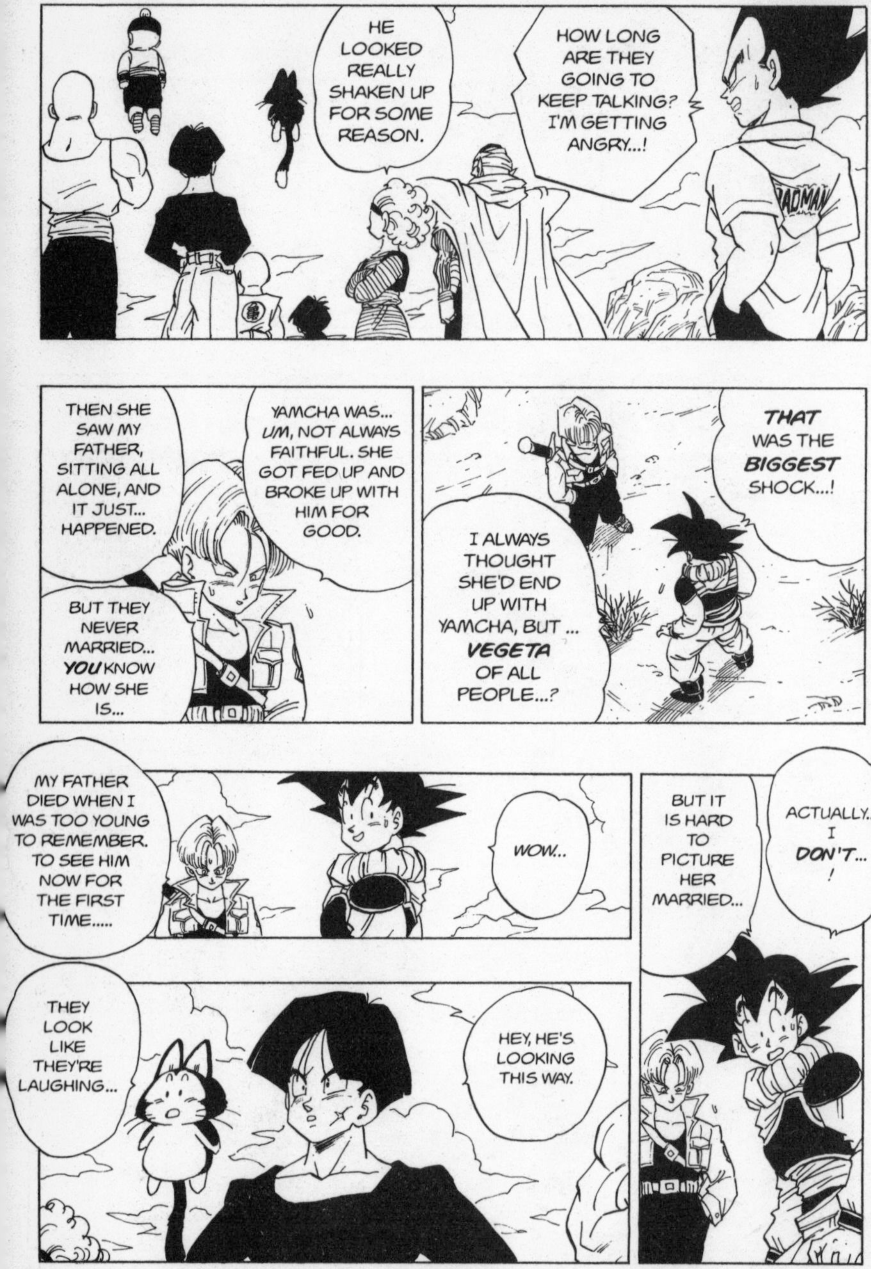
HOW LONG ARE THEY GOING TO KEEP TALKING? I'M GETTING ANGRY...!
HE LOOKED REALLY SHAKEN UP FOR SOME REASON.
THAT WAS THE *BIGGEST* SHOCK...!
I ALWAYS THOUGHT SHE'D END UP WITH YAMCHA, BUT ... *VEGETA* OF ALL PEOPLE...?
YAMCHA WAS... *UM*, NOT ALWAYS FAITHFUL. SHE GOT FED UP AND BROKE UP WITH HIM FOR GOOD.
THEN SHE SAW MY FATHER, SITTING ALL ALONE, AND IT JUST... HAPPENED.
BUT THEY NEVER MARRIED... *YOU* KNOW HOW SHE IS...
ACTUALLY... I *DON'T*...!
BUT IT IS HARD TO PICTURE HER MARRIED...
WOW...
MY FATHER DIED WHEN I WAS TOO YOUNG TO REMEMBER. TO SEE HIM NOW FOR THE FIRST TIME.....
HEY, HE'S LOOKING THIS WAY.
THEY LOOK LIKE THEY'RE LAUGHING...

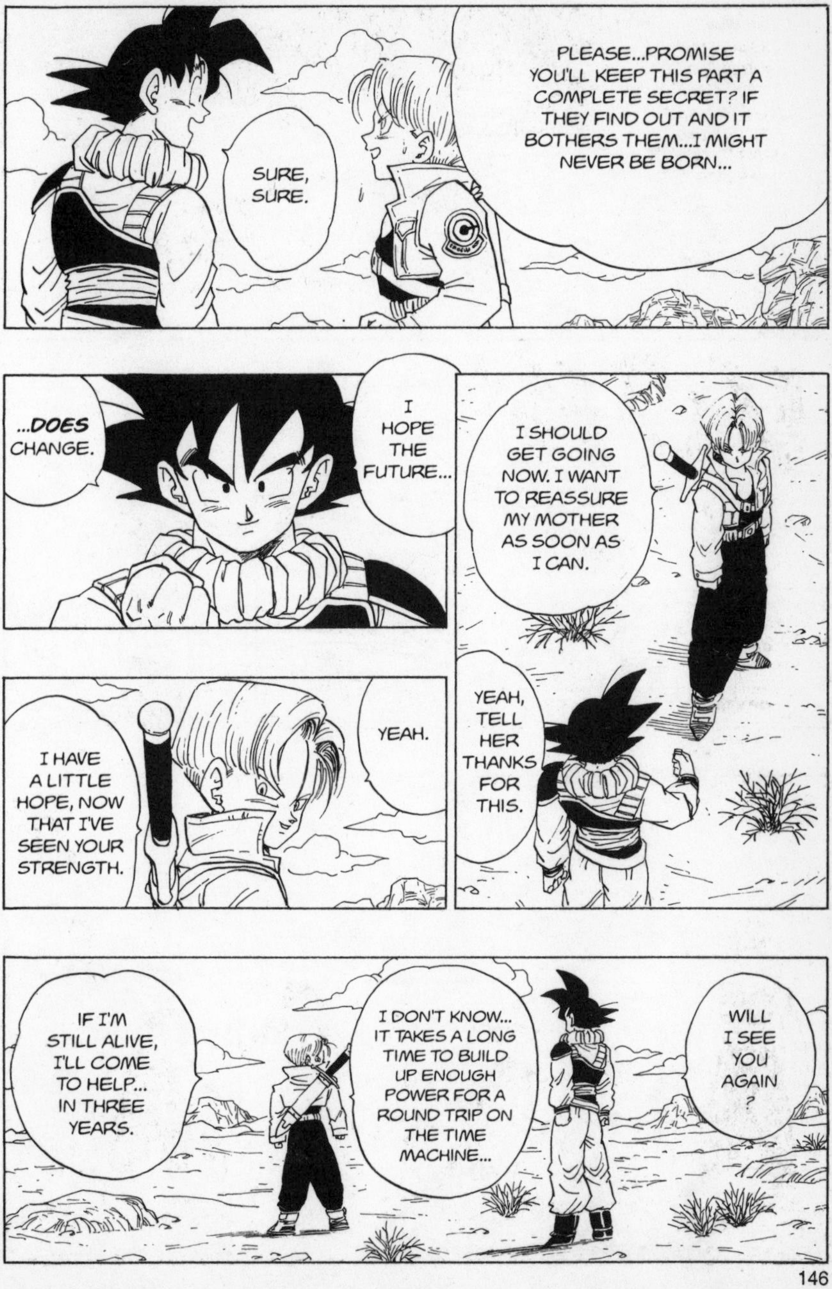
PLEASE...PROMISE YOU'LL KEEP THIS PART A COMPLETE SECRET? IF THEY FIND OUT AND IT BOTHERS THEM...I MIGHT NEVER BE BORN...
SURE, SURE.
I SHOULD GET GOING NOW. I WANT TO REASSURE MY MOTHER AS SOON AS I CAN.
YEAH, TELL HER THANKS FOR THIS.
I HOPE THE FUTURE...
...**DOES** CHANGE.
YEAH.
I HAVE A LITTLE HOPE, NOW THAT I'VE SEEN YOUR STRENGTH.
WILL I SEE YOU AGAIN?
I DON'T KNOW... IT TAKES A LONG TIME TO BUILD UP ENOUGH POWER FOR A ROUND TRIP ON THE TIME MACHINE...
IF I'M STILL ALIVE, I'LL COME TO HELP... IN THREE YEARS.

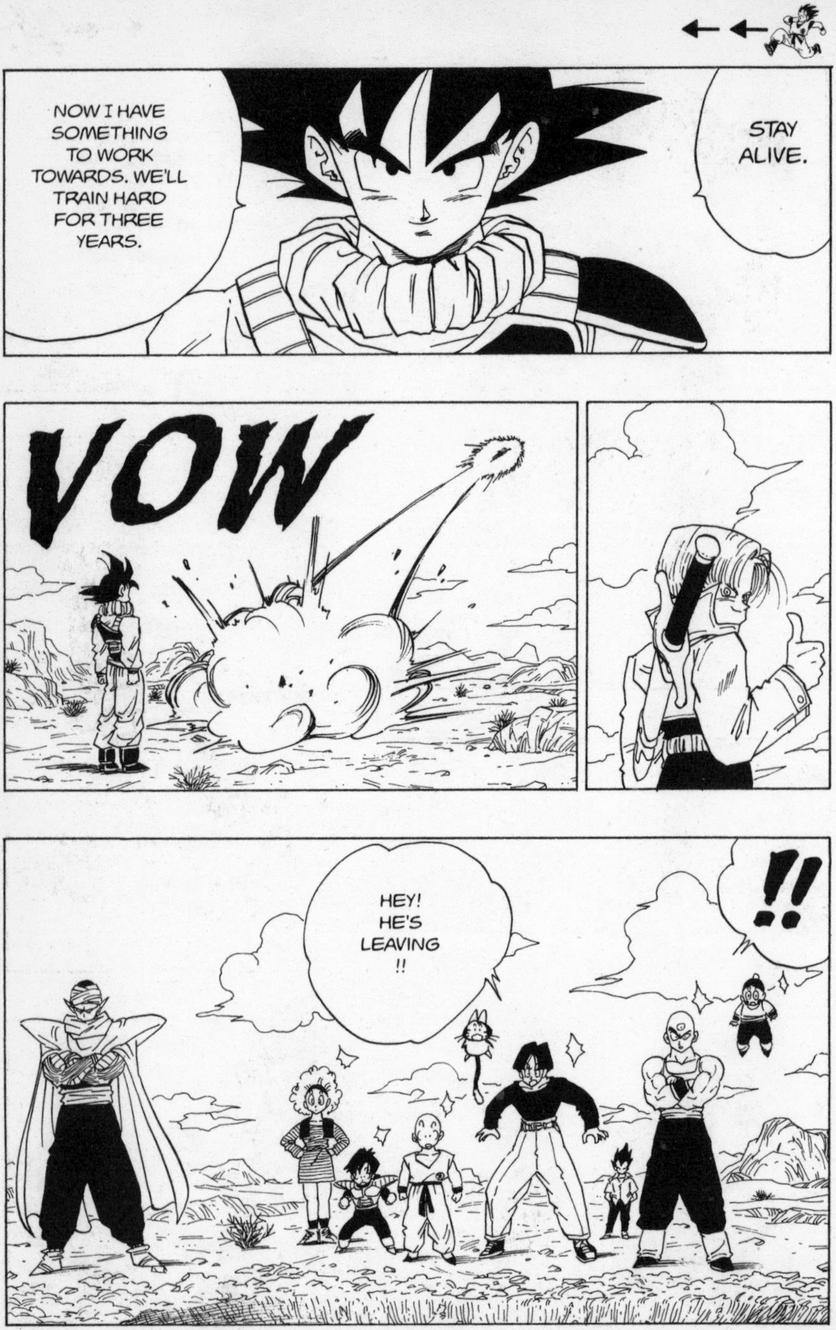
STAY ALIVE.
NOW I HAVE SOMETHING TO WORK TOWARDS. WE'LL TRAIN HARD FOR THREE YEARS.
VOW
!!
HEY! HE'S LEAVING !!

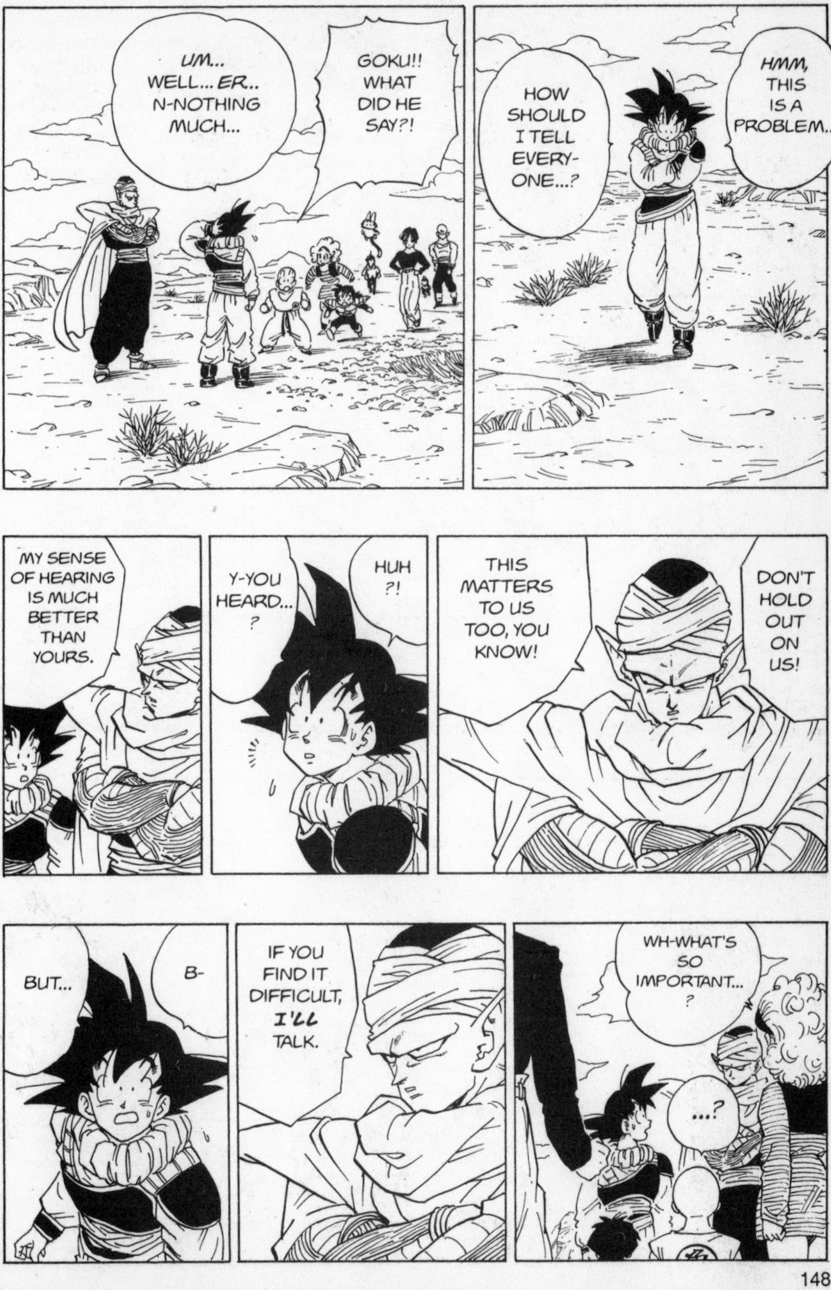
HMM, THIS IS A PROBLEM...
HOW SHOULD I TELL EVERY-ONE...?
GOKU!! WHAT DID HE SAY?!
UM... WELL... ER... N-NOTHING MUCH...
DON'T HOLD OUT ON US!
THIS MATTERS TO US TOO, YOU KNOW!
HUH ?!
Y-YOU HEARD... ?
MY SENSE OF HEARING IS MUCH BETTER THAN YOURS.
WH-WHAT'S SO IMPORTANT... ?
...?
IF YOU FIND IT DIFFICULT, **I'LL** TALK.
B-
BUT...

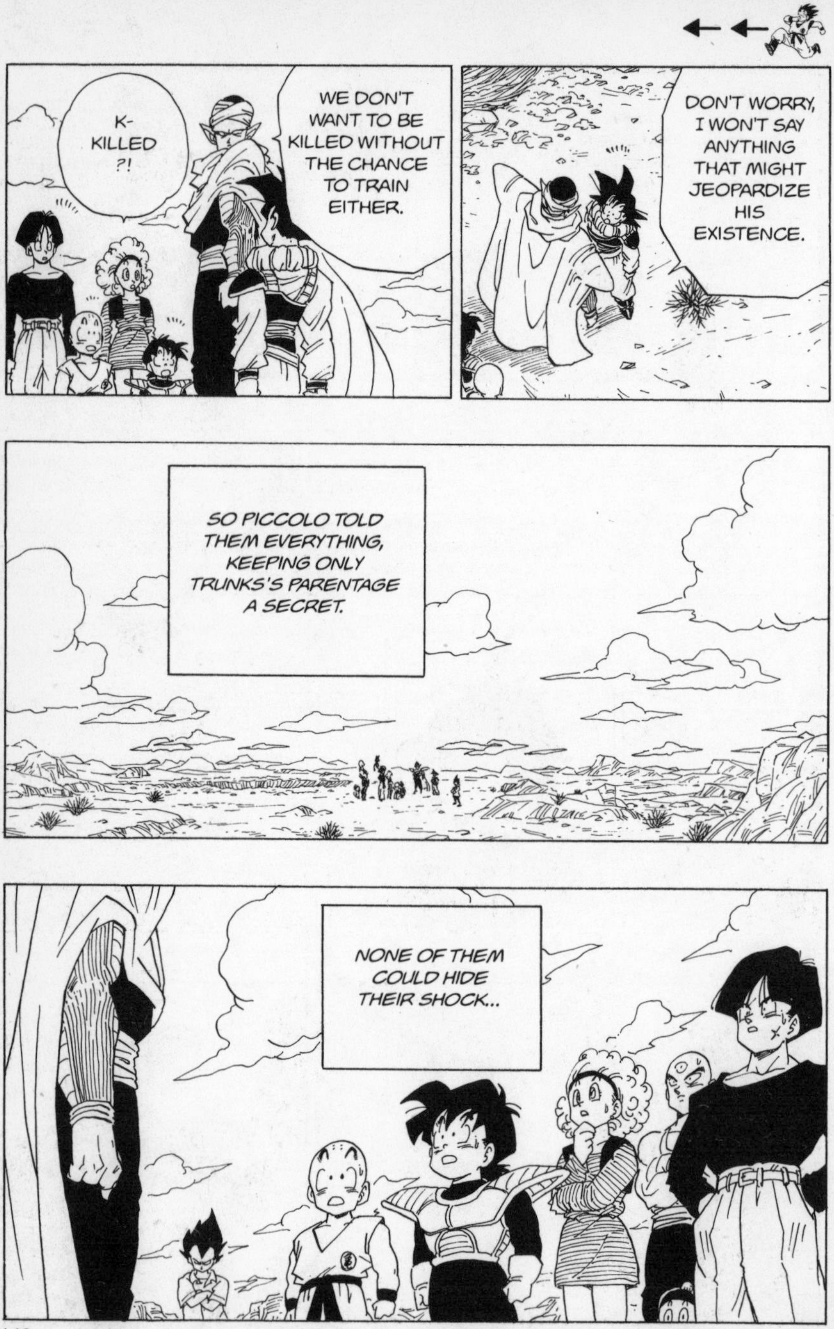
DON'T WORRY, I WON'T SAY ANYTHING THAT MIGHT JEOPARDIZE HIS EXISTENCE.
WE DON'T WANT TO BE KILLED WITHOUT THE CHANCE TO TRAIN EITHER.
K-KILLED ?!
SO PICCOLO TOLD THEM EVERYTHING, KEEPING ONLY TRUNKS'S PARENTAGE A SECRET.
NONE OF THEM COULD HIDE THEIR SHOCK...

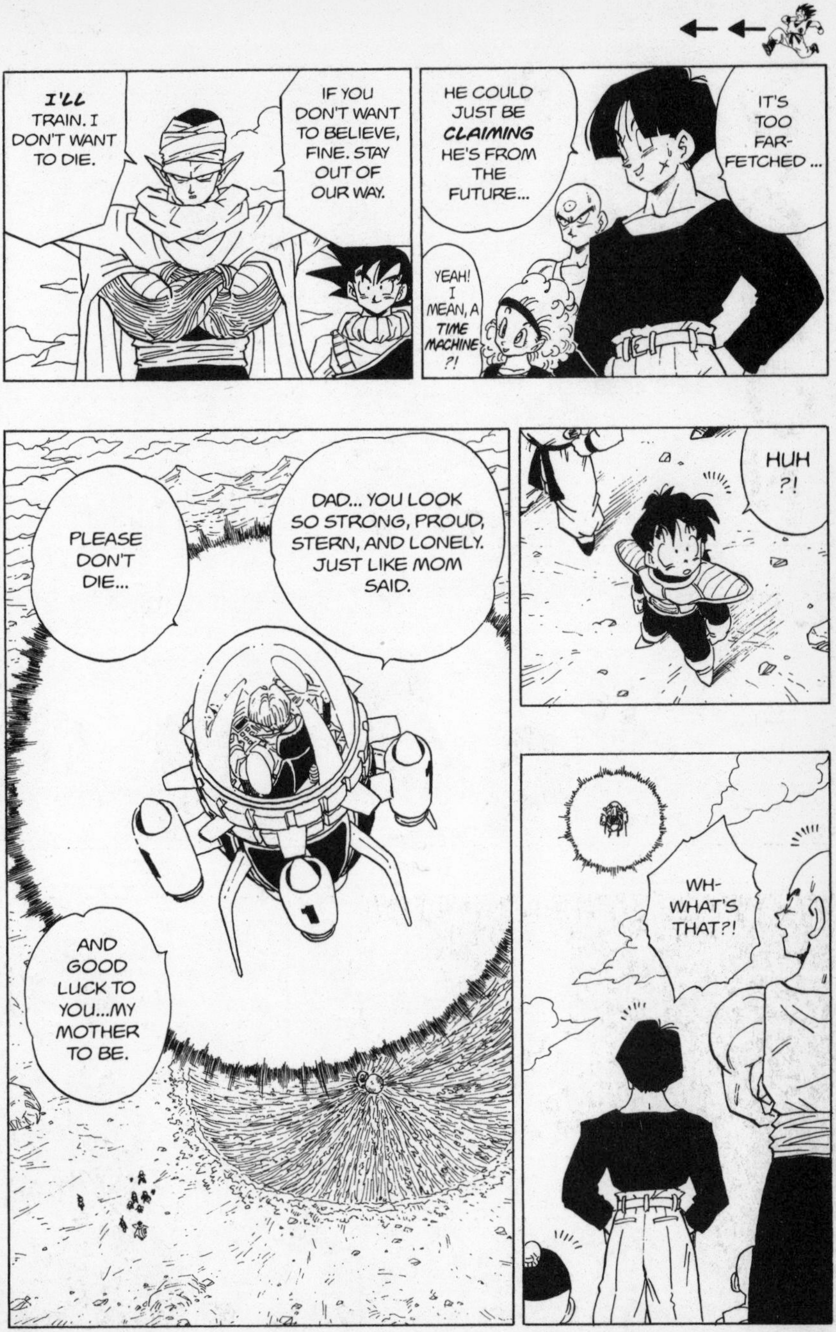
IT'S TOO FAR-FETCHED...
HE COULD JUST BE CLAIMING HE'S FROM THE FUTURE...
YEAH! I MEAN, A TIME MACHINE?!
IF YOU DON'T WANT TO BELIEVE, FINE. STAY OUT OF OUR WAY.
I'LL TRAIN. I DON'T WANT TO DIE.
HUH?!
WH-WHAT'S THAT?!
DAD... YOU LOOK SO STRONG, PROUD, STERN, AND LONELY. JUST LIKE MOM SAID.
PLEASE DON'T DIE...
AND GOOD LUCK TO YOU...MY MOTHER TO BE.

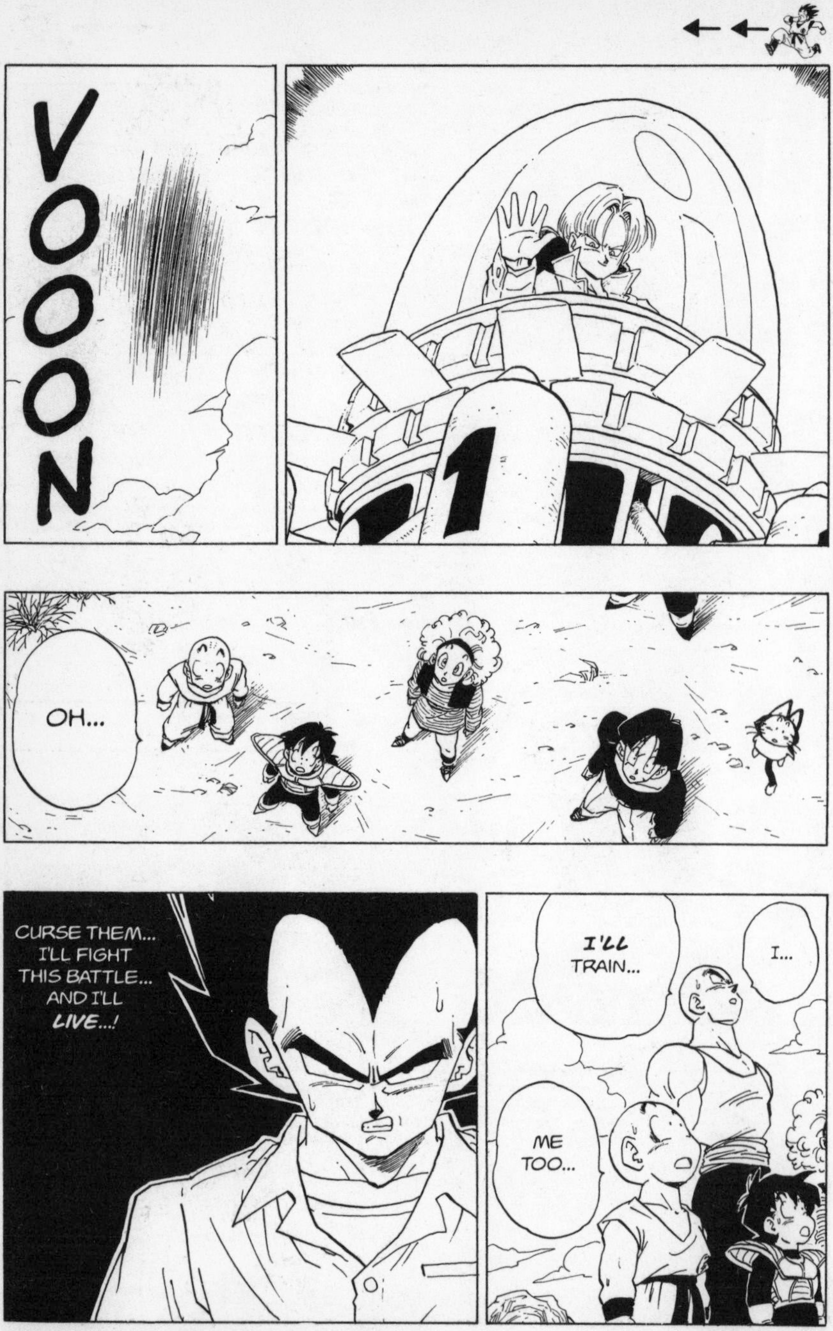
VOOON
OH...
I...
I'LL TRAIN...
ME TOO...
CURSE THEM... I'LL FIGHT THIS BATTLE... AND I'LL *LIVE*...!

NEXT: PREPARING FOR THE FUTURE

DBZ:142 • The Risky Decision

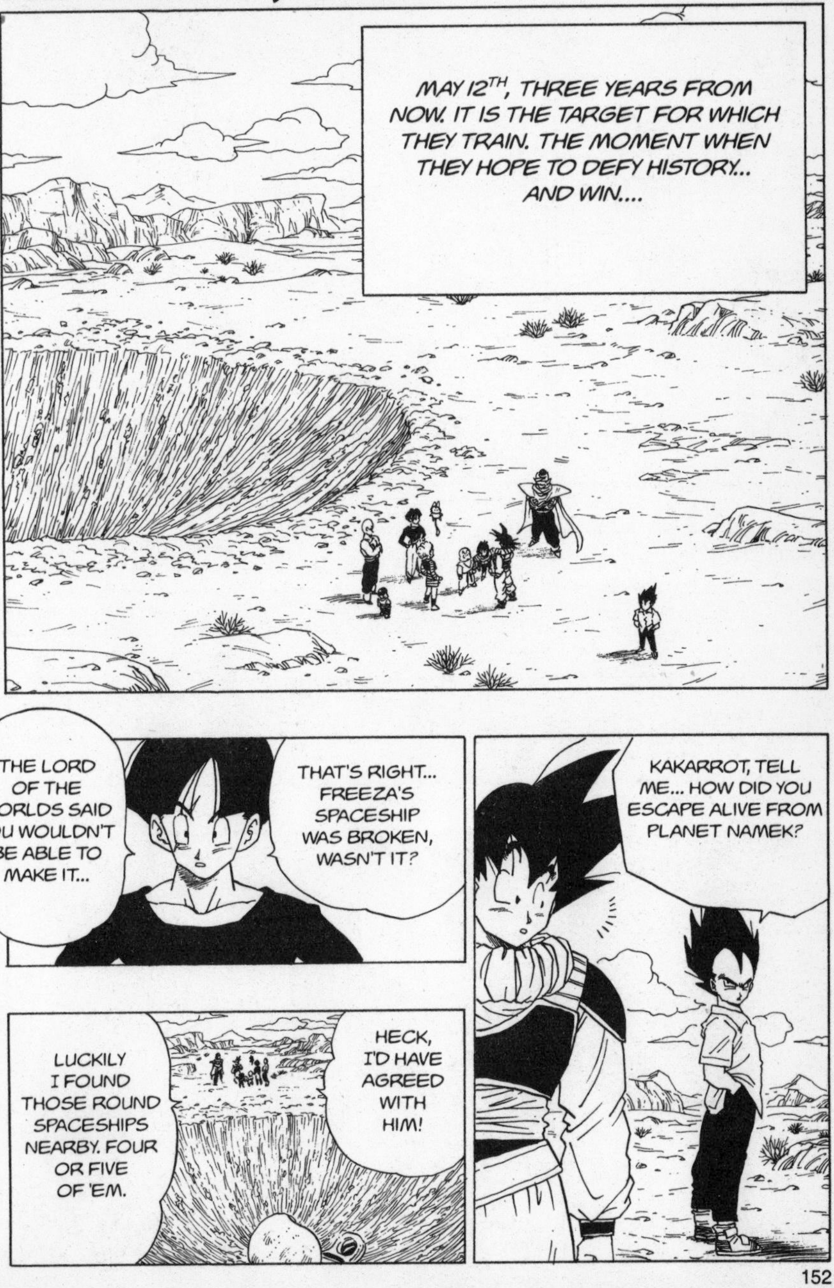
MAY 12TH, THREE YEARS FROM NOW. IT IS THE TARGET FOR WHICH THEY TRAIN. THE MOMENT WHEN THEY HOPE TO DEFY HISTORY... AND WIN....
KAKARROT, TELL ME... HOW DID YOU ESCAPE ALIVE FROM PLANET NAMEK?
THAT'S RIGHT... FREEZA'S SPACESHIP WAS BROKEN, WASN'T IT?
THE LORD OF THE VORLDS SAID 'OU WOULDN'T BE ABLE TO MAKE IT...
HECK, I'D HAVE AGREED WITH HIM!
LUCKILY I FOUND THOSE ROUND SPACESHIPS NEARBY. FOUR OR FIVE OF 'EM.

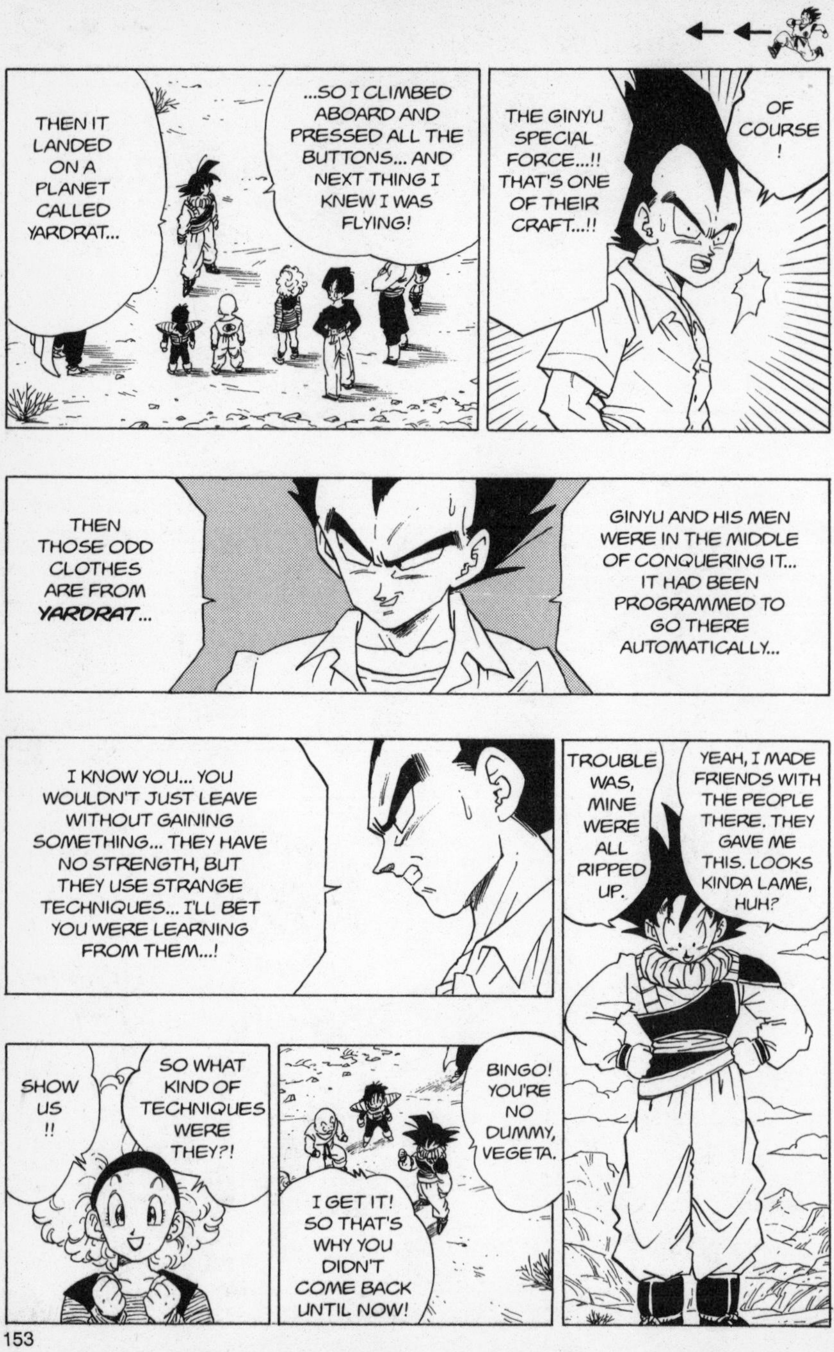
OF COURSE!
THE GINYU SPECIAL FORCE...!! THAT'S ONE OF THEIR CRAFT...!!
...SO I CLIMBED ABOARD AND PRESSED ALL THE BUTTONS... AND NEXT THING I KNEW I WAS FLYING!
THEN IT LANDED ON A PLANET CALLED YARDRAT...
GINYU AND HIS MEN WERE IN THE MIDDLE OF CONQUERING IT... IT HAD BEEN PROGRAMMED TO GO THERE AUTOMATICALLY...
THEN THOSE ODD CLOTHES ARE FROM *YARDRAT*...
YEAH, I MADE FRIENDS WITH THE PEOPLE THERE. THEY GAVE ME THIS. LOOKS KINDA LAME, HUH?
TROUBLE WAS, MINE WERE ALL RIPPED UP.
I KNOW YOU... YOU WOULDN'T JUST LEAVE WITHOUT GAINING SOMETHING... THEY HAVE NO STRENGTH, BUT THEY USE STRANGE TECHNIQUES... I'LL BET YOU WERE LEARNING FROM THEM...!
BINGO! YOU'RE NO DUMMY, VEGETA.
I GET IT! SO THAT'S WHY YOU DIDN'T COME BACK UNTIL NOW!
SO WHAT KIND OF TECHNIQUES WERE THEY?!
SHOW US!!

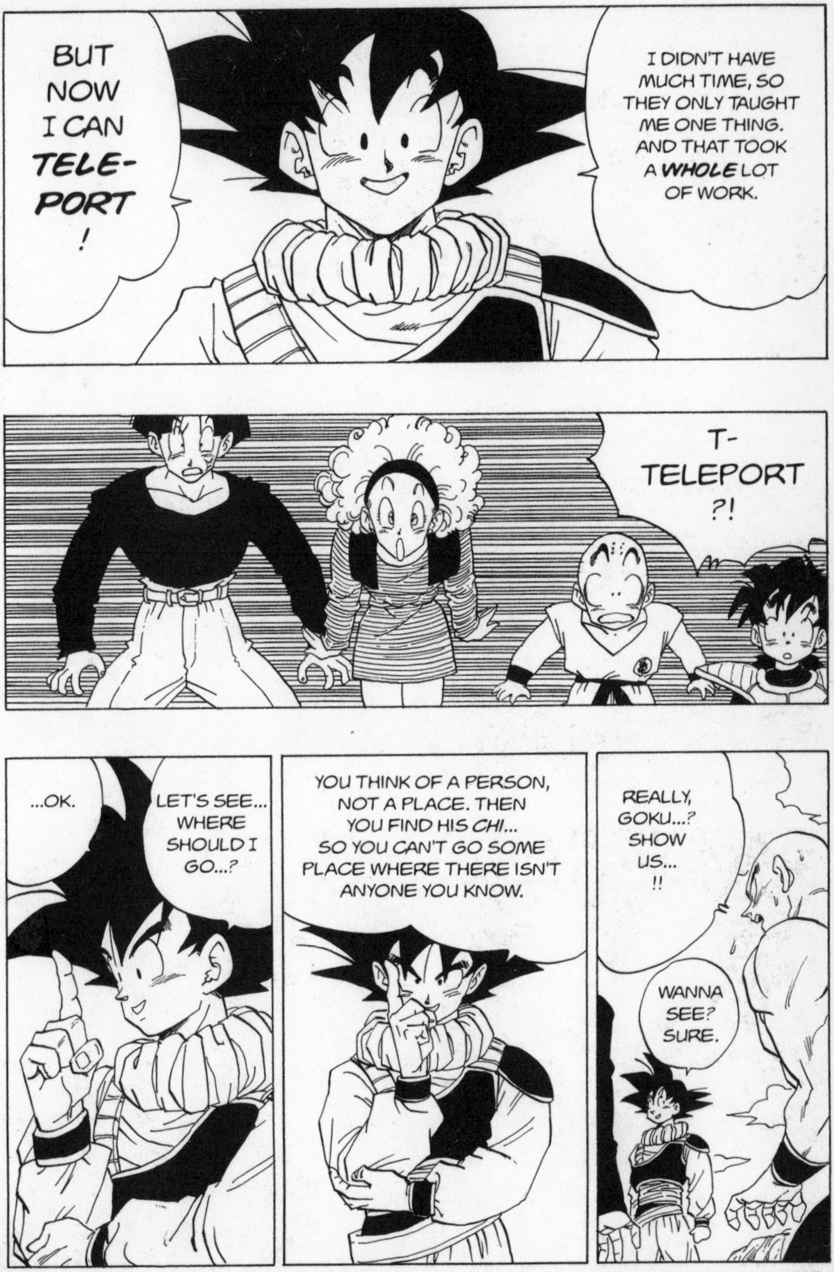
I DIDN'T HAVE MUCH TIME, SO THEY ONLY TAUGHT ME ONE THING. AND THAT TOOK A WHOLE LOT OF WORK.
BUT NOW I CAN TELE-PORT!
T-TELEPORT?!
REALLY, GOKU...? SHOW US...!!
WANNA SEE? SURE.
YOU THINK OF A PERSON, NOT A PLACE. THEN YOU FIND HIS CHI... SO YOU CAN'T GO SOME PLACE WHERE THERE ISN'T ANYONE YOU KNOW.
LET'S SEE... WHERE SHOULD I GO...?
...OK.

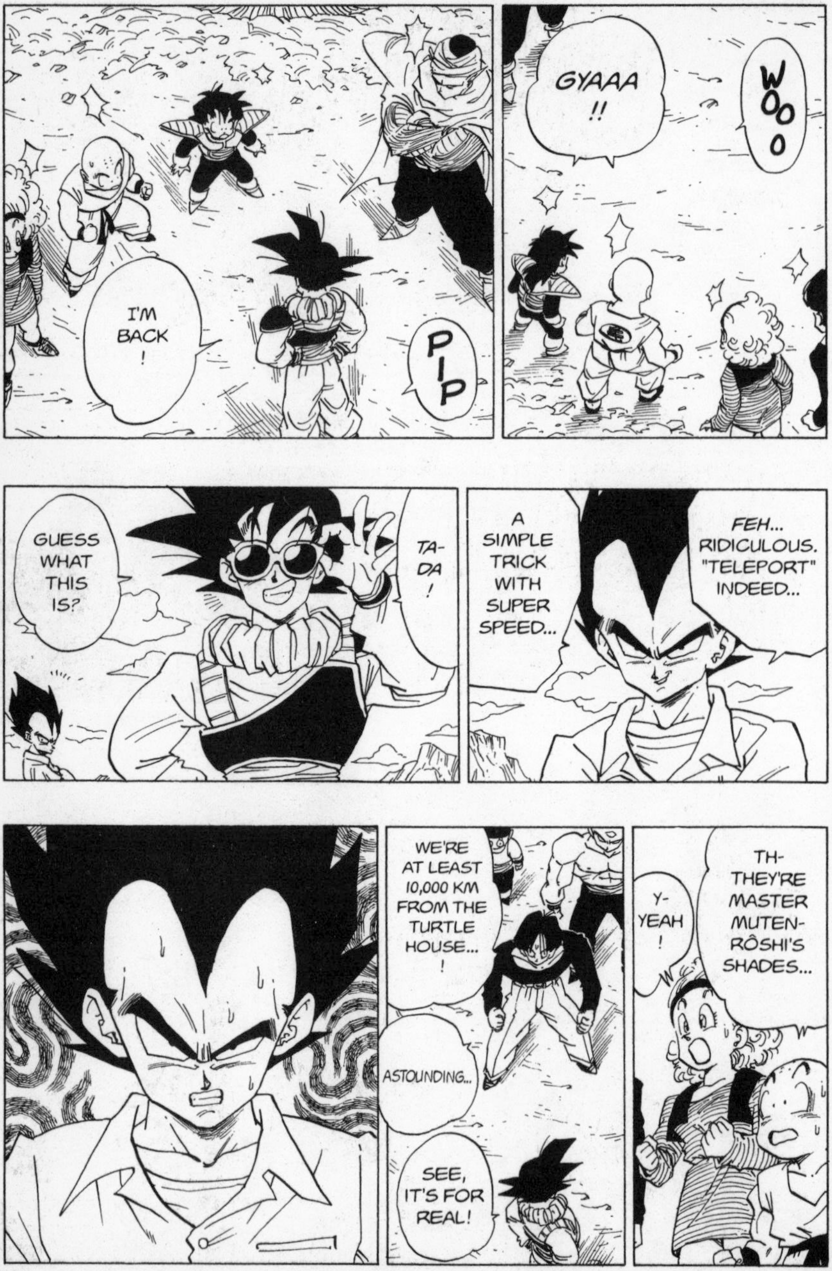
WOOO
GYAAA!!
PIP
I'M BACK!
FEH... RIDICULOUS. "TELEPORT" INDEED...
A SIMPLE TRICK WITH SUPER SPEED...
TA-DA!
GUESS WHAT THIS IS?
TH- THEY'RE MASTER MUTEN-RÔSHI'S SHADES...
Y-YEAH!
WE'RE AT LEAST 10,000 KM FROM THE TURTLE HOUSE...!
ASTOUNDING...
SEE, IT'S FOR REAL!

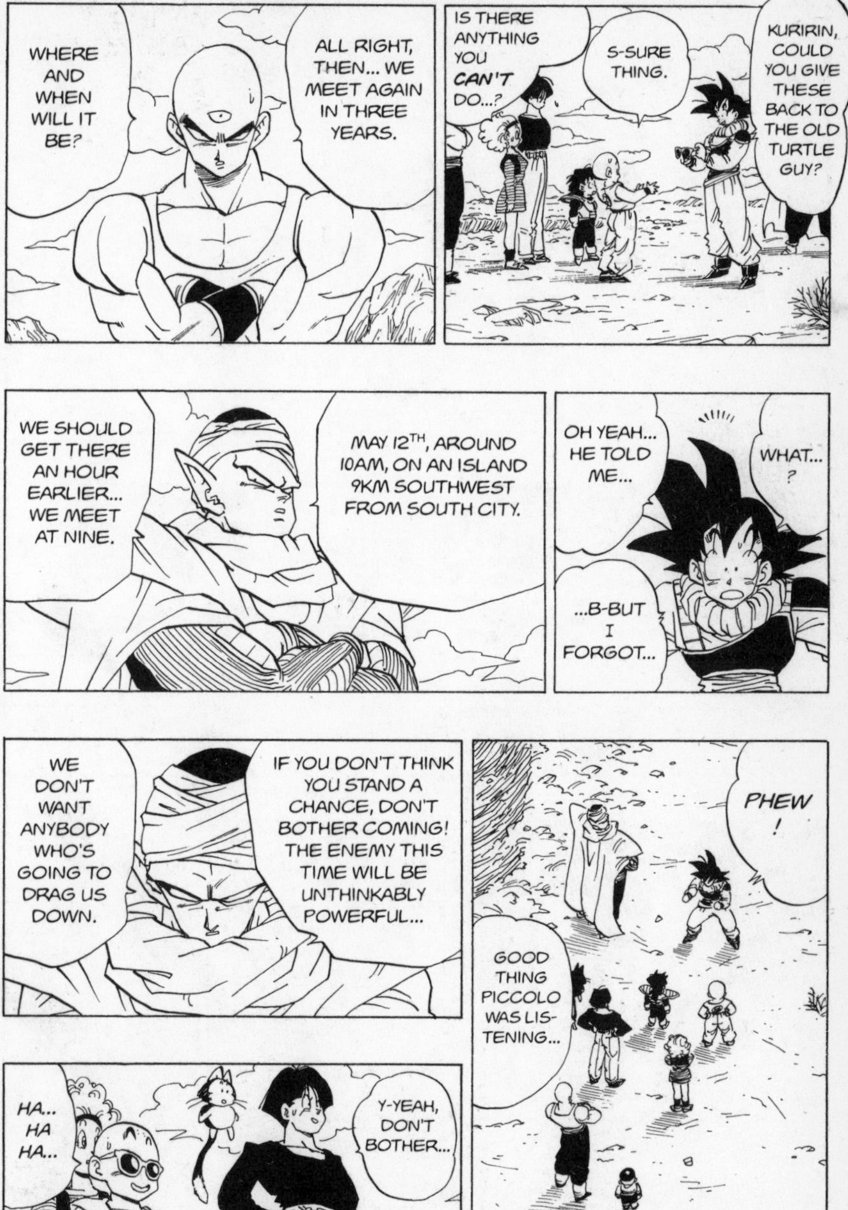
KURIRIN, COULD YOU GIVE THESE BACK TO THE OLD TURTLE GUY?
S-SURE THING.
IS THERE ANYTHING YOU *CAN'T* DO...?
ALL RIGHT, THEN... WE MEET AGAIN IN THREE YEARS.
WHERE AND WHEN WILL IT BE?
WHAT...?
OH YEAH... HE TOLD ME...
...B-BUT I FORGOT...
MAY 12TH, AROUND 10AM, ON AN ISLAND 9KM SOUTHWEST FROM SOUTH CITY.
WE SHOULD GET THERE AN HOUR EARLIER... WE MEET AT NINE.
PHEW!
GOOD THING PICCOLO WAS LIS-TENING...
IF YOU DON'T THINK YOU STAND A CHANCE, DON'T BOTHER COMING! THE ENEMY THIS TIME WILL BE UNTHINKABLY POWERFUL...
WE DON'T WANT ANYBODY WHO'S GOING TO DRAG US DOWN.
Y-YEAH, DON'T BOTHER...
HA... HA HA...

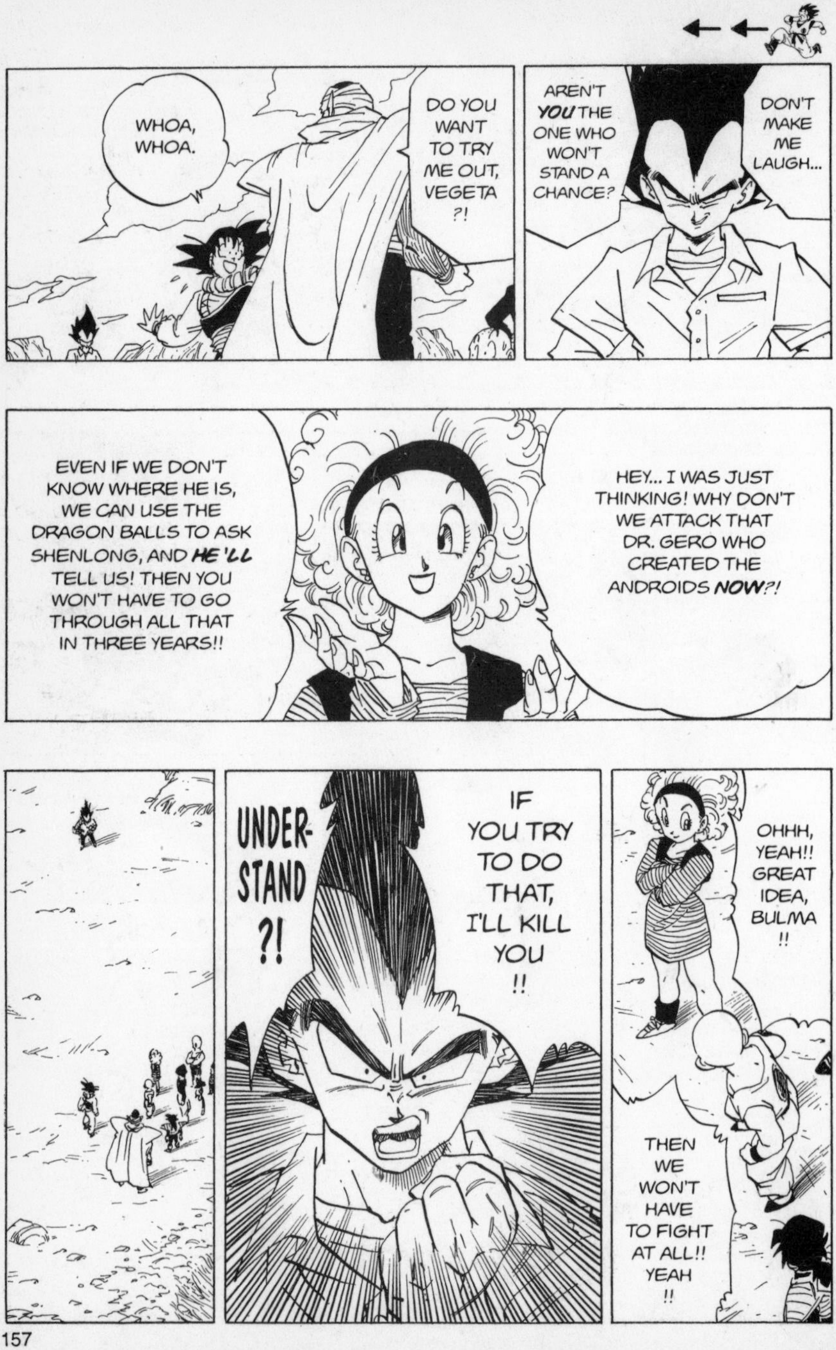
DON'T MAKE ME LAUGH...
AREN'T *YOU* THE ONE WHO WON'T STAND A CHANCE?
DO YOU WANT TO TRY ME OUT, VEGETA?!
WHOA, WHOA.
HEY... I WAS JUST THINKING! WHY DON'T WE ATTACK THAT DR. GERO WHO CREATED THE ANDROIDS *NOW*?!
EVEN IF WE DON'T KNOW WHERE HE IS, WE CAN USE THE DRAGON BALLS TO ASK SHENLONG, AND *HE'LL* TELL US! THEN YOU WON'T HAVE TO GO THROUGH ALL THAT IN THREE YEARS!!
OHHH, YEAH!! GREAT IDEA, BULMA!!
THEN WE WON'T HAVE TO FIGHT AT ALL!! YEAH!!
IF YOU TRY TO DO THAT, I'LL KILL YOU!!
UNDER-STAND?!

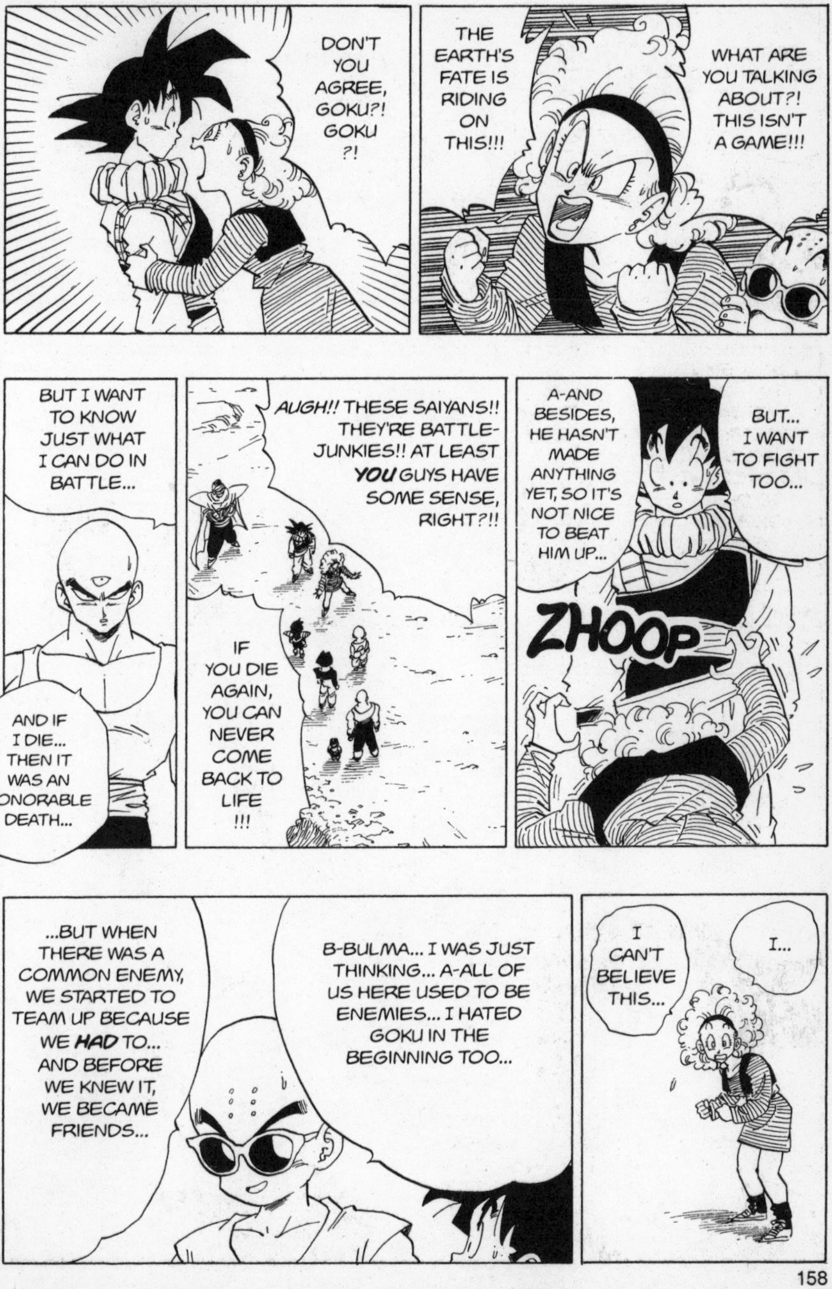
WHAT ARE YOU TALKING ABOUT?! THIS ISN'T A GAME!!!
THE EARTH'S FATE IS RIDING ON THIS!!!
DON'T YOU AGREE, GOKU?! GOKU ?!
BUT... I WANT TO FIGHT TOO...
A-AND BESIDES, HE HASN'T MADE ANYTHING YET, SO IT'S NOT NICE TO BEAT HIM UP...
ZHOOP
AUGH!! THESE SAIYANS!! THEY'RE BATTLE-JUNKIES!! AT LEAST YOU GUYS HAVE SOME SENSE, RIGHT?!!
IF YOU DIE AGAIN, YOU CAN NEVER COME BACK TO LIFE !!!
BUT I WANT TO KNOW JUST WHAT I CAN DO IN BATTLE...
AND IF I DIE... THEN IT WAS AN HONORABLE DEATH...
I...
I CAN'T BELIEVE THIS...
B-BULMA... I WAS JUST THINKING... A-ALL OF US HERE USED TO BE ENEMIES... I HATED GOKU IN THE BEGINNING TOO...
...BUT WHEN THERE WAS A COMMON ENEMY, WE STARTED TO TEAM UP BECAUSE WE HAD TO... AND BEFORE WE KNEW IT, WE BECAME FRIENDS...

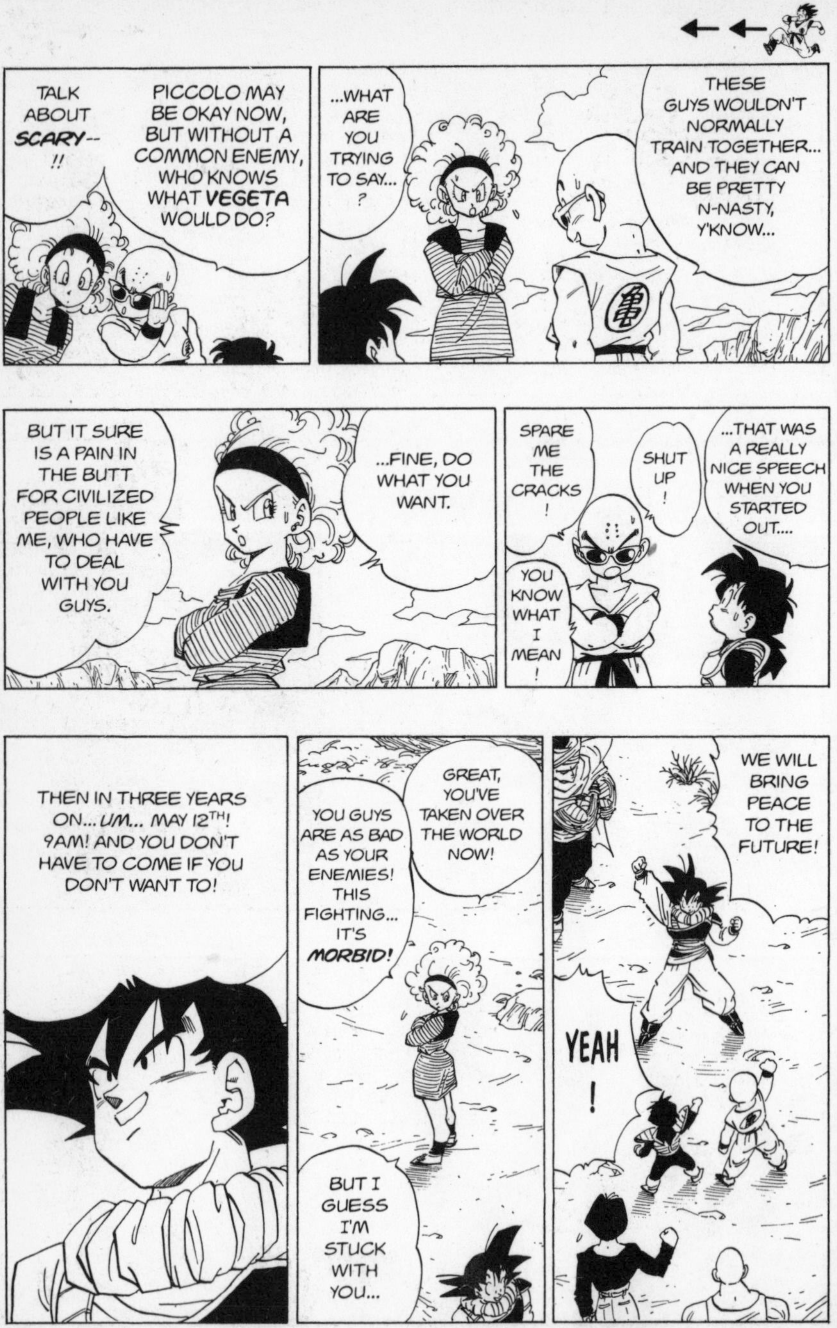

THESE GUYS WOULDN'T NORMALLY TRAIN TOGETHER... AND THEY CAN BE PRETTY N-NASTY, Y'KNOW...
...WHAT ARE YOU TRYING TO SAY...?
PICCOLO MAY BE OKAY NOW, BUT WITHOUT A COMMON ENEMY, WHO KNOWS WHAT **VEGETA** WOULD DO?
TALK ABOUT ***SCARY***--!!
...THAT WAS A REALLY NICE SPEECH WHEN YOU STARTED OUT....
SHUT UP!
SPARE ME THE CRACKS!
YOU KNOW WHAT I MEAN!
...FINE, DO WHAT YOU WANT.
BUT IT SURE IS A PAIN IN THE BUTT FOR CIVILIZED PEOPLE LIKE ME, WHO HAVE TO DEAL WITH YOU GUYS.
WE WILL BRING PEACE TO THE FUTURE!
YEAH!
GREAT, YOU'VE TAKEN OVER THE WORLD NOW!
YOU GUYS ARE AS BAD AS YOUR ENEMIES! THIS FIGHTING... IT'S ***MORBID!***
BUT I GUESS I'M STUCK WITH YOU...
THEN IN THREE YEARS ON... *UM...* MAY 12TH! 9AM! AND YOU DON'T HAVE TO COME IF YOU DON'T WANT TO!

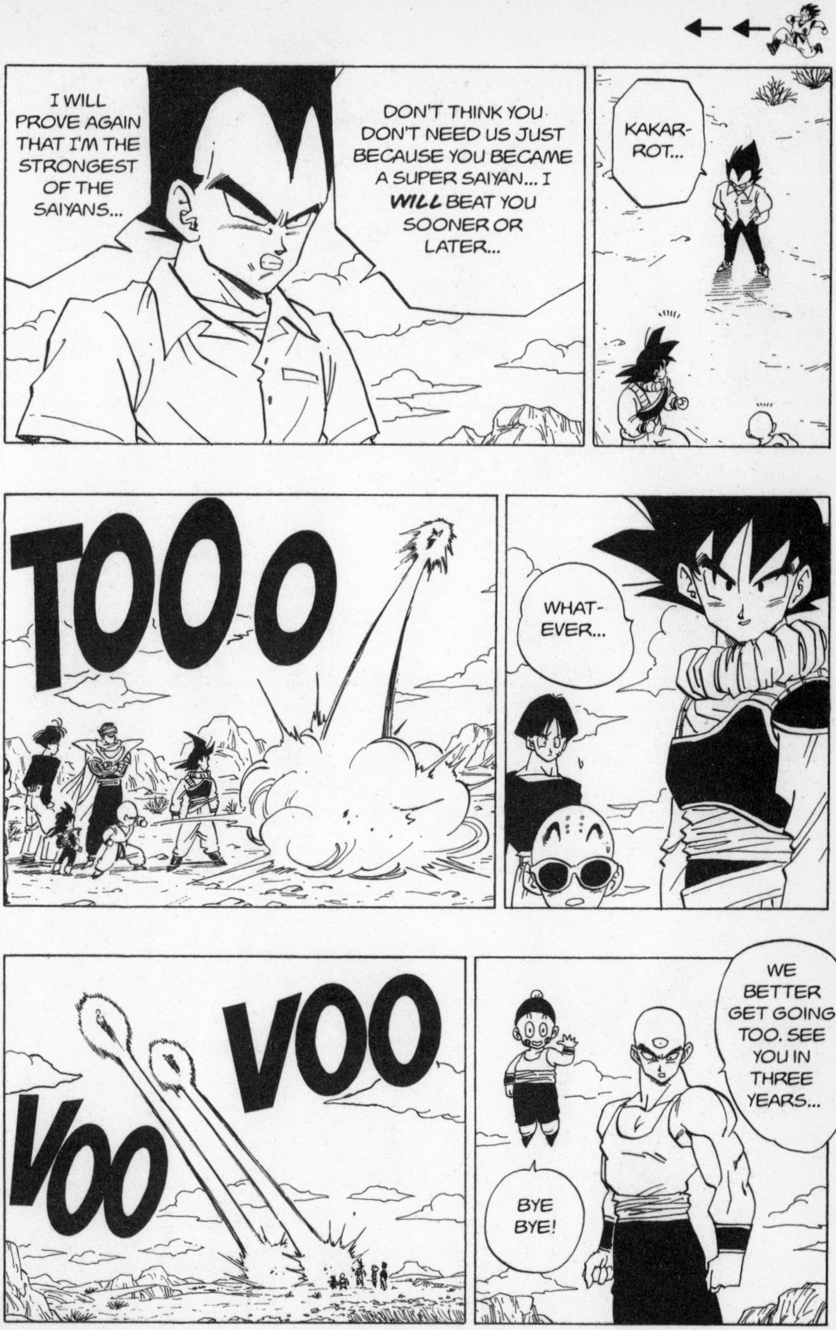
KAKAR-ROT...
DON'T THINK YOU DON'T NEED US JUST BECAUSE YOU BECAME A SUPER SAIYAN... I **WILL** BEAT YOU SOONER OR LATER...
I WILL PROVE AGAIN THAT I'M THE STRONGEST OF THE SAIYANS...
WHAT-EVER...
TOOO
WE BETTER GET GOING TOO. SEE YOU IN THREE YEARS...
BYE BYE!
VOO
VOO

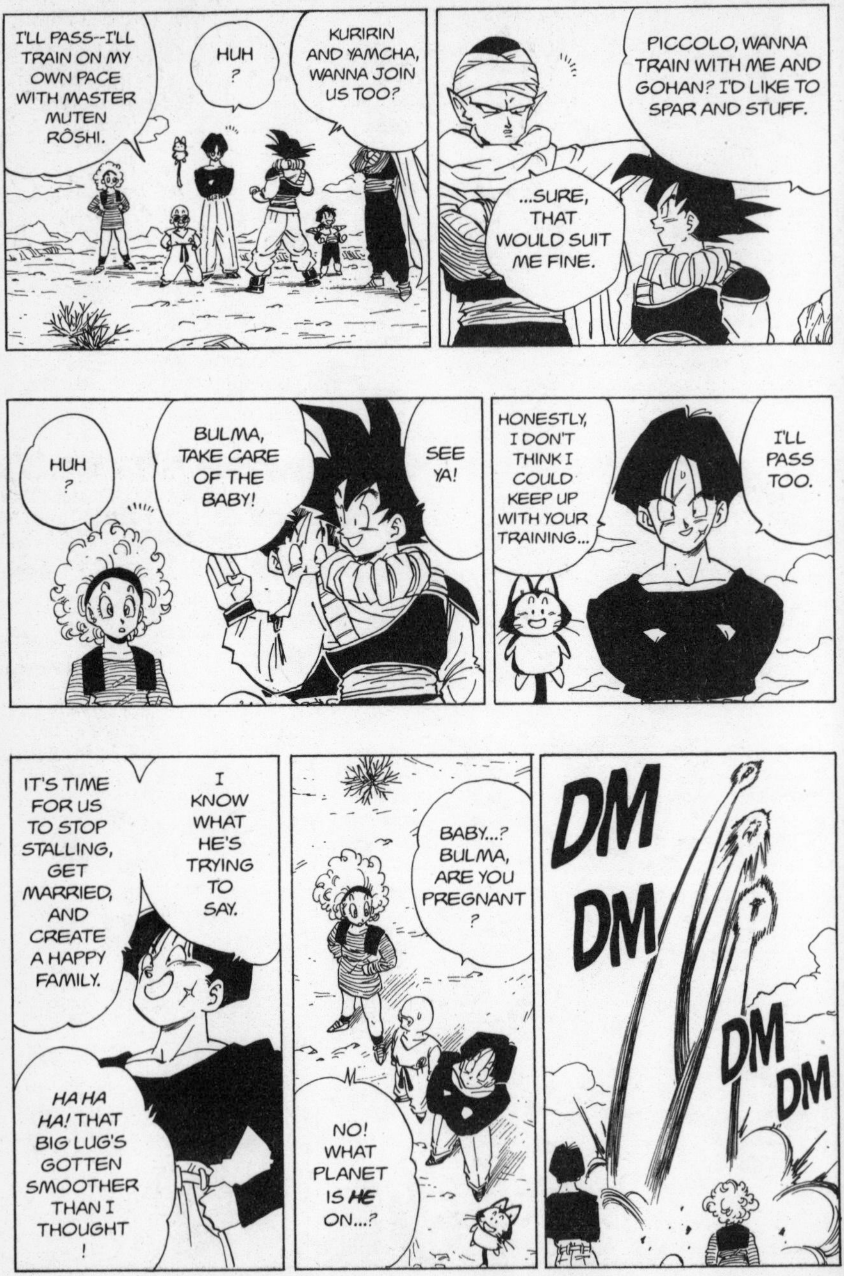
PICCOLO, WANNA TRAIN WITH ME AND GOHAN? I'D LIKE TO SPAR AND STUFF.
...SURE, THAT WOULD SUIT ME FINE.
KURIRIN AND YAMCHA, WANNA JOIN US TOO?
HUH ?
I'LL PASS--I'LL TRAIN ON MY OWN PACE WITH MASTER MUTEN RÔSHI.
I'LL PASS TOO.
HONESTLY, I DON'T THINK I COULD KEEP UP WITH YOUR TRAINING...
SEE YA!
BULMA, TAKE CARE OF THE BABY!
HUH ?
DM
DM
DM
DM
BABY...? BULMA, ARE YOU PREGNANT ?
NO! WHAT PLANET IS *HE* ON...?
I KNOW WHAT HE'S TRYING TO SAY.
IT'S TIME FOR US TO STOP STALLING, GET MARRIED, AND CREATE A HAPPY FAMILY.
HA HA HA! THAT BIG LUG'S GOTTEN SMOOTHER THAN I THOUGHT !

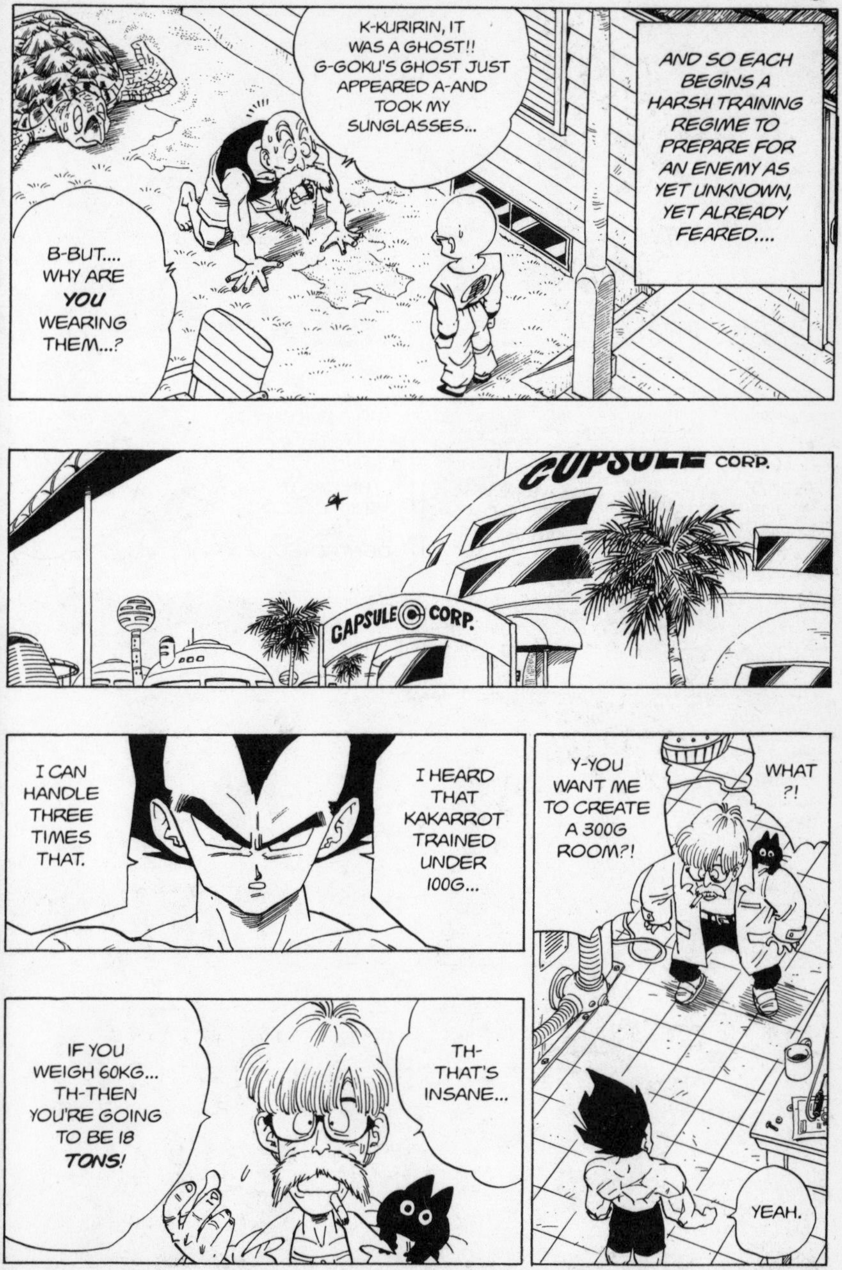
AND SO EACH BEGINS A HARSH TRAINING REGIME TO PREPARE FOR AN ENEMY AS YET UNKNOWN, YET ALREADY FEARED....
K-KURIRIN, IT WAS A GHOST!! G-GOKU'S GHOST JUST APPEARED A-AND TOOK MY SUNGLASSES...
B-BUT.... WHY ARE *YOU* WEARING THEM...?
CAPSULE CORP.
CAPSULE CORP.
WHAT ?!
Y-YOU WANT ME TO CREATE A 300G ROOM?!
YEAH.
I HEARD THAT KAKARROT TRAINED UNDER 100G...
I CAN HANDLE THREE TIMES THAT.
TH- THAT'S INSANE...
IF YOU WEIGH 60KG... TH-THEN YOU'RE GOING TO BE 18 *TONS*!

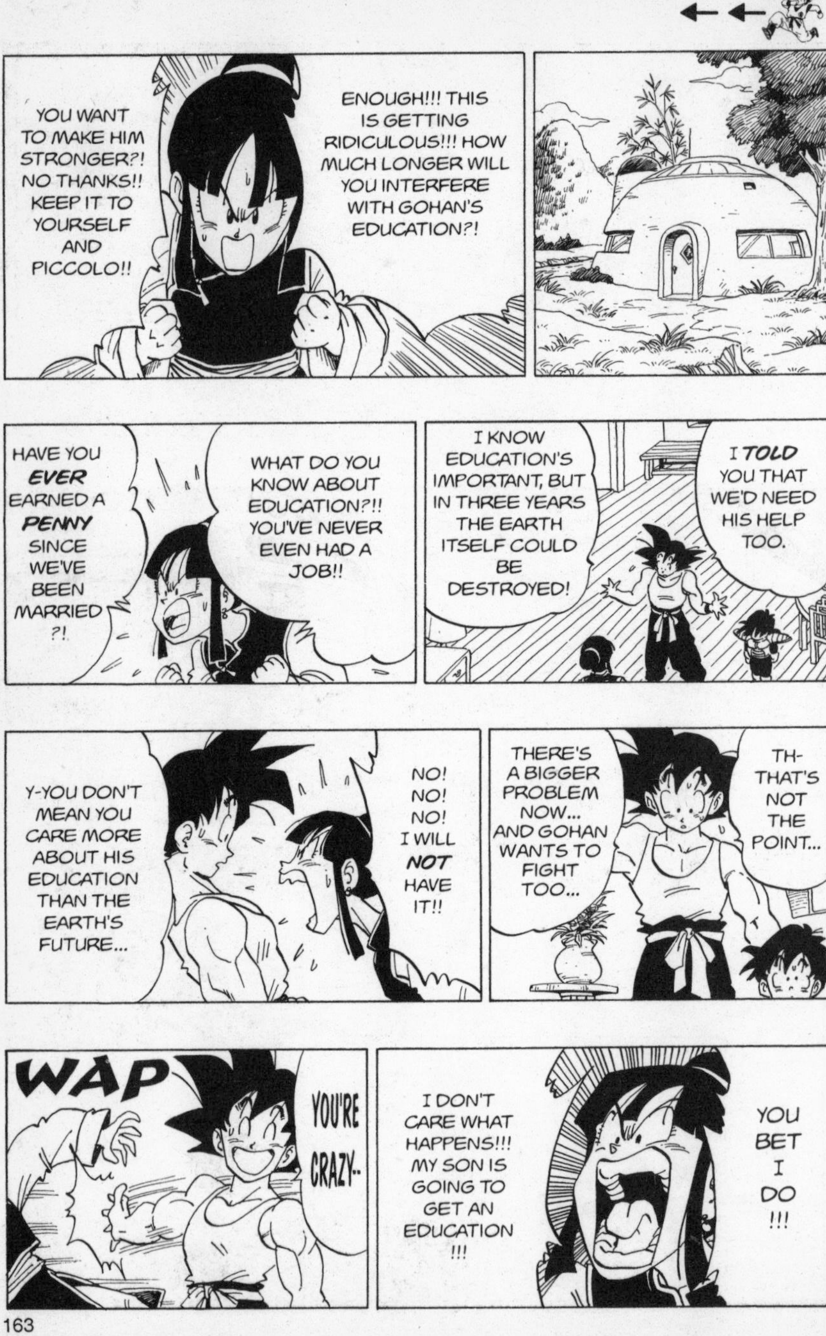
ENOUGH!!! THIS IS GETTING RIDICULOUS!!! HOW MUCH LONGER WILL YOU INTERFERE WITH GOHAN'S EDUCATION?!
YOU WANT TO MAKE HIM STRONGER?! NO THANKS!! KEEP IT TO YOURSELF AND PICCOLO!!
I TOLD YOU THAT WE'D NEED HIS HELP TOO.
I KNOW EDUCATION'S IMPORTANT, BUT IN THREE YEARS THE EARTH ITSELF COULD BE DESTROYED!
WHAT DO YOU KNOW ABOUT EDUCATION?!! YOU'VE NEVER EVEN HAD A JOB!!
HAVE YOU EVER EARNED A PENNY SINCE WE'VE BEEN MARRIED ?!
TH- THAT'S NOT THE POINT...
THERE'S A BIGGER PROBLEM NOW... AND GOHAN WANTS TO FIGHT TOO...
NO! NO! NO! I WILL NOT HAVE IT!!
Y-YOU DON'T MEAN YOU CARE MORE ABOUT HIS EDUCATION THAN THE EARTH'S FUTURE...
YOU BET I DO !!!
I DON'T CARE WHAT HAPPENS!!! MY SON IS GOING TO GET AN EDUCATION !!!
YOU'RE CRAZY..
WAP

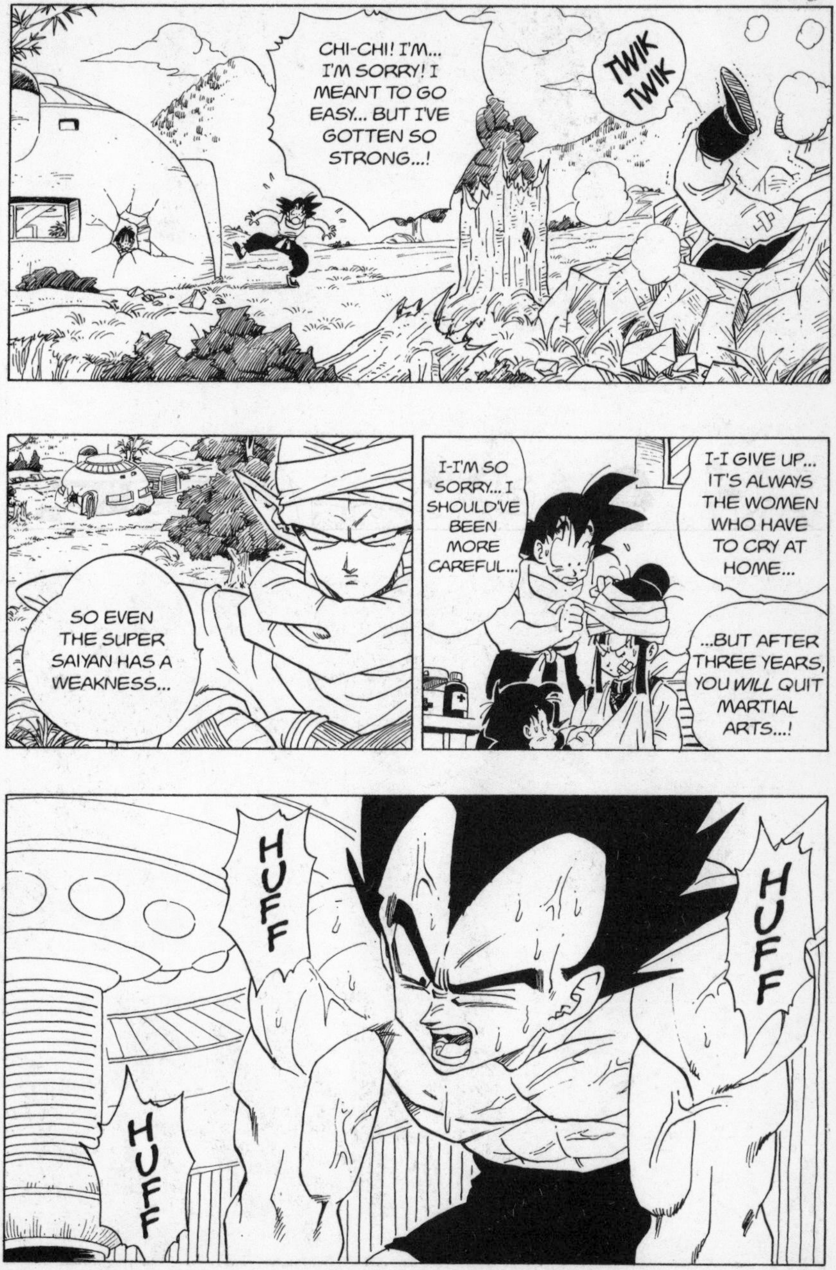
TWIK TWIK
CHI-CHI! I'M... I'M SORRY! I MEANT TO GO EASY... BUT I'VE GOTTEN SO STRONG...!
I-I GIVE UP... IT'S ALWAYS THE WOMEN WHO HAVE TO CRY AT HOME...
I-I'M SO SORRY... I SHOULD'VE BEEN MORE CAREFUL...
...BUT AFTER THREE YEARS, YOU *WILL* QUIT MARTIAL ARTS...!
SO EVEN THE SUPER SAIYAN HAS A WEAKNESS...
HUFF
HUFF
HUFF

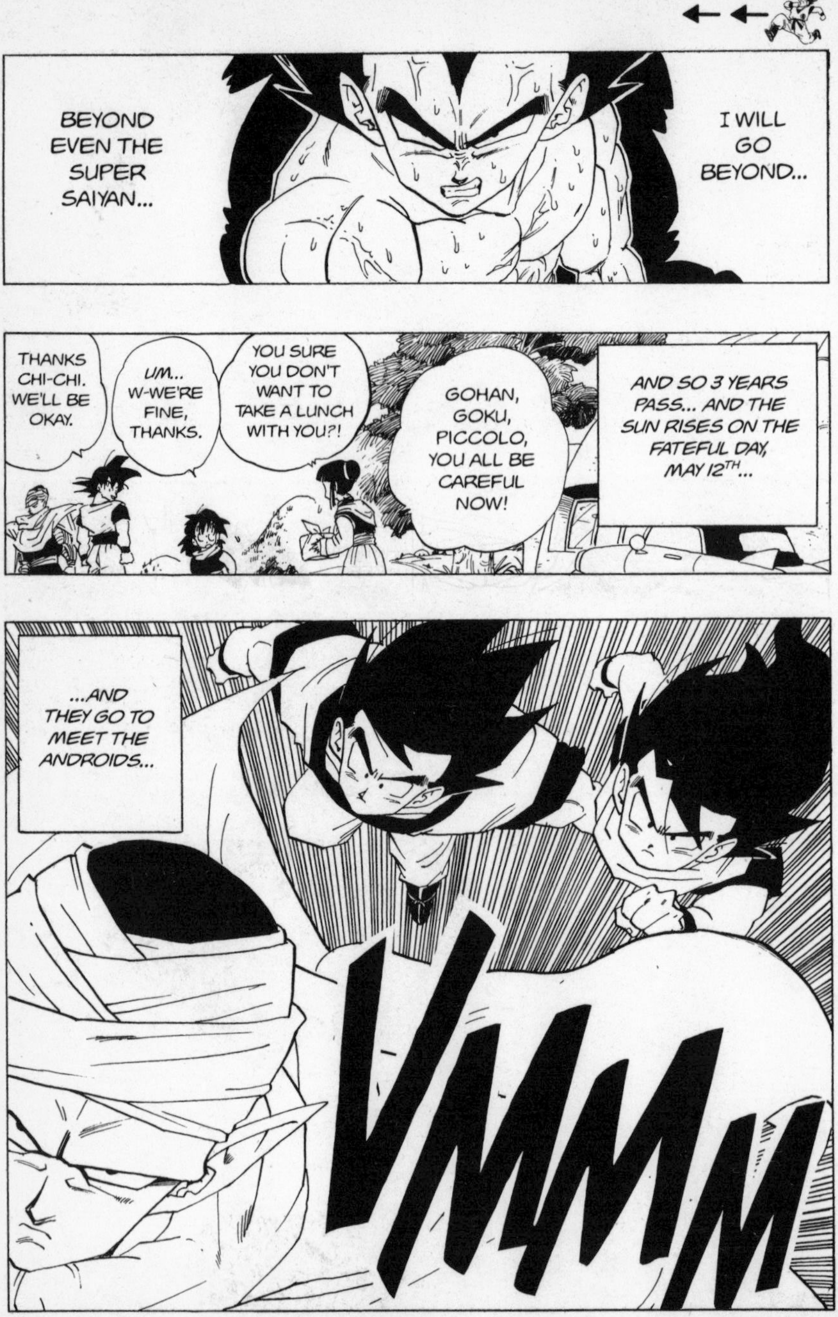
I WILL GO BEYOND...
BEYOND EVEN THE SUPER SAIYAN...
AND SO 3 YEARS PASS... AND THE SUN RISES ON THE FATEFUL DAY, MAY 12TH...
GOHAN, GOKU, PICCOLO, YOU ALL BE CAREFUL NOW!
YOU SURE YOU DON'T WANT TO TAKE A LUNCH WITH YOU?!
UM... W-WE'RE FINE, THANKS.
THANKS CHI-CHI. WE'LL BE OKAY.
...AND THEY GO TO MEET THE ANDROIDS...
VMMM

NEXT: SUPER WARRIORS, GET READY!

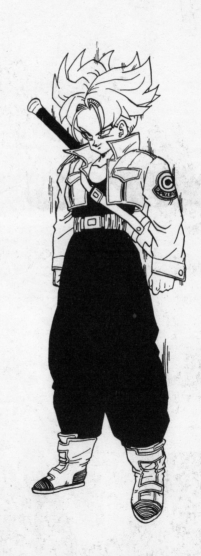

DBZ: 143 • The Gathering of the Warriors

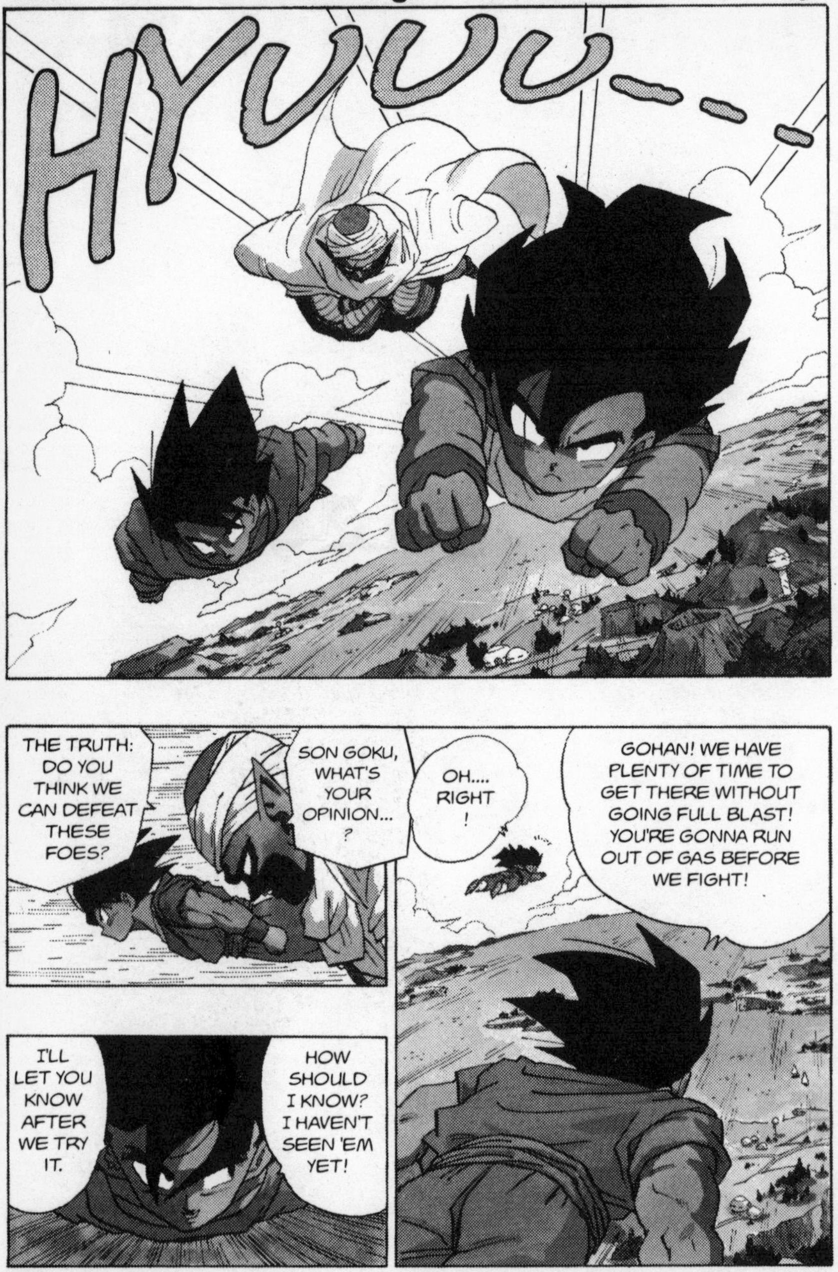
HYUUU---
GOHAN! WE HAVE PLENTY OF TIME TO GET THERE WITHOUT GOING FULL BLAST! YOU'RE GONNA RUN OUT OF GAS BEFORE WE FIGHT!
OH.... RIGHT!
SON GOKU, WHAT'S YOUR OPINION...?
THE TRUTH: DO YOU THINK WE CAN DEFEAT THESE FOES?
HOW SHOULD I KNOW? I HAVEN'T SEEN 'EM YET!
I'LL LET YOU KNOW AFTER WE TRY IT.

by AKIRA TORIYAMA

DBZ:143 • The Gathering of the Warriors

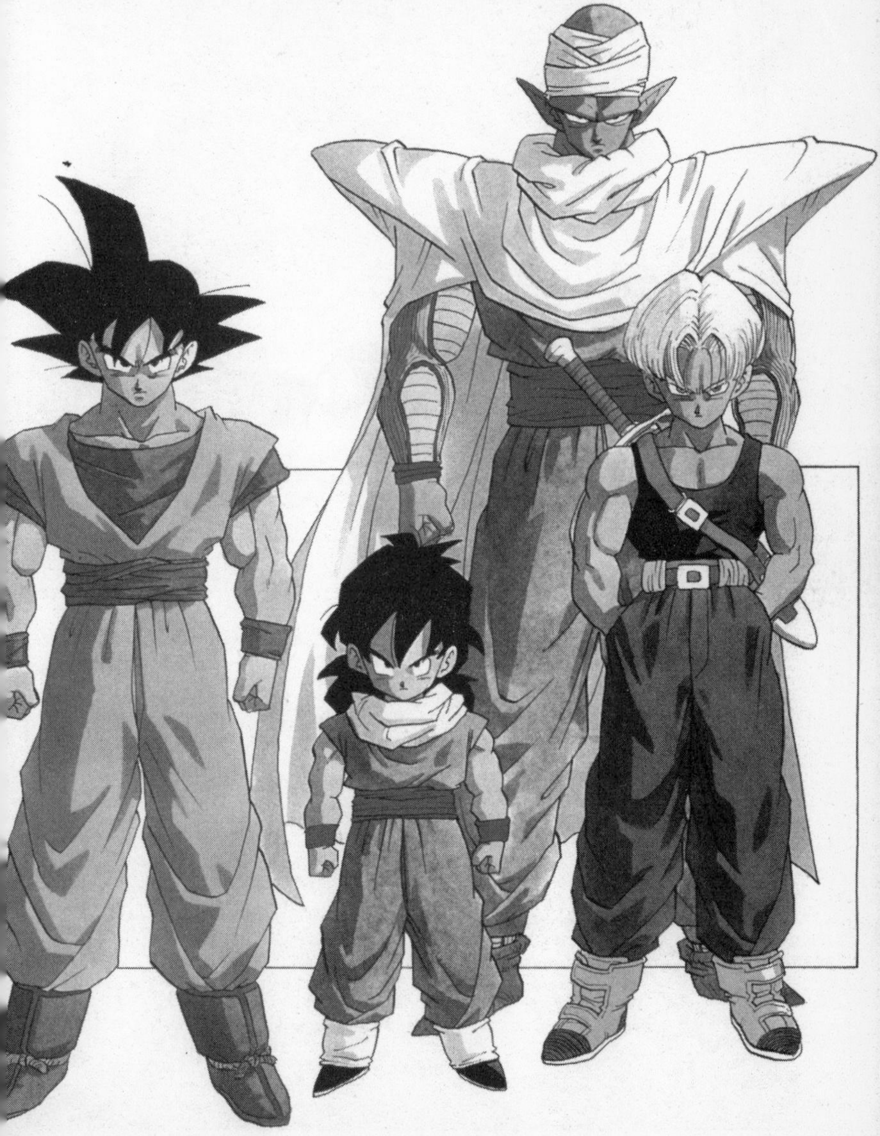

DRAGON BALL Z

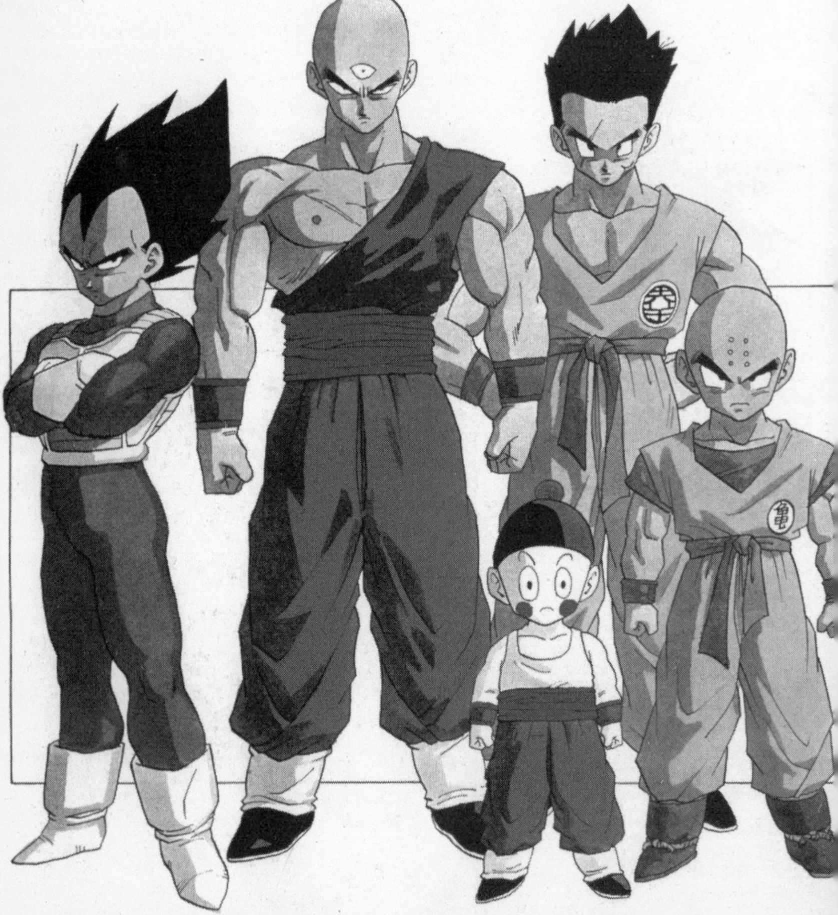

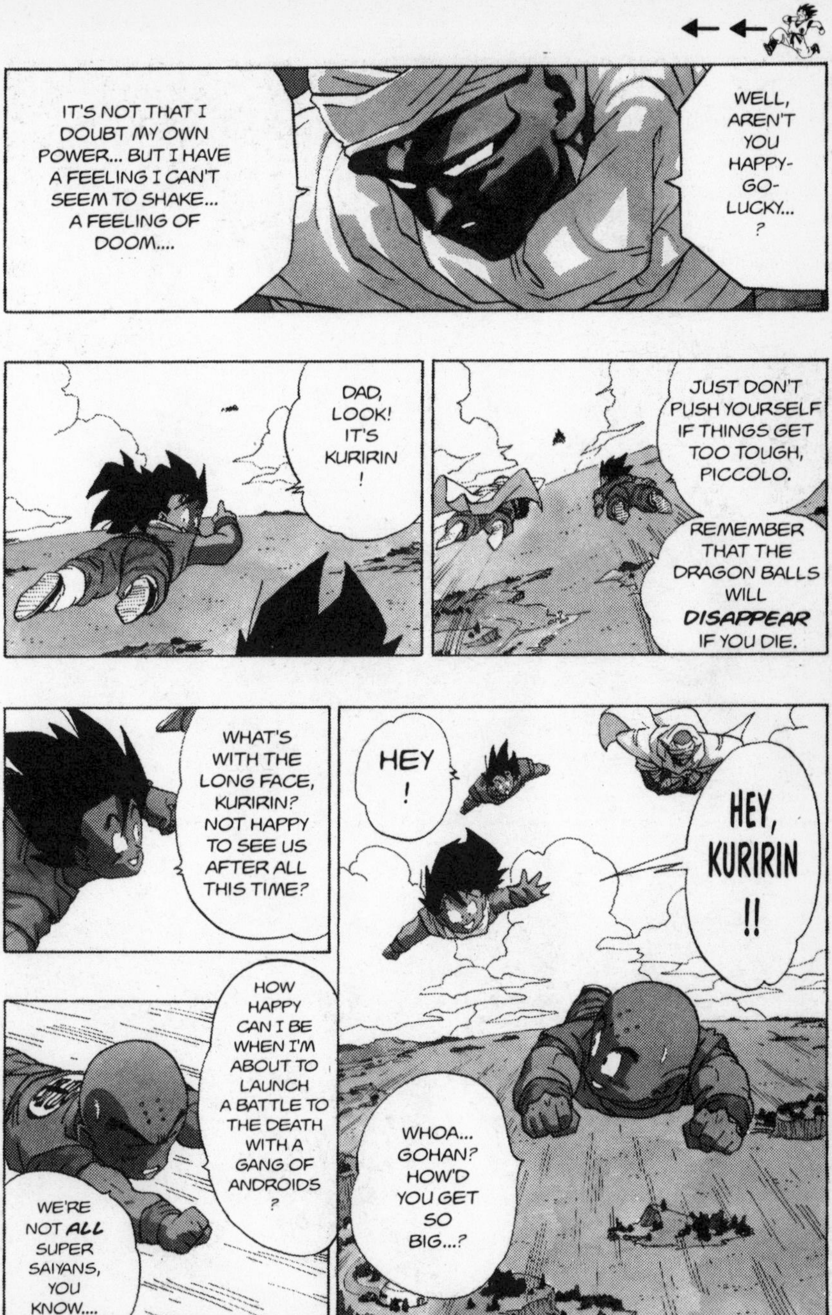
WELL, AREN'T YOU HAPPY-GO-LUCKY...?
IT'S NOT THAT I DOUBT MY OWN POWER... BUT I HAVE A FEELING I CAN'T SEEM TO SHAKE... A FEELING OF DOOM....
JUST DON'T PUSH YOURSELF IF THINGS GET TOO TOUGH, PICCOLO.
REMEMBER THAT THE DRAGON BALLS WILL **DISAPPEAR** IF YOU DIE.
DAD, LOOK! IT'S KURIRIN!
HEY, KURIRIN!!
HEY!
WHOA... GOHAN? HOW'D YOU GET SO BIG...?
WHAT'S WITH THE LONG FACE, KURIRIN? NOT HAPPY TO SEE US AFTER ALL THIS TIME?
HOW HAPPY CAN I BE WHEN I'M ABOUT TO LAUNCH A BATTLE TO THE DEATH WITH A GANG OF ANDROIDS?
WE'RE NOT **ALL** SUPER SAIYANS, YOU KNOW....

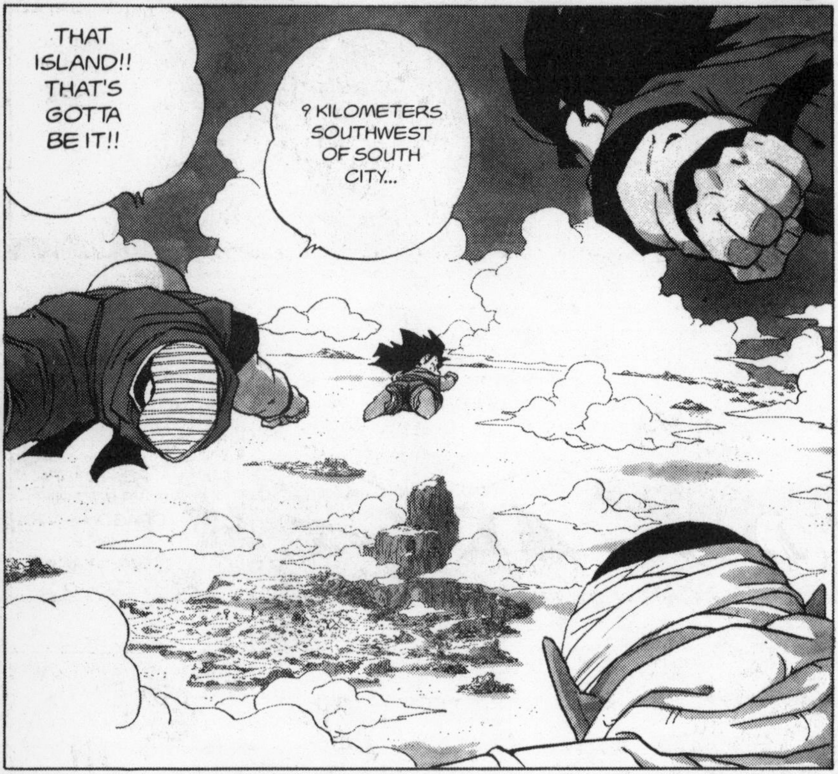
9 KILOMETERS SOUTHWEST OF SOUTH CITY...
THAT ISLAND!! THAT'S GOTTA BE IT!!

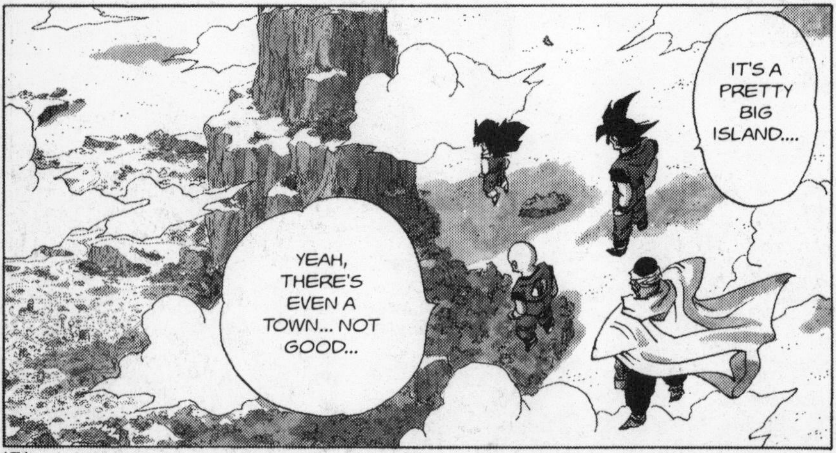
IT'S A PRETTY BIG ISLAND....
YEAH, THERE'S EVEN A TOWN... NOT GOOD...

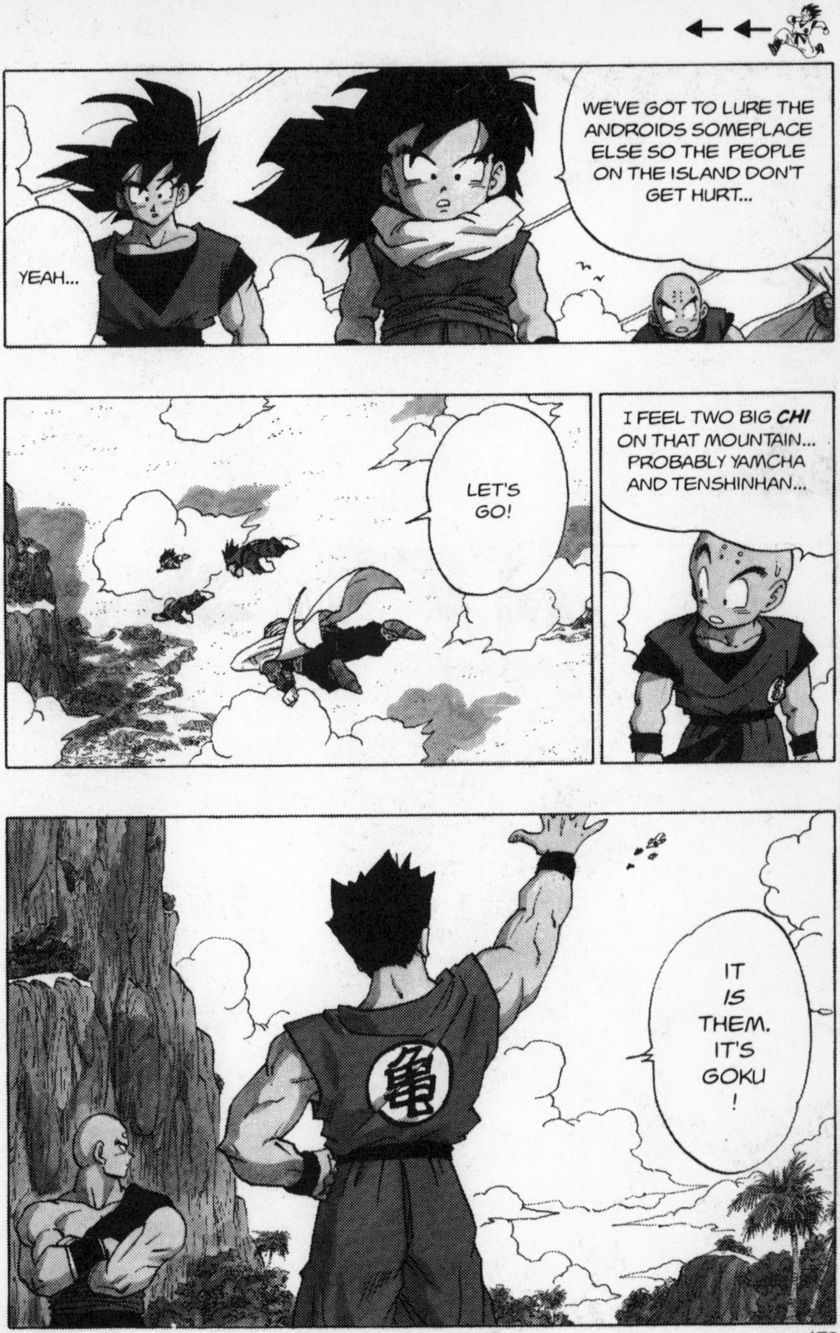
WE'VE GOT TO LURE THE ANDROIDS SOMEPLACE ELSE SO THE PEOPLE ON THE ISLAND DON'T GET HURT...
YEAH...
I FEEL TWO BIG *CHI* ON THAT MOUNTAIN... PROBABLY YAMCHA AND TENSHINHAN...
LET'S GO!
IT *IS* THEM. IT'S GOKU!

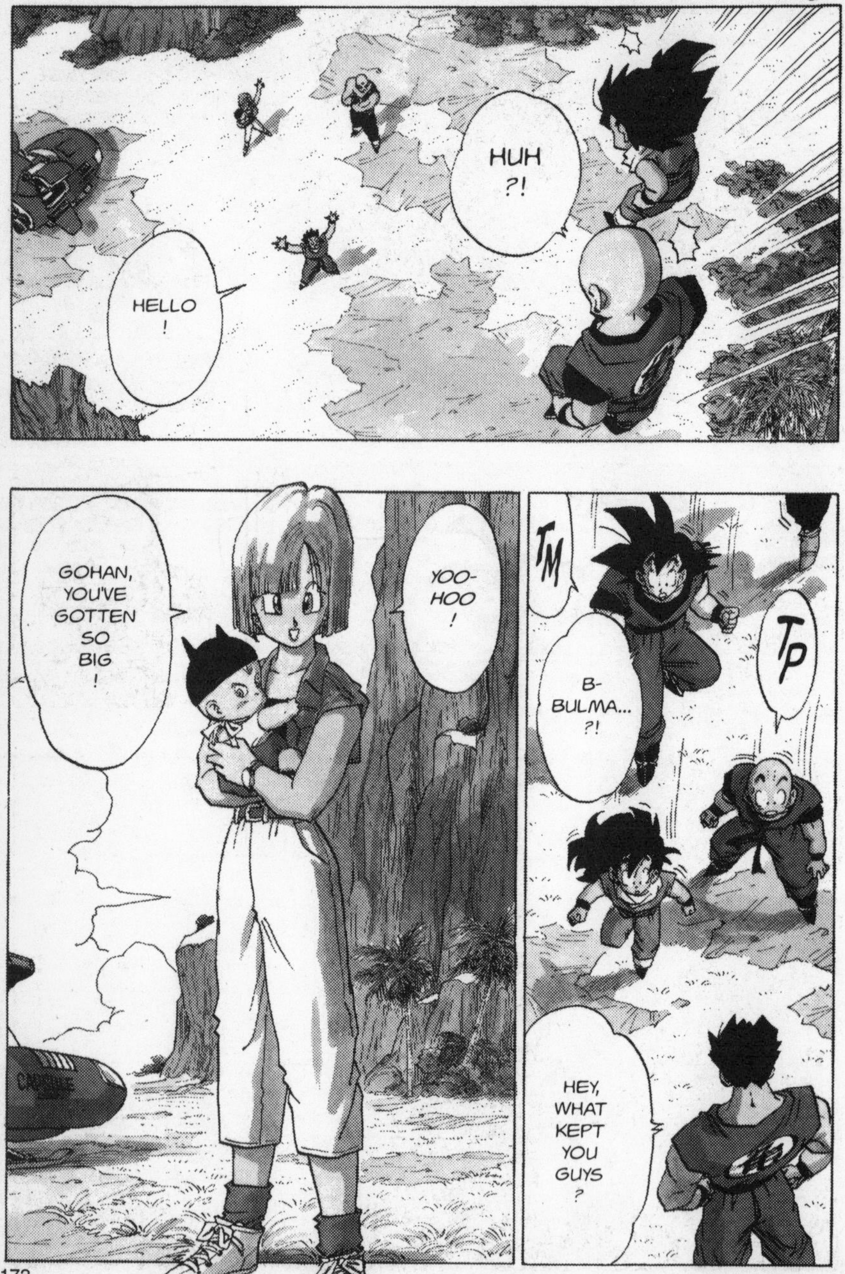
HUH ?!
HELLO !
TM
TP
B-BULMA...?!
HEY, WHAT KEPT YOU GUYS ?
YOO-HOO !
GOHAN, YOU'VE GOTTEN SO BIG !

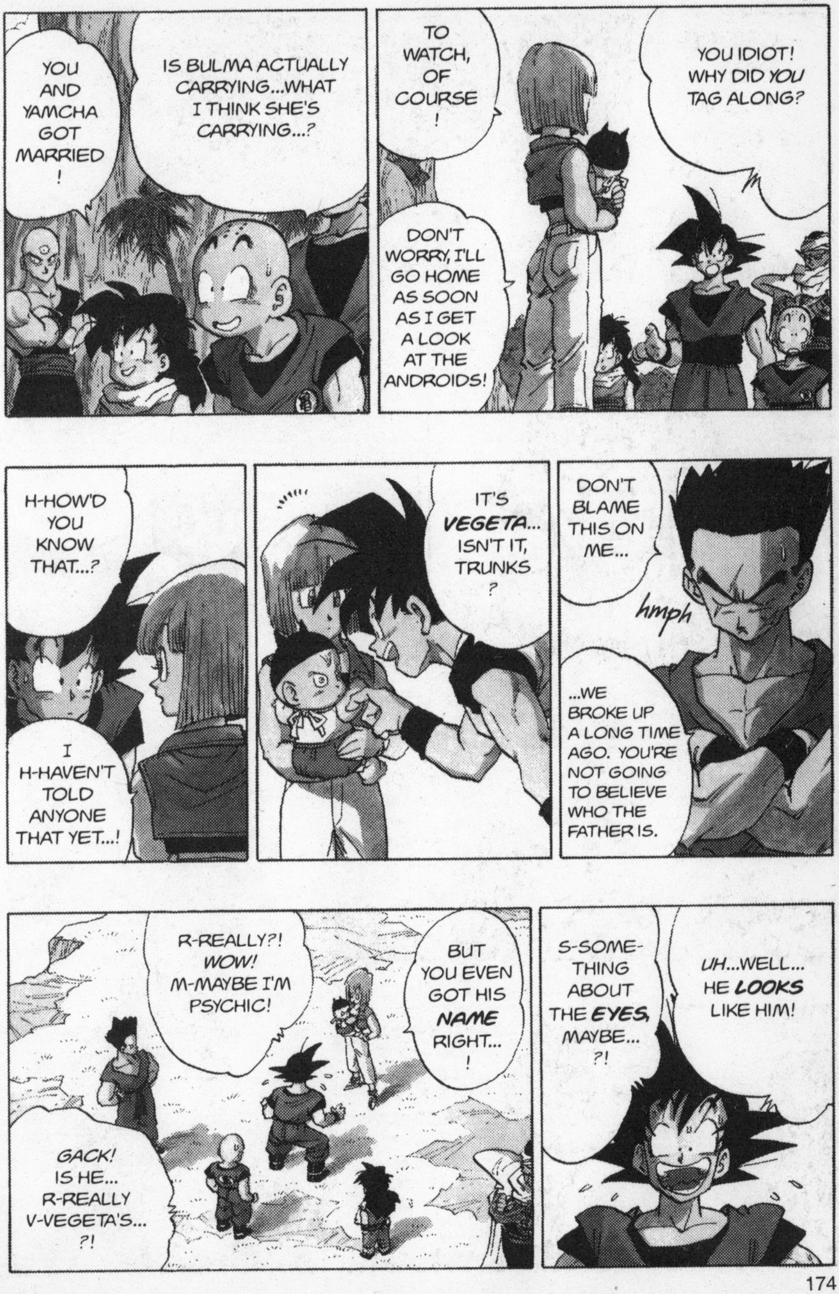
YOU IDIOT! WHY DID *YOU* TAG ALONG?
TO WATCH, OF COURSE!
DON'T WORRY, I'LL GO HOME AS SOON AS I GET A LOOK AT THE ANDROIDS!
IS BULMA ACTUALLY CARRYING...WHAT I THINK SHE'S CARRYING...?
YOU AND YAMCHA GOT MARRIED!
DON'T BLAME THIS ON ME...
hmph
...WE BROKE UP A LONG TIME AGO. YOU'RE NOT GOING TO BELIEVE WHO THE FATHER IS.
IT'S ***VEGETA***... ISN'T IT, TRUNKS?
H-HOW'D YOU KNOW THAT...?
I H-HAVEN'T TOLD ANYONE THAT YET...!
UH...WELL... HE ***LOOKS*** LIKE HIM!
S-SOMETHING ABOUT THE ***EYES,*** MAYBE...?!
BUT YOU EVEN GOT HIS ***NAME*** RIGHT...!
R-REALLY?! *WOW!* M-MAYBE I'M PSYCHIC!
GACK! IS HE... R-REALLY V-VEGETA'S...?!

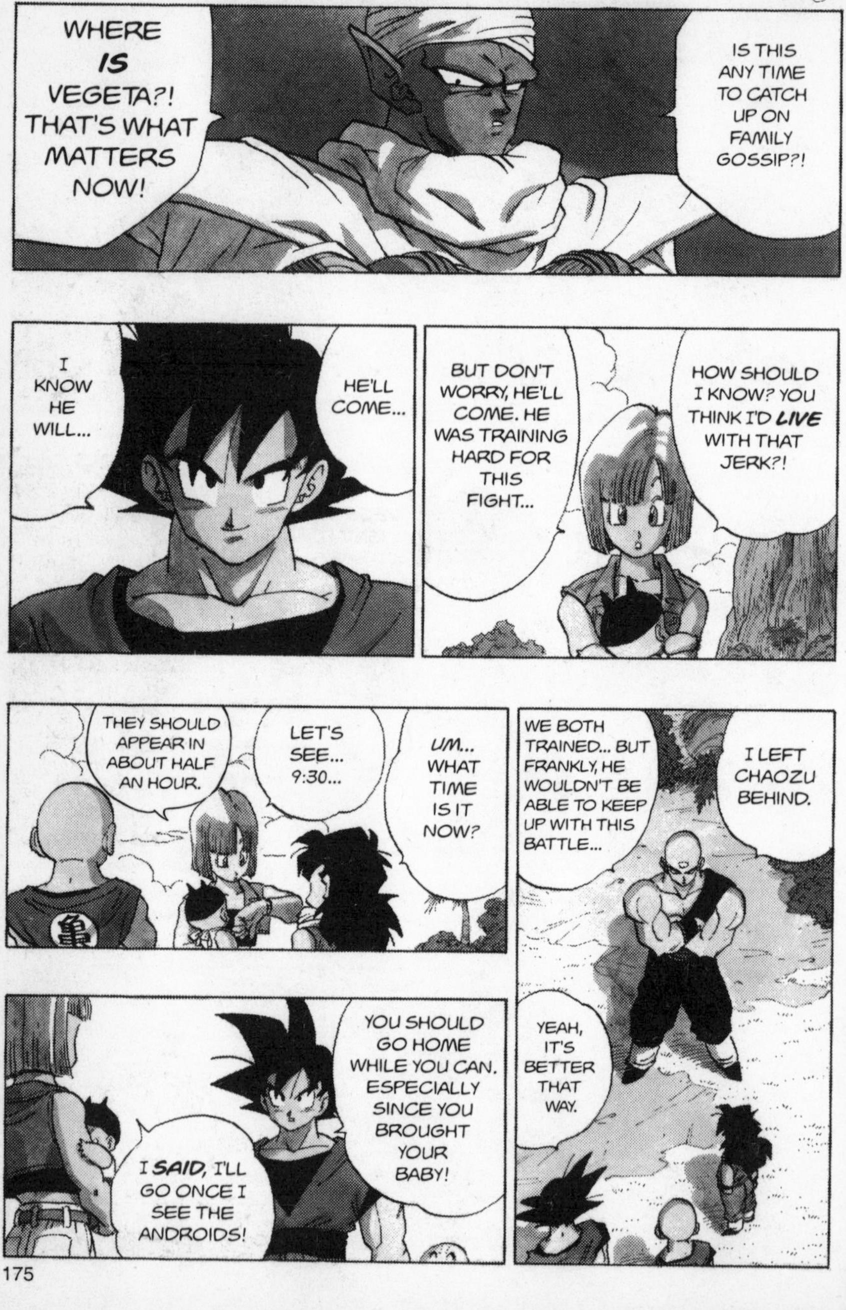
IS THIS ANY TIME TO CATCH UP ON FAMILY GOSSIP?!
WHERE IS VEGETA?! THAT'S WHAT MATTERS NOW!
HOW SHOULD I KNOW? YOU THINK I'D LIVE WITH THAT JERK?!
BUT DON'T WORRY, HE'LL COME. HE WAS TRAINING HARD FOR THIS FIGHT...
HE'LL COME...
I KNOW HE WILL...
I LEFT CHAOZU BEHIND.
WE BOTH TRAINED... BUT FRANKLY, HE WOULDN'T BE ABLE TO KEEP UP WITH THIS BATTLE...
YEAH, IT'S BETTER THAT WAY.
UM... WHAT TIME IS IT NOW?
LET'S SEE... 9:30...
THEY SHOULD APPEAR IN ABOUT HALF AN HOUR.
YOU SHOULD GO HOME WHILE YOU CAN. ESPECIALLY SINCE YOU BROUGHT YOUR BABY!
I SAID, I'LL GO ONCE I SEE THE ANDROIDS!

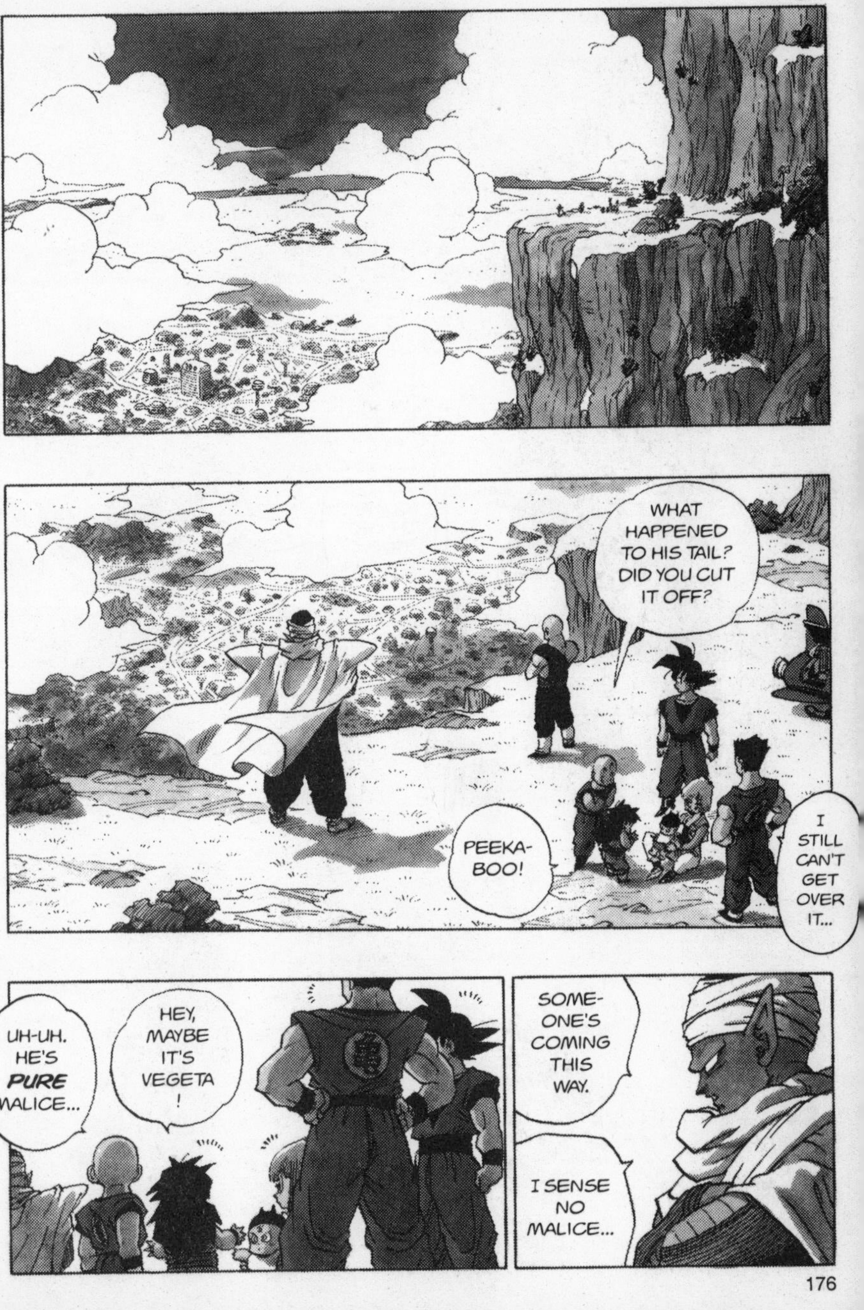
WHAT HAPPENED TO HIS TAIL? DID YOU CUT IT OFF?
I STILL CAN'T GET OVER IT...
PEEKA-BOO!
SOME-ONE'S COMING THIS WAY.
I SENSE NO MALICE...
HEY, MAYBE IT'S VEGETA!
UH-UH. HE'S **PURE** MALICE...

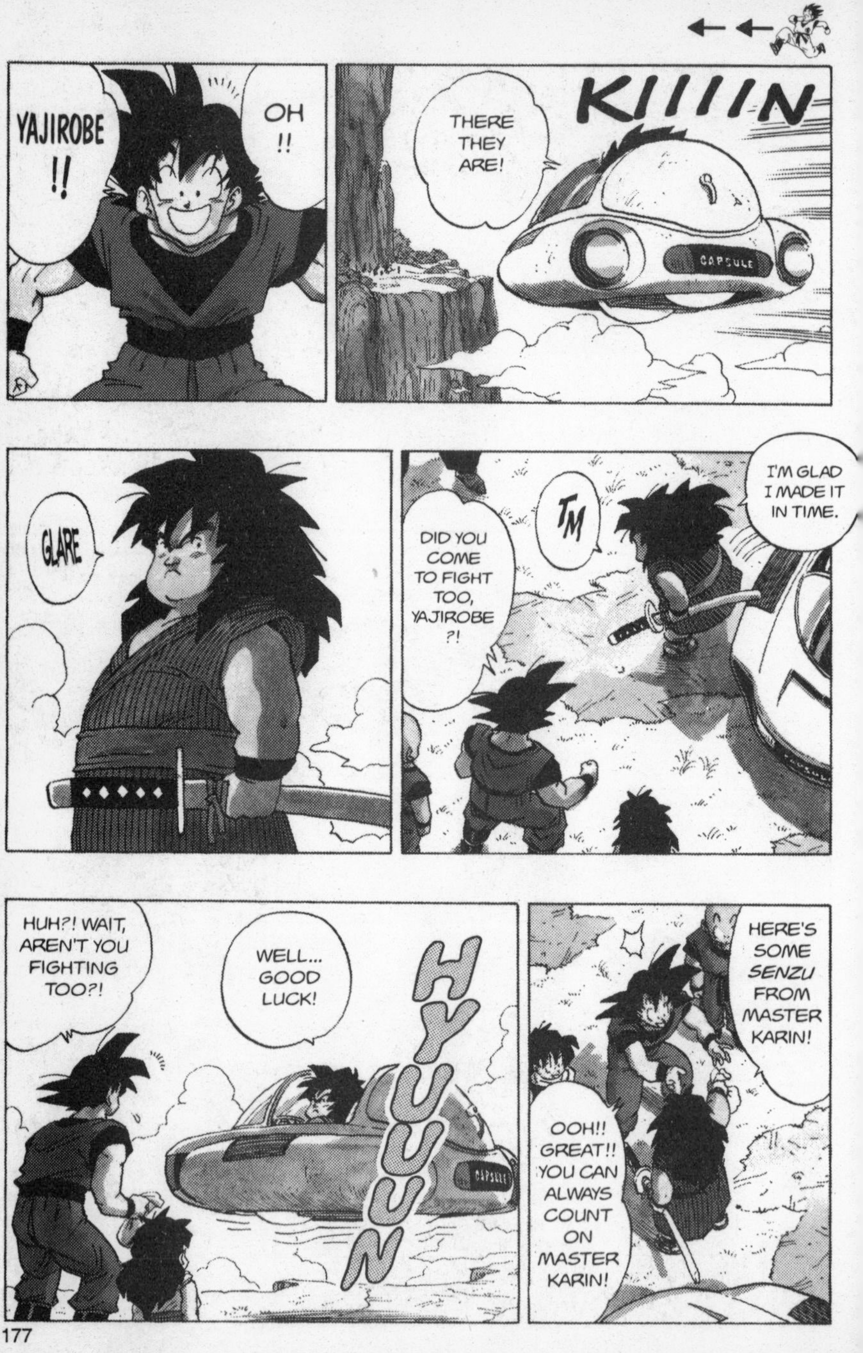
KIIIIN
THERE THEY ARE!
OH !!
YAJIROBE !!
I'M GLAD I MADE IT IN TIME.
TM
DID YOU COME TO FIGHT TOO, YAJIROBE ?!
GLARE
HERE'S SOME SENZU FROM MASTER KARIN!
OOH!! GREAT!! YOU CAN ALWAYS COUNT ON MASTER KARIN!
HYUUUN
WELL... GOOD LUCK!
HUH?! WAIT, AREN'T YOU FIGHTING TOO?!

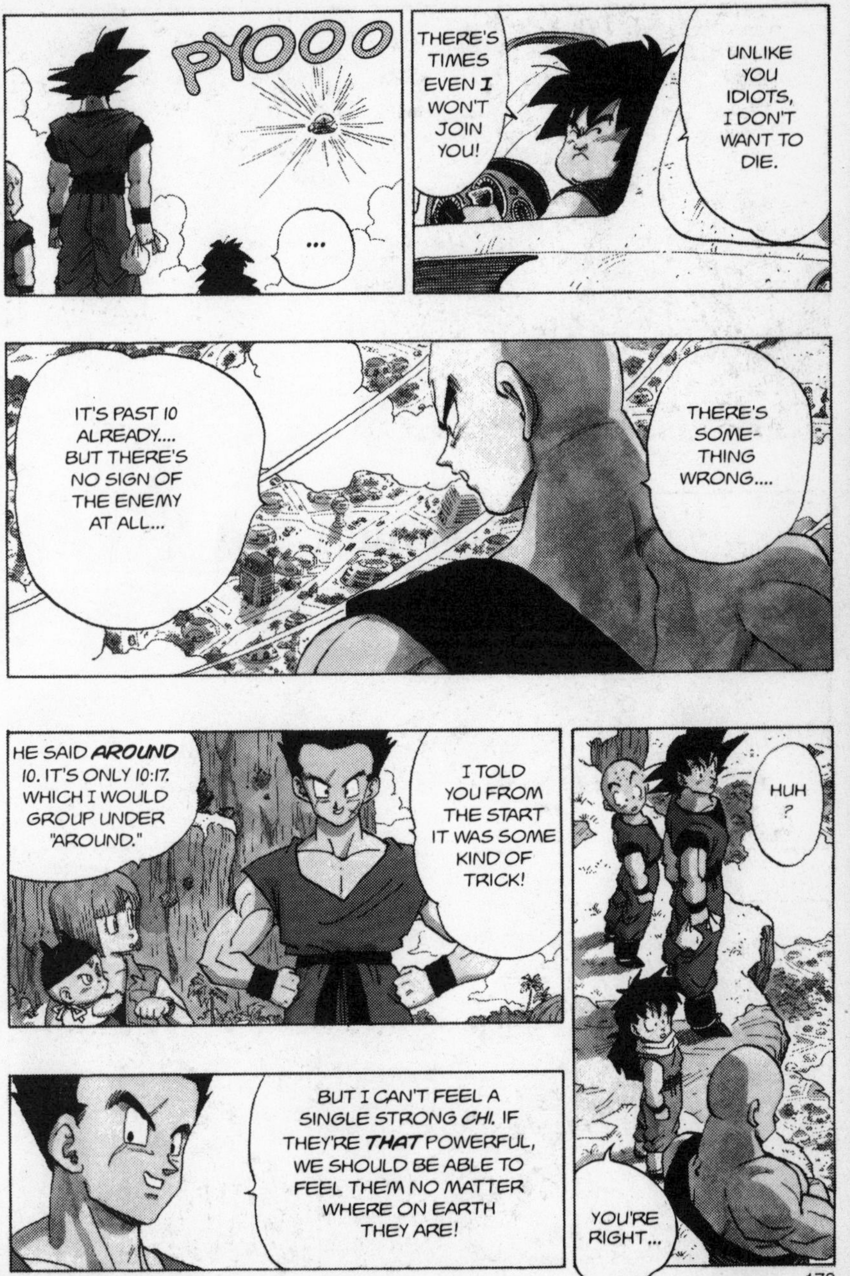
UNLIKE YOU IDIOTS, I DON'T WANT TO DIE.
THERE'S TIMES EVEN I WON'T JOIN YOU!
PYOOO
...
THERE'S SOME-THING WRONG....
IT'S PAST 10 ALREADY.... BUT THERE'S NO SIGN OF THE ENEMY AT ALL...
HUH?
YOU'RE RIGHT...
I TOLD YOU FROM THE START IT WAS SOME KIND OF TRICK!
HE SAID AROUND 10. IT'S ONLY 10:17. WHICH I WOULD GROUP UNDER "AROUND."
BUT I CAN'T FEEL A SINGLE STRONG CHI. IF THEY'RE THAT POWERFUL, WE SHOULD BE ABLE TO FEEL THEM NO MATTER WHERE ON EARTH THEY ARE!

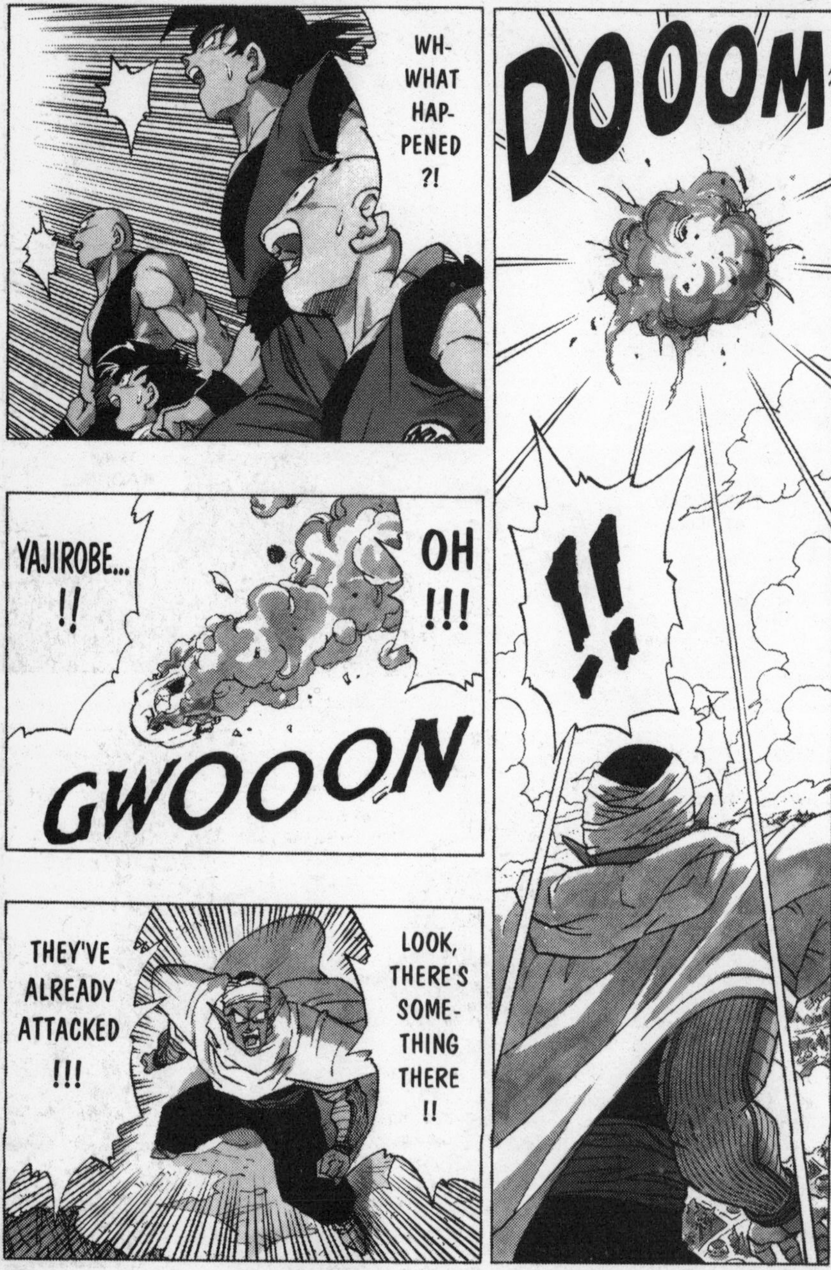
DOOOM
!!
WH-WHAT HAPPENED?!
OH!!!
YAJIROBE...!!
GWOOON
LOOK, THERE'S SOMETHING THERE!!
THEY'VE ALREADY ATTACKED!!!

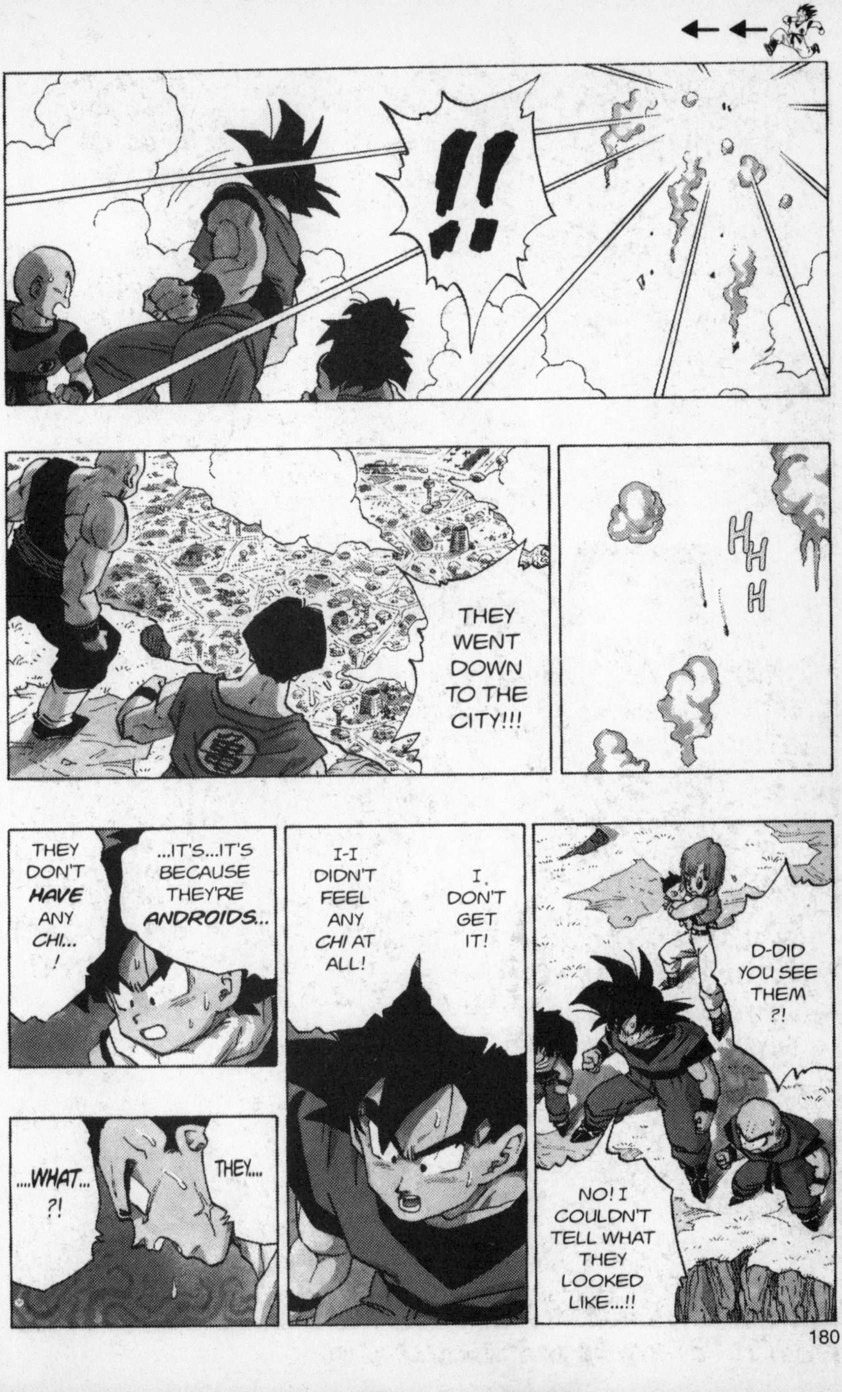
!!
HHH
THEY WENT DOWN TO THE CITY!!!
D-DID YOU SEE THEM ?!
NO! I COULDN'T TELL WHAT THEY LOOKED LIKE...!!
I DON'T GET IT!
I-I DIDN'T FEEL ANY *CHI* AT ALL!
...IT'S...IT'S BECAUSE THEY'RE *ANDROIDS...*
THEY DON'T *HAVE* ANY *CHI...* !
THEY....
...WHAT... ?!

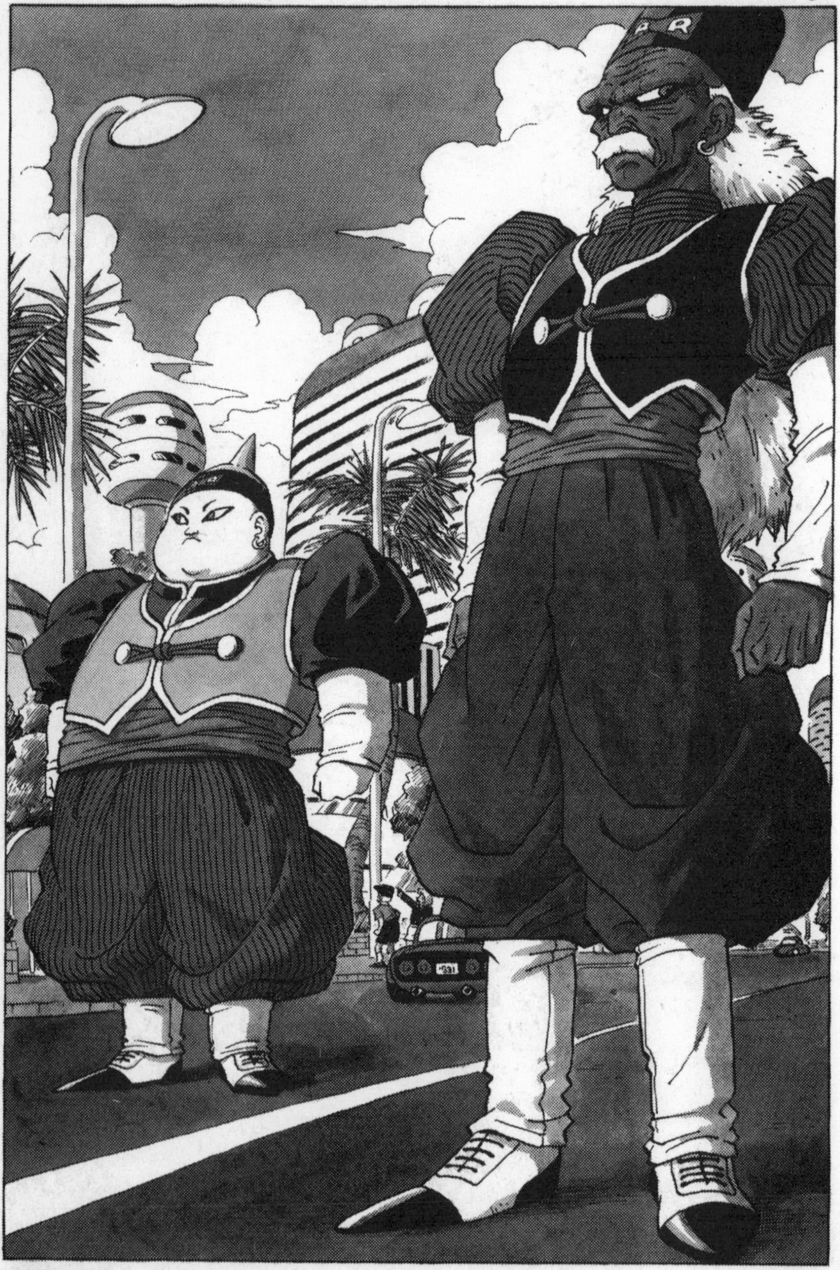

NEXT: Slaughter in South City

TITLE PAGE GALLERY

DRAGON BALL

BIRD STUDIO 鳥山明 Akira Toriyama

CLASH OF THE SUPER POWERS!

DBZ:119 • Kaió-ken times 20!!!

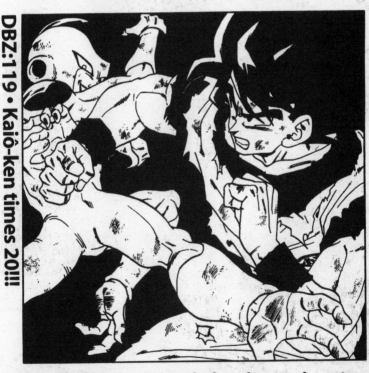

These title pages were used when these and previous chapters of Dragon Ball were first published in Japan in 1991 in Weekly Shonen Jump magazine.

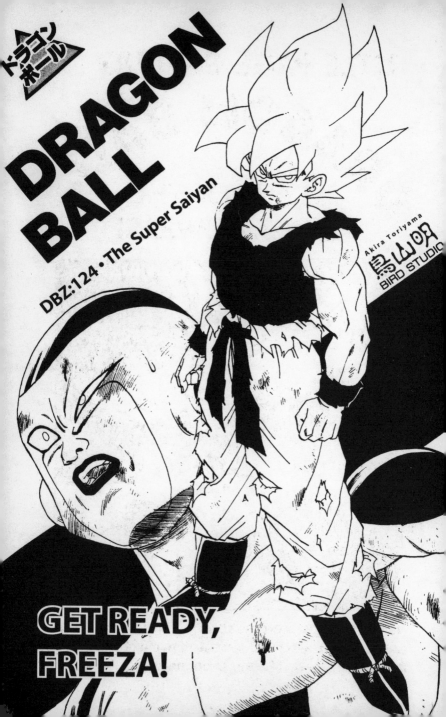

ドラゴン・ボール

DRAGON BALL

DBZ:124 • The Super Saiyan

Akira Toriyama
鳥山明
BIRD STUDIO

GET READY, FREEZA!

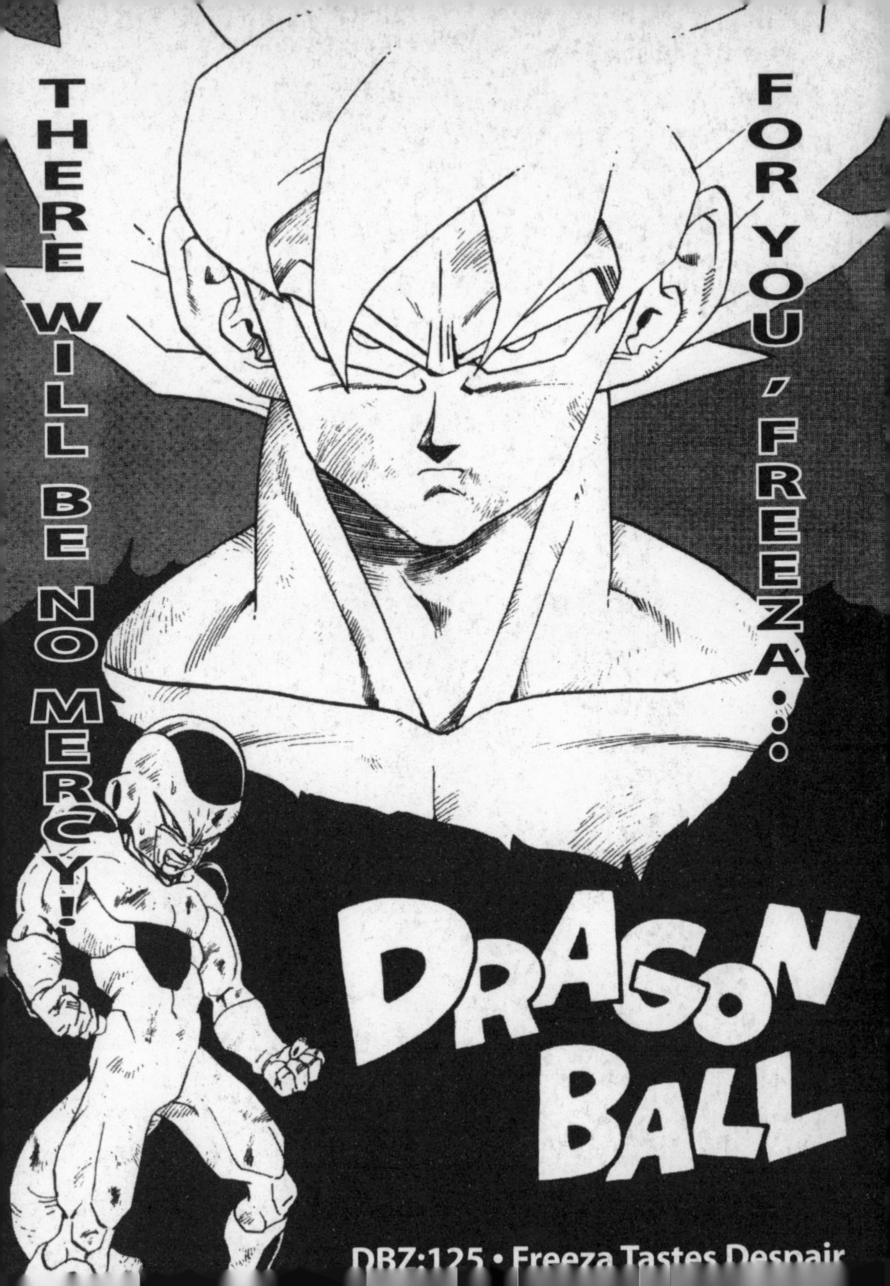

DBZ:125 • Freeza Tastes Despair

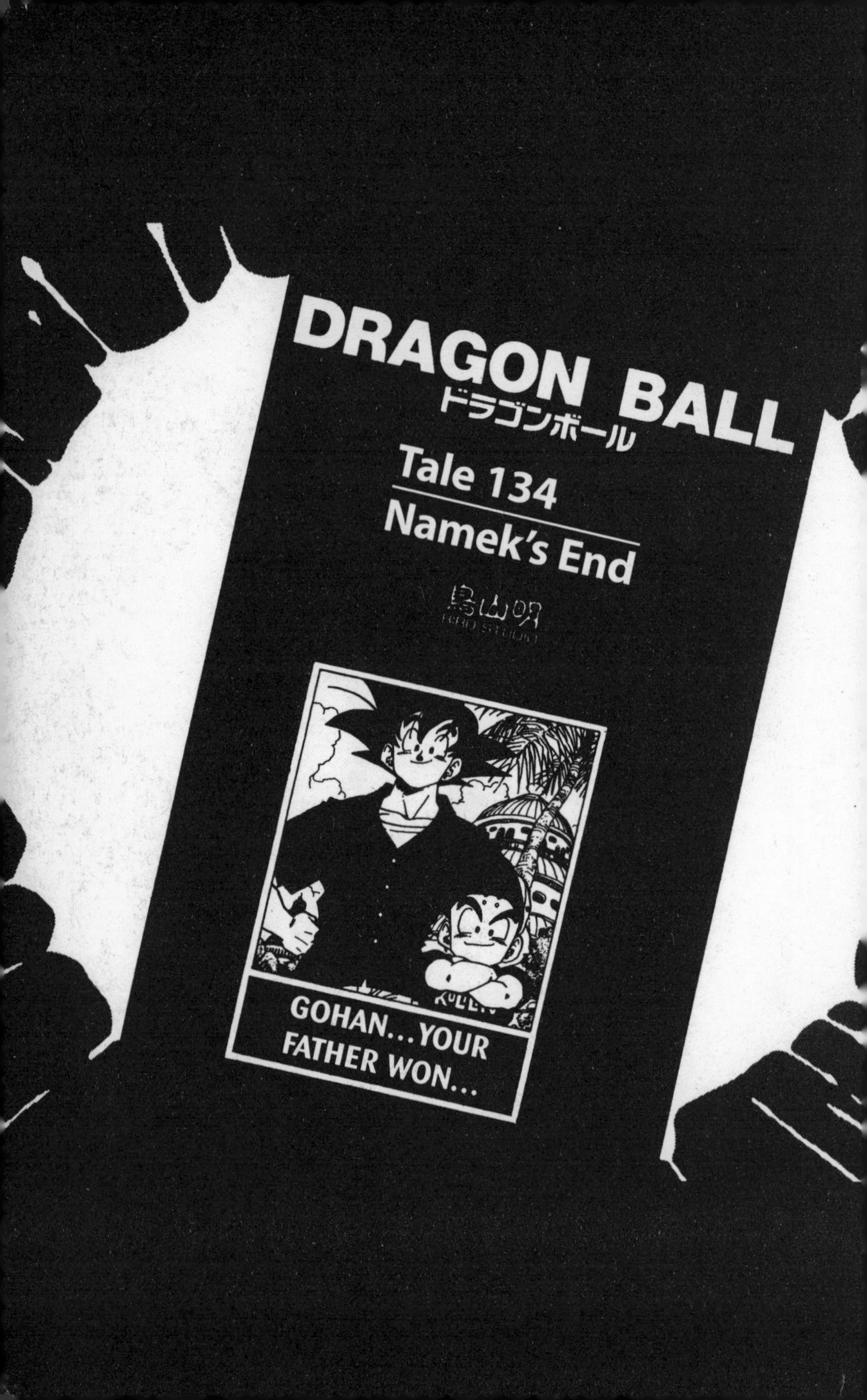
DRAGON BALL
ドラゴンボール
Tale 134
Namek's End
鳥山明
BIRD STUDIO
GOHAN...YOUR FATHER WON...

DRAGON BALL

DBZ:135 •
Where is Goku?

Akira Toriyama
BIRD STUDIO. 鳥山明

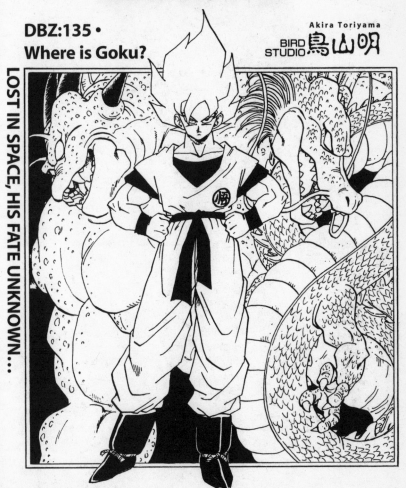

LOST IN SPACE, HIS FATE UNKNOWN...

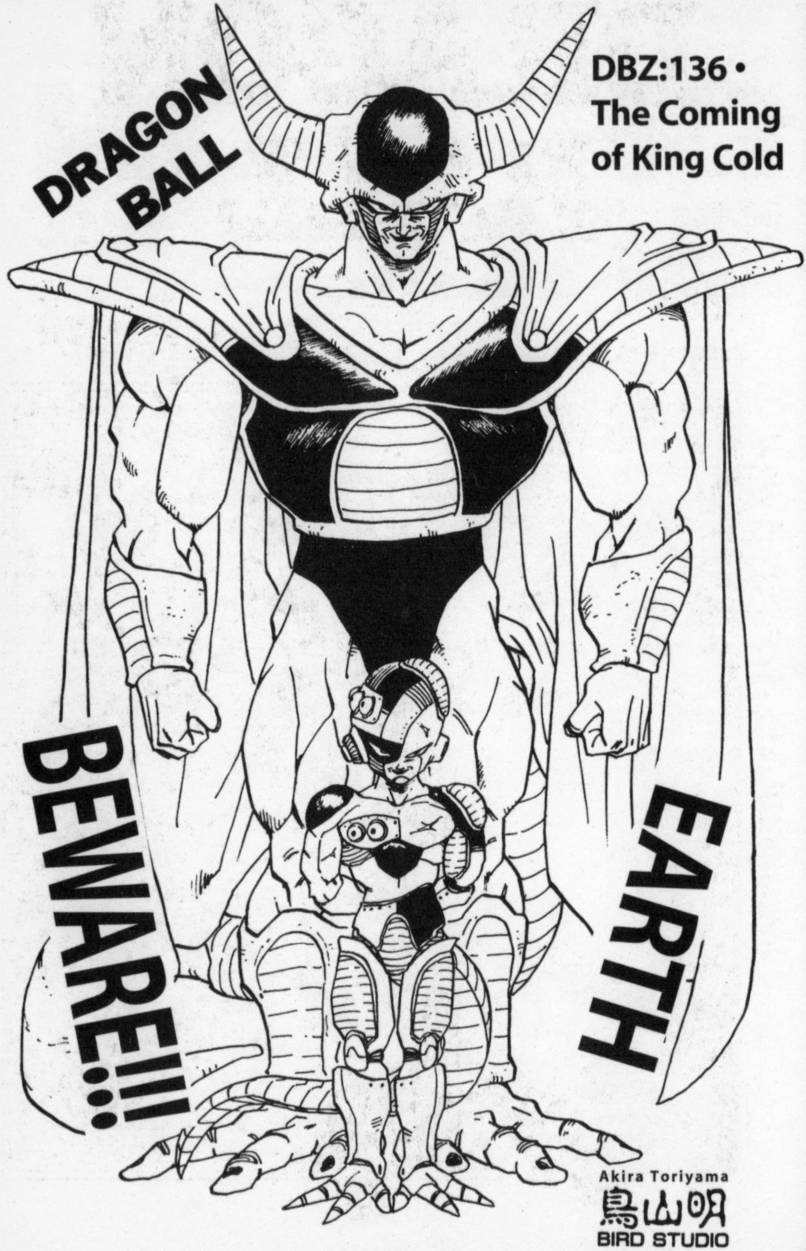

DRAGON BALL
DBZ:136 • The Coming of King Cold
EARTH BEWARE!!!
Akira Toriyama
鳥山明
BIRD STUDIO

DRAGON BALL

DBZ:137 • The Young Man of Mystery

Akira Toriyama
鳥山明
BIRD STUDIO

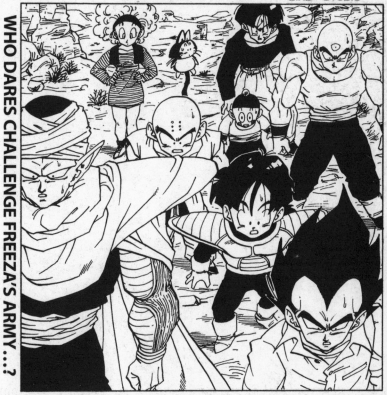

WHO DARES CHALLENGE FREEZA'S ARMY....?